THE MYTH OF THE EASTERN FRONT

From the 1950s onward, Americans were quite receptive to a view of World War
Two propagated by many Germans on how the war was fought on the Eastern
Front in Russia. Through a network of former high-ranking Wehrmacht and current Bundeswehr officers who had served in Russia, Germans were able to convince
Americans that the German army had fought a "clean" war in the East and that
atrocities there were committed solely by Nazi organizations. This view fit well
with the prevailing anti-Communism of the Cold War and continues to this day
in a broad subculture of general readers, German military enthusiasts, wargame
aficionados, military paraphernalia collectors, and reenactors who tend to romanticize the German military.

Professor Ronald Smelser is the author of *The Sudeten Problem, 1933–1938: Volk-
stumspolitik and the Formulation of Nazi Foreign Policy* and *Robert Ley: Hitler's
Labor Front Leader*. Both books have been translated into German. In addition, he
has published seven edited or co-edited books and numerous articles on modern
German history. He is also editor-in-chief of the four-volume *Learning about the
Holocaust: A Student Guide* and has worked closely with the Holocaust Education
Foundation. Smelser is former president of the German Studies Association and
the Conference Group for Central European History as well as a former member of
the American Advisory Board of the German Historical Institute in Washington.

Professor Edward J. Davies II is the author of the *Anthracite Aristocracy* and *The
United States in World History* and has also served on the advisory board for
National Geographic's *Concise History of the World*. He has published articles in
professional journals such as the *Journal of Social History* and *Journal of Urban
History* and reviewed manuscripts for the *Journal of Military History* and university
presses.

The Myth of the Eastern Front

The Nazi-Soviet War in American Popular Culture

RONALD SMELSER

University of Utah

EDWARD J. DAVIES II

University of Utah

Amazon 11/07

CAMBRIDGE
UNIVERSITY PRESS

CAMBRIDGE UNIVERSITY PRESS
Cambridge, New York, Melbourne, Madrid, Cape Town, Singapore, São Paulo, Delhi

Cambridge University Press
32 Avenue of the Americas, New York, NY 10013-2473, USA

www.cambridge.org
Information on this title: www.cambridge.org/9780521833653

First published 2008

Printed in the United States of America

A catalog record for this publication is available from the British Library.

Library of Congress Cataloging in Publication Data

Smelser, Ronald M., 1942–
The Myth of the Eastern Front : the Nazi-Soviet war in American popular culture / Ronald Smelser,
Edward J. Davies, II.
    p.   cm.
Includes bibliographical references and index.
ISBN 978-0-521-83365-3 (hardback)
1. World War, 1939–1945 – Campaigns – Eastern Front.   2. World War, 1939–1945 – Public
opinion.   3. Propaganda, German – United States.   4. Germany – Foreign public opinion,
American.   5. Public opinion – United States.   6. Myth.   I. Davies, Edward J., II, 1947–   II. Title.
D764.S569   2007
940.54′217 – dc22   2007017716

ISBN   978-0-521-83365-3 hardback
ISBN   978-0-521-71231-6 paperback

Dedicated to
Edward J. Davies, 1925–2003
Ruth Smelser

Contents

Illustrations

Preface

We would like to express our gratitude to those who have helped us along the way in researching and writing this book. We are grateful to the staff members in the archives where we have worked and to colleagues who have helped us with materials and advice. The Bundesarchiv/Militärarchiv in Freiburg, the Institute für Zeitgeschichte in Munich, and the Staatsarchiv in Nuremberg provided us with invaluable documentation. Similarly, library and staff members in archives and libraries in this country have been helpful: the National Archives of the United States at College Park as well as, at long distance, the staffs of the Cornell Law Library (William Donovan Papers), the Herbert Hoover Presidential Library (Truman Smith Papers), the Seeley G. Mudd Manuscript Library at Princeton University (Allen Dulles Papers), and the University of Notre Dame Archives (George Shuster Papers). We have profited enormously from discussions with colleagues, including Peter Black, Jürgen Förster, Joseph Bendersky, Robert Gellately, Johannes Hürter, MacGregor Knox, Geoff Megargee, Dieter Pohl, Bruce Siemon, and Charles Sydnor.

We would like to thank Antonio Munoz for his generous permission to use photographs from his many publications. In the spirit of true scholarship, he also sent us additional materials that we incorporated into the book.

Our indexers, Robin Hill and Tressa Friend, completed an essential task with skill and grace; we are grateful for their help.

We are also grateful to our home institution, the University of Utah, for its support. The University Research Committee provided us with vital computer equipment; the College of Humanities was generous with release time, and the Tanner Humanities Center hastened the appearance of this book by making one of the authors, Ronald Smelser, a Center Fellow.

The writing of this book was in many ways a personal journey. Many decades ago, I came across a title, *Hitler Moves East*, by Paul Carell, in a local bookstore in my hometown. Having little knowledge of the war in Russia, I purchased the book and quickly became enthralled with the scope of the war and its centrality in defeating the Germans. Carell's dramatic prose and his gift for storytelling soon created immense sympathy on my part for the Germans and their plight in the vast landscapes of Russia. My interest aroused, I continued to buy as many books as possible on the Eastern Front and by the late 1990s owned several hundred. My desire to learn as much as possible about the titanic struggle in the East also led me into the world of war games, and over the years I also came to own dozens of games. Well versed on the war, or so I believed, I began to discover the Russian side of that vast conflict and realized that my understanding was at best incomplete and at worst terribly exaggerated. Soon I turned to my colleague, Professor Ronald Smelser, an expert on Nazi Germany, for more effective explanations of the war and thus started our collaboration that led to the present book.

My one regret as I now finish the last stages of the book is the absence of my father, Edward J. Davies, whose death in 2003 took him from me. He and my mother, Mary V. Davies, have been constant sources of support and inspiration over the long years of my career and I now dedicate this book to his memory. I also want to extend my thanks to my wife, Liliana, who has stood by me throughout the completion of this book, and to my daughters, Erin and Mary Anne, who have been with me in good and bad times. Dad, I finally did finish the book!

— Edward J. Davies II

The book began with reminiscences of growing up in Pennsylvania in the 1950s, when the first documentaries began to appear on television. We remembered how boys came to school every morning after these showings full of enthusiasm about German dive-bombers and armored formations. These memories led us to find and investigate the phenomenon of "romancing" the German military in American popular culture from that day to this.

I would like to dedicate this book to my wife Ruth, who has been a source of support, encouragement and love.

—Ronald Smelser

THE MYTH OF THE EASTERN FRONT

Introduction

For most Americans, the Western Front – defined as North Africa, Italy and France, and western Germany – was decisive in defeating Nazi Germany during World War Two. After all, this was the arena in which our military dominated in terms of manpower, material, and planning. It was the front that received the most exhaustive coverage in the media, despite thorough wartime reporting from Russia. It was from this front that the names, which would highlight our struggle, echo down through several generations – Kasserine Pass, Anzio, Normandy, Huertgen Forest, the Bulge. And it was this long series of military engagements that would figure most dramatically in postwar presentations – right down to today. Television series such as *Combat* during the 1960s featured American soldiers defeating Germans on a weekly basis. Movies, most notably *The Longest Day*, *Patton*, and *The Battle of the Bulge*, reminded Americans dramatically of the triumphs of U.S. arms. A stream of books from *Company Commander* to *Eisenhower's Lieutenants* gave the general public detailed accounts of our wartime exploits. Media fascination with World War Two gained renewed impetus in the 1990s, as we commemorated various fiftieth anniversary events. Tom Brokaw's *The Greatest Generation* celebrated and romanticized in print and on television those rapidly disappearing men and women who saved the world from Hitler. *Saving Private Ryan* brought the same message to movie audiences and *Band of Brothers* continues to do so on television as we enter the twenty-first century. A controversial monument in Washington, DC, enshrines our wartime triumphs in stone. But one looked in vain during those celebrations for any mention of the Soviet contribution to victory in Europe. Even the D-Day fiftieth commemorations in 1994, appropriate in their extensiveness, largely failed to mention that a gigantic Soviet offensive unleashed on June 22, 1944, took enormous pressure off Americans, who still had not broken out of the Normandy Pocket. This omission is all the more unfortunate in light of the fact that it was Soviet arms that really broke

1

the German army, no less than 80 percent of which was fighting on the Eastern Front. Even those Americans with a passing familiarity with the war in Russia have insisted that the Red Army only triumphed because of enormous supplies sent to them by America through the Lend Lease program.

Only recently have the widespread awareness of the Holocaust and revelations about the barbaric depredations of the *Schutzstaffel* (SS) and its *Einsatzgruppen* altered this fundamental misunderstanding. Still, the legacy of the Cold War and all it entailed – fighting the evil empire with the Germans as our friends and allies – continues to cast its spell on American perceptions of World War Two in the East. Those who have taken the trouble to learn about that titanic struggle, ironically enough, tend to view it, not as the agony and eventual triumph of an important ally, but rather through the lenses of our common enemy.

The thesis of this book is that from the early 1950s on, Americans were uncommonly receptive to a view of World War Two as it was fought in Russia that was remarkably similar to that of many Germans, particularly leading circles of former German military and even National Socialists. In fact, this view of the war in the East in many respects contained elements of the Nazi worldview as applied to this theater of the war.

That it was possible for Americans to adopt the outlook of their late enemies on a crucial theater of World War Two to the detriment of their former allies derives in part from the imperatives of the Cold War. After all, if the Germans were not only to be our friends, but also our armed allies, it was important to erase at least some aspects of the recent war from the public memory and to revise the terms of discussion of other aspects, particularly with regard to our new enemy – and former ally – the Soviet Union.

Many Germans stood ready to help us in this regard, and they had certain advantages in doing so. For one, we had a long record of anti-Communism, which pre-dated World War Two, and therefore an established antipathy toward the Russians, which was easily revived after that conflict was over. Toward the Germans, Americans had always had a deeply ambivalent attitude. During wartime, negative sentiments readily emerged. In more normal times, the wellspring of positive attitudes was just as easily recalled and used to shape the public outlook (with the surviving negative ones attaching themselves exclusively to Hitler and the Nazis). Large segments of the American public also harbored certain attitudes, among them cultural, economic, racial, and aesthetic, which bore a disturbing similarity to those of fascism in general and Nazism in particular, which could be tapped in shaping a new view of the war in the East. Finally, by the 1950s, Americans, who, during the war, had followed events in Russia on a day-to-day basis, remembered little about the

Eastern Front and were thus open to new interpretations, which faced little competition in becoming established.

These factors permitted opinion-making members of the former German military, busy creating their own mythologies about World War Two, to take advantage of the Cold War climate to work on their receptive American "friends" and colleagues. This book is the story of how the Germans, through a network of former high Wehrmacht officers and Bundeswehr officers who had served in World War Two, created in the minds of the American military, then journalists and popular writers, an interpretation of World War Two in the East disturbingly similar to that projected by Hitler's regime during the war itself and that left the Wehrmacht with a largely "clean" reputation as to its conduct of that war. This view, which the Americans gradually absorbed during the 1950s, continues in the popular literature and part of the media to this day, and indeed delineates a broad subculture of general readers, German military enthusiasts, war game aficionados, military paraphernalia collectors, and reenactors.

Clearly, academic scholarship in America has always studied the war in Russia. During the past thirty years, scholars have gradually exposed the role of all the agencies of Nazi Germany, including the military, in Hitler's war of racial enslavement and extermination in the East. Still, mainstream academic scholarship has focused on a narrow spectrum of professorial readers and has ignored the general public, whose views were shaped by German writers and their sympathizers.

To be sure, awareness of the Holocaust is quite widespread today. Yet this awareness seems to be compartmentalized in the minds of many Americans, who continue to admire the German performance in Russia during World War Two despite the obvious involvement of the German military in the crimes of the regime.

As our research reveals, a more specific American subculture composed of military officers, historians employed by the military, and popular historians has really succeeded in shaping the broad popular view of the German military. This view makes the German army appear as if it had operated independently of the genocidal policies and practices of the Nazi regime in the East and only played the traditional role of a military force fighting honorably for its country. Indeed, given our view of the Russians, which quickly emerged early in the Cold War, the Wehrmacht is often viewed on a heroic scale, as if its role in Russia were only a prelude to our own struggle against Soviet Communism. In this context, the defeat of the German army in 1945 *on the Eastern Front* shapes up to have been something approaching a tragedy. Indeed, one can observe in this popular literature something very close to a "lost cause" romanticism that, in many respects, parallels that which appeared in the United States decades after the Civil War with respect to the Confederate cause. The South lost the Civil War on the battlefield, but, in many ways, won it in the history books and in the popular imagination. With regard to a sizable number of Americans, this also appears to be the case with the Nazi war against the Soviet Union.

Given the dramatic change in historical memory initiated during the Cold War, it is necessary to look at how familiar Americans were with the war on the Eastern Front during World War Two itself. In Chapter 1, we review the very extensive, indeed ubiquitous, coverage aimed at Americans of the war in Russia. This coverage ranged from newspapers, magazines, books, and movie newsreels to popular radio programs and mass rallies and collections. Americans were quite familiar with the campaigns in the East from the invasion of the Soviet Union on June 22, 1941, to the capture of Berlin in May 1945. Russian leaders, including Stalin and a number of top Soviet generals, were household names for Americans. By the end of the war, Americans were nearly as familiar with the German-Russian war as that of our own.

Chapter 2 deals with the changing historical perspectives wrought by the Cold War. Within a short time, as the Cold War broke out, the memory of the Eastern Front in World War Two began to fade. As we made the psychological shift from viewing the Russians as allies to seeing them as (potential) enemies and the Germans from enemies to clients and, eventually, allies, a conscious attempt was undertaken to change the historical memory of the American public; to create a "lost cause" myth with regard to the Eastern Front, one that cast the German army in the role of a heroic adversary to the Communist monolith. Former German generals were more than happy to help create the myth – especially Franz Halder, whom we discuss in some detail.

Chapter 3 continues this story by examining the so-called Halder group, which, commissioned by the U.S. army, provided us with hundreds of studies, especially of the war in Russia, as seen from the German perspective. We, who were facing a possible land war with the Soviet Union, were an eager audience. Later, ties were cemented with former German officers through a complex network of relationships throughout the 1950s and 1960s, particularly among the Bundeswehr, the West German army, and U.S. forces in Germany, and the myth achieved wider popularity. The chapter concludes with parallels between the myth creation during the Cold War and that undertaken, also for political reasons, in the United States after the Civil War, in order to reintegrate the white American South back into the Union on the grounds of a heroic "lost cause" fought by the Confederacy.

Chapter 4 examines how the myth of the "clean" Wehrmacht in the East during the Second World War was brought to the general public in the United

States by a series of widely selling memoirs, written by former German generals such as Erich von Manstein, Heinz Guderian, Hans Rudel, Hans von Luck, and others, as well as novels, such as those by Swen Hassel, and popular histories like those written by Paul Carell. The chapter also debunks many of the myths, especially those propagated by Manstein and Carell. It concludes by examining the revival of Wehrmacht popularity, especially in the U.S. military after the debacle in Vietnam. We felt, once again, that the Germans had valuable things to tell us, both regarding how to maintain the integrity of an army in wartime and how to defend against a possible Russian attack in the revived Cold War of the 1980s. This new popularity of and respect for the Wehrmacht seeped out into the broader culture and created the foundation for popular activities that fascinate several American subcultures to the current day – such as wargaming, reenacting, Internet websites, and chatrooms.

If Chapter 4 examines and debunks the myths developed by the German generals, Chapter 5 explores more specifically just what messages the German generals in their earlier publications, as well as lower-ranking officers and ordinary German soldiers in more recent memoirs, were trying to communicate to a broader American audience.

Chapter 6 examines the gurus. These authors, mostly but not exclusively American, have picked up and disseminated the myths of the Wehrmacht in a wide variety of popular publications that romanticize the German struggle in Russia. The gurus, men like Mark Yerger, Richard Landwehr, Marc Rijkmans-poel, and Franz Kurowski, who insist on authenticity in their writings, combine a painfully accurate knowledge of the details of the Wehrmacht, ranging from vehicles to uniforms to medals, with a romantic heroicization of the German army fighting to save Europe from a rapacious Communism. There is little in the way of historical context in the writings of these men. They honor particularly the soldiers of the Waffen-SS, without bothering to tell us of the war of racial enslavement and annihilation these men pursued in the East.

In Chapter 7, we examine the popular culture of what we have termed the "romancers," that is, a wide subculture of Americans who have embraced the message of the gurus and indulge in wargaming and Internet chatting to a degree that reveals an identification with the values of courage, honor, and self-sacrifice they see in the German soldier of World War Two. The romancers also show an alienation from what is viewed as the crass materialism, selfish egotism, and moral ambiguities of the current world.

The book concludes with Chapter 8, which investigates similar people who choose to more actively carry out their fantasies of the "clean" Wehrmacht by donning the uniforms of their heroes and spending weekends and vacations in reenactments. They, like the gurus and other "romancers," also insist on authenticity in uniforms, equipment, and organization. One authenticity they lack is that of historical accuracy; they also dream of a different outcome of World War Two, if only the mistakes made by Hitler, but never the generals, could have been avoided. The chapter ends with a brief discussion of "what-if-history," like that written by R. H. S. Stolfi, which envisions the possibility of a German victory in the East under different circumstances. The "what-if" histories fuel the imaginations of the romancers in all the subcultures.

1 Americans Experience the War in Russia, 1941–1945

Opening: The Story of the First Russian–American Encounter

On April 25, 1945, an American patrol in the small town of Leckwitz, Germany, learned from freed Allied prisoners of war (POWs) that the Russian army was in the immediate neighborhood. Shortly, the GIs came upon a young Russian cavalryman who told them Soviet troops were on the eastern bank of the Elbe. The Americans crossed the Elbe near Streha and soon met the Russian soldiers. This meeting marked the first encounter between American and Russian troops (Figure 1). The GIs, part of an advanced patrol, fraternized with their Russian counterparts for ten days. Both sides managed to communicate with each other and the U.S. soldiers received superb treatment.[1]

Here were American soldiers sharing bread, stories, and comradeship with their fellow Russian allies, about whom the Americans had been curious for years. Both reveled in their celebration of the impending victory over their bitter enemy, Nazi Germany.

Within a few years, soldiers from the Soviet Union and the United States would again face each other – not in friendship but in anticipation of war. The tensions of the Cold War might be understood in light of our past histories. The friendship of 1945 demands thought and reflection. Hostile opponents in 1939, tentative partners in 1941, the Union of Soviet Socialist Republics (USSR) and the United States of America (USA) had become staunch allies by 1945, to the surprise of many and the disappointment of some Americans.

The Russian–American Relationship, 1917–1941

The tortured relationship with the Soviet Union began with the birth of the Soviet state in 1917, when the Bolsheviks, under the leadership of Vladimir

Figure 1. American troops (left) reach out to grasp hands with Soviet soldiers after the historic junction at Torgau, Germany. (Reprinted by permission, United Press International Photo.)

Lenin, seized power. The capitalist and democratic United States immediately identified the Bolsheviks and their Marxist ideology and authoritarian style of rule as inimical to our system. This hostility only intensified during the interwar years as the U.S. media mounted a sustained attack on the Soviet experiment. For most Americans, the Soviet Union remained a distant and menacing power. Soviet policies during the 1930s – Stalin's brutal collectivization and ruthless purges – heightened the already strong distrust.

The 1930s also witnessed the rise of another hostile regime – the Nazi Germany, one that would join the USSR as an enemy of America's democratic principles. By the late 1930s, this new threat, in fact, overshadowed the danger posed by the USSR. Accordingly, Hitler temporarily replaced Stalin as the major international villain in American minds.[2]

The unexpected Nazi-Soviet Pact in August 1939 and the subsequent conquest of Poland by these two powers revealed Hitler's aggressive plans, and, again, reminded Americans of Stalin's duplicity. This deed also opened the final flurry of anti-Soviet and anti-Communist activity before our own involvement in the war. The 1940 Soviet invasion of Finland only added fuel to the fire. Americans were outraged over this attack on a small, defenseless country by a neighboring giant.

June 22, 1941 dramatically transformed the landscape. The Nazi surprise invasion of the USSR suddenly made the Soviet Union appear as a victim rather than as a victimizer. Moreover, any potential Soviet threat to the United States and the West gave way to the larger awareness that if Hitler conquered Russia, he might be unstoppable.

U.S. policy makers reacted to the new situation by moving rapidly to support the Soviet Union in its fight for survival. Isolationists in America were unconvinced of the need to aid Russia, so recently our foe. Most Americans were ambivalent. President Franklin Delano Roosevelt (FDR) and his advisors proposed applying the policy of Lend Lease to the Russians, much as we were doing with the British. Isolationists bitterly opposed this move.[3]

Pearl Harbor and Hitler's subsequent declaration of war undercut this opposition. Now, the Americans and the Russians faced the same enemy in Nazi Germany. Americans could no longer safely observe the struggles in Europe from across the Atlantic Ocean, for the war had become their fight as well. The new allied relationship with the USSR was reflected in the changed attitudes of the American press toward the Soviet Union; increasingly the media would portray the Russians in positive and, often, heroic terms.

The newspaper of record, the *New York Times*, brought from the outset highly detailed reporting of the conflict, including daily maps noting the locations of the battles and the advances or retreats of the Germans and Russians. *New York Times* reporters also provided incisive analysis of the battles and key decisions by both armies. The paper even printed the often-conflicting communiqués from Berlin and Moscow in its stories. The paper carried numerous photographs of action in Russia, even of Soviet training exercises before the outbreak of the war. Clearly, the *New York Times* brought sophisticated, in-depth analyses of the war, along with often, in retrospect, surprisingly accurate prognoses of its future course, to which stories by journalists such as Hansen Baldwin attest.[4]

For the more general public, there were *Look, Life, Time, Liberty*, and the *Reader's Digest* – and above all, the radio. These accounts often characterized the Russians in terms that made their plight compelling to an increasingly compassionate American public, itself now deeply embroiled in the conflict. The media humanized Russians for Americans. Russians facing the departure of family members for battle or the real possibility of the deaths of sons, fathers, and even daughters struck a chord with Americans who shared the same experiences as their loved ones went to war.[5]

Correspondents, authors, and radio announcers described the modern character of Soviet society and its daily struggles for survival. The media wrote extensively of the proficiency of Russian armies and their heroic soldiers who steadfastly faced a brutal enemy capable of cruel deeds. Readers and viewers in the United States came to learn how vicious and inhumane the Germans behaved toward the Russian people. The American media shocked American audiences with accounts of German atrocities against even the most innocent of Russians. Pictures in magazines as well as newsreels in theaters highlighted the written descriptions.[6]

As time went on, Americans became quite familiar with the course of the conflict, with the nature of the belligerents involved, and with the top leadership in both Germany and the Soviet Union, as well as with the devastation being wrought. Above all, from the beginning, Americans had little doubt as to the enormous scale of the conflict and the implications of a Nazi victory.

Radio programs listened to by millions of Americans, especially favorites like The Great Gildersleeve, Fibber McGee and Molly, and The Jack Benny Show, frequently made reference to the valiant fighting of the Russians.

Initial coverage focused almost exclusively on battlefield operations as the momentous struggle between Nazi invaders and Soviet defenders unfolded. Gradually, however, coverage broadened to include a wealth of stories on wider subjects, including social, economic, political, and human-interest themes, all vital for an American public whose knowledge of the Soviet Union was sketchy and cliché ridden at best.

Americans also tried from the outset to contextualize the war, attempting to find a sense of the war's direction and eventual outcome by comparing it to earlier conflicts. Stories abounded about the classic invaders of Russia and their fate, ranging from the Swedes under Charles XII to Napoleon to Hindenburg. Nor did analysts miss the parallels between the Nazis and the Teutonic Knights. These attempts to furnish context provided Americans a way to deal with a conflict in which an early awe of German military prowess combined with a fundamental lack of respect for Soviet war potential could be molded into some hopeful expectations about how the war would conclude. As the Russian fortunes of battle went first one way, then another; as the Germans advanced and the Soviets retreated, but did not collapse; as the Germans renewed their offenses, again driving the Soviets back, but not to the point of defeat; as the Soviets gradually stopped the Germans, then began their own painfully slow advances; as the momentum of war passed from German to Soviet hands, American attitudes toward the Soviet Union shifted and a growing respect for the Russians and their capabilities emerged. These changing fortunes of war, in turn, combined with our own participation in the conflict to prepare Americans to accept and even admire a country that, until recently, they had regarded with extreme skepticism and suspicion – and with good reason.[7]

After our entry into the war, the newfound alliance with the USSR encouraged a growing respect for the Soviet Union and even a lionizing of the Russians that would, in retrospect, seem naïve and unseemly. Whereas stories on the Russian front no longer quite dominated the headlines, they remained imbedded in a larger coverage of the war, which linked our own fortunes on the battlefield with those of our Russian ally in a common struggle against an odious enemy.

Within this context, the American media carefully followed the major battles on the Eastern Front and recognized from the outset the decisive nature of these violent encounters. The German defeat before Moscow in December 1941, the Soviet successes at Stalingrad and Kursk in 1943, and the Soviet breakthrough into Eastern Europe in the wake of the Minsk "pocket" in summer 1944 created a frame of reference for Americans. The media and public opinion polls clearly acknowledged these Russian victories as crucial way stations for the allies in this gruesome conflict.[8]

A pattern emerged during the war as well, as events on the battlefield in Russia shaped American attitudes. The dramatic successes of the Nazis early in the war, the long string of Soviet defeats which slowly turned into successful resistance, the gradual Allied seizure of the initiative were all mirrored in an evolving American attitude toward the Soviet Union and its peoples. Americans shifted slowly from pre-war hostility, or at least ambivalence, to the entire Soviet experiment, to sympathy in light of the shock of the Nazi juggernaut terrorizing the Russian people. Then Americans grudgingly came to accept a vital, if uncomfortable ally, and, finally, to embrace enthusiastically cooperation with a power that we came to imagine, however unrealistically, as similar to ourselves. Near the end of the war, we reverted to our old suspicions as the Nazi threat receded and the Soviet advances brought a powerful new Soviet presence into Eastern Europe. In retrospect, the peak of the enthusiasm for our Russian ally came in 1943 and 1944, as flattering cover stories on Joseph Stalin in major news magazines and positive articles on the Soviet Union in the usually reliably conservative *Reader's Digest* attest.[9]

Red Army Leaders

American hopes for and confidence in its Soviet ally grew dramatically in the course of the conflict. Opinion after battles such as the defeat of the Germans at Moscow in 1941 and Stalingrad in 1943 departed dramatically from what had been U.S. assessments of the Red Army at the beginning of Barbarossa. Americans had been at least vaguely familiar with Stalin's purges of the Red Army officer corps in the late 1930s and could attribute the colossal early Soviet defeats in 1941 in part to the deficits left by the absence of roughly 80 percent of the officers at the rank of colonel and above. It was unlikely, though, that Americans would have been aware of the dire consequences left by the loss of, for instance, a Tuchachevsky, a brilliant innovator and one of the few Soviet commanders who readily grasped the potential of armored warfare of the sort that the Germans were to use with such success.[10]

As the German onslaught against the Soviet Union began to bog down in late 1941 and as the battered Red Army survived its initial setbacks, and even fashioned successful counterassaults, Americans, long familiar with the German commanders, now began to read about Soviet military leaders. Profiles of these officers were an opening wedge into the general prevailing ignorance about a Soviet system, which, by and large, had been held, not without reason, in general disregard. When the Soviet Union did not collapse in 1941, Americans wanted to know why. The media answered that curiosity with a plethora of reports over the coming years, which, taken together, sketched a portrait of surprising competence in the Soviet system.

Frequently featured early in the war were emerging Soviet commanders such as Semyon Timoshenko and Georgi Zhukov, both members of the Stavka (general headquarters of the Red Army) and effective, high-level field commanders. Both men exhibited traits appealing to the American public: They emerged from humble circumstances to achieve success through ability and performance. Zhukov rose from an illiterate youth to become the best mind in the Red Army. Similarly, Timoshenko rose from the dire poverty of a Bessarabian peasant background to become Commissar for War. The American press praised him for his courage and his martial abilities. He "transform[ed] the Red Army into a smooth-working machine," enabling it to withstand the German onslaught. "Twice he . . . met and defeated Hitler's best – before Moscow in 1941 and at Lake Ilmen near Novgorod in the winter of 1943." These men shared other traits that made them appealing to Americans: They were young – usually in their forties – and fiercely patriotic. In every sense of the word, these Russian commanders resonated with the American public.[11]

American journalists were also surprised at the openness, accessibility, and informality of Soviet commanders. Wallace Carroll, a Moscow-based correspondent, visiting the front lines at Vyazma, noted that General Sokolovsky "spoke as freely as any officer ever speaks about military operations."[12]

Red Army Soldiers

Correspondents and writers also wrote about the rank and file of the Red Army. The average soldier emerged as an important element in the Russian war machine, the one who actually did the fighting and dying. Again, writers placed the rank and file in the larger context of Russian military history. Readers came away impressed that the Soviets, unlike their Tsarist predecessors, made sure that all the soldiers could read and write. Literacy made them better soldiers and enabled the Red Army to devote its training to more crucial matters now accessible to literate soldiers. In fact, the troops had libraries of their own where they could read the works of Russia's leading authors such as Tolstoy. Reading clubs, according to Marshal Voroshilov, were common in the Red Army, with some 1,900 in operation containing a total of 25 million books.[13]

The Red Army also spent significant resources keeping its men in good health. American readers were informed that the rank and file were certainly better clothed and equipped than their World War One counterparts and could handle the vast extremes of weather that marked the seasons in Russia' northern latitudes. The Russians often conducted attacks in fierce snowstorms, while the Germans were wont to hide in the safety of their bunkers.[14]

Another account took readers through field hospitals where the wounded first received treatment. Americans could read and see in photographs that the Red Army devoted significant resources to treating its wounded. These installations were impeccable, according to Carroll, and they provided effective care for the troops. American writers favorably compared these medical stations with their American counterparts.[15]

Readers could see pictures of Russian soldiers in action in several venues. *Life* published a photograph of Russian infantry attacking a German strongpoint. Moviegoers could see the same shot but as part of the "March of Time" series film, *One Day of War*. *Time* also carried a photo of Soviet troops in action during a campaign in 1943. Its editors noted that this army represented a much-improved version of its 1942 predecessor and, by implication, was fully capable of defeating the Wehrmacht.[16]

Walter Kerr, commenting on the determination of the Russian soldiers for his American audiences, wrote:

> I wish you could have seen those men back in Moscow or at the front, men of medium height, stocky build . . . all in fine physical condition. They were not fighting animals who cared little whether they lived or died. They wanted to live. They wanted to go home to their families. But they were not afraid to die."[17]

Other observers picked up and repeated the German reaction to Russian stubbornness early in the war, when the Germans lamented that the Russian soldiers fought on against impossible odds even when surrounded. Many of the soldiers trapped behind enemy lines transformed themselves into partisans who constantly harassed the Germans. Russian infantry also performed effectively whether working in formations or isolated and on their own. By contrast, German infantry, according to one Western correspondent, floundered when cut off from their units, just as they often struggled inadequately when confronted with winter weather or difficult terrain.[18]

Weapons of the Red Army

Accounts of the actions of Red Army soldiers and their officers also included an appreciation for the weapons the Russians developed and deployed against their German adversaries, ranging from tanks to artillery to airplanes. These weapons proved essential to Russian survival and success. The weapons were designed and produced under the constant pressure of German victories. Commentators noted the new and often improved tanks the Soviets introduced as the war progressed. The medium T-34 tank, which the Russians would produce by the thousands, became the workhorse of the Red Army and spearheaded its offensives from 1942 onward, along with various assault guns such as the SU-85 and SU-100.[19]

As these weapons appeared in large numbers, the Soviets developed effective combined arms doctrine based on the tactical innovations of the 1930s and battlefield experience. Given the inadequacies of early tank models and the initial inability of the Russians to appreciate combined arms tactics until the Germans used them so effectively, this achievement was no mean feat. As commentators observed for American audiences, by 1944, the Russian commanders had developed impressive skills in handling these weapons. Marshall Konev, for instance:

> used his tanks both to fight and transport. His favorite tank is the T-34, with its broad treads, high belly clearance, tommy gun crews and fuel barrels strapped to the side."[20] [This quote indicates how little American correspondents knew about military matters. Fuel barrels strapped to the sides of tanks were disasters waiting to happen and having troops ride the outside of the tank was a tactic of desperation made necessary by lack of trucks.]

Photographs also captured the strength of the T-34 in leading Russian troops into enemy territory later in the war. *Time* featured a picture of Russian tanks and tommy gun crews mopping up in East Prussia, the first German territory occupied by the Red Army. Another photo showed Russian armor over the dramatic caption: "They make mincemeat." American audiences gradually became aware that the Russians had become masters of mobile, armored warfare every bit as effective as the Germans had been in the initial stages of the war.[21]

Americans also came to appreciate the role of Russian artillery, especially under its commander, the tough and experienced General Gennady Voronov. Artillery had proven itself time and again to be the rescuing arm of the Red Army. Under Voronov's command, the artillery, which had held prominence in the Red Army since the Civil War of 1919–21, really came into its own. In the early days of the war, when the Russians faced one calamity after another, artillery proved the one branch able to save the situation time and again, despite constant shortages of weapons. Voronov's effective leadership markedly improved the caliber of the artillerymen. He removed incompetent officers, rewrote the artillery manuals, and demanded innovative tactics: He urged his men to conduct close fire and to resist at all costs when encircled by Wehrmacht troops. Americans repeatedly learned of his critical role, first in front of Moscow in 1941–42, then in the Stalingrad operation and in the successful Soviet offensives later in the war. Articles also described the types of artillery the Russians used and Voronov's favorite weapon, the Katyusha, rocket artillery appropriately nicknamed "Stalin's Organ." In fact, American moviegoers in the spring of 1944 saw the unleashing of these ferocious weapons in the Red Army attack on Gomel in the Ukraine. Few could leave the theaters unimpressed with the might of this combat arm.[22]

Finally, Americans also followed the exploits of the Red Air Force. In a dramatic picture in May 1942, Americans saw a determined Russian flyer bearing down on a German target in what the caption labeled the "Mighty Sturmovik." The caption also detailed the features of the Sturmovik, one of the Soviet's most successful combat fighters, which included the innovative "rocket bomb," and a powerful engine.[23]

Correspondents told the American public that the Soviets faced the enormous task of rebuilding their air force, shattered by the surprise German attack in June 1941. Air cover was crucial on the battlefield, so that the air force represented a high priority to the Russians. By 1944, Americans learned of the designers who developed the new planes and discovered that the Soviets pioneered air power theory during the 1930s and were the first major power to practice large-scale drops of paratroopers. Soviets improvised on designs and materials and then mass-produced these new planes, which finally gave them air superiority midway through the war. Americans often encountered stories about the pilots who flew these planes – as well as planes manufactured by American companies – and their exploits against the Germans.[24] In fact, already in July 1943, Larry Bell, president of Bell Aircraft Corporation, sent a letter of congratulations and a pocket watch to Col. Alexander Pokryshkin, top-scoring Soviet ace and three-time recipient of the "hero of the Soviet Union" medal for his exploits flying the P-39 Bell AirCobra.[25]

In 1944, *Time* devoted a major article to the Red Air Force and its innovative commander, Marshal Aleksandr Novikov, whose picture appeared on that month's cover. Understanding Russia's plight, he rejected ideas of a strategic bombing air force and successfully urged the building of close-support planes. He wanted simple designs and as many planes as possible. His ideas proved to be on target.[26]

The Soviet Economy

The battlefield successes of the Red Army rested squarely on the productive capacity of Soviet agriculture to feed its soldiers and people and its industry to arm the soldiers at the front and the partisans operating behind German lines. The American media in all its forms took great care to describe the Soviet economy, its background, strengths, and weaknesses, and its overall manufacturing power. Americans did learn a great deal about the Soviet efforts to build a successful agricultural system and an industrial infrastructure. Reporters and other observers gave the American public as detailed a picture as possible, given wartime security and the ever-present secretive Soviet state. Certainly, Americans came into the war with some grasp of Soviet efforts to industrialize the economy and also reorganize agriculture along collectivist lines during the 1930s. American engineers, auto makers, skilled workers, and occasionally tourists worked in and visited the Soviet Union during this decade and saw first hand the results of these efforts, or at least what Soviet authorities wanted them to see. Still, in 1941, *Fortune* writers argued that Americans had relatively little understanding of the Soviet economy, how it functioned, its location, and its capacity.[27]

More popular magazines such as *Readers' Digest* and *Life* carried articles describing the Soviet economy for a broader readership. These pieces appeared throughout the war and explained to the general public the dynamics of Russian industry and agriculture. *Life* featured a Russian village and the people who worked on the local collective. The description of this community, while not uncritical of the destruction of the Kulaks during collectivization, nevertheless accepted this violent transformation as fundamental to the Soviet Union's capacity to feed its armies and its people. The writer also reminded Americans that each family on the collective had their own house and private plot of land to cultivate vegetables. The large-scale collectives, such as the one portrayed in *Life*, capitalized on the availability of farm machinery. This union of machine and large-scale farming led to rich harvests, which sustained the Russian people and soldiers in wartime.[28] The author of the piece entitled it "Collective Farms Feed the Nation." Readers came away with both images and descriptions of Russian agriculture, so very different from its American counterpart, yet still apparently quite productive.[29] Nonetheless, occasionally the American media could not resist the temptation, despite the great differences in the two systems, to make the Russians seem like Americans. A good example of this was the Academy Award-winning war film *North Star*, released in 1943, in which the residents of a Soviet collective farm closely resemble family farmers in Kansas.

By far the most frequently covered story dealt with the Soviet achievement in the Ural region of Siberia. Here, the Russians had constructed whole new industrial regions designed to exploit the rich natural resources of the region, from coal and iron ore to manganese and tin. Correspondents gave Americans a history of the region and its ongoing centrality to the very survival and eventual victory of the Soviets. From maps pinpointing the major industrial centers and large deposits of raw materials, American readers could see for themselves the abundance of the region and its undiminished capacity to support the Soviet war effort.[30]

Americans were regaled with photos of these cities and their giant industrial operations. They saw photographs of workers in sites, such as Magnitogorsk, engaged in the production of tanks, locomotives, and other wartime essentials. No one could misread the critical role of this production in sustaining Russia's armies. Americans could also see in these same photos the efforts of women as a vital part of the heavy manufacturing process. Total war demanded that every able-bodied individual must participate. Americans were reminded of pictures of their own Rosie the Riveter. In an attempt to show the more human side of these industrial cities, editors also included extensive shots of river walks, homes, and parks where workers and their families enjoyed what little free time their grueling schedules allowed.[31]

Stalin's decision to build industry far from the reach of a Western enemy enabled the USSR to survive calamities of the war. Because a portion of Russia's raw materials and many of her industrial sites and hydroelectric operations were situated west of Moscow and in the Ukraine, they quickly came under German occupation. Without the vast resources and economic reality of the Ural region, Russia would never have been able to cope with losses of this magnitude and meet the incredible economic demands of total war.[32] Prominent Americans visiting the USSR confirmed the journalistic appraisals of Soviet achievements during the war. The head of the U.S. Chamber of Commerce, Eric Johnston, and journalist/author Richard Lauterbach, visited the Ural region of the Soviet

Union in 1944. Touring key urban industrial centers from Magnitgorosk and
Novosibirsk to Omsk and Tashkent, they concluded that "the Russians had
done a magnificent job." The two encountered numerous young men and
women who had journeyed to the region to work in its factories, mines, and
other industrial sites. They drew familiar parallels for American audiences
when they compared the manufacturing center of Novosibirsk to Chicago and
claimed the Russian city ranked as one of the great urban centers of the world.
Mikhail Kulagin, Communist Party Secretary in Novosibirsk, emerges from
their description virtually as an American prototype:[33]

> ... tough, wiry, 44-year old. ... He looks and acts like a cross between Jim
> Cagney and a Rotary greeter. Politically, he is a sort of Russian Jim Farley,
> slapping backs, shaking hands, everyone knows him, wants a private word with
> him. He sends his regards to his old pals, Hank Wallace and Don Nelson, who
> met him during their travels in Russia.[34]

Men as reputable as Johnston and the well known Lauterbach gave credence
to the claims about Soviet industrial might and helped convinced American
readers of the new-found economic power of our ally.

Stalin

At the beginning of World War Two, Stalin had the well-deserved reputation of
being the latest in a long line of tyrants going back from Lenin all the way to Ivan
the Dread. Eugene Lyon, editor of the conservative *American Mercury*, referred
to Stalin in a book as "a dark-visaged, pockmarked, slow moving Asiatic [who]
dominates the landscape of world affairs today."[35]

With the invasion of the Soviet Union in 1941, however, and in particular
after Pearl Harbor and Hitler's declaration of war on the United States, which
made the Soviet Union an ally, American attitudes toward Stalin began to
change. Given the American tendency to personalize countries about which
we know little in the form of their leaders, Stalin soon came to embody the
virtues of a Russian people resisting the depredations of the Nazi predator. He
assumed the character of benign ruler.

This, it turned out, was an understatement. One British correspondent
observed: "He looks like the kindly Italian gardener you have in twice a week."
For millions of Americans, Stalin became simply "Uncle Joe." Cover stories
on Stalin that appeared in such widely read magazines as *Time, Look,* and
Life strengthened this benign impression. In fact, a 1944 *Look* cover story was
entitled "A Guy Named Joe: Stalin's Knowledge Includes Airplanes, Soap."

In his military tunic, "he made Churchill in his siren suit look positively shabby.... "Few who have been privileged to talk with Stalin came away without being impressed by his mind, his remarkable grasp of information." He knew aeronautics; he knew soap wrappers; he knew all the specs for the Sturmovik fighter; he had read James Fenimore Cooper; he had been a youthful poet.[36]

Beyond his newly discovered personal characteristics and virtues, Stalin above all enjoyed an enormously great reputation for his performance, and, by extension, that of his people, in the war against Hitler. It was this feat that prompted *Time* to make him its Man of The Year for 1942. The article began: "The year 1942 was a year of blood and strength. The man whose name means steel in Russian, whose few words of English include 'tough guy' was the man of 1942. Only Joseph Stalin knew how close Russia stood to defeat in 1942, and only Joseph Stalin fully knew how he brought Russia through." Even the accomplishments of leaders much more familiar to us, Roosevelt and Churchill and Chiang Kai-shek, did not stand up to those of Stalin. "But the 1942 accomplishments of Chiang, of Churchill and of Roosevelt will not bear fruit until 1943. And, worthy though they may prove, they inevitably pale by comparison with what Joseph Stalin did in 1942."[37]

In March 1943, *Life* devoted an entire issue to Russia. Stalin adorned the cover. Astonishingly, considering the well-known anti-Communist stance of Henry Luce, the publisher, this was, in the words of one historian, "a bulging issue praising Communist Russia as one would hesitate to praise his native land lest he be accused of chauvinism."[38]

Americans were flattered by passing references to Stalin's knowledge of America, particularly its military history. "Timoshenko is my George Washington," he told an American general in 1942. "Zhukov is my George B. McClellan. Like McClellan he always wants more men, more cannon, more guns. Also more planes. He never has enough. But... Zhukov has never lost a battle," Stalin cannily concluded, too polite to point out that McClellan had never won a major one. Prominent Americans who had met the Soviet leader reinforced the positive image of Stalin. Wendell Willkie, whose book *One World* was a huge best seller in 1943, had visited Moscow for two weeks the previous year, where he met Stalin. In one of many spin-off articles from the book, the former candidate for president described his meeting with Stalin, from the dictator's greeting: "Glad to see you, Mr. Willkie" (the title of the article) to final assessment: "These I thought were wise words from a sagacious man."[39] But then, Willkie, who mercifully passed away in 1944, was a hopelessly romantic dreamer next to Eric Johnston, president of the U.S. Chamber of Commerce (Figure 2). Johnston's impression of Stalin, however, did not differ substantially

Figure 2. Left to right: Eric Johnston, president of the U.S. Chamber of Commerce and visitor of Joseph Stalin; and Thomas E. Dewey, Republican presidential nominee, Albany, NY, July 21, 1944. (Reprinted by permission, United Press International Photo.)

from that of Willkie, although he was somewhat more skeptical of the future. "As we motored along Moscow's blacked-out streets, I was still aware of this man's presence. His bluntness, his frankness, his humor intrigued me. He was coldly practical throughout. He rarely used an adjective or a superlative . . . Yes, Stalin was right. War has brought us together."[40]

That all of these encomiums trickled down to the common man there can be little doubt. Applauding *Time*'s decision to make Stalin Man of the Year, an American Seaman 2nd Class wrote to the magazine:

> In choosing Joseph Stalin Man of the Year, *Time* not only hit the nail on the head, but sunk a spike in one blow. Stalin stands for the Russian people, for what they are and for all they have done, the way they've done it, their guts, patriotism and downright loyalty to him as a leader in a country at war. The Germans fight like devils, but the Russian people, all of them, are fighting like hell and their fight is in the name of Stalin. Whether or not we agree with his form of government, let us in 1943 look toward this giant, take heed of his meaning and fight like hell.[41]

Humanization

Hollywood films about Russia in the 1930s usually drew clear distinctions between the Soviet regime and the people (something that did not happen in the 1950s, when the two were viewed as virtually synonymous). This fact enabled us to humanize the Russian people during World War Two (and, correspondingly, to dehumanize them during the Cold War). We did so in a number of complex ways, not the least of which was to draw parallels between them and ourselves.[42] One *Life* article on unity in diversity credited the Great Russians with being:

> prolific, gregarious, productive, aggressive and friendly. . . . They will go anywhere and try anything. They were one hell of a people long before the revolution. To a remarkable degree, they look like Americans, dress like Americans and think like Americans.[43]

Russians, moreover, also resembled the much-admired English. Other articles complimented the high morale and stiff upper lip of the Russians, comparing them to the English during the blitz: "The people of Moscow . . . were going about their business as calmly as Londoners. . . ."[44]

Despite the terrible onslaught of the Germans, who, in the fourteenth week of the war, seemed close to victory, Americans perceived an image of a tough people determined to prevail.

> Behind each Russian face, though, there was something more than these anxieties: there was determination. . . . With all his guts [each Russian] would help demonstrate to the Germans that an idea is harder to conquer than a nation and that the Russian nation is harder to conquer than any other."[45]

Little had changed a year later, in the desperate late summer of 1942, when *Time* again observed: "Fighting, working, making love, hanging out their clothes to dry, the Russians carried on" and quoted approvingly a Soviet writer reflecting on the nature of his own people: "there is a point in all Russians beyond which they seem to become oblivious of pain and fatigue. Up to that point, they are stolid and slower to react than most Europeans. Beyond it, they perform feats of endurance far beyond the usual human measure."[46]

The Russians, always possessed of a certain inferiority complex about their technological backwardness, have taken special pride in their cultural achievements, and linked those to their survival in the war, in which the Nazis, now cast in the role of barbarians, were trying to destroy the Russian people and their culture. Many articles brought home to Americans a sense of the great cultural legacy of the Russians and the great national pride invested in those achievements. Gone now were the crude "boy meets tractor; boy falls in love with tractor" jokes of the 1930s (they would return in the Cold War). *Time* quoted Stalin, who offered a virtual litany of Russian cultural heroes with whom he thought Americans should be familiar and whom he held up as a contrast with Nazi barbarity.

> These people, devoid of conscience and honor, people with the morale of beasts, have the impudence to call for the destruction of the Great Russian nation, the nation of Plekhanov, of Lenin, of Belinsky and Chernyshevsky, Pushkin, Tolstoy, Glinka and Tschaikovsky, Gorki, Checkhov, Sechewnov and Pavlov, Repin and Surikov, Suvorow and Kutuzov. . . . [47]

One clear area of Soviet achievement, as the sputnik shock of the late 1950s would demonstrate, lay in education. Soviet regimes of the 1920s and 1930s went a long way toward erasing the almost universal illiteracy that had been Russia's lot for centuries. American magazines took note of this fact. *Life* profiled the education system in Russia, pointing out how the Soviet regime had boosted the literacy rate to 80 percent in twenty years. In Moscow, bookstalls were as common as fruit stands in New York. Major libraries contained millions of volumes; the Literary Museum in Moscow alone was responsible for more than a million rare volumes.[48]

It is one indication of the complexity of coverage that the American press did not just convey the Russian people, virtues, and blemishes, as a faceless, anonymous mass; rather, countless articles singled out specific groups in the Soviet population for detailed attention. Family values and cohesion, always high on the scale of American priorities, appear frequently as themes in articles about the Russians. Despite the social upheavals of revolution and collectivization, Russians were depicted as being dedicated to family and hence to the larger unit in which the family was seen to flourish – the fatherland. As one author put it:

> The war has lifted the family to a new eminence and a new appreciation. Were anyone now to speak of it as a relic of a bygone age and fit for oblivion and annihilation he would be deemed a maniac or an outcast. Now there are no more hallowed words than semya (family) and rodina (fatherland). Life and happiness, the greatest man can know, emanate from these as inevitably as light and warmth emanate from the sun. Without the family and the fatherland there are only emptiness and futility, even as without the sun there is only darkness and death. The fatherland makes the family secure, the family makes the fatherland invincible – such is the view and the attitude now.[49]

Resistance against the Nazis was also often conveyed in family terms, as in the *Time* article entitled: "Come, Grandson, Let Us Cut Down the Orchard," which depicted a village of Cossack families carrying out the scorched earth policy against the Germans.[50]

One sea change in American coverage of Russia that occurred during the war involved Russian women. Now they appeared no longer as dumpy, frowsy Kolkhozniki, but rather as three-dimensional women – feminine and combative, nurturing and fierce, fashionable and covered with mud and blood. Often they were compared with members of the U.S. Women's Army Corps (WACs) and British Women's Royal Navy Service (WRNS, or Wrens), the difference being that Russian women actually served in combat roles, a fact that often amazed and appalled Americans and contributed to the tendency on the part of correspondents whenever possible to glamorize the Russian female. Walter Graebner, as he toured Russia, was particularly struck by the beauty of the women he saw. Already, at the airport upon his arrival, he observed mostly women.

> Physically they were superior in every way to any women I had seen since leaving America. [One wonders where he had been in the meantime.] They were perfect specimens of fitness – sturdy, erect of posture, bright-eyed, with healthy hair and clear peach-colored skin. They walked with the firm, determined steps of athletes . . . a few wore lipstick.

Graebner was all the more impressed because he had expected "an abundance of ordinary peasant types with poor figures and ill-fitting clothes." In fact, the clothes of his interpreter "were as smart as the dresses worn by most Chicago and New York secretaries."[51] Soviet women were depicted to the U.S. reader in a variety of roles, including coal miner, factory worker (the Russian equivalent of "Rosie the Riveter"), the shop foreman, and collective farm administrator. Indeed, the horrific losses of manpower, particularly early in the war, pressed women into virtually all jobs. The desperation for soldiers, given the huge losses suffered by the Russian armies, even pressed women into military service, including combat roles. As one American woman visitor observed:[52]

> Ballerina Olga Lepeshinskaya dances in a rickety shed within the sound of artillery. Nina Dubadze trains Red Army men to throw grenades. Natalia Dmitrievna designs a ship and it is built amid falling bombs by girls in their Teens.[53]

Photographs that humanized and personalized Soviet women for U.S. readers usually accompanied these stories, which often led the reader to believe that the postwar goals of Soviet women were the same as those of their American counterparts – domestic bliss and/or professional success. "'And what'll you do when the war ends?' one woman was asked. 'Become a school teacher again.' 'And get married?' 'Yes, of course!' she laughed gaily. 'A husband, children, a career – that's my idea of a woman's place in the world.'"[54]

If Russians were prouder of anything more than their culture it was their children. Russians traditionally dote on children, protect them, and hope for great things for them. Children in large numbers were evacuated from cities such as Leningrad, Smolensk, and Minsk as the Germans approached. The regime was at pains to build child care centers for mothers in war industry, something which particularly caught the attention of American women workers concerned about the care of their own children while on the job. Margaret Bourke-White, famous journalist and photographer for *Life* magazine, frequently described the creche system in the USSR and photographed a number of these sites.[55] But such was the all-consuming nature of the war in Russia that not even normally coddled children could escape some kind of participation, and a number of articles highlighted their occasionally mundane roles as janitors and cleaners, occasionally heroic ones as parachute spotters for the partisans. Visiting one school in session, an observer from America wrote of the children:

> They knew the meaning of the war only too intimately. Hardly one in School 255 but had a father or a brother in the Army. Not a few were already orphans. Others had had no news for months from fathers or brothers and were slowly reconciling themselves to the worst. Never, said the teachers, had the children been so mature and so sensitive.[56]

Always and everywhere there was, of course, the Russian soldier. Jamming the railroad stations on the way to the front and, often horribly wounded, returning home. In the American press, the Russian soldiers were not just one of a mass – neither in long lines of prisoners stretching to the horizon depicted in German newsreels, nor the Russian 'juggernaut' of late wartime legend. Nor were they the dirty, ignorant, brutalized, treacherous peasants of Nazi mythology. Rather, the picture of the Russian soldier that emerged was that of a patient, long-suffering, but also frequently a handsome, literate, innovative soldier who was capable of demonstrating great individual initiative.

The same applied to the Russian worker. "The Germans called those Russians 'mechanically inept and stupid' 'congenitally unfitted for industry,'" lamented Walter Rhys Williams, writing for *Survey Graphic*, who then asked rhetorically:

How then did it come to pass that in so short a time they became masters of the machine? To understand this, we must erase from our minds that image of the peasant – a clumsy, ox-like, shambling, dull witted creature . . .

Indeed, the Russian worker, he continued, had a lot in common with his American counterpart. "In terms of blueprints, pistons, kilowatts, amperes, the workers in Kharkhov and Leningrad have a common language with their contemporaries in Detroit and Pittsburgh."[57]

Bridges

These comments get to the heart of the motivation of journalists and many others who tried to interpret Russia and its peoples to the American reader: to build bridges that would link the two allied peoples and aid them in understanding one another. In doing so, there was a deliberate effort made to stress the commonalities that bound Russians and Americans together; to stress how alike they were under the veneer of vastly different social and economic systems.

Time and again, observers high and low ascertained how alike in character Russians and Americans were. Vice President Henry Wallace, one of the great boosters of the Russians during the war, set the tone for this exercise in many publications. In one article: "Two Peoples–One Friendship" he observed: "The Americans and the Russians are both frontier peoples. Both are continental peoples, with imagination and faith in the future. I have every reason to believe that Russia is the natural friend of the Americans in the years ahead."[58] A long-time observer of the Russians noted: "My first impression of the Russians . . . is how like Americans they are in certain aspects of their character and temperament, in their sense of humor, even in their sins and shortcomings." Then, in a veritable litany, he drew out the common traits, which one would see again and again in many publications throughout the war. Both people are multinational, machine-minded, pioneers, friendly, peace loving and given to hospitality, and interested in sports, athletics, and big game. They even have their vices in common. Both are "given to hard liquors rather than light ones."

Time, in a cover story on Stalin, also took pains to underscore the common features of both peoples:

The two peoples who talk the most and scheme the biggest schemes are the Americans and the Russians. Both can be sentimental one moment, blazingly angry the next. Both spend their money freely for goods and pleasures, drink too much, argue interminably. Both are builders.[59]

Part of the intense identification with the Russians stemmed from an American desire to see in them an ally fighting for his very life. Later in the war, this motive was joined by the desire not to have to face another conflict with an emerging superpower. This hope for peace came out clearly in a *Look* article on "Hometown-Russia" in 1944. Speculating on future peace, the writer opined: "The answer lies in the hearts and minds of both peoples. Each is strong, destined to be stronger. Each has much to teach the other. Today each wants peace. But lasting peace depends on how well both, together, can solve their differences, rivalries and mutual suspicions."[60] That they did not succeed in doing so became apparent in the emergence of the Cold War, in which the once intense identification with the Russian people dissolved into hostility and negative stereotype.

Russia's swift industrialization during the 1930s and the miracles of war production apparent after 1941 helped journalists establish another similarity between the two nations: their modernity. Americans were enamored of modernity and easily attributed this feature to their ally. The hope was that modernity would bring postwar prosperity, mutual trade, and a gradual convergence of the two societies. Americans have always thought that other peoples and societies had the potential – and the desire – to become like them and this fantasy was given free rein during the war.

Observing that the traditional beard had all but disappeared in Russia, one observer claimed that the country "is becoming one of the most clean-shaven nations in the world. . . . " Of course, as was often pointed out, Peter the Great, the first Russian modernizer, had gone after the beards of his nobles as a symbol of the triumph of the modern over the traditional. As Russia became more modern, it had to become more like us. "In their external appearance," this same observer continued, "the Russians are becoming more and more Westernized, more and more attuned to the machine age which they have so indefatigably espoused and which they so openly exalt."[61]

Walter Graebner, out in the "Wild East' visiting Russian industrial installations, could not help but wax eloquent over his modern hotel room in Baku. "It had two comfortable, spring-mattressed beds, electric lights, telephones and a connecting bathroom with a good tub, hot-cold running water, and a toilet that didn't smell."[62] Americans, in fact, were mightily impressed with the feats of war production that came precisely from the plants east of the Urals, and saw the prodigious efforts as a perfect complement to the Lend Lease products – food, medical supplies, and, above all, hundreds of thousands of Ford trucks. It was easy to extrapolate from this production to the streets of Soviet metropolises like Moscow, with its wide boulevards and miles of modern apartment buildings. Even traditional village life – always a touchstone for Russian backwardness – seemed to be transformed under the impulse of war. Russian villages, American visitors found, as they were carefully guided to model cases, far from resembling their sometimes crude traditional names – like pig snout or mare's cunt – were clean, neat, and well laid out. Everywhere, Lenin's dream of rural electrification seemed to prevail.

Even the "Hollywoodization" of Russia seemed to be proceeding apace, as a profile of Russia's movie queen, Lyubov Orlova, and her director/husband demonstrated. As photographed by Bourke-White, Orlova, fashionably attired and coifed, leaning on a fireplace mantel, cigarette in hand, in intense conversation with her husband, as her pet dog, equally fashionably coifed, looked on approvingly, could easily have been Greta Garbo in a Beverly Hills mansion.[63]

Religion and the Soviet Regime

But the clincher for many devout Americans must have been Russia's apparent emergence from atheism. In 1942, Stalin suddenly resurrected the Orthodox church, which had been savagely persecuted for years, as part of the war effort. The Metropolitan Sergei was brought out of mothballs and permitted to issue pronouncements for the national cause. Stalin even admitted to the British ambassador that "he too believed in God."[64] Eric Johnston, president of the U.S. Chamber of Commerce, was taken aback in his interview with Stalin, when the dictator, referring to a well-known American industrialist, said: "May God protect him." *Pravda* even began to capitalize God.[65]

These signals from Russia were encouraging to millions of Americans, of whose main objections to the Soviet system one had been its official atheism. Now a multitude of articles attested to a spiritual resurgence in Soviet Russia. Two-thirds of the peasant population and a third of the urban workers allegedly remained attached to their faith. "If this evolution continues," wrote one observer ecstatically, "we may hope that Soviet Russia will establish complete religious freedom as it exists in America and England."[66] Countless Russian mothers were depicted as sending their sons off to battle with a blessing. Even one young soldier, Alexej, raised under the Soviet system and not exactly steeped in the faith, was heard to say, "One may believe or be an infidel, but a mother's blessing is always sacred."[67]

At Christmas 1944, *Time* visited the religious scene in Moscow. "Moscow's fifty churches were jampacked. Patriarch Sergei . . . celebrated the Christmas service in Moscow's Bogoyarlevsky Cathedral. Worshippers were packed so tight that few of them could raise their arms to make the sign of the cross."[68]

Margaret Bourke-White had already visited this same cathedral two years earlier and begun a lengthy photo essay on the religious revival in Russia by writing movingly about her experience there. She described seventy-four-year-old Patriarch Sergei in great detail, noting his few words of English and his Soviet-built M3 car ("which is similar to our Ford"). She visited Metropolitan Vedensky and his wife at home – a considerably younger man and "witty, worldly, and a bit of a flirt." She also attended a service held by the large Baptist community in Russia. "They were delighted when I answered yes [to the question whether there were many Baptists in America] and especially pleased when I told them that my grandmother was a Baptist."[69]

Countless other stories emphasized common interests and pursuits. Russians were as crazy about sports as Americans. Maps in U.S. magazines demonstrated the depth of German penetration into Russia as well as the feat of moving Soviet industry eastward beyond the Urals. The cartographic displays incorporated economic and political data that helped readers understand the Soviet economy and political system. The maps also depicted the titanic battles that raged on the Eastern Front and showed the movement of armies across the Russian landscape. *Look* even superimposed a German invasion of the United States on the same scale the Third Reich conducted against the Russians. The magazine placed Russian cities on the U.S. landmass to show Americans the extent of the German thrust into the USSR. Readers could see how far the German armies had advanced by measuring it against the United States. These maps enabled Americans to follow the course of the war and the fortunes of their Russian allies, who bore the majority of the suffering and destruction mercilessly dished out by the German military upon its foes. Geography lessons were obviously not lost on Americans.[70]

Finally, even months after the war ended, this pattern of stressing similarity was firmly enough established; the bridge still sufficiently intact that *Look*, in a photo essay entitled "They're Coming Home in Russia, Too," brought a number of candid shots demonstrating that "Red Army Soldiers Act Like Our Own GI's."[71]

Aiding The Russians

U.S. citizens responded to the Russian crisis with unexpected generosity, given the long-standing animosities and misunderstandings that existed between the two countries. Public officials, ordinary Americans, and even children gave of their own resources to aid the Russians in their fight against the Nazis. The contributions to the Soviet war effort ranged from clothing to medical supplies and complemented the far larger official American Lend Lease policy, which gave the Russians war and war-related materials.

Often, U.S. delegates accompanied these genuine demonstrations of good will and support. Americans such as Corliss Lamont and Edward Carter of the American Council on Soviet Relations and the Russian War Relief group, respectively, made the long and arduous journey to the Soviet Union.[72] Even defeated Republican presidential candidate Wendel Willkie toured the Soviet Union extensively early in the war and wrote numerous articles in such popular magazines such as *National Geographic* and *Reader's Digest*, which praised the Russians and their heroic accomplishments in resisting the German invaders. The mere name of Willkie legitimized these accounts and made the USSR and its peoples far more real to American audiences accustomed to traditionally hostile descriptions of the Communist regime and its supporters.

Willkie also appeared at pro-Soviet rallies in the states. In November 1942, he joined David Dubinsky, President of the International Ladies' Garment Workers' Union (ILGWU), in a rally "dedicating 100 hospital tents" donated by the ILGWU to the Russian cause. The presence of Juri Okov, member of the Russian Consulate General; Marcia Davenport, chair of the Russian War Relief Society; and Newbold Morris, president of the New York City Council, lent a sense of legitimacy to Willkie's talk. His speech expressly linked the Russian and American wartime goal of defeating the Nazis. The crowd gathered in the New York City streets to hear Willkie enthusiastically cheered him throughout his talk. The *New York Times* also captured this crowd jammed into the intersection of 40th Street and 7th Avenue in a black-and-white photo prominently displayed alongside the story line. Upon closer inspection, one can see the ILGWU banners proclaiming support for the USSR. In New York, at least, the Soviet cause was capable of bringing out large and enthusiastic crowds.[73] Coincidentally, New York City Mayor Fiorella LaGuardia proclaimed November 8, 1942, as Stalingrad Day in honor of the twenty-fifth anniversary of the founding of the USSR and the great battle raging in southern Russia. The fierce struggle on the Volga River gripped millions of Americans, many of whom recognized it as a crucial battle of the war. LaGuardia declared the memorial day to underscore the bonds of friendship between the Russians and Americans, and to extend a "tribute to our Russian ally. . . ."[74]

Open support for the Soviet Union came both from the liberal left and the conservative right. In September of the same year, some 200 of the nation's business leaders gathered at the Bankers Club in New York City to hear speeches praising the Russian war effort. Thomas Lamont, senior vice-president of the powerful J. P. Morgan and Company, and Leon Freser, president of the First National Bank of New York City, demonstrated the caliber of the men who attended this event. They listened to Assistant Secretary of War for air, Robert Lovett, admonish them to abandon the old, hostile attitudes toward our ally. A similar gathering in Washington, D.C., hosted "government notables" on the estate of Joseph E. Davies. The meeting also praised the Russian war efforts and served as a prelude to the mass rallies planned for November of that year in New York City to demonstrate American support for the Soviet Union and its peoples.[75]

Noted columnist James Reston brought the message home to Americans on the seriousness of the war in Russia with his book *Prelude to Victory*. This work explained to American audiences the dangerous and real threat the German armies posed to the Russian people. It became one of the most widely read pieces of the war. *Prelude* appeared in paperback and was sold in outlets from drugstores to bus stops where ordinary Americans congregated on a daily basis. Reston's name gave the piece credibility, while his engaging style attracted millions of American readers.[76]

On a more somber note, Rabbi Jacob Hertz, speaking to the United Jewish Committee, issued a call to Jews all over the world to contribute in whatever way they could to the Russian cause. He was quoted in a *New York Times* article declaring that Adolf Hitler was "the murderer and destroyer of peoples and countries, the exterminator of the Jewish people." As a representative of the Aid Russia Fund, he reminded his listeners that the USSR "was the first country where anti-Semitism was outlawed" and now deserved all the help possible to defeat the Germans. Although addressed to the Jewish community, the call was certainly heard by many in the American public who perceived the first intimation of the genocidal campaign the Germans were conducting against the Jews.[77]

Ordinary Americans also expressed their feelings toward the Russian people and their struggles to defeat the Germans. In June 1943, *Time* carried samples of letters that Americans had written to individual Russians. One letter writer, George MacLellan, went so far as to declare his willingness to give the very clothes he wore each day. He even listed his measurements so a potential recipient would know the fit. MacLellan's response to Russia's plight was part of the Russian War Relief (RWR) campaign to encourage Americans to correspond with individual Russians. Russell G. Idle of Collinsville, Ill., wrote, "Most of us laboring people have confidence in you. We think you are a fair and helping ally, or what we call 'square shooters.' We feel you are nearest like us, than any other people." Veteran E. G. Sabatan, a merchant in tiny Dwight, Neb.: " . . . I did my part in 1918. I was in France for a year fighting those Germans but I guess we didn't stay long enough. . . . Give the Germans hell. . . . "[78]

By June 1943, U.S. citizens had sent some 1.2 million letters to Russia. Usually the plan was for an individual to communicate with someone in the USSR who held the same type of job. So, for example, thousands of farmer's wives in the United States sent letters to Russian peasant families. Industrial Bridgeport, Conn. sent greetings to the citizens of industrial Gorki.[79]

The RWR organization, formed by leading U.S. citizens and supported by committees across the country, became the most well-known organization in support of Russia. As the letter-writing campaign demonstrated, its members helped sparked the growing concern of Americans for their counterparts in Russia. It began as a donor of medical supplies and grew into an all-purpose organization as American participation in the war accelerated after the Pearl Harbor attack.[80]

RWR benefited immensely from the fact that it had been founded, run, and supported by prominent members of America's corporate elite. These men included Edward C. Carter, secretary-general of the Institute of Pacific Relations and president of the RWR, and C. C. Burlingame, one-time president of the New York City Bar, to F. W. Gehle, vice-president of Chase National Bank, Thomas D. Thacker, former solicitor general of the United States, and Al Smith, former New York state governor and 1928 Democratic Party presidential candidate. A network of local and regional elites drawn from a variety of locations, ranging from Georgetown, D. C., to Evanston, Ill., joined in support of the RWR. These men clearly identified with FDR's pro-Soviet Lend Lease policy and used their weight and connections to good effect to promote the Russian cause.[81]

The RWR established its headquarters in New York City and then set up branches in thirty-five American cities. The RWR also ran subcommittees in many smaller communities, so that its activities reached into the smallest corners of American society. On example – Stamford, Conn. – will demonstrate the range of the RWR measures in garnering support for the Russian war effort. In 1944, the RWR marked the opening of its local branch in Stamford with a celebration that drew community luminaries and hundreds of urban residents. Once up and running, the RWR sponsored a local campaign, "Share Your Clothes with Russia," that drew some $20,000 worth of clothing from Stamford donors. The Stamford Country Club, local financial institutions, the Slavonic League, and Stamford Women's Clubs, among other organizations, all gave their support to this campaign. The RWR also held Sunday afternoon garden parties where residents of Eastern European descent sang Slavonic songs and played the Russian balalaika. In more public affairs, the RWR sponsored local parades that featured the singing of the "Our Father" in Russian. Commenting on such events, Lois Miller wrote in *Reader's Digest*, "John Doe's pennies, dimes, and quarters are helping to fight Hitler right now along the Russian front."[82]

Such examples of individual Americans giving of their own money and time generated national coverage. The RWR passed out some one million small piggy banks for Americans to fill with their change. One mother attached her bank to her child's baby carriage. While she walked her child, passers-by filled the bank with nickels and dimes. A Midwestern banker fixed his bank to the dashboard of his car and asked for fares when giving his friends rides. Pictures carried by *Survey Graphic* showed Louisville children carrying donations to the RWR branch. Another photo depicted local supporters in Sheboygan, Wisconsin, gathering clothing intended for the Russian people.[83] Edward C. Carter's visit to the USSR in 1943 was intended to demonstrate to the thousands of Americans who generously gave of their resources that such gifts were being effectively used for their intended purposes. He wrote back that Russian children now enjoyed donated American clothing, and demonstrated their gratitude by planting victory gardens with some 450 tons of seeds sent by Americans. Russian families would shortly be able to enjoy Idaho potatoes or New England squashes. He also assured ordinary Americans that the Soviets were keeping careful records on exactly where the donated items were being sent – whether to Kharkhov or Rostov. Carter even appeared with partisans, who had made the dangerous journey from behind enemy lines to Moscow in search of American aid.[84]

RWR also held rallies during the war. In June 1942, it hosted a rally at Madison Square Garden, which included noted speakers such as Russian Ambassador Maxim Litvinoff and U.S. Director of Lend Lease, Harry Hopkins. The rally also commemorated the anniversary of the founding of the USSR. The Ambassador spoke on the tremendous sacrifices of the Russian people in fighting the Nazis and their ongoing ability to stay in the war. He assured his listeners that the combined resources of the USSR, America, and Great Britain would prove decisive. Hopkins, who had already journeyed to Moscow to see first-hand the Russian war effort, also told an audience of 20,000 about Russian determination to carry on the struggle, although he warned that the Red Army was still in great danger. William Green, head of the American Federation of Labor (AFL), praised the Red Army, which he declared had exposed the myth of German invincibility. Members of the AFL wholeheartedly supported the Russian cause.[85]

The rally was also a fundraiser. The RWR had already collected some $2 million toward a goal of $6 million. Carter eloquently reminded the audience that "it was the little people who started the RWR, the steel workers, housewives, office workers . . ." among others. The ILGWU and the National Maritime

Union gave generously. So, too, did the International Business Machine Corporation and steel giant, U.S. Steel, and other major corporations. John D. Rockefeller, Jr. personally sent a $50,000 check "with a letter declaring it was 'an expression of my admiration of what the Russian army was doing – their heroism, their courage and their sacrificial devotion to their homeland.'" Members of the audience made donations from "$5,000 to one dollar"; no donation was too small.[86]

Cultural exchanges also enhanced American understanding of the USSR and promoted better relations. These ranged from academic visits to chess matches. Russian music also generated great interest in the United States. Shostokovich's wartime symphonies were performed throughout the United States, as were those of other Russian composers. Shostakovich's Seventh Symphony was smuggled out to the West and premiered on American radio under the baton of Toscannini. The piece, written during the siege of Leningrad, became a symbol of resistance to the Nazis. Shostakovich appeared on the cover of *Time* on July 20, 1942.[87] American jazz and films enjoyed great popularity in the USSR. Such exchanges also built on a twenty-year history that included tourism and the transfer of American technology and American ideas.[88]

The good will apparent in these exchanges lasted only as long as the viability of the alliance. Once that came into question, as it did so dramatically in 1945–1946, changes were swift. The most visible bellwether for this fragile comradeship appeared in the *Reader's Digest*, an intensely conservative and patriotic magazine that reached a significant readership – millions – among ordinary middle class Americans. In terms of support for the beleaguered Russians, the *Reader's Digest* was, in a sense, the last in and the first out. The *Reader's Digest* had always reflected the rock-ribbed conservatism of the Wallace family, which started publishing the immensely popular monthly in 1927. The reprinted or abridged articles almost inevitably came from other conservative magazines such as *The American Mercury* or *The Saturday Evening Post*. The Wallaces even republished essays from cautious provincial newspapers, including the *Baltimore Sun*.

Throughout its early years, the *Reader's Digest* had rarely shown even a shred of support for the Soviet experiment and, indeed, had often gone to great lengths to vilify the USSR and its leaders. This attitude only intensified after Roosevelt's recognition of the USSR in 1933. Stalin's brutal collectivization, his purges of thousands of Soviet citizens, and his invasion of tiny and seemingly defenseless Finland sustained the magazine's hostility during the entire decade. This antagonistic stance persisted even after the Nazi invasion of the Soviet Union in June 1941. While opinion makers called for vigorous aid to the USSR, the *Reader's Digest* poignantly included articles such as the critical

"Silent Soviet Revolution" (July 1941) from *Harpers* written by Bertram Wolfe, a widely recognized expert on Russia. In the same year, the Wallaces reissued "Academy of High Treason" (August 1941), extracted from *The American Mercury*, in which Jan Vatlin purported to expose a Communist plot against the U.S. defense effort.[89]

The magazine's editors did occasionally relent, as the war in Russia reached an early turning point near Moscow. They grudgingly acknowledged the Soviet Union's tremendous effort in combating the Nazis and the stubborn resistance of its peoples against the brutal Nazi onslaught. In January 1942, *Reader's Digest* republished an article from *Life* by Russian front-line correspondent, Alexander Poliakov, who extolled the guerrilla war behind German lines. In February 1942, American journalist John Scott, who had worked in the Soviet Union during the 1930s in the Ural industrial region, wrote a piece for *Barrons* entitled "Stalin's Ural Stronghold." This piece drew an encouraging picture of Russia's wartime industrial plant capable of supplying her armies with unlimited martial resources yet safely beyond the reach of the Nazi armies. Despite its continuing suspicion of Stalin and his regime, *Reader's Digest* did include this article, authenticated by its American author, in the February issue.[90]

Still, the editors never abandoned their hostility and continued to release pieces critical of the USSR and its leadership. In December 1941, *Reader's Digest* published an essay written by one-time Communist and, by that date, bitter enemy of Marxist-Leninism, Max Eastman. His article, "Stalin's American Power," from the *American Mercury* issued in the December 1941 *Reader's Digest* created a menacing image of the Communist threat in the United States.[91]

Eastman would later join the ranks of Cold War warriors who once admired the Soviet experiment, encountered its darker side, and then moved sharply to the right of the political spectrum. Eastman experienced firsthand the Soviet Union during the early 1920s when he met Lenin and other Communist leaders. He smuggled out Lenin's testament after Stalin assumed power in the USSR. Ironically, his activities in the Soviet Union and longtime familiarity with Communism and the Soviet regime authenticated his position as a critic of the USSR. By World War Two, his essays had assumed a place as a staple of conservative journalism on the experiment in Russia. Then, in 1941, his critical piece, which the *Reader's Digest* labeled as one of the most important articles in months, explained how the Communists were infiltrating liberal organizations and playing Americans, including President Roosevelt, for suckers. The editors anticipated such a favorable reaction that reprints were offered to the readership. Caught between the distrust for Stalin and his war against the Nazi invaders, Eastman revealed the wartime dilemma of conservatives.

He warned that "Stalin is the weaker of the two gangster-tyrants and common sense demands that we support this resistance to Hitler. But common sense also warns us against the added strength of his American agents with their own more subtle plot against our way of life."[92]

After Pearl Harbor and our own entry into the war, the gigantic conflict in Russia assumed increasing importance for Americans; Russia now stood, despite our misgivings, as a critical, if not *the* critical American ally. News of the Russian front dominated the headlines. Few Americans could miss the significance of the war in the Soviet Union. In the words of one scholar: "Hardly an hour would pass between the summer of 1941 and June of 1944 when the progress of the Russian defense of the homeland was not mentioned on most radio stations." During the last week of June 1941, the Russo-German war and American-Russian relations occupied 72.3 percent of the front page of the average American newspaper. . . . Until Pearl Harbor, and then beginning again a month later for another two years, the Russo-German war . . . usually occupied a major portion of every front page of United States newspapers and held the lead off story on radio broadcasts."[93]

American attitudes toward the Soviet Union began to change under the impact of almost continuous news coverage. In October 1941, only 22 percent of Americans ranked Russia along with Britain as a partner; by February 1942 this figure had jumped to 41 percent. By the spring of 1943, *Time* captured the rising pro-Russian sentiment when it carried a cartoon from the St. Louis *Dispatch* that showed a vulture with a German Army officer's hat and a Nazi symbol on its chest sitting on a sign that read "I am protecting Europe from Bolshevism." In keeping with this spirit of wartime allies, the *Reader's Digest* featured articles favorably disposed to the USSR. This change in policy proved no longer risky given that even the violent anti-Communist extraordinaire, Colonel McCormick, owner of the *Chicago Tribune*, wrote, no doubt with clenched teeth, that although Communists remained both cockeyed and dangerous, "we should draw not upon their dangerousness, but upon their cockeyedness." For McCormick this position was as close as he ever got to domesticating Communism.[94]

Typical, then, for the *Reader's Digest* in 1942 and 1943 were articles strongly supporting Russian war relief, extolling the incredible Russian war effort and the price the Russians were paying, and taking note of the remarkable fortitude of the Russian peasant.[95]

In early 1942, the *Reader's Digest* also printed selections from former Ambassador Joseph Davies' intensely pro-Soviet and highly controversial book, *Mission to Moscow*, which had appeared after Pearl Harbor. Typically, Davies wrote

"Those who fear Russian communism here in America grossly underrate the strength of their own country and its institutions." In that same issue, Milton Mayer referred to the Soviet Foreign Minister, Maxim Litvinov, as "Little Papa Litvinov," who joined the now avuncular Stalin ("Uncle Joe").[96]

A year later, *Reader's Digest* published, among other articles, a piece by Wendel Wilkie, "Life on the Russian Frontier," which not only expressed admiration for the Russian war effort but also for the accomplishments of the Soviet system.[97]

> Any man who visits a part of the Soviet Union today may well dislike its godlessness, or be disturbed about its communist themes: but no man can look at these people and talk to them without realizing that they have built one of the most effective societies of modern times.

> Wilkie, unsuccessful Republican opponent of Roosevelt in 1940, reflected the American tendency to be impressed by anything modern. He donated his royalty check for the article to Russian relief. Wilkie, whose book *One World* outsold even Davies' *Mission to Moscow*, stood as a major spokesman for both wartime alliance and postwar cooperation with the Soviets, with whom, he believed, we could create a peaceful world.

Several months later, at the height of the popularity of the wartime alliance, *Reader's Digest* felt constrained, perhaps again out of contrition, to offer another corrective from Max Eastman. Referring to Davies and Wilkie, he noted of the ambassador, "[His] performance only points up by the extreme example the epidemic of hysterical adulation of a tyrant state which is sweeping so many influential Americans off their feet." And of Wilkie: "The mushheads and muddleheads are doing us in. We turn naturally to Wendel Wilkie." He issued dire warnings against "our self-deluding Leftists." Against Christian ministers who "go all out to convince America that Russia enjoys religious freedom. . . ." and against the Vice President, Henry Wallace, who had become "another apologist for Communism. . . ."[98]

Having done its conservative duty, the *Readers' Digest* went on to publish relatively positive pieces for the rest of 1943 and 1944. Typical was "The last Days of Sevastopol" by a Russian journalist, Boris Voyetkov, extracted from the *Saturday Evening Post*. Even Max Eastman saw the necessity of postwar cooperation with the Soviets, so that *Reader's Digest* also opened its pages to a number of pieces speculating about that possibility, especially during 1944, as the victorious Red Army drove westward. Eric Johnston reported on his conversation with Stalin, whom he found to be a practical, straightforward fellow. William White, war correspondent and editor of the *Emporia Gazette*, who had accompanied Johnston on his six-week trip to the Soviet Union, wrote a two-piece essay, "Report on the Russians" which, in retrospect, proved quite clear and critical, but balanced. It ignited a controversy, as some thought the piece an inappropriate critique of a wartime ally. *Reader's Digest* defended White's right to publish his views.[99]

Still, the controversy signaled the fraying of the allied coalition as the war drew to a close. *Reader's Digest* published one more article in tune with the wartime admiration of the Russian war effort, in retrospect a swan song. Richard Lauterbach's article, "Russia's Number One Soldier," taken from *Life* and published the same month as the German surrender, was the last positive piece that *Reader's Digest* would ever release about the Russian war effort against the Nazis. Lauterbach profiles General Zhukov, whom he characterized as "one of the greatest generals of World War Two." A combination of Marshall, Eisenhower, and Bradley, "Zhukov has a record of military achievement without parallel in modern war;" "no single counterpart" emerged "in either the Allied or Axis armies." Adjectives characterizing him included "Cunning, imaginative, prophetic . . . audacious, imperturbable, unconquerable." The article culminates in the assessment: "Zhukov is a good communist. He does not believe in God. But he does believe in history, in progress, in decency. For these things, for his home, his wife, his children, and for Russia, he has fought an unbeatable war." These comments proved a remarkable tribute given that we would soon adopt the German vision of the war in the East and the Wehrmacht generals would, ironically, attain the mythic stature of Zhukov. He and other much-lionized Russian generals such as Timoshenko would vanish from the American consciousness they once dominated. Signaling this dramatic shift in attitudes, *Readers' Digest* republished Leigh White's *Saturday Evening Post* essay, "The Soviets' Iron Fist in Rumania" three months after the Zhukov article. The Cold War had begun.[100]

We have taken perhaps an inordinate amount of time to discuss the *Readers' Digest* offerings during the war. Yet, we believe it important to lay the foundation for a dramatic shift in memory that would ensue during the Cold War. Americans encountered a flood of information about the war in the East during the years 1941–1945. This information included detailed narratives about the battles, particularly the decisive Stalingrad conflict and the final chapter, the seizure of Berlin. The chapter also incorporated material from the media – books, newspapers, popular magazines, and radio – which examined with great sympathy the tragedy visited upon Russia by the Germans. These media forms also personalized this suffering and glorified the triumphs of Russian arms and the Russian people. Soon after the war, this memory faded under the strains of emerging USSR–USA tensions, then disappeared to be replaced by a pro-German version, one that stressed Russian atrocities, German heroism, and even a superhuman sacrifice to defend Western culture from the Eastern hordes. Soon, a sizable body of Americans would embrace this German view, profoundly at odds with our wartime understanding. Such a transformation occurred only because of the deep ambivalence Americans always held toward the Communist regime and for Slavic peoples in general, even at the height of the wartime alliance. Nowhere did this ambivalence appear more evident than in the pages of the *Reader's Digest*.

2 The Cold War and the Emergence of a Lost Cause Mythology

At the end of World War Two, there was no question but that the German army was in complicity with the regime's war crimes. While the war was still going on, in November 1942, the Soviets created the Extraordinary State Commission to investigate Nazi war crimes. As a result, several Soviet military tribunals were held the following year: in July and August at Krasnodar, in September at Mariopol, and, most dramatically, in December at Kharkov. The trials drew a great deal of publicity. Foreign journalists were invited and the transcript was translated into a number of languages. There was a good deal of coverage in the Western press. Already, in the Krasnodar trial, which dealt with collaborators, serious accusations were levied against the German 17th Army under Colonel General Richard Ruoff. The Kharkov trial brought together as defendants a Soviet collaborator, a German army captain, an SS officer, and a 6th Army corporal, all of whom had been involved in massacres of civilians, including Jews; four of the accused were executed. Already, here, the pattern of cooperation between SS and Wehrmacht was being established.[1] After the war, the Soviet government staged a number of show trials, which ran parallel to the International Military Tribunal (IMT) trial in Nuremberg. These included trials in Smolensk and Bryansk in December 1945 and in Riga in February 1946. Again, both German military officers and SS were tried and executed for mistreatment of Soviet prisoners of war (POWs) and for murdering civilians. At Riga, for example, seven generals were executed for their crimes. The Russians also hanged the infamous Friedrich Jeckeln, Higher SS and Police Leader on several fronts in Russia, who, among other crimes, carried out the massacre at Babi Yar and the annihilation of the Jews of Riga. A number of other Soviet trials of German officers ran through 1947, based on the mandate of the Allied Control Commission Law #10 and resulting in many convictions and executions prior to the official abolition of the death penalty in the Soviet Union in May 1947.[2]

The Soviet liberation of the largely intact Majdanek camp at Lublin in August 1944 also received widespread coverage in the western press and introduced the West to the Nazi death camps.[3]

The conviction that the Wehrmacht stood in the service of the racial goals of the Nazi regime was most clearly and forcefully expressed in the various post-war trials, beginning with the International Military Tribunal at Nuremberg in 1945–46. Among the groups which Justice Robert Jackson, the first U.S. prosecutor at Nuremberg, wanted to have indicted as a criminal organization was the German General Staff. There was strong support for this in the Administration and the task was handed over to the man who would later succeed Jackson, Telford Taylor. Taylor came up with the "General Staff and High Command of the German Armed Forces" as the umbrella term for the indictable organization. This decision reflects in part our interpretation of German "militarism" as the main force behind both World Wars. During World War Two, the Nazi regime itself had often been viewed as an expression of German militarism, and, at the end of the war, public opinion agreed that German militarism should be extirpated forever. Even General Eisenhower, who would later exonerate the Wehrmacht, initially agreed most forcefully. In July 1944, he was recorded as saying "that the German General Staff regards this war and the preceding one as merely campaigns in their dogged determination first to dominate Europe and eventually the world. He [Eisenhower] would exterminate all of the General Staff [which he estimated to number about 3,500]. Or maybe they could be concentrated on some St. Helena . . . "[4] On April 27, 1945, as the war was just days from ending, Allied Supreme Headquarters urged the U.S. government to "exile all General Staff officers and all generals forever, and imprison them for life in an area under the control of one or all of the United Nations."[5]

Interestingly enough, there was not unanimity on this question. A number of U.S. army officers (including, Taylor thought, William "Wild Bill" Donovan) apparently identified with and respected their German counterparts enough to reject the idea of trying them as a group. This did not apply to trials of Japanese generals, however, leading Taylor to observe wryly that "apparently in old-line military circles yellow generals did not rank as high in the scale of virtue as Nordic white ones."[6] Although support for the trials remained high in the upper levels of the Administration and the Pentagon, combat-grade officers tended to object to the proceedings against their German counterparts. Former German officers would later capitalize on this atttude as they tried to shape American attitudes toward the war.[7] By the time the trials were under way, even Eisenhower (and his former colleague, Field Marshal Montgomery) got a bit nervous about the proceedings, imagining themselves in the place of

Wilhelm Keitel and Alfred Jodl.[8] More ominously, the British rejected the idea out of hand.

In the end, Taylor was not able to satisfy the court that there was a collective entity called the "High Command," so that trials of individuals became necessary after the main Nuremberg IMT trials. However, in making his case for declaring the High Command a criminal organization, Taylor aired much of the dramatic evidence that would later be forgotten about Wehrmacht complicity in war crimes. In particular, he offered documents, including messages to the troops, issued by high-level military commanders, among them Walther von Brauchitsch, Walter von Reichenau, and Erich von Manstein, in which they urge the ruthless extirpation of the "Jewish-Bolshevik" system.[9] The first issue of the Wehrmacht propaganda series left no doubt as to the army's stance toward the Soviet regime. "Anyone who has ever looked into the face of a red commissar knows what Bolsheviks are. . . . It would be an insult to animals to describe the features of these slave drivers, a large percentage of whom are Jewish, as bestial. They are the embodiment of everything infernal, the incarnation of insane hatred for all that is noble in man. These commissars are the revolt of the subhuman against the nobility of blood."[10]

On October 10, 1941, Field Marshal von Reichenau, 6th Army commander in Russia, issued instructions to his troops that clarified their mission. "The most essential aim of war against the Jewish-Bolshevistic system is a complete destruction of their means of power and the elimination of Asiatic influence from the European culture . . . The soldier in the Eastern territories is not merely a fighter according to the rules of the art of war, but also a bearer of ruthless national ideology and the avenger of bestialities which have been inflicted on the German and racially related nations. Therefore, the soldier must have full understanding for the necessity for a severe but just revenge on subhuman Jewry."[11] No wonder, then, that the Nuremberg Tribunal, although not recognizing the existence of such an entity as the "High Command," except in the language of the indictment, nevertheless noted that the high German officers were "responsible in large measure for the miseries and suffering that have fallen on millions of men, women and children" and recommended individual trials for the accused.[12]

Two German generals were among the twenty-two major Nazi war criminals tried at Nuremberg: Alfred Jodl and Wilhelm Keitel. Keitel, chief of the High Command of the armed forces, had participated in Hitler's planning for every invasion and had signed off on some of the most odious orders issued by Hitler, including the Commando Order, the Commissar Order, the Night and Fog Decree, the Hostage Order, and the Jurisdictional Order, to name only the most egregious. Typical was his order of September 16, 1941, which read that the "death penalty for 50–100 Communists should generally be regarded in these cases as suitable atonement for one German soldier's death. The way in which sentence is carried out should still further increase the deterrent effect."[13] Jodl was chief of the Operations Staff of the High Command and technically subordinate to Keitel. He also had signed many incriminating orders involving Nazi invasions and atrocities, which led him (like Keitel) to be indicted and convicted for crimes against humanity and war crimes. Both men were sentenced to death and hanged.[14]

A great deal of testimony was offered at the Nuremberg trial and subsequent trials that was devastating to the German military and subsequently forgotten during the Cold War. When it came to the war in the East against the Soviet Union, the prosecutors were clear in their own minds as to the role of the German army in genocide, and the testimony of even many Nazis themselves confirmed this judgment.

In his statement to the court, Telford Taylor, moving from a discussion of events in the West, turned to the Eastern Front:

> I propose to show here that the activities of the German Armed Forces against partisans and other elements of the population became a vehicle for carrying out Nazi political and racial policies and a vehicle for the massacre of Jews and numerous segments of the Slav population which were regarded by the Nazis as undesirable . . . I will show that the Armed Forces supported, assisted, and acted in cooperation with the SS groups . . . [15]

Here, in his opening statement, Taylor alludes to German military and SS culpability for war crimes that would soon be denied or forgotten, only to be rediscovered thirty years later by historians and just reach public consciousness in the 1990s and beyond. It is, however, a culpability repressed by those who would romanticize the Eastern front.

Taylor had lined up devastating testimony to make his case. First came Otto Ohlendorf, chief of Einsatzgruppe D, which had murdered, by Ohlendorf's own admission, 90,000 people between June 1941 and June 1942. Ohlendorf went on in excruciating detail to describe the murder of men, women, and children, including Jews, by his men and the disposal of their possessions and bodies. Ohlendorf, under questioning, confirmed the knowledge and active support of the German army in this process. "Himmler told me that before the beginning of the Russian campaign Hitler had spoken of this mission [to exterminate Jews and Communist functionaries] to a conference of the army groups and . . . the commanding officers – and had instructed the commanding generals to provide the necessary support." They not only provided support;

they got into the spirit of mass murder. "In Simferopol," Ohlendorf said by way of example, "the army command requested the Einsatzkommandos in its area to hasten the liquidations, because famine was threatening and there was a great housing shortage." The commander of the nearby 11th Army was Field Marshal Erich von Manstein, whose later statement that he was shocked to hear about the murder of the Jews is belied by the fact that the only conflict he had with the SS was over who should get the wristwatches of murdered victims. Manstein won that one. Ohlendorf: "At the request of the Army, watches were made available to the forces at the front."[16]

Then came Erich von dem Bach-Zelewski, Hitler's favorite SS general. Bach-Zelewski, Higher SS and Police Leader for central Russia until the end of 1942, who was in charge of the grisly task of combating partisans in Russia, and then of suppressing the Warsaw uprising in 1944, testified to the widespread involvement of the Wehrmacht in atrocities carried out by SS and police in the East. He frequently conferred with the commanders of army groups and with the district commanders of the Wehrmacht and advised them on the methods that should be used to combat partisans. He named "General of the Cavalry Bremer, Wehrmacht commander in the East; General Field Marshal Küchler, commanding general of Army Group North; the commanding generals of Army Group Center, Kluge and Busch; the Wehrmacht commander in the Ukraine, General of the Luftwaffe Kitzinger; General Field Marshal Freiherr von Weichs, commanding general in Serbia . . . " among those with whom he had worked. Under cross-examination by the Russian prosecutor Colonel Pokrovsky, Bach-Zelewski added Major General Hartmann and Colonel General Reinhardt to the list. Lest one get the impression that tough, even brutal antipartisan activities were justified, Zelewski admitted that "the struggle against the partisan movement was a pretext for destroying the Slav and Jewish population." Asked by Pokrowsky whether "the Wehrmacht Command [was] aware of the methods adopted for fighting the partisan movement and for destroying the Jewish population," Bach-Zelewski replied: "The methods were known generally, and hence to the military leaders as well." He also confirmed what we know today as "Generalplan Ost" (General Plan for the East), when he admitted that the measures taken by the German military were designed to lead to the extermination of thirty million Slavs in the Soviet Union.[17]

Walter Schellenberg, former major general in the Waffen-SS and chief of Office VI (foreign intelligence branch) of the Sicherheitsdienst (Security Service or SD) in the RSHA (Reich Main Office for Security, the umbrella organization of the Nazi police state), also implicated the Wehrmacht. Schellenberg was present and kept the minutes at a meeting between his boss, Reinhard Heydrich, and Quartermaster General of the German Army, General Eduard Wagner, at

the end of March 1941, at which the two men signed an agreement detailing
future cooperation between Wehrmacht and SS Einsatzgruppen.[18]

The Commissar Order, the directive issued by the Wehrmacht to German
troops just before the invasion of Russia, ordering that all Communist military commissars who fell into German hands be shot, was also presented into
evidence at Nuremberg.[19]

Finally, an affidavit from Ernst Rode, former SS brigadefuehrer and major
general of the Police and Waffen-SS as well as former chief of command staff
of Himmler himself, highlighted the close cooperation between SS and army.
Referring to the activities of the Einsatzgruppen, Rode said,

> the [military] commanders were . . . thoroughly cognizant of the missions and
> operational methods of these units. They approved of these missions and oper-
> ational methods because, apparently, they never opposed them. The fact that
> prisoners, such as Jews, agents, and commissars, who were handed over to the
> SD, underwent the same cruel death as victims of so-called purifications, is a
> proof that the executions had their approval.

Rode also admitted that it was clear to him "that anti-partisan warfare gradually became an excuse for the systematic annihilation of Jewry and Slavism."
Again, he, like the others, named names. In the course of his work, he had discussions with the leading officers of the Wehrmacht and Army Operations Staff,
including "General Warlimont, General von Butlar, Colonel General Guderian,
Colonel General Zeitzler, General Heusinger, General Wenk, Colonel Graf Kielmannsegg . . . and General von Bonin."[20] Interestingly enough, several of these
officers would be instrumental either in building the lost cause myth (Guderian) or in the creation of the Bundeswehr in the 1950s (Kielmannsegg).

And what were the generals saying about these accusations as the trial
proceeded? A few were admitting to them. In conjunction with the attempt to
indict the German military High Command, General Johannes Blaskowitz, a
field commander early in the war, and Field Marshal Werner von Blomberg,
Commander in Chief of the Wehrmacht prior to 1938, signed affidavits to the
effect that virtually all General Staff officers supported Hitler's war policies,
including the invasion of Poland.[21]

As to the specifics of Wehrmacht complicity in mass murder, one former
general who admitted the truth was General Hans Röttinger, general of Panzer
troops and Chief of Staff of the German 4th Army and later of Army Group
Center on the Eastern front. He was involved from time to time with antipartisan activities. Taylor submitted his affidavit at the trial. "At the beginning,"
Röttinger wrote, "in accordance with orders which were issued through official channels, only a few prisoners were taken. In accordance with orders Jews,

political commissars, and agents were delivered up to the SD." Röttinger was well aware of the larger purposes behind "partisan warfare." He had come to "realize that the order from the highest authorities for the harshest conduct of the anti-partisan war can only have been intended to make possible a ruthless liquidation of Jews and other undesirable elements by using for this purpose the military struggle of the Army against the partisans."[22]

After the Nuremberg IMT, no more trials were held involving the four Allied powers. The twelve successor trials of further Nazi war criminals were held instead before American military tribunals at Nuremberg in 1947. One hundred eighty-five defendants were involved as the accused, including representatives of the SS and Gestapo, government ministries, doctors, industrialists, and the SS Einsatzgruppen.

Two of these cases again involved German generals: Case Seven and Case Twelve. In Case Seven, the "Hostage Case," twelve officers who had been assigned to southeastern Europe were charged with criminal disregard of the civilized rules of warfare with respect to the treatment of hostages and civilians. Focus of the case was shootings of civilian hostages in Yugoslavia and Greece. In part, these shootings were carried out as reprisal for alleged partisan activities. But they were also (as we know today) part of the Final Solution, given that many of the hostages were Jews or Roma and Sinti. Part of the accusation also involved the deportation of civilians to be slave laborers in Nazi concentration camps or, as it turned out, to their deaths in extermination camps. Ten were convicted, including Wilhelm List, Walter Kunze, Lothar Rendulic, Wilhelm Speidel, Helmuth Felmy, Ernst von Leyser, Hubert Lanz and Ernst Dehner. Their sentences ranged from life to time served.[23]

In Case Twelve, the "High Command or OKW Case," fourteen defendants were charged with personal responsibility in ordering the mistreatment and murder of POWs as well as the abuse and deportation of civilians in occupied areas. Eight of these officers served on the Eastern Front. They were viewed by the court as representative of the military elite of the Wehrmacht. Eleven of these generals, including Wilhelm von Leeb, Georg von Küchler, Hermann Hoth, Hans Reinhardt, Hans von Salmuth, Karl Hollidt, Karl von Roques, Hermann Reinecke, Walter Warlimont, Otto Wöhler, and Rudolf Lehmann, were convicted in October 1948 of war crimes and crimes against humanity. Central to these convictions was the role these generals played in the formulation and carrying out of the Commissar and Commando orders, their role in the deportation of war prisoners and civilians to be slave laborers in Germany, their role in crimes against civilians as well as POWs, particularly Soviet war prisoners, and their role in the killing of Jews in the East. Sentences ranged from life to three years.[24]

In this trial in particular, the evidence demonstrates the whole breadth of Wehrmacht complicity in crimes in the East – evidence that faded as new legends were concocted in subsequent years. One of the great ironies of the post-IMT trials carried out by the Americans, particularly the OKW trial, was that they were meant to prevent precisely what happened in the 1950s and beyond – the rewriting of history and the manufacturing of legends. The U.S. prosecutor, Walter H. Rapp, said as much in a 1948 radio interview, when he asserted that the most important effect of the trial was meant to be the "prevention of legends." Without accusations against "two or three general field marshals and a dozen or a dozen and a half colonel generals," he said, the same thing would happen as it did after the last war, namely, the population would get the impression that generals were "gracious, old, highly educated fine gentlemen," who couldn't possibly have anything to do with what they were accused of doing. Unfortunately, Rapp, although correct in his assessment, was wrong in his prediction.[25]

We have discussed at some length and quoted from the testimony at Nuremberg against the German military. There is little that is new here. American and German historians, in particular, have researched and written exhaustively since the late 1970s on this theme – and on the Holocaust generally. But, lest one think that we belabor the obvious, it is important to note, that for the better part of three decades, the clear connection drawn out at Nuremberg and subsequent trials, which linked the SS and the German military to the Holocaust (although the term did not come into widespread usage until the 1970s) in the East was lost, repressed, and forgotten. Indeed, if one thinks in terms of the general public, it is only in the 1990s, partly through publicity focused on the "Crimes of the Wehrmacht" exhibit, that what the general public clearly knew and acknowledged in 1945 once again became part of its historical consciousness. In the interim, the emergence of the Cold War and the radical realignment it promoted made a change in historical memory necessary. And out of this change came the lost cause mythology, which characterized the German role in the East in vastly different terms.

The changing international context was decisive. Our view of the Russians altered as soon as we came into close contact with them. Then, joint governance of Germany broke down. Finally, hostility provoked the Cold War.

First, it is important to deal with personal experiences, both negative ones with respect to the Russians and positive ones with respect to the Germans. There was great joy on the occasion of the first meeting of American and Soviet troops at Strehla and Torgau on the Elbe on April 25, 1945. The U.S. troops at the former meeting stayed for some days with the Russians and one of the outcomes was a joint oath taken under the stark impact of a devastating war to do all in their power to avoid another war. That moment was later remembered "as a unique moment, a punctuation point between the virtual end of one war, the Good War, the Great Patriotic War; and the beginning of another, the Cold War."[26] One of the few who had clung to that moment in time and recognized the tragedy of allies becoming enemies was Joe Polowski, a Chicago taxi driver, who every year on April 25, appeared on the Michigan Avenue bridge in Chicago with a sign: "Halt the spread of nuclear weapons."[27] When he died in 1983, he was buried on his explicit instructions at Torgau. At a 1985 reunion, the veterans laid a wreath on his grave and the following year German filmmaker Wolfgang Pfeiffer produced a film on Polowsky, "an American Dreamer." That reunion and film generated little attention, because we had long been at odds with the Soviet Union and Cold War rhetoric dominated our relationship. The original meeting was virtually forgotten; the alliance scarcely remembered.

In July 1945, as the joint occupation of Berlin was just beginning, an American Civil Affairs officer, John J. Maginnis, was already frustrated with the Russians, whom he was just getting to know:

> I found the Russians to be a baffling combination of childishness, hard realism, irresponsibility, churlishness, amiability, slovenliness, and callousness. It became a continuing problem to remind myself that the Russians, who were giving us trouble, were our friends, and the Germans, who were giving us cooperation, were our enemies.[28]

Looking back from the perspective of fifty years later, a former British intelligence officer, Noel Annon, agreed:

> The Soviets continued to treat their allies as they had during the war. They were suspicious, ungenerous, disagreeable, uncooperative and obstructive.[29]

Characteristic as well was the reaction of the American interrogators at Mondorf in July 1945, when a small group of Russians arrived to do some interrogating of their own. After all, there were some big fish there, including generals Walter Warlimont and Albert Kesselring. Clearly, the Americans had more sympathy for their German captives than for their Russian allies. As one of them, Major Kenneth Hechler, later wrote: "These Russians came to their tasks with grim, vengeful looks. I watched them at breakfast with us, and began to get a little concerned about what effect their presence would have on the reactions of the prisoners I was interrogating. Hardly had they set foot within the prisoner of war enclosure before Gen. Warlimont and others began to ask excitedly whether they were Russian war crimes investigators." But Hermann Göring managed to jolly the Russians into leaving in good spirits. "Shortly thereafter," Hechler continued, "they left Mondorf throroughly happy and there were fifty sighs of relief – forty from the detainees and ten from the investigators."[30] It is not surprising that Warlimont was concerned about war crimes investigators; he was later tried, convicted, and sentenced to life for war crimes.

In September 1945, *Look* magazine took cognizance of the negative impressions Americans were already gathering from the Russians, including that they were "arrogant, domineering, uncooperative and suspicious," but reminded its readers what difficulties the Russians had faced during the war and that they would cooperate in the future.[31] One month later, the same magazine carried an article by a French woman resistance fighter who was concerned about U.S. soldiers fraternizing with Germans. "Have the GIs forgotten so soon that the frauleins they hold in their arms are Germans – the atrocity experts?" she asked. The story, tellingly entitled "Have We Already Forgiven the Germans?", was replete with tales about and pictures of victims of Nazi torture.[32]

Many people could not bring themselves to believe the reports of Nazi atrocities and backed away from the realization. Soon, the U.S. soldiers, who had actually liberated the camps and were eyewitnesses to the horrors perpetrated by the Nazis, were replaced by young soldiers who had seen neither combat nor the camps. In them, the wellspring of positive cultural images of Germans and Germany reemerged. Fairly quickly, as the war drew to a close, American combat veterans who had little truck with the Germans gave way to younger occupation soldiers who found the Germans to be a quite normal, indeed hospitable people, an image many Germans tried to reinforce. Many young Americans felt more at home in Germany – among their recent enemies – than in Allied countries.

A *Reader's Digest* article of March 1946 entitled "Why So Many GIs Like the Germans Best" asserted that "Roughly four out of every five returning soldiers preferred Germany to any of the Allied countries they had seen." This preference had ominous consequences; it caused many to reject or deny stories they read in the press about Nazi atrocities during the recent war. "Incredible though it may seem, many an American soldier carried his defense of the Germans to the point of accusing the American authorities of having invented the atrocity stories . . . All he knew was that the people about him now looked like those he had known at home. He could not connect them with the stories of torture and murder he had heard and read." Indeed, only 43 percent of U.S. soldiers held the German people responsible for the war and only 25 percent for the concentration camps.

The juxtaposition of starved, dirty survivors of the camps, now displaced persons (DPs), and well-fed German hausfraus, who reminded them of mom, only strengthened the positive image of the Germans in the minds of the

American soldiers. Already, here, we can see the foundation being laid for what was to follow a few years later. "It was not uncommon to hear an American soldier say that if there were another war in Europe he would rather be a German ally."[33] The stark contrast between the condition of the Germans and that of DPs was not just one of positive and negative image in the eyes of many American soldiers and officers; it brought out cultural prejudices, including anti-Slavism and antisemitism. In the words of one Jewish-American officer who dealt with DPs, "About June of 1945, I began to feel and see a change in attitudes in the American military towards refugees and displaced persons, especially towards Jews." Many U.S. soldiers "carried their homegrown prejudices against Jews and Eastern Europeans around with them. DPs were seen "as scum and dirt" while the Americans treated Germans as "the salt of the earth."[34]

An important aspect of changing attitudes on the part of American soldiers toward both the Germans and the Russians came by way of fraternization. As the war was still raging in 1944, U.S. military authorities imposed a strict policy of nonfraternization on U.S. soldiers, who, from the outset, had been handing out chewing gum and chocolates to eager German children. Already, at this point, the authorities were becoming concerned about "the perplexities of the American soldier on finding that the enemy whom he had been taught to hate and fear was a people with a culture and living habits so much like his own had already become evident." But the policy, which was widely circumvented, was relaxed in mid-1945 and reversed by 1946, when, as the processes of democratization and de-nazification got underway, the authorities actually encouraged contact between U.S. soldiers and German civilians. The contacts took many forms: church services, movie theaters, bars and taverns, black market contacts, and sexual relations, to name only a few of the most important.

By 1948, the German Youth Assistance program had reached almost 1.7 million German young people. German-American clubs and discussion groups were also important. The first of these was the Cosmopolitan Club in Bad Kissingen, formed on June 19, 1946. Among its members was a former colonel in the German air force, an interesting portent of things to come. Former German soldiers also figured prominently in U.S. military employment; nearly 35 percent of all German soldiers repatriated from camps in the U.S. found employment on U.S. bases.[35]

The myriad contacts between Americans and Germans from 1945 on not only created a growing sympathy, respect, and even kinship between the two peoples, which softened wartime antagonisms, they also created a vital opportunity for the Germans to educate us at the grass roots military (and civilian) level about the Russians. Our own growing distrust and dislike for our "allies" was tremendously reinforced by our new German friends – and created an

important foundation on which the former German military could "educate"
us on the nature of the war in the East. From the beginning, Germans regaled
Americans with tales of the barbaric Russian soldier – crude, animal-like, backward, bestial, childlike, and cruel. Typical was the anecdote about the Russian
soldier who, discovering a water tap for the first time in his life, yanked it out of
the wall and stuck it in his backpack so he could have water any time. These were
racial images and stereotypes that the Nazi regime had promulgated during the
war and which now became part of the American image as well.

The central Asian "Mongol" sexual predator became emblematic for all
Russian troops, and U.S. soldiers, many of whom had grown up with anti-Slavic
prejudices, quickly absorbed the German imagery. The Russians did not help
themselves in this regard, it should be noted. Another universal German story
for our consumption was that of the Russian soldier as looter and rapist. In fact,
the entrance of the Russian soldiers into Germany had been accompanied by
rape on a gigantic scale. Hundreds of thousands of German females from eight
to eighty were ravished by Russians, who were often in a drunken condition.
Gang rapes were ubiquitous. Nor did the raping end with the war. Well into
1947, raping of German women by Russian soldiers was common, to the point
at which German Communists, anxious to create a positive image of the Soviet
brother, were seriously concerned. Only when Russian military personnel were
segregated from the German population in their zone in mid-1947 – not to
protect German women, but for reasons of politics and widespread venereal
disease – did the raping largely cease. Soldiers of all armies rape in war, but
the Russian example went beyond the usual scale, largely because of feelings of
revenge on the *Herrenmenschen* for the terrible depredations of the Germans
in the Soviet Union.

What is interesting – and ironic – here is how the relationship between
Americans and the Germans in their zone and the Russians in theirs took
opposite trajectories after the war. Initially, as we have seen, Americans were
enjoined strictly not to fraternize; the Russians had no such injunctions. As
time went on, however, Americans communicated more and more freely at
many levels with their German friends, while the Russians isolated themselves
increasingly from their zonal inhabitants. The policy of isolation represented
the most radical form of nonfraternization. Official policies aside, from the
outset, the typical American, having suffered little at the hands of the Germans
and sharing a material culture with them, were amenable to friendly conversations, which the Germans used to "educate" them about the Russians (among
other things).

In the Soviet zone, the opposite was happening. After terrorizing the Germans in their zone with years of rapine (sexual and otherwise), the Russians

disappeared into their compounds and cut off any dialogue with "their" Germans. Moreover, even prior to that isolation, little in the way of dialogue had opened up anyway, because, unlike the American, the average Russian hated the Germans for the barbarism of the occupation during the war and shared little in the way of material culture with them anyway. In fact, the discovery on the part of Russian soldiers of just how well Germans lived in contrast to the average Soviet citizen fueled the hatred that led to rape at the end of the war.[36] Unlike the young American occupation soldiers of 1946 and beyond, who quickly forgot about a war in which they had not fought anyway, every young Russian soldier carried an indelible memory of the war in his heart, one reinforced continually by Soviet observances. For the Russian soldier in 1946 or 1950 or 1960, the memory of the "Great Fatherland War" changed very little; for the Americans memories of the "War in the East" changed fundamentally.

All this notwithstanding, the American people as a whole, both during the war and for some time afterward, wanted the most severe kind of justice for German war criminals. Popular surveys indicated that the vast majority of Americans approved of a policy to convict and execute chief Nazi officials. "Almost no American in the postwar period thought that the program of denazification and punishment was too harsh," one scholar has suggested. One indication of this was the universally hostile reaction to Senator Robert Taft's condemnation of the trials in an October 1946 speech, in which he said the "hanging of the eleven men convicted will be a blot on the American record which we shall long regret." But the wrath of the American people would soon be turned away from the Germans and diverted elsewhere under changing circumstances, as illustrated by the fact that by 1948, "Taft's stand was considered not a burden but a political asset by Republican leaders."[37]

The breakdown of Allied cooperation in the governance of Germany and the outbreak of the Cold War mark a radical change in these circumstances. International events gradually both formed the context for the changing attitudes described earlier and part of the reason for those changes. Postwar Germany was supposed to be jointly controlled by an Allied "condominium," a phrase attributed to Hans Kelson, an anti-Nazi German émigré.[38] That is, the new tenants threw out the old; each controlled his own condo, but shared responsibility for the whole building. Each Allied power controlled its own zone autonomously, but agreed that Germany be run as an economic unit through an Allied Control Council. But the tenants soon fell out among themselves. Joint rule did not work, first because of the French, then the Russians. Fundamental issues, such as reparations and structural reform, helped to dissolve the condominium. But, given the profound distrust between the western Allies and their Russian colleagues – even during the war – and the vast differences in systems between East and West, the hope of joint governance was probably a chimera from the start. It is hard for a communist and a capitalist to share the same apartment building.

The reversal of roles was already becoming apparent in the fall of 1946, when Secretary of State James Byrnes, in a speech at Stuttgart, said: "The American people want the German people to win their way back to an honorable place among the free and peace-loving peoples of the world."[39] The key events of the following years, which marked the division of Germany, the emergence of the Cold War, and a fundamental transformation of our attitudes toward both the Germans and the Russians, are a familiar litany. So are the establishment of "Bizonia" by the West in January 1947; the failure to settle the reparations question at the Moscow Four Power conference in March; the inauguration of the Marshall Plan in June of that year; and the London Conference of the Big Four Foreign Ministers in December, a watershed in the East-West split, at which no compromise on Berlin or Germany was reached.

The following year – 1948 –witnessed the introduction of a new currency – the Deutschmark – signifying two separate economic systems for Germany, the introduction of which in the western sectors of Berlin triggered the Russian blockade of the city, which was to last for a year. The dramatic events surrounding the blockade and the western response – the Berlin airlift – put a stamp on our changing attitudes. The heroism of the airlift, the truculence of the Russians and the pluck of the Berliners finished a process already underway in which the Russians now became the enemy and the Germans, if not allies – that would come soon enough – at least clients to be protected. The West Germans, for their part, now increasingly identified with the West and were inclined to throw in their lot with it, while defining for their new friends a part of the war in which they had been so recently engaged as enemies. By 1949, two German states had come into existence as clients of the former allies, now rapidly becoming enemies. When the Russians finally did lift the blockade in June of that year, the division of Germany had been sealed. Just two months earlier, the North Atlantic Treaty Organization (NATO) was founded, heralding a further step in the evolution of a part of the German people from enemies to clients to allies.

In June 1950, North Korea launched an invasion of its southern neighbor. The United States was quickly drawn into the conflict, necessitating yet another step in our evolving relations with the (West) Germans – a step that would have been unthinkable just three or four years earlier – the revival of a German military. Now the clients would become full-fledged allies. As Germans emerged as potential allies and military partners, we were obliged to deal with the question of World War Two crimes and their punishment from a different perspective.

In June 1949, military occupation of the United States zone of Germany, under the aegis of General Lucius Clay, was replaced by a civilian authority, a High Commissioner. John J. McCloy was a complex man under great pressure on the war crimes issue. A Wall Street lawyer and Henry Stimson's right hand man in the War Department, McCloy was courageous, but not free of the prejudices of his class and time. He had Jewish friends, but was mildly antisemitic and refused to believe the reports he received on the extent and nature of the Nazi mass murder of the Jews. His inaction on that issue was partly responsible for the failure to push through an order to bomb the Auschwitz-Birkenau death camp.

However, he was no friend of the Germans either. A veteran of World War One, he hated the specter of Prussian militarism. He agreed with the Potsdam accords on the division of postwar Germany and strongly supported the Nuremberg trials. At the beginning of his tenure as High Commissioner, although he saw the need to build up West Germany politically and economically, he had, by his own admission, to "fight back his revulsions [sic]."[40] To a German, who had requested that he forget about the concentration camps, he replied, "So far as I am concerned, I cannot forget the Auschwitzes and Dachaus and I do not want the German people to forget them either. If they do, they will start their new German state in an atmosphere of moral degeneration and degradation."[41]

It was not easy, however, to act on this moral resolve in the changing climate of 1949 and beyond. General Clay, the zonal military commander, had left for McCloy the task of executing fifteen convicted war criminals as well as deciding on the commutation or reduction of sentences of many more. McCloy initially favored harshness. However, as time went by, the growing leniency of his decisions was a barometer of changing attitudes toward the Germans as the Cold War became a prime frame of reference for the United States. This was particularly the case after the outbreak of the Korean War and the ensuing discussions on German rearmament, in the course of which McCloy began to tilt toward increasing lenience.[42]

Of those Nazis convicted in the post-Nuremberg trials, carried out by the United States between October 1946 and April 1949, about 100 came under McCloy's jurisdiction, including the fifteen capital cases. (The 1,600 defendants in the "Dachau" trials prosecuted by the U.S. Army were not McCloy's responsibility.) To aid him in his decision-making, McCloy appointed a clemency review panel chaired by Justice David Peck. On August 25, 1950, the board delivered its report, which recommended reduction in sentences or clemency in seventy-seven of ninety-three cases under consideration, including commutation of seven of the fifteen death sentences. This represented a considerable softening.[43] On January 31, 1951, McCloy, although under a great deal of pressure to be even more lenient, not the least from the new Adenauer government of West Germany, did hold the line on five of the fifteen death sentences, but reduced the sentences of, or paroled completely, seventy-nine of eighty-nine war criminals at Landsberg prison. Here, McCloy was inconsistent in his decisions. He did confirm the death sentences of SS Major General Otto Ohlendorf; SS Colonels Paul Blobel (Babi Yar and Operation 1005), Werner Braune, and Erich Naumann in the Einsatzgruppen cases; and Oswald Pohl, director of the SS Economic and Administrative Main Office, which had overseen the economic exploitation of concentration camps. These sentences were carried out on June 6, 1951. At the same time, however, he released others, who were directly involved in Einsatzgruppen killings. Among these was Martin Sandberger, former chief of Einsatzkommando 1a of Einsatzgruppe A, later commander of the Security Police and SD in Estonia, where, in 1941 and 1942, he had busied himself directing the shooting of thousands of Jews, communists, and others.[44] Another, whose sentence McCloy reduced from twenty to ten years, was Franz Six, former head of SD foreign intelligence and Einsatzgruppe operative. Most controversial of those released was Alfried Krupp, the big armaments industrialist who had, among other things, widely used slave labor during the war. His release raised a firestorm of criticism in the United States, indicating that the road to amnesia did have some potholes. Time and events, however, favored leniency. One of Krupp's executives, also released at the time, put his finger on the matter when he said: "Now that they have Korea on their hands, the Americans are a lot more friendly."[45]

Interestingly enough, when it came to the generals, who would soon begin the process of rehabilitating themselves, McCloy was not inclined to leniency. List and Kunze, who had murdered hostages in the Balkans, were denied clemency, as were Reinicke, who had killed POWs, and Reinhard and Hoth, who had transmitted the "Commando" and "Commissar" orders. The Adenauer government, and especially its military advisers, as well as former German veterans, were very upset about McCloy's refusal to grant clemency to the generals. Some of it was, frankly, personal: Some of the pressure on McCloy came from former General Hans Speidel, soon to become a leading Bundeswehr figure, whose brother, former General Wilhelm Speidel, was serving out his sentence at Landsberg.[46]

In the end, McCloy's actions set in motion a train of events that led to the release of all remaining war criminals in American custody by 1958. In a sense, McCloy had seen this development coming early on. In September 1950, he told

President Truman that because of political exigencies like German rearmament and the Cold War, "certain of the things we would like to see done in Germany will not be completed."[47] What he perhaps did not see was the full magnitude of the changes that his actions helped to bring about. His commutations and releases, McCloy's biographer suggests, "allowed the Federal Republic to slip into amnesia about its past. Without McCloy's intending it, his Landsberg decisions contributed to the German *Schlusstrich* [draw a line under the past] mentality about the war criminals."[48] Many Germans, in turn, then seduced us into a similar amnesia as a prerequisite for a reformulation of memory. The trials precipitated some American criticism from the outset, and this criticism only intensified as the Cold War emerged in the late 1940s. We recall Senator Robert Taft's resistance to the very idea of a tribunal. Iowa Supreme Court Justice Charles Wennerstrum, presiding judge at *US vs. List*, criticized the war crimes program in February 1948.[49]

Some objections were strictly legal, based on what was generally referred to as "victor's justice." A number of jurists saw severe procedural problems in the trials, especially the lack of any appeal mechanisms. Concern was also expressed over violations of the rights of the accused. Many saw dubious practices in the extraction of confessions. Misgivings arose that the trials violated U.S. legal traditions and constitutional safeguards. Hence the resort to executive clemency and sentence review.

Other objections were largely political in nature. Many Republicans latched onto the trials in general from 1947 on as a way to discredit the Democratic Administration, by characterizing the trials as unfair, as un-American, even as tainted by Communist bias. More specific protests often combined principled objections with state or regional politics and, disturbingly, centered on defending one or another Nazi war criminal, often on specious grounds. A good example was Senator William Langer of North Dakota, many of whose constituents were of German-American background. Langer thought that the trials of all but the most prominent Nazis were in error; that they violated U.S. legal traditions and aided Communism. Langer used his power on behalf of Martin Sandberger, appointed commander of Einsatzkommando 1a of Einsatzgruppe A in 1941, and then, later that year, commander of the Security Police and SD in Estonia. Units under Sandberger's command had, as their charge, murdering Jews, Communists, and members of the intelligentsia in Estonia. In September 1947, a U.S. military court, in the Einsatzgruppen trials, sentenced Sandberger to death. The sentence was commuted by McCloy, partly thanks to Langer's efforts, and Sandberger was released in January 1953.[50] It was one of the unfortunate outcomes of the objections to the trials on whatever grounds that, "By the end of the 1940s, many in the United States had come to accept the conservative argument that the convicted Nazi perpetrators were not criminals, but were instead the victims of the Allied war crimes program."[51]

One could not create a better atmosphere for a reconceptualization of a major part of World War Two. Ready to capitalize on the opportunity were many high-level officers in the Wehrmacht, who soon turned to the dual task of rehabilitating their reputations and educating us on the war in the East. Emblematic of both tasks was the work of the "Operational History (German) Section," otherwise known as the Halder group.

The man we chose to head the military research program was former general Franz Halder. Halder seemed to have ideal credentials for this kind of responsibility. As chief of the army General Staff from 1938 to 1942, he had been at the center of operational planning for the first three years of the war. Even though his office increasingly lost responsibility as Hitler took over more and more command functions, in the minds of his American handlers, Halder seemed to be in the tradition of the great von Moltke, who once headed the great Imperial General Staff.[52] Moreover, Halder seemed to be as much at a distance from the Nazi regime as any senior German officer. His name had been linked with the resistance as early as 1938 and 1939. In September 1942, he was cashiered by Hitler as General Staff chief over alleged fundamental disagreements over military policy. The icing on the cake came when Halder was arrested in the wake of the July 20, 1944, abortive assassination attempt on Hitler's life and incarcerated in several concentration camps up to his liberation by Americans at the end of the war. As much as any former general officer, Halder seemed to be untainted by the crimes of the Nazi regime. He was, moreover, in an ideal position to relay to the respectful Americans the view of the war and the Nazi regime now being constructed by large numbers of former German officers, whose interest in setting the record straight dovetailed nicely with exculpatory motives. Moreover, Halder, although he refused to compose his memoirs, did publish, in 1949, a tendentious pamphlet entitled *Hitler als Feldherr* (Hitler as Commander) which contained most of the myths about the war in the East which would be the stuff of memoirs and histories from the pens of many from that point on.[53]

Making fun of the title ascribed to Hitler: *Grösster Feldherr aller Zeiten* (Greatest Commander of all Times or *Gröfaz* for short), Halder sets up an idealized version of a commander and compares Hitler invidiously to it. Within this context, Halder mixes truth, half truth, myth, and lies to establish the wisdom and innocence of the German military – and thus himself – in contrast to the miscalculating, feckless, dangerous amateurishness of Hitler.

Among his points as they relate to the East: that he desperately tried to get the Western powers to stand up to Hitler ("to bang on table by Hitler")[54]; the army was against the war, against the attack on Poland, and certainly against the Russian campaign; operational plans for a war with the Soviet Union were prepared only at Hitler's orders; the military men warned Hitler against an "adventure" in the East; Hitler did not understand the military potential of the Russians, while the generals did; the war was really a preventive war to fend off a Soviet attack; Hitler's decision to attack Russia was primarily a political one, although Hitler never made his goals in conquering the Soviet Union clear to the military; and Hitler, in contrast to his generals, thought the Russian campaign could be completed in eight weeks and the winter clothing demanded by the army would not be necessary. Then, of course, all the strategic and operational mistakes of the war in the East were also laid at Hitler's door. Hitler's amateurishness contrasted at every point with the professionalism of the soldiers. Hitler's *Wahnsinn* (lunacy) contrasted with the simple patriotism of the army. Hitler's complete immorality contrasted with the traditional moral code of the officer.

Nowhere here does Halder mention the genocidal crimes of the regime and the army's cooperation in carrying them out. Where he does mention them in his earlier affidavit during the Nuremberg trials – he notes that after Hitler explained the future nature of the war in Russia – including the Commissar Order – "listeners on the part of the army were of course outraged by this speech of Hitler's" and some officers complained to Brauchitsch, who recommended that "we, of the OKW [Oberkommando der Wehrmacht, High Command of the Armed Forces], could never execute such orders."[55]

A closer look at the Halder the Americans did not know about (or, it would later turn out, care about) reveals the sharp contrast between the emerging mythology of the war in the East and the truth that, although it was recognized in part at Nuremberg, would soon be forgotten, only to be revealed decades later by historical research. To be sure, Halder was linked with a circle of officers who already, since the Munich crisis, had toyed with the idea of overthrowing Hitler (men like Ludwig Beck, Hans Oster, and Helmuth Grosscurth) because of their fear that Hitler was leading them into catastrophe. In the end, however, by the turn of the year 1939–40, Halder pulled back from the group and from any idea of a military coup to overthrow Hitler, particularly during wartime. Instead, he focused on his duties as operational planner for whatever the "Fuehrer" might decide to undertake.

In any event, Halder's contemplation of resistance seems to have derived more from military turf battles with the political leadership than with any moral scruples about the nature or direction of the regime.[56] Where the regime was headed became clear already during the Polish campaign, when the SS and Security Police were busy annihilating the Polish intelligentsia, something that outraged many German officers, but not apparently Halder, who was well informed about the killings, but refused, as did Brauchitsch, to make an issue of them. Unlike members of the resistance, who were deeply disturbed about the emerging nature of Hitler's war plans and the beginning genocide in Poland, Halder played down the crimes as an aberration and responded negatively to the plans of one general to declare a state of emergency in occupied Poland in order to go after the SS and police perpetrators.[57]

Later, Halder would similarly accept the depredations of the Einsatzgruppen and delude himself that he was keeping the army out of the murder game, although his actions led to the opposite result.[58] With respect to the fateful campaign against the Soviet Union, contrary to his later assertions, Halder (a) supported it fully, (b) laid plans for it well in advance of any orders from Hitler, (c) had no concerns about a Soviet attack on Germany – that is, did not consider the war to be "preventive" at the time, (d) was well aware of what Hitler envisioned as the true nature of the war, (e) helped lay the operational foundations for genocide, both against POWs and civilians, and (e) shared Hitler's assumptions about quick victory.

There is no question today that the German generals shared much of Hitler's vision of German continental hegemony and that this dominance was to be achieved in large part by a war of conquest in the East. Already in the 1920s – long before Hitler came to power – the German military was planning for an expansion of the army far beyond any defensive needs. The so-called "Great Plan" of 1924–25 foresaw a war of expansion, which would create a German imperium far greater than that of the Kaiser. Halder shared this view. During the Sudeten crisis in September 1938, the new General Staff Chief ordered the earlier plans for an offensive war retrieved from the archives.[59] With regard to the conquest of the East, the generals' vision did not differ substantially from that of Hitler, although they only gradually accepted, as they had not yet during the Polish campaign, the idea of a primarily racial basis for conquest. Drawing on a long Prussian-German military tradition, which had always viewed Russia as backward and technologically inept, a tradition more recently reinforced by Russia's (temporary) loss during World War One, and a more recently acquired anticommunism, the German military viewed a war of conquest in the East as a legitimate way to achieve German primacy on the continent.[60]

In a number of interviews just before the war, Halder had informed Western observers that Germany did not want war in the West and could avoid it if Western powers would not block Germany's foreign policy desires in the East.[61] In planning the original version of Barbarossa in summer 1940,

Halder's order to his staff of planners was to test the idea that "The [East] must be viewed chiefly with reference to the requirements of a military intervention which will compel Russia to recognize Germany's dominant position in Europe."[62] Indeed, Halder's parting of the ways with other resistance members in 1939–40 signaled his willingness to go wherever Hitler might lead. A leading military historian, Jürgen Förster, maintains that Halder was at the "center of the preparations of the army leadership for the struggle against the ideological enemy."[63]

Halder was not just at the center of developments; he was way ahead. Scholars have demonstrated that the German generals not only supported Hitler in his offensive plans in the East, but had, in many cases, already laid these plans themselves – and influenced Hitler in how he carried them out. Halder is a prime example. In May 1940, on the eve of the German victory over France, German eyes were already turning to the East. But it was not Hitler who, at this point, was looking to a swift campaign against Russia (he was considering a large-scale demobilization) – but Halder! The first major plan for a war against the Soviet Union – "Operation Otto" – was drafted by Halder's staff on his orders beginning on July 3, 1940, partly out of strategic considerations, partly to counter the very demobilization which Hitler was contemplating. Halder's instructions came at just the time when he was distancing himself from his former comrades in the resistance.[64] Heinz Guderian, another postwar apologist for the Wehrmacht, also took part in the planning, projecting a march route that would take his divisions to Kiev, then to the Dnepr River and thence to Odessa on the Black Sea.[65]

Moreover, in contrast to postwar claims made by Halder and others, that their plans for an invasion of the Soviet Union were essentially defensive – that they were merely anticipating a Soviet attack and preparing a defensive war – it was clear at the time that Germany was playing the role of aggressor. On February 28, 1941, almost four months before the German assault, Halder wrote in his diary: "Russia: Isolated reports on Russia's unfriendly attitude towards us received lately, are of no importance. Russia has made no protest against our measures, nor against Bulgaria's attitude." Halder felt that a Russian attack was "completely improbable."[66] Two days later, he wrote: "*Disposition of Russian forces*: Strong concentrations in the Ukraine are noteworthy. Would be right for an offensive against Hungary and the Bukovina, but I feel sure this possibility can be discounted."[67]

Furthermore, there was little doubt in Halder's mind as to the kind of war Hitler was about to unleash. After a major conference on March 30, 1941, where, in a two-and-a-half-hour tirade, Hitler made his goals and methods clear to an assemblage of 250 German officers, Halder recorded the gist of Hitler's remarks in his diary. Under the intriguing heading of "Colonial tasks!" Halder writes, referring to Hitler's remarks:

> *Clash of two ideologies.* Crushing denunciation of Bolshevism, identified with asocial criminality. Communism is an enormous danger for our future. We must forget the concept of comradeship between soldiers. A Communist is no comrade before or after the battle. This is a war of extermination. If we do not grasp this, we shall still beat the enemy, but 30 years later we shall again have to fight the Communist foe. We do not wage war to preserve the enemy.
>
> *Future political gains of Russia*: Northern Russia goes to Finland. Protectorates: Baltic States, Ukraine, White Russia.
>
> *War against Russia*: Extermination of the Bolshevik Commissars and of the Communist intelligentsia. . . . We must fight against the poison of disintegration. This is no job for military courts. The individual troop commanders must know the issues at stake. They must be leaders in this fight. The troops must fight back with the methods with which they are attacked. Commissars and GPU men are criminals and must be dealt with as such. This need not mean that the troops should get out of hand. Rather the commander must give orders, which express the common feelings of his men. This war will be very different from the war in the West. In the east, harshness today means lenience in the future. Commanders must make the sacrifice of overcoming their personal scruples.[68]

In the margins, Halder makes a notation: "Embody in the ObdH (Army High Command) order."

What is clear here is not only that Halder and the top generals were made aware of Hitler's barbaric plans for the East, they also now were cognizant of the fact that the military itself would be integrated into a process of murder that ignored all moral scruples and international laws. Far from protesting this, Halder set about drafting a series of orders that anticipated Hitler's desires and laid the foundation for a barbarous war without mercy – not only to Communist functionaries, but to vast numbers of civilians and POWs as well.

Two "criminal orders" preceded the Nazi invasion of the Soviet Union. The best known is the "Commissar Order," which commanded that all Communist functionaries be summarily shot. Less known was the "Barbarossa" or "Jurisdictional" Decree, which largely suspended all the rules of military justice with regard to the conduct of the troops in the East. Halder's staff was instrumental in drafting these orders; Lieutenant General Eugen Müller, who reported directly to Halder, was the author.[69] The practical outcome was expressed in the "Guidelines for the Conduct of Troops in Russia," which basically declared open season on large, vaguely defined segments of the Soviet population, including "Bolshevik agitators, irregulars, saboteurs, Jews" among others, who were to be dealt with ruthlessly.[70] What these orders and guidelines laid the basis for was eventually the mass murder of Soviet civilians, Jews and Soviet POWs, a grim task in which the army had implicated itself from the outset. As one historian has noted: "It is remarkable that the predominant view of Russia of the Nazi party and SS leadership was reproduced by the high command of the Wehrmacht."[71]

Halder also presided over negotiations between his Quartermaster General Eduard Wagner and Reinhard Heydrich, head of Himmler's police empire about cooperation between the army and the Einsatzgruppen in rear areas of the front. Halder clearly knew about the activities of the Einsatzgruppen, given that their depredations in occupied Poland were generally known by the military, and protested by only a few officers. This same Wagner would later reveal the calloused attitudes of the German military toward Russian POWs when he said at a conference on the exploitation of prisoners as labor: "Non-working war prisoners . . . are supposed to starve. Working prisoners may be fed from army rations in individual cases."[72] That Halder himself was indifferent to the fate of POWs emerges from one of his diary entries: "Typhus camp of Russian PWs (20,000), doomed to die. . . . Ghastly picture, but relief appears impracticable at the moment."[73]

That not all German officers shared these views or wanted to be involved in the process in which the army became implicated in a lawless war of aggression can be seen in the diary of active resistance leader, Ulrich von Hassell: "What the documents reveal as having been communicated about orders issued to the troops and signed by Halder regarding our conduct in Russia – and the systematic perversion of military justice vis-à-vis the population into a caricature mocking all law – is enough to make one's hair stand on end."[74] But Hassell's view was not that of most of the generals. As one scholar noted: "On June 22, 1941, Hitler and the Wehrmacht presented themselves in a rare unanimity which was hardly ever seen before".[75] In drafting the "criminal orders" without Hitler's explicit instructions or interference, what the army had accomplished in its fecklessness was to take the lead in its own weakening vis-à-vis the regime, in expanding the power of the SS, and in opening the door to the barbarization of the coming war in the East.[76]

Again in contrast to postwar assertions on the part of the German military, the generals, Halder included, far from opposing the invasion of the Soviet Union, looked forward to the campaign with alacrity, elated as they were about the swift victories in the West. In doing so, they vastly underestimated the war-making potential of the Soviet Union, grievously overestimated the capabilities of the German armed forces, and projected time spans for the campaign in the East that appear, in retrospect, to be pure fantasy. Already in July 1940, as he undertook planning for what would become "Operation Barbarossa," Halder estimated that 80 to 100 German divisions would be sufficient to overwhelm the Russians, who, he thought, had only had fifty to seventy-five good divisions.[77] (Ultimately, the Germans would attack with 152 divisions and discovered that the Russian had more than 300.) This attests to an overwhelming failure on the part of German military intelligence. This mindless optimism continued in the early days of the campaign, which was launched on June 22, 1941. Dramatic early successes led Halder to record in his diary on July 3:

> On the whole, then, it may be said even now that the objective to shatter the bulk of the Russian Army this side of the Dvina and Dnepr, has been accomplished. I do not doubt the statement of the captured Russian Corps CG that, east of the Dvina and Dnepr, we would encounter nothing more than partial forces, not strong enough to hinder realization of German operational plans. It is thus probably no overstatement to say that the Russian Campaign has been won in the space of two weeks.

From the start, the generals had engaged in incredible self-delusion to the point where, as the Russian campaign drew nearer and then got underway, they constantly revised downward [!!!] how much time it would take.[78] Not even Hitler was as confident as his generals.[79] Thus, Halder's later claims that he had opposed the war in the East belong in the realm of legends.[80] Finally, it must be said of those top German officers, including Halder, who claimed after the war that their motivation in sending millions of men to their deaths down to the bitter end was simple patriotism, that their motives were not just patriotic, but pecuniary as well. The fact is that from 1940 on, Hitler regularly bribed his top generals, including Halder. The going rate was RM 4,000 per month in tax-exempt payments to field marshals and RM 2,000 per month for colonel generals, effectively doubling their already considerable salaries. These payments were secret and conditional on behavior. Halder was promoted to *Generaloberst* (colonel general) in July 1940 and began receiving his bribes as of that date. The payments continued even after he was dismissed as Chief of the General Staff in September 1942, because he did not retire, but was reassigned to the "Fuehrer-Reserve." Only in the wake of the abortive assassination attempt on Hitler in July 1944 were Halder's payments stopped because of his alleged foreknowledge of the plot.[81]

Halder was, to be sure, arrested after the July 20 plot and placed in several concentration camps, including Dachau, Ravensbrück and Flossenbürg. One should not imagine, however, that he was breaking stones in a quarry. He later admitted to having no complaints about provisions and quarters. Toward the end, he found himself in VIP company, including former Reichsminister

Hjalmar Schacht, former French Premier Leon Blum, and former Austrian Chancellor Kurt Schuschnigg. Only at the end of January 1945 was he even officially discharged from military service. He was captured by advancing American troops on May 5, 1945.[82]

Franz Halder embodies better than any other high German officer the dramatic difference between myth and reality as it emerged after World War Two, particularly with regard to the war in the East. His postwar apologia and his service to the Americans and to their understanding, particularly, of the war in the East stand in marked contrast to the reality of his career.

3   The German Generals Talk, Write, and Network

The Operational History (German) Section

George N. Schuster, a prominent lay Catholic and president of Hunter College, who would become High Commissioner for Bavaria under John J. McCloy, had written extensively on German culture. Partly for this reason he was appointed chairman of the War Department Historical Commission, which was organized to interview high-level Nazis who had fallen into American captivity. Schuster and his colleagues would interview twenty-five of these men from July to November 1945, including military men such as Albert Kesselring, Karl Doenitz, and Heinz Guderian, with whom Schuster was quite impressed.[1]

One outgrowth of the Schuster Commission interviews in 1945 was the creation, by the United States Army Historical Division, of the Operational History (German) Section under the aegis of Colonel H. E. Potter. The victors had conducted thousands of interrogations of captured German officers. Now it seemed wise to go on to the next step and recruit from that same pool Germans who might write about their experiences in the war, so as to round off our own future studies. Such writings might also have potential for gathering intelligence. Our initial focus was on those fronts where we had fought the Germans. As time went on, however, the unfolding Cold War and the possibility of war with the Soviet Union shifted our interest to the Eastern front and the German–Soviet war.

Already in the summer of 1946, Franz Halder was involved in the emerging flood of studies – to his and to our benefit. He had been captured by the Americans and initially treated, as he saw it, as a "criminal."[2] From October 1945 to January 1946, he was turned over to the British for interrogation. In August 1946, he was brought to Nuremberg and interrogated as a witness in the war crimes trials there, and then was sent, as one of a number of high-ranking German officers chosen to write about their war experiences, to Steinlager near

Marburg in Hessen. On June 20, 1947, he was officially released from custody. Obviously, he was no longer a "criminal." Although he was relieved at not being put on trial in Nuremberg as a member of a criminal organization (the German High Command), he was not yet home free. As part of the de-nazification effort, he still had to face a German-conducted court (*Spruchkammer*) in Munich. He had to defend himself against the accusation of having aided and abetted the Nazi regime in its war making, and therefore shared responsibility "for all the unspeakable suffering which the war and its consequences caused for this generation." The trial, conducted in October 1948, was followed closely by the press in Germany and abroad and aroused much attention. Halder denied any knowledge of SS crimes behind the lines and portrayed himself as having been outside the loop of decision-making in the regime. Halder's attorney entered as mitigating factors his connection with the resistance and his later arrest and incarceration by the Nazi regime. In the end, the court declared him to be "*unbelastet*" (guiltless) and released him.[3] The prosecutor, however, appealed the ruling to the appeals court (*Kassionshof*) in the Bavarian Justice Ministry. In the meantime, the prosecutor had gained access to Halder's detailed war diaries, which, among other things, revealed his role in formulating the "criminal orders." His exoneration from the first trial was suspended and it looked as though he was in deep trouble.

His friends, the Americans, came to his rescue. The appeals court tried in vain during the ensuing months to set a hearing date. The Americans would not release him, however, claiming that his work for the "Historical Division" made him indispensable. He remained under U.S. protection and never went to Munich for the second trial. The Bavarian government finally gave up and the original verdict was reinstated in September 1950. Halder was free to continue work with the Americans.

Indeed, by 1948, he had thoroughly ingratiated himself with the U.S. Army. In July 1947, he had received the assignment to take command of the German internees (former German officers were termed "civilian internees") in the camp at Neustadt, near Allendorf. As the history project became more elaborate, these former officers were moved in the summer of 1948 to Königstein in the Taunus and Halder was made director of the "Control Group" of the Historical Division. He and his group now oversaw the production of what would eventually become 2,500 major manuscripts written by more than 700 former German officers. In June 1954, Halder transferred the operation to Karlsruhe and continued its work until 1961.[4]

What were Halder's motives in securing for himself such a central role in educating the Americans about the Eastern Front in World War Two? By his own admission, one goal was to continue the war against Bolshevism.[5] Halder proclaimed this goal already in October 1946, not so much because he foresaw the Cold War, but rather against the background of outrage on the part of most German officers at the Nuremberg verdict, especially that of Generals Jodl and Keitel, who received a death sentence. The goal of fighting Bolshevism was meant to mollify particularly these officers writing for Halder and thus allow the project to continue.[6] Later the anti-Communist motive fit quite nicely into the Cold War context.

Another Halder goal – perhaps the one nearest to his heart – was to rescue the honor of the German officer corps by disassociating it from Hitler, Nazism, and the atrocities of the war. This was a goal that went back to the end of the war and would continue to animate Halder. The Americans were not ignorant of this motive. They had already heard of it as a result of the fact that Halder's conversations with other generals while in captivity had been secretly recorded. One intelligence memo stated: "He [Halder] is extremely frank on what he thinks should be suppressed or distorted, and in particular is very sensitive to the suggestion that the German General Staff is involved in anything, especially planning for war."[7] It was a view the Americans came to share as part of the myth-making process. Finally, Halder was anxious to prepare the histories from a German perspective for a future German Wehrmacht and for the purpose of making such an entity once again acceptable to the German people.

To aid him in his work, Halder demanded – and got – from the Americans substantial documentation from the records seized by the Allies. This produced a two-fold advantage. It enabled the men writing for Halder to ground their narratives in documentation. It also permitted the Control Group to make incriminating evidence disappear.[8]

In appointing his "Control Group," which would vet all submitted studies, Halder was careful to choose mostly high-ranking former staff officers whose views would be in accord with his own.[9] The same principle would apply to the many authors he would employ. These men were also picked for their varied experience, which would make their contributions valuable to the Americans, who by now were anxious to get German insights into both operational planning and troop training. Thus, Halder's purposes and those of the Americans meshed nicely. Asked later how he could work with Americans so soon after the war, Halder replied that,

> There were no difficulties because there was good will on both sides. In the initial period it was a matter of laying out the decisive relationships among organization, mobilization, training etc. in the German army and in explaining experiences undergone, in particular in the struggle with the eastern foe, with which the US Army had no personal experience at all. Later our work evolved into histories of the war and here as well the East stood in the foreground.[10]

Halder supervised the officers writing histories for him quite closely and did not hesitate to "coach" them if their work did not fit closely enough into the interpretive framework Halder was trying to develop. Often, after receiving a manuscript, he would write quite lengthy letters back suggesting editorial changes in content or emphasis.[11] Themes that were deemed particularly sensitive, especially where politics intruded on the military, Halder reserved for himself.[12]

Halder picked a number of men who connected decisively with both past and future: Many had been leading commanders, especially in the East, during the war; some had been charged as war criminals. Some would make careers in the West German army after 1955; others would achieve notoriety and popularity, especially with the Americans, with published books and memoirs. Interestingly enough, the categories do not sort out as neatly as one might surmise. A sizable number had been combat leaders on the Eastern Front: Gotthard Heinrici (4th Army and 1st Panzer Army, 1941–45), Guenther Blumentritt (4th Army, 1940–42), Heinz Guderian (2nd Panzer Army, 1941–42; inspector general of Panzer troops, 1943–44), Albert Kesselring (Luftwaffe commander in Russia, 1941; later Wehrmacht commander south in Italy), Hasso von Manteuffel (7th Panzer Army and Grossdeutschland division, 1943–44), Oskar Munzel (Panzer brigade commander, 1944–45), Erhard Rauss (15th and 3rd Panzer Armies), Hans von Greiffenberg (chief of staff for General Fedor von Bock in Russia, 1941), Lothar Rendulic (2nd Panzer Army in Yugoslavia; commander, Army Group South in Russia), Georg Küchler (commander, Army Group North in Russia), Geyr von Schweppenburg (commander XXXX Panzer corps), and Adolf Heusinger (chief of operations, OKW, 1943–44). These men and many more represented a deep wellspring of knowledge and experience about the Eastern Front. At the same time, a number of them were accused or convicted war criminals, including Küchler and Rendulic, for their activities in the Balkans, as well as Kesselring, who had hostages shot in Italy, and Manteuffel, convicted by a German court later for having a nineteen-year-old German deserter shot. Hans Speidel, who would later lead the West German army, was no war criminal, but his brother Wilhelm, who was military commander in Greece, was; as was Alexander von Falkenhausen, who had hostages killed and Jews deported while running occupied Belgium.

Many of these men would go on to write books, including memoirs, which would exert a strong influence on generations of Americans and help to perpetuate the myth of the Eastern Front. They included Erhard Rauss, Heinz Guderian, Alfred Toppe, Walter Warlimont, and Albert Kesselring as well as Oskar Munzel, who had led a Panzer brigade on the Eastern Front and later rose to high rank in the Bundeswehr. Perhaps the most problematic in some ways was Adolf Heusinger. He was chief of the Operations Division for the

German army and thus had a good overview of everything that was happening in the East. He was by Hitler's side during hundreds of wartime conferences; in fact, he was injured during the July 20, 1944, assassination attempt on Hitler. Arrested as a possible accomplice, he was quickly released and put into the Führer reserve. His name appeared on initial United Nations war criminal lists, but then mysteriously disappeared. He was engaged as a witness at Nuremberg and defended his former comrades, then worked with the Americans briefly before joining Reinhard Gehlen's West German intelligence agency. He was a leading figure in the campaign to release German officers still in custody in the late 1940s and early 1950s. In 1950, he became military adviser to Chancellor Konrad Adenauer, who named him – as well as Hans Speidel – to the post of lieutenant general of the Bundeswehr, upon its establishment in 1955. In 1957, he became the first general inspector of the Bundeswehr – in effect, its top commander. He finished his career in the early 1960s as chair of the "Nato Military Committee" in Washington, and contributed to the development of the American "flexible response" doctrine.[13] Like the group as a whole, Heusinger ran the gamut from possible war criminal to U.S. helper to Bundeswehr leader.

A look at the many titles on the Eastern Front generated by the Halder group reveals a great deal of depth and breadth at the tactical, operational, and strategic levels. At the strategic level, we have, for example, "The German Campaign in Russia: Planning and Operations (1940–1942)" and "Decisions Affecting the Campaign in Russia, 1941–42", the latter written by Halder himself. These studies established the myth of the Eastern Front by laying the responsibility for Barbarossa squarely at Hitler's feet, with the German army leaders being both chagrined and doubtful. At the operational level, we have studies such as "The Battle of Moscow, 1941–42" by Hans von Greiffenberg; "Operational 'Citadel', the Battle of Kursk in July 1943" by Theodore Busse, et al.; "The Collapse of Army Group Center, 1944" by Peter von der Groeben; and "The Pomeranian Battle and the Command in the East, 1945" by Erhard Rauss. These studies strengthen the general point of view of German operational superiority confronting in the end masses of men and materiel. Finally, at the tactical level, there is a plenitude of studies, such as "Tactics of Mobile Units: Operations of the 5. SS Panzergrenadier Division 'Viking' at Rostov and Maikop Oilfields" by Felix Steiner; "Combat in Deep Snow" by Lothar Rendulic; and "In Snow and Mud: 31 Days of Attack Under Sedlitz during early Spring of 1942" by Gustav Hoehne. The last two titles suggest the German propensity to blame setbacks on the Russian weather.

The Americans were especially interested in the German defensive battles during the last two years of the war, for the West anticipated seeing itself at least temporarily in a similar situation if the Soviet Union unleashed its sizable army against Central and Western Europe. Halder's men were happy to oblige with titles like: "Operations of Encircled Forces: German Experiences in Russia" by Oldwig von Natzmer and "German Defense Tactics Against Russian Breakthroughs" by Erhard Rauss. Here, the Germans could serve a double purpose: to perpetuate the myth of the Eastern Front and to salvage their pride by drawing on their wartime experiences to advise the Americans.[14]

At a deeper level, a number of the studies convey to the Americans the German view of the Soviet Union, its peoples, and its soldiers. Though often frank about the fighting qualities of the Russian soldier and the leadership of the Red Army, once it had mastered the techniques pioneered by the Germans, the studies also portray a racial view of the Russians that had diverged little from Nazi racial doctrine. One sees this in studies such as "The Fighting Qualities of the Russian Soldier" by Lothar Rendulic and the aforementioned "Small Unit Actions." One often runs into generalizations about Slavs that are outright racist. For example, "The Slav psyche – especially where it is under more or less pronounced Asiatic influences – covers a wide range in which fanatic conviction, extreme bravery, and cruelty bordering on bestiality are coupled with childlike kindliness and susceptibility to sudden fear and terror."[15] In another article, the Russian soldier, termed a "semi-Asiatic," "possesses neither the judgment nor the ability to think independently. He is subject to moods, which to a Westerner are incomprehensible; he acts by instinct. As a soldier, the Russian is primitive and unassuming, innately brave but morosely passive when in a group." . . . "Disregard for human beings and contempt of death are other characteristics of the Russian soldier." . . . "Because of his simple and primitive nature, all sorts of hardships bring him but few emotional reactions. His emotions run the gamut from animal ferocity to the utmost kindliness."[16] General Rendulic, in his pamphlet "On the Fighting Qualities of the Russian Soldier," poses a purely racial argument: that the Russians represent a racial mixture in which "there can also be traced a weak Germanic blood strain from the Gothic period and the Middle Ages. Of special importance, however, I consider the infusion of Mongol blood during the 300 years of the Tartar domination, since it very definitely put its stamp on the Russian national character." What characteristics did this infusion of blood produce? "The greatest patience and endurance of suffering, a certain inertness and submissiveness to life and fate, little initiative, and in many of them . . . an easily aroused inclination toward cruelty and harshness which may be considered as part of the Mongol heritage in view of the good-natured disposition of the people."[17] Halder himself could not resist weighing in with his own assessment: "Frequent insensate cruelty is found coupled with attachment, fidelity, and good nature under proper

handling."[18] In this manner, the Germans could hope to forge another connection with the Americans. Together they were "Westerners" facing not only
an ideological and military threat, but a racial one as well.

The many studies composed by the German officers had a strong impact
on the Americans. Particularly after the outbreak of the Korean War, many
U.S. agencies developed what one author has called "an insatiable appetite
for information on Soviet military organization and operations in World
War II . . . More than 1,182 requests had been received from the general staff
and from service schools, and of these 972 had been furnished." A large number of high-ranking American officers also read these studies and many, left
untranslated, were used in German classes at the military academies. Some
were also published and used in the training of U.S. troops in Europe.[19]

As the U.S. Army prepared to meet a possible Soviet attack in 1948 and
thereafter, new strategies were necessary to meet that threat. Original planning
was based on a position defense, which would hold the enemy at the Rhine.
This tactic changed after 1949 as the concept of "mobile defense" was adopted.
This allowed for an enemy thrust deep into Allied territory, which would then
be cut off and destroyed in a series of counterattacks by highly mobile armored
units with devastating firepower. This change in tactics was strongly influenced
by the German accounts of their own flexible defense in the East during the
last years of the war. With the publication of Field Manual 17–100 in 1949, the
U.S. Army acknowledged that its position in Central and Western Europe was
strongly analogous to that of the Germans on the Eastern Front after 1943.[20]

It is some indication of the extent to which Americans recognized the
influence of the Halder group that Halder himself and a team chosen by him
were invited, on February 28, 1952, to embark on a year-long study of the Field
Manual 100–5 and expose it to a critique based, in part, on the experiences of
the group in the East.[21] Halder was happy to do so. As he wrote to General
Blumentritt soon after the invitation was issued: "I have undertaken this task,
because I am of the opinion, that with a serious handling of this task, we will
be in a position to make an intellectual contribution to the defensive potential
of the West, which no one else can do. I'll also not conceal the fact that the
old German General Staff, which is still rejected in public, is at least valued
behind the scenes as unparalleled experts."[22] The U.S. Army increasingly would
agree with the self-assessment of Halder and would become convinced that the
German generals would have achieved victory but for Hitler's usurpation of
their authority.

In the end, the German contribution to U.S. operational doctrine would
turn out to be short lived. The combination of economics (armor was too

expensive) and nuclear weapons caused the doctrine of mobile defense to remain on the books, but not on the battlefield.[23] The real and lasting German influence, as it turns out, was the rehabilitation of the German officer corps and the establishment and perpetuation of the myth of the Eastern Front in the minds of, first, the U.S. military, then widening circles of government and politics, and, finally, millions of Americans.

Franz Halder stands as the living symbol of this success. His popularity, generated through networking with ever larger circles of the military, political, and diplomatic elites of the United States – and eventually with ordinary Americans – was symptomatic of the successful establishment of the Eastern Front myth as well as the reestablished reputation of German arms. Halder's papers redound with complimentary letters from U.S. military personnel, not the least those with whom he worked in the Historical Division. Many of them not only appreciated his labors, but became convinced of his slant on World War Two, not just by the manuscripts he delivered but also by his translated book, *Hitler as Warlord*, which most of them had read and which was in great demand.[24]

As the 1950s wore on, Halder's influence grew. He not only continued to supervise the generation of historical manuscripts; he also facilitated lectures on the part of former German officers to the United States and to U.S. bases in Germany. This becomes clear from his daily calendar. A sampling: "Heidelberg . . . is looking for a German general who speaks Russian. He is to give lectures to American officers who speak Russian about his personal war experiences in Russia . . . The seminar is to last 10 days"; "Meyer meets with a representative of the U.S. 7th Army and three French officers. Discussion on the nature of partisan warfare and our experiences in Russia and in the Balkans"; or:

> Reichhelm reports in prior to a lecture tour in America. (Theme: the Russian soldier"); "A proposal from the USA on lectures of German officers, especially v. Puttkammer. There is the intention of holding the lectures, which have found such resonance over there, in Europe as well with the 7th army . . . At a time when many American officers are taking pains with the German Bundeswehr, I would welcome it, if German officers would do a service for the 7th army. This army has a particular interest in our German experiences with Russia"; "Philippi reports on his lecture to the Americans on the Eastern campaign (in the context of an American university course) Apparently successful."[25]

From November 27 to December 8, 1955, Halder was invited to the United States by the Office of the Chief of Military History (OCMH), run by his old boss, P. M. Robinett. Halder visited West Point, Annapolis, New York, and Mt. Vernon. Near the end of his trip, he also addressed a group of top-ranking officers, including General and Chief of Staff Maxwell D. Taylor, at the OCMH. He emphasized the value of military history as an integral part of German General Staff planning, praised the work of the Historical Division, and then urged caution in the evaluation of the documentation coming out of World War Two – particularly written orders. Undoubtedly the "criminal orders," on which his staff had worked, were in his mind as he urged future historians to consider the "atmosphere" in which orders were generated – one increasingly dominated by Hitler's usurpation of military command. "The entire work methods, the exchange of ideas, the decision making and the issuing of orders at the top levels of the German command were increasingly influenced, if not entirely pervaded, by Hitler's attitude of mind (*Geisteshaltung*). They are only understandable if one is familiar with the atmosphere of mutual distrust and mutual reservations," Halder said, and once again contrasted "the unbridgeable gap between Hitler's demonic nature (*Ungeist*) and the old military concepts in the German army."[26] That Halder was taken seriously is reflected in the letters of thanks he received from members of his audience. The Chief Historian, for example, said, "Your visit was a stimulation and encouragement to all of us, and your address on the last day gave us an experience that we shall long remember as a landmark in our own history."[27]

As the work of the Historical Commission gradually drew to a close by the late 1950s, encomiums of praise poured in to Halder from high and low. One major wrote from the Pentagon that, "I believe that your contribution to Germany and the United States since the war is incalculable and that it will stand as an everlasting monument to your career as soldier, man and world citizen."[28]

The Commander in Chief of the U.S. Army in Europe wrote "to express my deep appreciation for your long and devoted service . . . The product of your labors is much more than mere pages of military history. Already it has provided valuable material for the organization and training of our military forces to meet the threat of communist aggression . . . Thus, your work has developed another area of alliance between our two great nations for the joint defense of our democratic ways of life."[29] Major General John P. Daley, Deputy Chief of Operations, wrote: "The studies prepared by the Control group under your supervision hold the distinction of being the ranking authoritative works available and will become more valuable with the passage of time."[30]

Halder was also rewarded in more material fashion. His close friend, Admiral Ansel, who had worked with him on researching Operation "Sea Lion," the plan to invade England in 1940, arranged for Halder to be named an associate member of the U.S. Naval Institute.[31] After his work had been completed, Halder was also awarded the "Meritorious Civilian Service Award" in November 1961 by Major General Doleman in the name of President Kennedy. It was the highest award a foreigner could earn working for the United States and the capstone of Halder's postwar career. It made Halder the only German general ever to be decorated by Adolf Hitler and an American president.[32]

During the 1960s, Halder became a kind of historical icon, especially after the publication of his diaries. Historians, academic and private, turned to him for advice and information, and he responded at great length to their queries.[33] Ordinary citizens wrote letters with every conceivable kind of question, and he patiently replied. Typical is that of Don Burkel of Batavia, N.Y., who wrote: "I was wondering if your [sic] not to [sic] busy if you could tell me the difference between the Knight's Cross and the Iron Cross or are they the same thing? I took the letter you sent to me and showed my history teacher and said that I was very lucky to be able to correspond with you about the war. I know your [sic] very busy and probably didn't have time to answer my second letter. I've put your first letter in a picture frame on the wall with the rest of my letters from famous people."[34]

Halder's fame and influence – first within the U.S. military, then within larger governmental circles, and, finally, with a fairly large general public interested in military history – parallel and express the gradual change in historical memory that happened in the United States in the course of the Cold War about the Eastern Front and the German military.

Networking with the Bundeswehr

Another conduit for Germans to deliver myths about the Eastern Front was created in 1955 – the West German army or Bundeswehr. There was a very important link between the formation of that armed force and the rehabilitation of the German army – a most important component in the myth of the Eastern Front. Five years earlier, after the outbreak of the Korean War, it became clear to the Americans that a German fighting force of some kind would have to be revived, for the eventuality that a hot war spread from Asia to Europe. U.S. military thinkers had been contemplating this eventuality since 1947, but now it took on a real urgency. Among large numbers of former German officers, however, there was the conviction that no future German fighting force would be possible without the rehabilitation of the Wehrmacht.

It was to this end on October 9, 1950, that a number of former senior German officers, including Hans Speidel, Hans Röttiger, Adolf Heusinger,

Hermann Foertsch, and Friedo von Senger und Etterlin, all five of whom had written manuscripts for us as part of the Halder group, met secretly for four days at a Benedictine abbey, Cloister Himmerod, in the Eifel mountains west of the Rhine to discuss the matter of German rearmament. The group advised West German chancellor Konrad Adenauer. Out of this meeting came a memorandum, known as the "Himmerod Memorandum," which would be the "Magna Carta" of the future West German army. The authors make it clear that they would only be involved with the founding of a West German military under certain conditions. All German soldiers convicted as "war criminals" would have to be released. The defamation of German soldiers, including Waffen-SS, would have to cease. Measures to change the public attitude toward military service would have to be implemented. The German federal government would have to issue a declaration to the effect that the German soldier had fought honorably. Suitable social measures would have to be taken to assure the material welfare of the former soldiers and their widows and orphans.[35]

Adenauer accepted these propositions and told the representatives of the three Western occupying powers that there could not be any West German contingent in the then-planned-for European Defense Community force as long as German soldiers remained in custody or were brought before courts. Part of Commissioner McCloy's willingness to commute a number of sentences of former German officers incarcerated at Landsberg prison undoubtedly went back to this condition.[36]

It was not enough for these former officers that the West German government "rehabilitate" them and their comrades. The Americans had to follow suit. An opportunity opened up with the visit to Germany in late January 1951 of the designated NATO commander, General Dwight Eisenhower.

Speidel and Heusinger seized the opportunity to speak to a man who was both former Allied commander and NATO commander. On his own initiative, Speidel went to Deputy Commissioner General George P. Hayes and convinced him to arrange a meeting with Eisenhower with the purpose of rehabilitating the German soldier. Together Heusinger and several members of the group worked out a document, which was presented to Eisenhower at a reception in his honor on January 22, 1951. Before signing it, Eisenhower told the German generals that he had been in error in his earlier assessments of the World War Two German military and offered an apology. In 1945, he had been of the impression that "the Wehrmacht and the Hitler gang were all the same." Recently, however, he had read a book about General Erwin Rommel, the "Desert Fox," which drew a sharp line between the army and the regime. The generals nodded their complete agreement with this distinction and noted that they had been well aware of it in their own experience during the war. Then, Eisenhower signed the document, which read as follows:

> I have come to know that there is a real difference between the regular German soldier and officer and Hitler and his criminal group. For my part, I do not believe that the German soldier as such has lost his honor. The fact that certain individuals committed in war dishonorable and despicable acts reflects on the individuals concerned and not on the great majority of German soldiers and officers.[37]

These words were coming from a man who had excoriated the German military in his book, *Crusade in Europe*, and who had written to his wife, Mamie, in late 1944: "the German is a beast . . . God, I hate the Germans."[38]

Several days later, Eisenhower met with President Truman, Vice President Alvin Barclay and most of the cabinet in the White House. There, he said "that too many Americans talked too much out loud about Germany. He, personally, would like to have German troops under his command. He had good reason to know what kind of fighters they made."[39]

The Germans were treated to icing on the cake when General Matthew Ridgeway, former U.S. commander in Korea, also exonerated the German officers of World War Two. Specifically, he urged the high commissioners to "pardon all German officers convicted of war crimes on the Eastern front [!]." He claimed to have issued orders in Korea "of the kind for which the German generals are sitting in prison" and that his "honor as a soldier" compelled him to insist on the release of these German officers from prison as a condition of his issuing "a single command to a German soldier of the European army."[40]

The Eisenhower and Ridgeway statements were important in the context of West German rearmament in the mid-1950s. Some months later, emboldened by the public statements of the two top U.S. generals, two former German generals, Hans Jürgen Stumpff and Hans-Georg Reinhardt, met with chancellor Adenauer to discuss the war criminal problem. Armed with a letter signed by twenty-six former generals and field marshals, including Halder, Kesselring, Rundstedt, and Guderian, the two officers insisted that no honorable German soldier could be expected to don a uniform as long as one innocent comrade was still incarcerated. They referred to those who had been convicted of the Malmedy massacre, the murder of captured American soldiers in Belgium, and compared those actions with events in Korea – undoubtedly a play on the Ridgeway statement. Adenauer found himself in agreement with the generals and noted that Eisenhower would soon be in the White House and then the whole question of war criminal verdicts could be settled "soldier to soldier." Reinhard concluded the meeting by saying that "the moment at which the first

German soldier puts on a uniform, must be the deadline for the resolution of the 'war criminal' problem."[41]

The Eisenhower and Ridgeway statements were thus important in the context of West German rearmament, but they were even more important in another context – the evolution of the myth of the Eastern Front. With the imprimatur of Eisenhower, a rehabilitated Wehrmacht could assume a central place in the portrait former German generals had been sketching since 1945. Now, the message could get out into ever widening circles, beyond the relatively small number of American officers and intelligence operatives who had been the first to adopt the myth.

The Bundeswehr

One institutional framework for spreading the myth of the Eastern Front was the West German army, which was established in 1955. Officers in this army would have many opportunities to network with American officers and civilians in the ensuing years. It is interesting to note that in 1955, 100 percent of the Bundeswehr officer corps consisted of former Wehrmacht soldiers (as late as 1967 it was still 41 percent).[42] Here was a large pool of men who had fought in World War Two and who were now comrades of the U.S. soldiers, many of whom had little or no memory of that conflict and were open to absorbing German memories. Within a short time, general collaboration was complemented by visits to American bases of German war heroes, who were admired and feted by their hosts. One particularly popular visitor was Erich Hartmann, the chief German ace of the war, who allegedly had shot down 314 Russian planes. In fact, in 1957, Hartmann graduated from a U.S. Air Force fighter course. This hosting continued in the United States itself, as Bundeswehr officers came over in significant numbers for training and maneuvers. For years, Hill Air Force Base in Ogden, Utah, hosted events involving former German and English pilots sponsored by the "Battle of Britain Society of Utah."[43]

In addition to myriad contacts between West German and American officers – as well as the base visits by Wehrmacht heroes – contacts were established at the top in the 1950s between former Wehrmacht generals – now top commanders in the Bundeswehr – and their U.S. equivalents. One typical example was Oskar Munzel. Munzel finished the war as a Major General, the commander of the 2nd Panzer division. (In 1944, he had commanded the 14th Panzer division in defensive action in the East). In American custody, he wrote for the Halder group, being a co-author of Department of the Army pamphlet 20–242, "German Armored Traffic Control during the Russian Campaign." After a stint as military adviser in Egypt, he joined the new Bundeswehr and was promoted to Brigadier General in 1956 and Lieutenant General in 1958. He wrote a book, *Panzertaktik*, which was very popular among American officers, as is illustrated by the many complimentary letters sent to him.[44] He was invited to the United States to speak and to tour bases. These visits usually earned him awards and expensive, leather-bound albums as gifts, as was the case with his tour of Fort Knox and Fort Benning in November-December 1958.[45]

He consulted with American officers on armored tactics and with his former colleagues, who were presenting lectures to U.S. officers.[46] Always, he and they stressed the factor of movement on the battlefield, including on the defense. One German officer, who sent Munzel the draft of a lecture he was going to give at Fort Knox, noted: "It was important to me to demonstrate to the Americans our mobility at the beginning of the [Russian] campaign and how through the loss of that mobility we also lost our superiority."[47] Munzel was also editor of a military journal, *Kampftruppen* (fighting troops), and corresponded with the editor of the U.S. counterpart *Armor*, Lieutenant Colonel Eugene Dutchak.[48] Munzel never quite became the magic figure represented by Halder, but he was not unknown to a public increasingly enamored of the Wehrmacht, as illustrated by a letter from the master at arms of the Ohio Valley Military Society requesting Munzel's picture and any Wehrmacht uniform which might still be in Munzel's possession, both of which the correspondent was willing to pay for.[49]

Not all Americans were favorably impressed by all the hobnobbing between high U.S. officers and former Wehrmacht generals, however. Outraged by a *New York Times* story which showed his former commander at Anzio, General Lucien Truscott, partying in Frankfurt with Kesselring, Bernard Burton, formerly with Co. K, 7th infantry regiment, Third Division, berated Truscott for this act, which was an insult to the families of the Italians whom Kesselring had had shot, and to the fallen American soldiers, none of whose widows would find themselves in the position of Truscott's wife in the photo that accompanied the story – with her hand resting on Kesselring's arm![50]

It was clear, though, that most U.S. officers were viewing the Wehrmacht and its officers with great respect. This was illustrated by one of the ironies of the nature of the Bundeswehr. A number of its younger founders – like Count Wolf von Baudissin, Count Johann Adolf von Kielmansegg, and Count Ulrich de Maiziere – wanted to distance the Bundeswehr from its Wehrmacht past and put it into the context of a modern democracy. They wanted to avoid resurrecting the old Prussian martial virtues, the old *Kommiss*, the strict spit and polish of the former German military and to create a "citizen in uniform," a soldier who would, in many ways, remain a civilian while serving; who would vote and even be politically active, something that was anathema to the apolitical Prussian tradition. Even the uniforms of the new Bundeswehr reflected the "antimilitarism" of these men. A dull gray and with no ornamentation, the uniforms were often mistaken for those of butlers or footmen. Nor was the goose step reintroduced.[51]

It is some indication of how enamored the Americans were with the old Wehrmacht, that they, who were allegedly teaching the Germans about democracy, either took no interest in the product of military reform or actually disparaged it. As Count von Baudissen discovered to his chagrin on a visit to the United States: "They simply wanted German soldiers – as numerous, competent and rapidly mobilized as possible."[52] Brigadier General John B. Murphy thought the idea of a democratic army absurd; it would be nothing more than an "undisciplined mob." "Any attempt at dictating our own concepts on a nation that has twice within a twenty five year period produced an awesome fighting force . . . would be doomed to failure." One is reminded of the standard words of the drill sergeant: "You are here to defend democracy, not to practice it."

Thus, though the Americans had high hopes for a West German defense force that could help defend Europe against the Soviet aggressor, they always doubted that the Bundeswehr measured up to the standards set by the Wehrmacht. As one German scholar put it: "In the final analysis, the nevertheless unshaken American faith in Germany's future military capability was fed by past experience with the German Wehrmacht. Although the Allies had severely criticized and punished . . . the Wehrmacht's involvement in Nazi politics of aggression and annihilation, their professional esteem for German fighting power, for the operative capabilities of the German general staff, and for the cohesion of the German troops outlived that criticism."[53] In a scathing review of the Bundeswehr in 1963, Truman Smith, the former military attaché to Berlin, who admired the old German military and who had brought Charles Lindbergh to Germany in 1937, wrote that: "The German army of 1963 is unworthy to stand comparison with any German army of the past two centuries." And it was precisely the democratic nature of the West German army, which led, according to Smith, to its weakness.[54]

From the early 1950s on, many former German officers increasingly felt free to offer ideas and criticisms at all levels of the U.S. military regarding its organization, strategy, and tactics. In part, they sensed their increasing credibility as Americans gradually accepted the myth of the "clean" Wehrmacht and expressed admiration for the World War Two German military effort. In part, the U.S. military also lost some of its own reputation among the Germans, partly because of its poor performance in Korea, and partly because of its inadequate equipment, which the Germans regarded as inferior to theirs in the previous war. And, in part, we kept asking them for advice, as in the case of Halder.

Already in 1950, Heinz Guderian, whose memoirs would be so popular later in the United States, in an interview with *U.S. News and World Report*, responded to the question of whether Russia's army could be beaten. "If there is one soldier in the world who could stop an aggressor's invasion into Western Europe, it is the German," Guderian replied. Moreover, drawing on his experience in Russia, Guderian insisted that mobile armored units were essential and, disparaging tactical nuclear weapons, that the decisive battles would still be fought on the ground. In response to the question of what defeated the German armies in Russia – space, Russian arms, or weather – [the question itself already limited the response to what Guderian wanted to say], Guderian blamed part of it on the Russian winter, but most on "the immense superiority in numbers of the Russian soldiers. With German soldiers I can defeat a three or even five-fold superiority of the enemy, but, if the proportion is one to ten or even one to eight, then, of course, even German soldiers have to capitulate." Asked why he did not join the resistance to Hitler, Guderian replied that the "only consequence of Hitler's removal would have been chaos among the leaderless German troops and the unchecked advance of the Russians. If the Russians are today at the Elbe river and not on the Rhine, then it is our merit." Finally, Guderian referred to his twenty-page memorandum for reform of the U.S. military, which urged a Prussian type system; it "seems to constitute a sort of Bible for the majority of American officers."[55] Here, Guderian managed to provide advice for the U.S. military on organization and tactics, which resemble those of the Wehrmacht after 1943, as well as to repeat myths about the Eastern Front and the relationship of the military to the Hitler regime. But this time he addressed a mass audience.

Two years later, in 1952, Guderian's twenty-page memorandum was again before the public, as it was announced in Germany that the new U.S. president, Dwight Eisenhower, was going to adopt Guderian's suggestion for an American version of the "Oberkommando der Wehrmacht." "Prussian dynamic would combine with American streamlining" to produce a new command structure, which, among other things, would combine the joint chiefs into a general staff as well as enhance the powers of the president as commander in chief.[56]

The participation of Bundeswehr officers in U.S. Army training programs also provided the basis for critique. A retired Lieutenant Colonel von Clear, taking part in a Command and General Staff Officer Course at Fort Leavenworth in 1955, wrote a detailed critique noting especially the fact that the Americans drastically underestimated the Russians and that their training for general staff operations was more drill than education. He did allow, however, that "our best ambassadors are American units returning from Germany" – one indication of the harmonious networking that had been going on.[57]

Finally, at a higher level, there is a 1958 critical report by former Major General Hermann Büschleb of the 1957 U.S. publication 7-100-2 "The Infantry Division" (referring to the so-called "Pentomic Division"). He compliments the Americans for combining for the first time tactics for conventional and atomic war, which makes an effort to take advantage of German experiences. Nevertheless, the tactics are still too stationary and not mobile enough; too many plans take the place of what should be one plan; and the report demonstrates "the missing experience with the tactics and mentality of the Red Army," one the Germans were still trying to impress on the Americans.[58]

German veterans were also sharing their advice not only with the American public and press, but also with U.S. intelligence, as the following story illustrates. Harry F. Kern, senior editor for foreign affairs for *Newsweek* magazine, was to write an article on what the behavior of former German officers might be, should a German army be reconstituted. The main source for the article was Geyr von Schweppenburg, another veteran of the Halder group, whom both Kern and the main editor of *Newsweek*, Robert A. Haeger, knew quite well. Kern would share the information acquired from Geyr with CIA chief, Allen Dulles, just as he had a previous article on the military in Germany with Dulles' predecessor, General Walter Bedell Smith. Kern was close to Geyr and a number of other former German officers and regularly sent them tear sheets from his *Newsweek* stories.[59]

The myth of the Eastern Front and the "clean" Wehrmacht percolated out to ever-wider military audiences. Much of the material appeared in the military journals, in which both former Wehrmacht officers and U.S. officers contributed articles. *Military Review*, for example, already in the early 1950s, was publishing articles such as "The Arctic Can Be Our Ally" by Lieutenant Colonel Joseph Peot (the Russian winter did the Germans in); "What Kind of Elephant Is Armor" by Lieutenant Colonel Paul Bogen; "Ground Force Mobility" by Paul Robinett (who had been Halder's handler); and by former German general Blumentritt, "Strategic Withdrawals."[60] Much of this amounted to a massive rewriting of history in the form of a "Lost Cause" mythology, which bore a close resemblance to another "Lost Cause" myth more familiar to Americans: that of the Civil War.

History, Memory, and the Civil War Analogy

The great German historian Theodor von Ranke thought that history should be written "wie es eigentlich gewesen," that is, as it really happened, shorn of myth and legend and based on documents that told the story. We know

now that this is a difficult, if not impossible, task, partly because the present is always intruding on the past. As David Thelen has put it: "So, the construction of memory [and, thus, of history] is a dynamic, ongoing process, which by and large serves the needs of the present. It is constantly shaped and reshaped as new information is assimilated, as new values and contexts come to the fore at a particular period of time, as our identity shifts, as we associate with new groups possessing a different orientation, as we are worked upon by different authorities determined to reshape our historical memory. It is a process both of selective remembering and of forgetting."[61] It is made possible by the fact that memory – even personal memory – is elusive, fleeting, transitory, and many-layered, with recent perceptions building upon and altering inherited ones. Thus, although events often have a powerful impact on people as they happen, memory fades rapidly and gives way to the needs of the present, including political exigency, personal or national validation, changed context, or the need for nostalgia. As David Lowenthal pointed out in his study *The Past Is a Foreign Country*: "Contrary to common belief, we forget most of our experiences; the greater part of what happens to us is soon irretrievably lost. . . . Memories are also altered by revision. Contrary to the stereotype of the remembered past as immutably fixed, recollections are malleable and flexible; what seems to have happened undergoes continual change. Heightening certain events in recall, we reinterpret them in the light of subsequent experience and present need."[62]

It is the main contention of this study that Americans have used a "Lost Cause" mythology for political purposes not once, but twice, in our history: first, as is well known, in the century after the Civil War in order to integrate the white South back into the Union; and then, during the Cold War, in order to wipe out the memory of the Soviet Union as our ally during World War Two, as well as to integrate our former enemies, the Germans, into the defensive structure of the West, and in doing so revalidate ourselves historically.

There is a rich literature on the Civil War "Lost Cause" upon which we can draw to make the analogy. In his fine study on the American Civil War and memory, David Blight points out one of the main features that apply to both cases. "Americans faced an overwhelming task after the Civil War and emancipation: how to understand the tangled relationship between two profound ideas: *healing* and *justice*. On some level, both had to occur; but given the potency of racial assumptions and power in nineteenth century America, these two aims never developed in historical balance."[63]

This was precisely the task the Adenauer regime faced in the late 1940s, after the founding of the Federal Republic of Germany. Justice required that the leaders and followers of the Nazi regime, including the military, face legal proceedings for their actions, that war crimes be expiated and that all traces of National Socialism be eradicated from the body politic. Healing, on the other hand, meant the integration of a whole generation of German veterans into society on terms by which they would accept democracy, unlike their predecessors after 1918, who became the bane of existence for the Weimar republic. As with the U.S. in the wake of the Civil War, the tasks of healing and justice did not proceed in balance. Healing took precedence over justice.[64] In the American case, North-South reconciliation was achieved at the expense of African Americans, for whom true emancipation and justice had to await another century. In the German case, reconciliation with the wartime generation was achieved at the expense of the victims of the Nazi Holocaust. The Americans basically accepted the Adenauer strategy, issued their own welcome to the former Wehrmacht soldiers, and began to build the myth of the Eastern Front.

Both the Civil War and World War Two ended with war crimes trials. In the latter case, there were many, beginning with the Nuremberg trials and continuing with the successor trials of the late 1940s. There was only one trial after the Civil War: that of the commander of the notorious Confederate prison at Andersonville, Ga., Captain Henry Wirz. At Andersonville, during the relatively short thirteen-month tenure of Wirz, more than 13,000 Union prisoners perished. But the ensuing battle for memory was similar in both cases. In the eyes of many observers, in retrospect, Andersonville resembled the later Nazi concentration camps. There were pictures of emaciated figures, half-starved prisoners who suffered from malnutrition, exposure, disease and mistreatment, just as in the German camps. If, in the eyes of the Nazis, concentration camps were a part of the war effort, so Wirz is supposed to have bragged that he was destroying more "Yankee soldiers than Lee was killing . . . "[65] Wirz was tried in Washington by a military court after the war, convicted of war crimes, and hanged.

But, just as agitation began in the late 1940s to rehabilitate and secure the release of German officers who had been convicted and imprisoned, a campaign to rehabilitate Wirz also began not long after his execution – led by former Confederate President Jefferson Davis – and continued for decades. Both sides fought for historical memory. In the South, a monument was built to honor "martyr" Wirz at Andersonville and the reason for the deaths of the prisoners laid at the door of the North, which had allegedly discontinued prisoner exchanges. The struggle continued into the twentieth century. In 1908, James Madison Page, himself a former prisoner at Andersonville, in collaboration with another former Union prisoner, M. J. Haley, wrote an exculpatory story about Wirz and the prison. Page was an admirer of the South, impressed with the bravery of the Southern soldier in battle, and advocated an emotional coming together of North and South. "For more than forty years we of the North have been acting unfairly. We charge the South with all the blame for all the horrors of the Civil War." As for Wirz: "I judge Henry Wirz from my personal knowledge of his character. Let us be fair and 'place ourselves in the other fellow's place.' Would you or could you have done better if you had been in his place under the same circumstances?" He concludes his book with the lines: "Then let us wipe out the so-called 'Mason and Dixon's line' and hang out the latchstring for each other."[66]

That publication prompted the former prosecutor of Wirz, N. P. Chipman, to respond three years later with his own book, justifying the trial and verdict. He concluded by saying: "The monument to Wirz may stand with its misleading and false inscriptions, the children in the schools of the South may be taught how atrocious was the conduct of the Union officials and how humane and just was the conduct of the Confederate officials. But the truth of history can never be effaced. The cruelty. The sufferings needlessly and wickedly inflicted upon hapless Union prisoners may be *forgiven* . . . but it is not in the nature of man to *forget* such sacrifices."[67] The struggle continues today in publications and on the Internet.[68]

There are other similarities as well. As indicated, establishing historical memory involves both remembering and forgetting. What is eradicated from historical memory is often as important as what remains. For example, in the establishment of the southern lost cause historical narrative, one seldom sees reference to slavery, ostensibly the main cause of the war; or, if it is mentioned, then it is in a romanticized context of happy slaves a la "Gone with the Wind." By the same token, the historical memory of the Eastern Front established over the past fifty years in popular culture never, until very recently, mentioned the Nazi racial genocide against Jews and Slavs. In both cases, issues and events that were central to the wars simply disappear from the narrative.

At the July 4, 1913, Gettysburg reunion of northern and southern veterans – a love feast between North and South – Governor William Hodges Mann of Virginia said: "We are not here to discuss the genesis of the war, but men who have tried to fight each other in the storm of battle are here to discuss this *great fight* . . . we came here, I say, *not to discuss what caused the war of 1861–1865*, but to talk over the events of the battle here as man to man."[69] This is basically the attitude of the American subcultures toward the war in the East. They are not interested in Hitler's vision of a war of racial conquest, subjugation, and annihilation. They are interested in Manstein's retaking of Kharkov in the spring of 1943; or in the exploits of one or another Waffen-SS division or of individual soldiers in that division. Grand strategy gives way to the operational and tactical levels, where one can avoid the difficult larger historical questions – the "whys" of history – and instead embrace the very malleable and romanticizable "how" and "what" of history at the basic human level. And in both cases – Civil War and Eastern Front – the reason is clear: By focusing on the fight itself, on the valor and achievements of individuals and their units, while leaving the terrible and complex issues aside, they can romanticize the conflict, cover it with a fog of sentimentality and a whiff of "what if." And just as there were no African-American veterans invited to attend the 1913 "Jim Crow" reunion and black newspapers regarded the reunion with sadness and scorn, so too might the survivors of the Holocaust view with similar emotions those who wax sentimental about black uniformed men with runes on their collar patches and death head symbols on their caps.

The reasons evinced for defeat in both cases are also quite similar. What Governor Charles Farrell of Virginia said at the dedication of the Confederate White House in Richmond on February 22, 1896, about the "Lost Cause" was later repeated by others with respect to the Wehrmacht in World War Two: "whose life was crushed out of it by superior numbers and merciless power." Or, as Georgian Charles Colcock Jones Jr. put it: "overborne by superior numbers and weightier munitions."[70] This was just the stance taken by the Nazis during the war and repeated by former German generals after the war, to explain the defeat of the vaunted Wehrmacht: the crushing of a viable culture by a materialistic civilization; or, as the language of the 1940s put it: the triumph of "Jewish materialism" of the Marxist and plutocratic variety over a culture which, at its core, celebrated opposing values, such as sacrifice, nobility, and idealism. As Blight characterizes the matter in the U.S. context: "Here, indeed, was the full blown myth of the Lost Cause – a glorious organic civilization destroyed by an avaricious 'industrial society' determined to wipe out its cultural foes."[71]

In both cases, former commanders willingly pardoned their counterparts on the other side in the interests of myth creation. Just as Eisenhower, in 1951, "sanitized" the Wehrmacht by saying that it had fought nobly for the Fatherland, despite the evil cause represented by Hitler, so Ulysses S. Grant in the concluding part of his memoirs, written just before his death in 1885, paid homage to the valor of his former enemy Robert E. Lee and to the Confederate army: "I felt like anything but rejoicing at the downfall of a foe who had fought so long and valiantly, and had suffered so much for the cause, though this cause was, I believe, one of the worst for which a people ever fought, and one for which there was the least excuse. I do not question, however, the sincerity of the great mass of those who were opposed to us ..." "The war was thus drained of evil, and, to a great extent, of cause or political meaning. A politics of forgetting attached itself readily to the Union hero's depiction of two mystic days at Appomattox ..."[72]

Figure 3. Jubal Early, promoter of the "Lost Cause."

There is also a close similarity between Confederate and German officers specifically involved in myth making: The most obvious parallel here is Jubal Early (Figure 3) and Franz Halder.[73] Both men set into motion campaigns to establish the historical memory of war. Early, an unrepentant former Confederate general, used the mechanism of the Southern Historical Society and its fourteen-year-long series of publications to present the Southern version of the war. As we have seen, Halder led a large group of former German officers in churning out reports and monographs for the United States Army Historical Division to promote the German version of the war, particularly in the East. Former Confederate general P. G. T. Beauregard's words to Early could just as easily have been said by Halder to his men: "After having taken part in *making* history . . . " the generals should now undertake the task to "see that it is correctly *written*."[74] The parallel goes on: both men (Early and Halder) were anxious to shape the views of future generations; both got into the fray very early after the war – Halder with his short book on Hitler as Commander, Early with his memoirs; both reached out to young people and foreigners; both pinpointed scapegoats for defeat – Early castigated General James Longstreet for the loss at Gettysburg, Halder blamed Hitler for the loss of the Second World War.

One of the differences between former Confederate and former German generals lay in the fact that the Confederates had no trust that Northerners would get the history right; the Germans believed early on that the Americans could be convinced to accept the German interpretation. In the end, however, both groups were largely successful.

Blight indicates five potent arguments Confederate Lost Causers used by the 1890s to plead their case at the national level. All five offer parallels to the post–World War Two period.[75] First, the Lost Causers wanted to "glorify the valor of the Southern soldiers and to defend their honor as defensive warriors." The gallant long-term defensive actions by the Wehrmacht from 1943 to the end of the war drew the respect and admiration of the Americans. Second, they "promoted the Confederate past as a bulwark against all the social and political disorder." The German contention that they were fighting in the name of Western civilization against the godless social and political revolution of the Bolsheviks is very similar. A third Lost Cause goal was to "guard the Confederate past against all its real and imagined enemies," strongly suggesting the romanticized revisionist history of the war in the East. Fourth was "arguing about the causes of the war." The German generals consistently argued that the invasion of the Soviet Union was really a preventive move intended to frustrate an invasion of Europe being planned by Stalin. Recent specious work has revived this allegation of Soviet aggression. Finally, the Lost Causers intended to "reinvigorate white supremacy by borrowing heavily from the plantation school of literature in promoting reminiscences of the faithful slave as a central figure in the Confederate war." Belated use by Nazi Germany of foreign auxiliaries, including from the despised *Untermenschen*, the Slavs, fits this mold to a degree. One thinks, for example, of the Vlassov army, recruited from among Soviet POWs toward the end of the war.

Both Lost Cause mythologies exerted a strong hold on popular culture. They withstood (and withstand) the test of time. It sometimes seems, with regard to popular literature, that academic historians have abandoned the field to the revisionist ones; or, if the academic studies do reach a broader audience, they tend to be rejected. This is typified by a letter to the editor penned by a retired U.S. military officer in response to Alan T. Nolan's critical study of Lee: *Lee Considered: General Robert E. Lee and Civil War History*: "I call upon every true student of the Civil War, every son and daughter of that war, both North and South, and every organization formed to study, research, reenact, perserve [sic] and remember our Civil War heritage not to purchase Nolan's book . . . If you have it already, burn it as it is not worth recycling."[76] By contrast, Lost Cause books like Winston Groom's *Shrouds of Glory. From Atlanta to Nashville. The Last Great Campaign of the Civil War*, appeared on many book club lists and enjoyed widespread popularity. Similarly, serious studies of the war in the East appeared as early as the 1960s and 1970s, like Alexander Werth's *Russia at War* and John Erickson's *Road to Stalingrad*, and soon went out of print, while the popular histories, for example, by Paul Carell, which romanticized the Wehrmacht in easy-to-read prose, sold in the millions.

In the popular literature and war gaming on the Eastern Front, the Germans are front and center, portrayed sympathetically, while the Russians hold a shadowy place in the background. Very often in war games, the German units are given their specific names, while the Russian ones are generic. For collectors and re-enactors, the memorabilia of the Germans – flags, uniform insignia, dog tags, weapons – assume an iconic significance, while one finds little from the Russian side. Similarly, the Union side – the winning side – suffers by comparison to the Confederate – the losing side. Lee and his generals have been the focus of a number of novels; Grant and his generals scarcely any. Lee and his generals dominate prints, sculpture, and art generally. From 1983 to 1995, *Civil War: the Magazine for the Civil War Society* carried thirty ads for Lee memorabilia, seventeen for "Stonewall" Jackson, three for the pair of them, and only two for Grant. As subjects for artists, Confederate topics outnumber Union ones by 3:1 and appreciate more rapidly in value.[77] Similarly, Nazi war art, for decades, was very popular, especially in the military, and the Air Force Academy, to take only one example, had a number of canvases in the mess hall. No example of Soviet socialist realism was present.

Public relations also play a role in both Lost Cause cases. Here one can cite the examples of George E. Pickett, leader of the famous "Pickett's Charge," memorialized as the high-water mark of the Civil War, and Erwin Rommel, the "Desert Fox," who led German troops conspicuously in North Africa in 1940–1942. Both North and South very quickly made Pickett famous, partly because of his dramatic defeat, and in part because of the valiant courage demonstrated even in failure. The creation of memory is quite dramatic in both cases. The final charge at Gettysburg could just as well have been called "Pettigrew's Charge," after General James Pettigrew, whose division played just as important role in the attack as Pickett's. But amateur historians, journalists, and, not the least, Pickett's very active widow, LaSalle Corbell Pickett, played an instrumental role in elevating Pickett to the all-embracing symbol of

Figure 4. "Jefferson Davis and His Generals," a popular Lost Cause engraving from 1890. Despite the title, Lee dominates the grouping. Each of the generals served all or part of his career in the eastern theater. Jackson is to Lee's right. Early stands at the far right. Collection of the author.

North-South reconciliation later in the nineteenth century.[78] Rommel, although an excellent commander, was also elevated to a status probably higher than he deserved, again for reasons of political expediency. Nazi public relations hailed him as the "people's general" after the dramatic victory over France in 1940. The British, more particularly Winston Churchill, played up Rommel as the ingenious "Desert Fox," partly to explain their embarrassing defeats in North Africa in 1941. After the war, Rommel kept his legendary status among both Germans and former Allies, in part because he operated on perhaps the only front where the Nazis did not practice wholesale genocide. Indicatively, General Eisenhower admitted, that it was after reading a Rommel biography that he began to change his attitude toward the German army.[79]

One should also take note of icons and totems, both inanimate and alive, in the larger picture of the "Lost Cause." We have mentioned Wehrmacht memorabilia. One should add to that still-living Wehrmacht veterans, who are welcomed into large numbers of Internet chatrooms by enthusiasts to expound their version of the war. Similarly, the recently deceased "world's oldest Confederate war widow" was transported from one occasion to another in the South in recent decades as a living symbol of the Lost Cause. It hardly needs to be stated that both the swastika and Confederate flags exert to this day a powerful influence both emotional and political.

It should also be noted that the two Lost Cause mythologies are intertwined. Civil War re-enactors exist not just in the American context, but in the German one as well, perhaps a subset of widespread German fascination with the American West and cowboys and Indians. One German professor, however, Wolfgang Hochbruck of the University of Stuttgart, observed laconically: "I think some of the Confederate re-enactors in Germany are acting out Nazi fantasies of racial superiority. They are obsessed with your war because they cannot celebrate their own vanquished racists. Most of these people are Bavarians, of course."[80]

4   Memoirs, Novels, and Popular Histories

A particular genre – the exculpatory memoirs of German officers such as Erich von Manstein, Heinz Guderian, Hans von Luck, F. W. von Mellenthin, and Hans Rudel – also feed the revisionist narrative. These books, far from being obscure rarities, have always been best sellers, often included as selections of national book clubs. The original and most influential are those by Manstein and Guderian, one the master of fluid tactical retreat, the other of lightning armored offense. These are perhaps the leading twin gods in the American pantheon of German war heroes.

Manstein's memoir, *Lost Victories*, has influenced Americans, particularly the military, for decades. Aware of the possibility of a Soviet attack on Western Europe during the Cold War with an accompanying U.S. retreat, the Americans viewed with awe Manstein's description of the series of fluid, tactical retreats of the Wehrmacht in Russia – at least those permitted by Hitler, who preferred to hold onto every inch of conquered soil. First published in English in 1958, it has maintained its popularity. The most recent edition is a 2004 paperback with a subtitle "Hitler's Most Brilliant General" and with the original laudatory foreword by the renowned British military historian, B. H. Liddell Hart. A new introduction by the award-winning American historian Martin Blumenson calls the memoirs "a magisterial, even noble account of the war from the German perspective," an all-important legitimization.[1] By the same token, a well-publicized edition of Guderian's *Panzer Leader* was re-released in 2002, on the fiftieth anniversary of its original appearance as a main book club selection (Figure 5).[2] How well do the influential memoirs of these two men square with their actual role in the war? To what extent do they perpetuate the myth of the "clean" Wehrmacht? As we shall see, in both books, half-truths, lies, omissions, and distortions coexist alongside truth.

Manstein became a "militärischer Kult- und Leitfigur"[3] (a commanding military presence raised to the cult level). He is a man much honored by

Figure 5. Heinz Guderian, the ultimate professional officer, on the cover of *Panzer Leader* (2002 edition).

postwar historiography, which he, second only to Franz Halder, influenced decisively, not the least through his memoirs. He was not only honored by many Germans and was called on by the West German government as an advisor when the new Bundeswehr was being conceptualized, but also by non-Germans, especially in U.S. Army circles. The Americans were impressed by his operational genius, specifically by his ideas on mobile defense against the Russians, who presumably, with their much greater numbers, would initially take the offensive in any war in Europe. The British, who would somewhat reluctantly try him for war crimes in 1949, were just as admiring. Liddell Hart, who would himself contribute much to the "clean" Wehrmacht myth with his book *The German Generals Talk*, called Manstein "the Allies' most formidable military opponent."[4]

Even today he is recognized as the most capable army leader of the Wehrmacht. That reputation enabled him, with some credibility, to devote himself after the war to his lifetime task of rescuing the reputation of the German army. His memoirs were only one tool in this enterprise. Manstein, indeed, put himself on a pedestal in advance of his admirers. He was the archetypal embodiment of the Prussian-German military tradition, who liked to compare himself with greats like Moltke the Elder and Schlieffen, chiefs of the imperial German general staff. It had been his ambition during the war – frequently vetted with Hitler – of becoming the supreme commander of the Russian theater with complete independence of command, with only Hitler, as chief of state, above him (Figure 6). As a person, Manstein could be – as many disgruntled colleagues agreed – arrogant, insensitive, cool, distant, and sarcastic.[5] He could also show courage and was very careerist, identifying himself with the new mobile style of warfare that had also been championed by Guderian.

At the outbreak of World War Two, he was chief of staff to Army Group South (von Rundstedt) and took part in that capacity in the short Polish campaign. Transferred to the West, he served as chief of staff to Army Group A in Coblenz, where planning was underway for a campaign against France and the Low Countries. The German High Command had formulated a plan, which very much resembled that of 1914, involving a massive drive through Belgium into northern France. Manstein developed an alternate plan, which involved using densely packed armor to sweep out of the Ardennes Forest across France to the channel coast. This was the plan Hitler eventually accepted and it worked brilliantly, partly through the efforts of Guderian. It was this "*Sichelschnitt*" (scythe cut) plan that would establish Manstein's reputation.

In February 1941, he was appointed commander of the 56th Panzer Corps (Army Group North) and took part in the massive invasion of the Soviet Union the following June. His corps cut through the Baltic and besieged Leningrad.

Figure 6. Erich von Manstein and Hitler in a friendly exchange.

On September 12, Manstein was given command of the 11th Army and assigned the task of conquering the Crimea with its enormous fortress at Sevastopol. This he succeeded in doing by July 1942, a success that won him a promotion to field marshal and marked another way station in his growing reputation as a field commander. It was also in the Crimea that he first became involved in war crimes.

Now a favorite of Hitler's, Manstein was given command on November 22, 1942, of Army Group Don (later renamed Army Group South). In spring 1942, this Army Group undertook a major German assault in southern Russia to reach the oil of the Caucasus and the city of Stalingrad. This task represented one of Manstein's greatest failures, for he underestimated the degree to which the German Sixth Army, which soon would be surrounded at Stalingrad, could be supplied by air and, thus, waited too long either to have them break out or to break in to their rescue. The result was the surrender of the Sixth Army, one of Germany's greatest military disasters in World War Two and, many think, a turning point in the war in the East.

Manstein was also involved in what would be the last time the Germans would take the strategic initiative in World War Two in the East – the battle of Kursk. In retrospect, the battle, which was initiated to cut off a giant salient in the German lines, made little sense. Guderian, for example, was against it; Manstein was in favor. The battle was begun in early July 1943 after many delays, which eliminated the element of surprise. A well-prepared Russian defense made slow going for the Germans and the offensive had to be broken off after a week, in part because of Allied landings in Sicily. Hereafter, Germany went on the defensive in Russia with Manstein, who realized that Germany could at best fight to a draw, but no longer win the war, advocating a fluid defense that would wear out Soviet offensive capacity. He still managed a success or two – he retook the city of Kharkov in March 1943 – but mainly now had to take charge of the long, bloody retreat westward. Here is where he found himself very much at odds with Hitler, who wanted to defend every piece of ground tenaciously. With Manstein constantly pushing for fluid defense and for the naming of an overall commander in the East (himself), Hitler, finally, while still appreciating his skills, dismissed Manstein in March 1944. Manstein hoped to be called back, but it never transpired. At the end of the war, the field marshal turned himself over to the British. He wanted at all costs to avoid capture by the Russians, who would have tried and executed him for war crimes – as indeed they tried in vain to do after the war.

Manstein's memoirs cover this entire period, ending with his dismissal in 1944.[6] He reveals early on that he is dealing almost exclusively with military affairs and is going to leave the political arena out. This is convenient, because it enables him to avoid entirely discussing the war in the East as one of racial enslavement and annihilation, as well as to avoid taking up any relationship he might have had with National Socialism. His presentations always put him in a positive light; he is central to all the military activities he presents.

He portrays the German military in a very favorable light and underscores the fact that German soldiers always outfought their enemies, even when faced with overwhelming material and manpower superiority. He emphasizes the leadership training in the German army, particularly at the lower levels. "Individual leadership was fostered on a scale unrivalled in any other army, right down to the most junior N.C.O. or infantryman, and in this lay the secret of our success."[7] What he is describing here is the famous *Auftragtaktik* (you reveal to your subordinates what has to be done and they take the responsibility for figuring out how to do it), which the Americans so admired and tried to institutionalize in the 1950s and again after the Vietnam conflict.

As for the Soviet enemy, Manstein admires the toughness of the ordinary Russian soldier, but never accords to the Soviet officer corps the ability to plan well on an operational level. He stresses time and again the Russian superiority in equipment, manpower, and reserves, especially in the last two years of the war, against which the Germans have only the superior fighting power of their soldiers. That the Russian Stavka (general staff) could develop and carry out complicated large-scale operations never occurs to him. It didn't occur to him during the war either and represented a blind spot, which, for example, allowed the Russians to fool him and retake Kiev in November 1943.[8]

He is critical of Hitler and lists his mistakes, as many others have done, including stopping the armored formations short of Dunkirk, thus allowing the major part of the British army to escape. Hitler also was mistaken in trying to win the initial campaign in Russia by attacking north and south on the flanks, instead of heading directly for Moscow. Hitler is criticized for focusing on Stalingrad in the first place, then for not evacuating the city in time to avoid losing a whole army. Hitler is faulted for delaying Operation Citadel (Kursk 1943) until all chance for success was lost and, most importantly, for his double failure to undertake a fluid defense in 1943–44 and for failing to name an overall independent commander in the East in the last two years of the war. That Manstein is being disingenuous in these criticisms is obvious. He failed to give orders to evacuate Stalingrad; he advocated Citadel; he failed to understand the economic side of the war, which is precisely what Hitler was taking into consideration in his overall strategy. Finally, Hitler, according to Manstein, had a gift for tactics, but he lacked any operational or strategic sense.[9] He lacked "military ability based on experience." Contrary to the common view of Hitler as gambler, Manstein maintains that Hitler was averse to taking risks, partly out of fear of humiliation; he tended to procrastinate endlessly when a decision was called for.[10]

Manstein is also critical of his colleagues in the army command (OKH). None of them come off well in these pages, especially his nemesis, Halder. Indeed, when *Lost Victories* appeared, many surviving generals were shocked to see how Manstein presented himself at their expense. They had all made mistakes; Manstein had made none.[11] That Hitler could come to dominate them so freely, said Manstein, lay in part in their own shortcomings. For example, after the Polish campaign, they wanted to go on the defensive in the West, which just handed the initiative over to Hitler.[12] "By further bowing to Hitler's will and putting out the orders for an operation with which its leaders privately disagreed, it *resigned* for all practical purposes as the authority responsible for land warfare."[13] This is also a self-serving argument, given that the very officers Manstein is talking about were those who also frustrated Manstein in his plans and ambitions. In making them appear to be passive and submissive to Hitler, Manstein only makes himself, by contrast, appear decisive and contrary. He highlights his disagreements with the dictator.

Those who, by and large, thought as he did, or functioned smoothly with him, or showed themselves to be equally decisive and independent, earn Manstein's approval in his memoirs. He is particularly approving of Guderian, especially during the French campaign. "Ultimately it was his élan which inspired our tanks on their dash round the backs of the enemy on the Channel coast. For me, it was a great relief to know that my idea of pushing large numbers of tanks through such difficult country as the Ardennes was considered feasible by Guderian."[14] As for the success itself, Manstein delivers a rare compliment to someone else. "... this success [defeat of enemy in France] is, I feel, primarily due to the tremendous verve with which General Guderian translated the Army Group's operational principles into action."[15] Manstein even liked Guderian's colorful sayings, such as in the use of armor – "klotzen, nicht kleckern" – Don't spatter 'em, boot 'em."[16]

In sum, then, Manstein's memoirs played such an important role in characterizing the German Wehrmacht and describing its campaigns from Manstein's viewpoint, that he created a "myth" "which critical military history writing of the last 20 years has for the most part been unsuccessful in puncturing."[17]

Manstein takes great pains to eliminate from his memoirs any discussion of politics. As noted, this allows him to focus entirely on the operational and tactical aspects of World War Two and to avoid discussion of the strategic level, which would have forced him to come to grips with the criminal nature of Hitler's war. But he was not above using political language when it served his career. One such example was a speech he made on the occasion of Hitler's fiftieth birthday, on April 20, 1939. There were parades and festivities at nearly all German garrisons that day, with the commanding officers having the opportunity to give a speech. These were entirely voluntary. There was no order to speak nor was there provision for speeches in the normal Wehrmacht celebratory protocol. Indeed, 42 percent of commanding officers chose not to speak that day. Manstein not only spoke, but offered paeans of praise for Hitler, who was sent by God to rescue Germany and make her great again. He concludes with fateful words, indicating that as a soldier he will follow the dictator wherever he might lead. "When it appears as if a hostile world wants to erect ramparts around Germany to block the way of the German people into their future, to hinder the leader in completing his work, so we soldiers pledge to our leader: in defiance of all the powers to protect his accomplishments, including in battle, to enforce his will, wherever he might lead us!"[18]

It is also interesting to note that nowhere in his memoirs or in any of his postwar writings did Manstein explicitly offer a condemnation of National Socialism.[19]

Hitler's notorious and criminal "Commissar Order," issued on June 6, 1941, merits only a paragraph in Manstein's memoirs.

> An order like the *Kommissarbefehl* was utterly unsoldierly. To have carried it out would have threatened not only the honor of our fighting troops but also their morale. Consequently I had no alternative but to inform my superiors that the Commissar Order would not be implemented by anyone under my command. My subordinate commanders were entirely at one with me in this, and everyone in the corps area acted accordingly.[20]

In fact, Manstein did pass the order along to his subordinate commanders as he was ordered to do – no commander could have so openly disobeyed a Hitler order. And, in fact, executions of commissars did take place in the area under Manstein's command, after he took over the 11th Army.[21] Nor would Manstein have been particularly surprised at the order, since he was present in March 1941 when Hitler laid out his plans for a war without mercy against the Soviet Union. In fact, one of the counts on which Manstein would be convicted in his 1949 trial involved precisely his carrying out of the Commissar Order.

Moreover, Manstein issued orders on his own initiative, which bear on the Holocaust in a larger sense. On November 20, 1941, Manstein issued an order, which does not focus on commissars, but rather on Jews. It read in part:

> Since the 22nd June the German people have been engaged in a life-and-death struggle against the Bolshevik system. This struggle is not being carried on against the Soviet armed forces alone in the established form laid down by European rules of warfare. Behind the front, too, the fighting continues. . . . Jewry

constitutes the middleman between the enemy in the rear and the remainder of the Red armed forces which are still fighting and the Red leadership. More strongly than in Europe it holds all the key positions in the political leadership and administration, controls commerce and trade, and further forms the nucleus for all unrest and possible uprisings. The Jewish-Bolshevist system must be exterminated once and for all. Never again must it encroach upon our European living-space . . . The soldier must appreciate the necessity for the harsh punishment of Jewry, the spiritual bearer of the Bolshevist terror. This is also necessary in order to nip in the bud all uprisings, which are mostly attributable to Jews.

Thus, Manstein is substantially in agreement with Hitler and with the Nazi belief that the Jews are behind Bolshevism and that Bolshevik equals Jews and Jews equal Bolsheviks. Nowhere in his memoirs did Manstein mention this order and, when confronted with it at Nuremberg by the American prosecutor, Telford Taylor, Manstein replied: "I must say that this order escapes my memory completely."[22]

The order helps to explain Manstein's role in the Holocaust, especially as commander of the 11th Army in the Crimea, a circumscribed peninsula where he had overall command responsibility. Even though he denied knowing anything about the murders being carried out by the infamous Einsatzgruppe D under Otto Ohlendorf, he was involved both passively (in that he received reports from his subordinates on the executions) and actively (in that he aided the Einsatzgruppe and actually gave orders for at least one massacre). Ohlendorf would be tried and executed for his activities after the war and gave incriminating testimony about the cooperation between his Einsatzgruppe and the Wehrmacht.

Manstein received regular reports on executions, most of which he ignored. One example serves here. A Captain Ulrich Gunzert was witness to the execution of Jewish men, women, and children, whose bodies were tossed into a ditch. Shaken by the incident, he reported the murders to Manstein immediately, urging him to take action. Manstein declined. He had no influence over what happened in rear areas, he maintained, which was not true, and besides he had other worries. He cautioned Gunzert against spreading the story. "It was a flight from responsibility," Gunzert wrote, "a moral failure."[23]

Often Manstein's troops would cooperate with the Einsatzgruppe by supplying transport, fuel, drivers, and military police to cordon off areas. The most egregious example of Manstein's active participation was the massacre of 11,000 Jews at the town of Simferopol in November 1941. More than 2,000 German soldiers took part in the action. Adding a grotesque note to a tragic incident, in the wake of the killing, Manstein's chief of staff, Otto Wöhler, who had regular contact with Ohlendorf, wrote on Manstein's orders to Ohlendorf instructing him to turn over to the army any wristwatches taken from the dead Jews. Ohlendorf, after some resistance, turned over 120 repaired watches to the army for distribution to the troops. Wöhler, by the way, was sentenced to eight years in prison for his cooperation with the Einsatzgruppe.[24]

While Manstein was in command of the 11th Army in the Crimea, Einsatzgruppe D killed more than 90,000 Jews, thus making the peninsula "judenfrei," something which Manstein denied at his trial and does not mention in his memoirs.[25] On another occasion, Manstein is reported to have ordered the shooting of 1,300 persons at Eupatoria as reprisal. Manstein denied giving the order, but maintained that reprisal executions were justified.[26] His aide-de-camp, Alexander Stahlberg, however, takes pains in his memoirs to tell how shocked and disbelieving Manstein was when he was told that 100,000 Jews had been murdered in his Group's rear area.[27]

Like most German generals, Manstein tries to underscore what good relations the German army had with Russian civilians, spoiled only by the predatory behavior of Nazi occupation officials. Even in the context of the "scorched earth" policy of the retreating German armies in 1943 and 1944, Manstein stubbornly clings to this mythology. He puts the best face on a set of brutal actions against the civil population, claiming that they were necessary to prevent the encroaching Red Army from availing itself of any resources as it pursued the retreating Germans at the Dnieper.

Naturally there was no question of our "pillaging" the area. That was something which the German Army – unlike certain others – did not tolerate . . . the Supreme Command had directed that the civil population would also be evacuated. In practice, this coercive measure was applied only to men of military age, who would have immediately been re-enlisted. On the other hand, a considerable proportion of the Russian population joined our withdrawal quite voluntarily in order to escape the dreaded Soviets, forming big trek columns like those we ourselves were to see later in eastern Germany. Far from being forcibly abducted, these people received every possible help from the German Armies and were conducted into areas west of the Dnieper in which the German authorities had arranged to feed and accommodate them. They were allowed to take along everything, including horses and cattle, which could possibly accompany them and wherever we could manage to do so we put our vehicles at their disposal. Although the war caused these people a great deal of misfortune and hardship, the latter bore no comparison to the terror-bombing suffered by the civilian population in Germany or what happened later on in Germany's eastern territories. In any case, all the measures taken on the German side were conditioned by military necessity.[28]

This is all sheer nonsense. Even in the days of victory in 1941, the German Army had, from the outset, behaved in bestial ways toward the civilian population. That was what living off the land was all about – predatory behavior. Now that the Germans were in full and desperate retreat, the thought of treating the civilian population any better than before was ridiculous. What the Germans were, in fact, doing here was taking everything they could use – including healthy adult civilians who could build their temporary fortifications and defensive lines, while destroying everything else, thus leaving the very young, the ill, and the elderly behind to suffer severe deprivation.

In August 1949, Manstein was brought to trial before a British military court in Hamburg on eighteen charges of committing war crimes. It was the last trial of a high Wehrmacht general. It is some indication of the emerging Cold War – the Berlin blockage had just been lifted – that the trial was quite controversial not only in West Germany, but also in England. The British had been reluctant to open proceedings, but had done so largely because the Russians and the Poles were demanding that Manstein be extradited for trial, and the British, mindful of relations with the Soviet Union, felt they needed to act judicially. But it was also a sign of the times that British conservatives took up a collection for Manstein's defense fund, with Churchill ostentatiously making the first donation of twenty-five pounds. The bishop of Chichester spoke out in favor of a general amnesty of German officers, as did the philosopher Bertrand Russell. The British were also aware that at some point in the future, West German manpower might be necessary to defend Europe and that most of the officers in that contingent would be former Wehrmacht officers. Indeed, the West Germans were signaling that no German troops would don a uniform as long as Wehrmacht officers remained in custody. The *Economist* wrote: "To hand over one of the ablest German wartime commanders to Russia or Poland would be quite incompatible with the rallying of German support for the West in the cold war . . . "[29] Once again, William Donovan, who had urged the generals to write their defense memorandum in 1945, stepped in and recruited his friend Paul Leverkuehn, who had stood ready to defend the generals at Nuremberg if necessary, to help in Manstein's defense.[30]

Manstein's defense attorney was Reginald Paget, a Labour Member of Parliament, assisted by the Germans and a British Jewish attorney, Sam Silkin. Paget based his defense of Manstein on the Nuremberg defense and did not fail to make the very political point that German officers would refuse to put on a uniform again as long as men like Manstein were still in custody.[31]

The defense presentations themselves helped strengthen the mythology of the "clean" Wehrmacht by becoming "an apologist for the Third Reich and its methods of warfare in Russia."[32] Paget claimed that many German acts, including using civilians and POWs in construction of fortifications and the shooting of civilians who were armed, were permitted by the Geneva Convention. He defended the "scorched earth" policy of the Germans in retreat because, as he said, no army in that situation is going to fight by Marquis of Queensbury rules. He claimed that both the British and American armies changed their code of military justice in 1944 from an obligation to obey all orders to an ambivalent stand. Worse, he substantiates the Nazi claim that Jews and Bolshevism are one and the same, thus trying to excuse Manstein's November 20, 1941, order. (There is no record of Silkin's response to this defense claim.) Moreover, Paget cast Manstein in the role of hero. His closing statement ends with the following words:

> The political purpose of this trial has been to condemn the reputation of the German army and of its greatest commander. It has failed utterly. When we met the Wehrmacht in Africa, Italy and France we found that they were decent soldiers. We believed, because we had absorbed much Russian propaganda, that the Germans had fought like savages in the East. That has not been the evidence in this case. On the contrary in circumstances of appalling savagery the German soldier, upon the evidence, showed considerable restraint and great discipline. For my part I am glad. If Western Europe is to be defensible these decent soldiers must be our comrades. Sir, it is not in the power of the conquerors to condemn the reputation of the vanquished. Manstein is and will remain a hero amongst his people. He was the architect of their victory and the Hector of their defeat, the man who commanded in their great retreat when in his heart and soul he knew that Troy must fall, and now before this court he has fought his last battle fearlessly for the honor of the army he served and of the men who died at his command. Whether or not you add to his stature the crown of martyrdom he will serve as a model of that which is best in the German character, courage, steadfastness, and what the Romans called 'gravitas' and for which we have no adequate word. It is not within your power to injure the reputation of Manstein, you can but injure your own.[33]

These words – Germans as honorable soldiers, Russians as the real savages, Wehrmacht commanders as the epitome of honor, Manstein cast in the mold of Hector of Troy – represent the core of the myth of the clean Wehrmacht.

Paget's pleas aside, the court found Manstein guilty on nine counts. They included neglect of duty in not preventing murders in his area of command; using Soviet prisoners and civilians to built fortifications and clear minefields; deporting civilians outside the area of his command; mistreating and shooting Soviet war prisoners; turning them over to the SD, carrying out the Commissar Order; and allowing subordinates to shoot civilians in reprisal. He was sentenced to eighteen years in prison.

But again, this was all happening within the context of the Cold War. Manstein secured early release in 1953, in part owing to high-level negotiations between Churchill and Adenauer, just in time to be adviser to the Blank Office, which was laying the groundwork for the new West German Bundeswehr.[34] Paget published a best-selling book on Manstein's career and trial, which cemented the defense version of the trial – and thereby the myth – in public memory. Added to this was the publication by Manstein's admirer, British historian Liddell Hart, of another best seller, *On the Other Side of the Hill* (published in the United States with the title *The German Generals Talk*), which lionized Manstein as the greatest operational genius and most effective enemy commander against the Allies. This, of course, prepared the groundwork for Manstein's own self-celebratory memoirs. The trilogy contributed enormously to the myth of the Eastern Front.

Unlike Halder, who produced no memoirs but made his own contribution to myth creation in the studies prepared for the U.S. Army, Manstein chose not to work with the Historical Division, preferring to make his contribution to the sanitizing of the Wehrmacht through his memoirs and other writings.[35] In doing so, he dedicated his life to a cause that he had already vowed to pursue during the Nuremberg trials. On October 2, 1946, one day after the court decided that the German High Command could not be grouped under "criminal organization," he wrote to his wife:

> It was of great satisfaction to me that at Nuremberg the general staff was not declared to be a criminal organization. So I was able during the ten months of working with the defense for the army, which has been the focus of my life's work, to perform one more service for it.[36]

He was to go on performing this service for the rest of his life. That he was successful is demonstrated by the enthusiastic, even reverential, reviews of his memoirs written by western scholars. A typical example is:

> Perhaps its [the memoirs] greatest value is that it mirrors faithfully the thinking and the tribulations of a great operational planner. The reader sees a genuine military talent at work and participated in the intellectual creation of first-rate solutions. The celebrations of this military logician who mastered all forms of land warfare and who was an outstanding leader of men, evoke admiration: they also school the mind of the reader.[37]

Already during the war, Manstein warranted extensive press coverage in Britain and the United States. On January 10, 1944, *Time* devoted its cover story to Manstein. The article focused on his tactical brilliance in fluid defense, something that the U.S. Army in the 1950s would also find impressive and

instructional. Despite the thrust of the article – that the Germans were ultimately doomed to defeat on the Eastern Front, as illustrated by the subtitle:
"Retreat may be masterly, but victory lies in the opposite direction" – the article praises Manstein for his "genius for war" and his "tactical brilliance." The
article concludes that "despite defeat and despair, the German burgher of today
has no greater military idol than Manstein."[38] This would very nearly be true
for the Americans as well in the context of the Cold War.

Heinz Guderian emerged during the 1930s as a strong advocate of armored
warfare. His reputation for being the father of the blitzkrieg, one which he himself later cultivated, is somewhat exaggerated given that other officers made their
own contributions. But Guderian was the great publicist. He wrote relentlessly
and, in 1937, published *Achtung Panzer!*, which became a best seller, to the
consternation of many more tradition-oriented officers.

Guderian commanded the XIX Army Corps during the Polish campaign,
and earned the Iron Cross 1st and 2nd Class for his daring exploits. His real
reputation he gained the next spring in the campaign against France, when he
drove his Panzers relentlessly from the Ardennes forest across France to the
channel coast. (Each of his tanks had a yellow "G" painted on it – Guderian
was not a modest man.) On the strength of that achievement, he was promoted to colonel general and made commander of the 2nd Panzer Army, which
he led successfully in the first months of the Russian campaign. Against
orders, however, he arbitrarily retreated before Moscow in December 1941, was
relieved of his command, and was placed in the reserve pool of the army high
command.

After Stalingrad, he was recalled as general inspector of Panzer troops in
order to beef up Germany's armored strength. In this capacity, working with
Albert Speer, the minister of armaments, he traveled the length and breadth of
Germany, visiting design and manufacturing facilities, in an attempt to develop
and build in larger numbers the tanks that were needed to fight on several fronts.
In this task he largely succeeded.

In July 1944, in the wake of the abortive officers' plot to assassinate Hitler,
Guderian was made chief of the army staff, a largely honorific post, given
that Hitler by this time had assumed virtually all command responsibilities.
Guderian was again relieved on March 28, 1945, when the war was virtually
over, ostensibly for health reasons.

In his memoirs, Guderian presents himself as a daring, innovative, audacious, hands-on commander who takes the initiative and pushes the envelope
in every campaign, all the while fighting those, especially in the German High
Command, who were too obtuse to see the potential of armored warfare and
who only tried to throw obstacles in his way. With regard to the French 1940

campaign, he writes: "All my decisions, until I reached the Atlantic seaboard at Abbéville, were taken by me and me alone. The Supreme Command's influence on my actions was merely restrictive throughout."[39]

His memoirs begin with a section on the development of the German armored forces, for the development of which he takes nearly full credit. Thanks to his stubborn initiatives, the first three Panzer divisions were created by fall 1935. All along the way, he faces resistance from less enlightened traditional officers, who stood in his way during the planning years, just as they would during the war. "The arguments often became extremely heated. But finally the creators of the fresh ideas won their battle against the reactionaries; the combustion engine defeated the horse; and the cannon, the lance."[40]

Turning to the war itself, Guderian, like virtually all the German generals who wrote after the war, is critical of many of Hitler's decisions and short-comings, the implication being that if the dictator had listened to him, the war would have turned out differently. He is just as critical of the German generals in the High Command. He contends that after the defeat of France, Hitler should have invaded North Africa immediately to engage England; that Hitler should not have invaded Russia in the first place; that in 1941 Hitler should have pushed directly on to Moscow; that Hitler should have ordered a general retreat to better defensive positions in December 1941, when the Wehrmacht failed to take Moscow; that Hitler should never have launched the Ardennes offensive in the West in 1944, but rather concentrated Germany's dwindling military resources in defensive operations in the East. This list names only the most glaring errors.[41]

As always, Guderian puts himself in a favorable light at the expense of some exaggerations and half-truths. For example, he exaggerates his unwillingness to continue the attack on Moscow in late 1941.[42] In fact, Guderian did advocate continuing the drive on Moscow in mid-November 1941, so that the gains of summer not be lost. Indeed, he was optimistic enough to set the goal for two divisions of his LIII Army Corps to reach Riason in order to cut off Moscow from the south. This meant marching 140 km, which Guderian estimated would take three weeks. Only a month later, he decided that they were overexposed and ordered a retreat on his own.[43] But this is a minor omission compared to the much more egregious untruths, half truths, and omissions in the memoirs.

Guderian claims only to have heard from Hitler on June 14, 1941, the reasons for attacking Russia and claims that all officers left the meeting in silence and with heavy hearts.[44] This is really quite disingenuous. Already on March 30, Hitler revealed to his commanders the nature of the coming campaign of racial annihilation against the Soviet Union. It is incredible that Guderian would not have heard about that speech.

He spends just one page on the very serious matter of the infamous criminal orders issued by Hitler at the beginning of Barbarossa – especially the Jurisdictional and the Commissar orders.[45] He condemns the "Jurisdictional Order," which pre-amnestied German troops for anything they might do to the Soviet population, not because it was criminal or inhumane, but because of the deleterious effect it might have on troop morale. At any rate, the order was never carried out by his troops, nor, he asserts, was the "Commissar Order." "The equally notorious, so-called 'Commissar Order' never even reached my Panzer group." He goes on to criticize the German High Command (OKH and OKW) for not blocking these orders, oblivious to the fact that these very agencies *drafted* the orders in the first place! His assertions here are simply not true.

He offers the old, highly questionable saws about the solicitude of the German army for Russian civilians, their religion, and culture. "While these winter battles went on" he writes about the period 1941–42, "we had to deal with the problem of supplying the homeland, the Army and the Russian population with food. The 1941 harvest had been a rich one throughout the country and there was ample grain for bread . . . the needs of our troops were assured as were those of the Russian civilians in the towns . . . "[46] He assures us that stocks were available until March 1942.

This is sublime nonsense. The 1941 harvest could hardly have been a rich one because the Ukraine, Russia's breadbasket, was the scene of ferocious battles during that period. Moreover, the German policy in Russia was precisely to channel all available resources back to Germany, assuming that the Russian population, especially in the cities, would largely starve. The General Plan for the East assumed an attrition rate of 14 million people. In Leningrad alone, 750,000 people would starve to death.[47]

He claimed to have visited the cathedral in Smolensk, only to be shocked that the Soviets had transformed it into a museum dedicated to atheism. Precious religious objects were scattered all over the floor. "It was not pretty." He ordered a Russian to be found who could take custody of the objects and returned the church to its intended purpose as a house of worship. "What later happened to the church I do not know. At that time we took trouble to see it came to no harm."[48] Similarly, he boasts about what good care he took of Tolstoy's estate at Yasnaya Polyana, which the Germans had requisitioned as their headquarters. "No stick of furniture was burned, no book or manuscript touched." All was put into safekeeping. Guderian even visited Tolstoy's grave to assure its preservation. Referring to Soviet broadcasts after the war, which told of the desecration of Tolstoy's estate, Guderian writes: "Any post-war statements to the contrary belong in the realm of fantasy."[49] As always, the Russian people are depicted as greeting the Germans as liberators. "The population of Nieswiez asked permission to hold a Thanksgiving service in celebration of their liberation; I was happy to be able to grant them this request."[50] And if that happiness did not last, then it was always the fault of Nazi civil administrators – particularly the very nasty ones like Erich Koch in the Ukraine.

Guderian claimed not to have known about the predatory behavior of the Nazi occupiers until 1943! At a meeting in February 1943, Guderian claims to have been informed for the first time by General von Prien, commander of Vinnitsa. "What Prien told me about the German administration was highly distasteful. German methods, particularly those of Reich Commissar Koch, had turned the Ukrainians from being friends of Germany into our enemies. Unfortunately our military authorities were powerless against this policy. It was carried out through Party and administrative channels, without the collaboration of the military and usually without the Army's knowledge and against its will."[51] This also was patently false. As we have seen, the army worked very closely with the SS and civil authorities in their pacification and plundering of Russia at any time – never mind as late as 1943 – as shown by the aforementioned postwar testimony of Ernst Rode, SS Brigadeführer and major general of the police, a member of Himmler's personal command staff. "My function was to furnish the forces necessary for anti-partisan warfare to the Higher SS and Police Leaders and to guarantee the support of Army forces. This took place through personal discussions with the leading officers of the Operations Staff of the OKW and OKH, namely with . . . " There follow eight names, one of which was Guderian's. Rode went on: "since police troops for the most part could not be spared from the Reich Commissariats, the direction of this warfare lay practically always in the hands of the army."[52]

The generals liked to emphasize their integrity and loyalty to Germany in their postwar writings, Guderian no less than the others. What they often forgot to mention was the fact that, in some measure, their loyalty was purchased. In many cases, Hitler showed his gratitude for services rendered – and expectations of future loyalty – by donating landed estates of varying sizes to his generals, field marshals and admirals; for example, Erich Raeder, Wilhelm von Leeb, Gerd von Rundstedt, Walther von Brauchitsch, Guenther von Kluge, and others. Guderian was one of the beneficiaries. At least Guderian, unlike many others, mentions the episode in his memoirs. But to divert any suspicion about his corruptibility, he places the gift in the most innocuous light. In spring 1942, Hitler, having heard that Guderian was contemplating buying property in southern Germany, suggested instead that Guderian settle in the Warthegau, the land of his ancestors. Announcing that he was giving a national donation to all men who had won the Oak Leaves to the Knight's Cross, the dictator told

Guderian to seek out a property. "When I heard this I realized that I could now put my grey uniform away and settle down once and for all to civilian life."[53] The truth is slightly less respectable. After receiving a list of more than a dozen estates, which he visited in turn, Guderian chose one which was not even on the list – a huge farm of 7,000 acres. The Gauleiter, Arthur Greiser, supported by Himmler, vetoed this estate, saying that where will they be with the field marshals, when a colonel general gets an estate of this size. Finally, given another list, Guderian found an estate, Deipenhof, which had been confiscated from a Polish family, and which was worth 1.24 million marks.[54]

It was possibly this reward for loyalty – not to mention his 2,000-mark monthly stipend – which helped govern Guderian's behavior in the wake of the July 20, 1944, officer's plot to assassinate Hitler. Guderian was not only appointed as chief of the general staff after the abortive plot, he also was asked to serve on a special Court of Honor (Ehrenhof), a military judicial body that had the duty of expelling the plotters from the army, so that they could be tried – and hanged – by the infamous Volksgerichtshof (People's Court). Guderian again depicts himself in the best possible light. He claimed he tried to get out of the duty, but was compelled to stay on by Hitler. He tried to be absent from as many sessions as possible – sessions that he called "repulsive." "What I heard was extremely sad and upsetting.... On the rare occasions when I was present I did my best to save any man who could be saved. Only in sadly few cases was this labor of love successful."[55] Yet he goes on to condemn the conspirators for what they did and suggests that the German people would have turned on them (the officer corps) for breaking their word of honor and assassinating the head of state in time of war.

Guderian's real feelings toward the plot, however, appear to come out in orders he issued on July 29 and August 24, 1944, which are not mentioned in his memoirs. The first directed all general staff officers to either become Nazi "leadership officers" or ask for a transfer.[56] The other stated:

> The 20th of July is the darkest day in the history of the German General Staff. Through the treason of several individual General Staff officers, the German army, the entire Wehrmacht, yes, the whole greater German Reich has been led to the edge of ruin ... Do not let anyone surpass you in your loyalty to the Führer. No one may believe more fanatically in victory or radiate that belief more than you ... Be an example to others in your unconditional obedience. There is no future for the Reich without National Socialism.[57]

Several months later, in a Home Guard (Volkssturm) rally on November 6, Guderian said that the elderly Volkssturm soldiers would prove to the enemy that there were "95 million National Socialists who stand behind Adolf Hitler.

We took our oath voluntarily and centuries from now one will still speak of the invincibility of our generation, which protected justice against all enemies."[58]

There is additional evidence to suggest that, although Guderian quarreled with Hitler on a number of occasions and portrayed himself as anti-Nazi after the war, he was really one of the most "Nazi" of the German generals. After all, despite these differences of opinion, Hitler kept coming back to Guderian to enlist his services again and again during the war. Hitler liked Guderian's gruff and earthy style; he appreciated Guderian's contributions to the theory and practice of armored warfare; but, above all, he realized the extent to which Guderian shared in the National Socialist value system. Indeed, Guderian has been characterized as a "National Socialist Leadership officer," partly because of the orders he issued to his officers after the July 20 plot.[59]

Goebbels certainly thought so. At the time when Guderian was recalled to duty to be inspector general of the Panzerkorps in March 1943, Goebbels noted in his diary:

> Guderian gave me the impression of an exceptionally wide-awake and alert commander. His judgment is clear and sensible and he is blessed with a healthy common sense. Undoubtedly I can work well with him. I promised him my unstinting support.

Just three days later he wrote: "I discussed Doenitz and Guderian at length with the Fuehrer; both enjoy his complete confidence."[60]

At a mid-day situation conference at the Wolfsschanze on September 1, 1944, Hitler said: "Under these circumstances [trying to figure out which detachments to send to reinforce the West wall] wouldn't it be useful to set up a racially pure detachment?" To which Guderian replied: "I'm for racial purity."[61]

Finally, even in captivity, Guderian had not shed his loyalty to Hitler and National Socialism. While in the hands of the U.S. 7th Army, Guderian was asked if he wanted to cooperate in writing the history of the recent war for Historical Section of the U.S. Army. He and one of his former subordinates, Leo Geyr von Schweppenburg, went to the most senior officer at their camp, Field Marshal Wilhelm von Leeb, to ask for advice and permission. The Americans secretly recorded the conversation. Leeb agreed that Guderian should cooperate, but warned Guderian that he "will have to consider your answers a bit carefully when approached on this subject ["Objectives, causes and the progress of operations"], so that you will say nothing which might embarrass the Fatherland." At the end of the conversation, the officers looked back reflectively on the twelve years of the Third Reich. Geyr allowed that "any objective observer will admit that National Socialism raised the social status of the worker, and in some respects even his standard of living as long as that was possible." To which Leeb replied: "This is one of the great achievements of National Socialism." Guderian chimed in with the words: "The fundamental principles were fine."[62] None of this, of course, appears in Guderian's memoirs. Nor does he even allude to the war of annihilation and enslavement that Hitler, fully supported by the Wehrmacht, fought in the East – with mass shootings, ravenous plundering, and slave labor.

After the war, Guderian escaped any trials aimed at the former German officer corps and began a process of rehabilitating the former Wehrmacht, a task made much less difficult by the opening of the Cold War and the prospect of needing German troops to help defend the West.

In 1950, shortly after the outbreak of the Korean War, Guderian published in Germany a short book entitled: *Can Western Europe Be Defended?*[63] He begins by placing Russia's gains after World War Two in the context of a centuries-long series of attacks from the East against which the West had to defend itself again and again. This time it was the Bolshevik menace. Unlike the Western powers, above all France and England, who mistakenly viewed the Soviet Union as just "another form of democracy," Hitler and National Socialism recognized from the outset the lethal danger posed by the colossus in the East. Convinced that Germany was in possession of the last opportunity to face down and destroy Bolshevism, Hitler constructed a dictatorship to fight the other dictatorship. Mistakenly thinking that he had a tacit deal with the West to give him a free hand in the East, Hitler was disappointed to see the West declare war on him, thus dooming his war to the death against Bolshevism. Guderian wrote:

> In the course of the war [against Russia] something happened that came so frequently in the history of Europe, which weakened the defensive power of Europe against the threat from the east: the western powers, later strengthened by the mighty power of the USA, allied themselves with Russia, landed at Normandy in the rear of the Germans and broke Germany's strength, even as it was fighting for its naked existence in the difficult struggle with the Soviet Union ... One had not recognized that they were dealing with a dictatorship compared to which Hitler's was a pale reflection ... With that a thousand years of German history, German colonization, German culture and civilization in Central Europe were erased.[64]

In other words, the alleged treachery of the West was responsible for Germany losing its war against the greatest threat to Western civilization. Not only that: The German soldier was only fighting for Europe. The Allies allowed the Russians to join in the verdict at the Nuremberg trials "in order to pass judgment on the defenders of Europe. For one may judge Hitler's acts as one will, in retrospect his struggle was about Europe, even if he made dreadful mistakes and errors [!]. Our soldiers fought and fell for Europe."[65] Such effrontery. There could be no better summary of Nazi propaganda in the years 1944 and 1945.

Guderian makes other points as well, which would reappear in his memoirs: Hitler as erratic and failed commander, the bad treatment of Russian civilians only by the Nazi civil administration, the scapegoating of the Russian winter. He also could not resist echoing Nazi racial propaganda (which he largely omits in his later memoirs):

> We see the completely unspoiled type of the east European, Russian and even more the Asiatic person possessed of a for western peoples almost unimaginable primitiveness in terms of their needs; hard, tenacious, inured to the punishments and rigors of the continental climate of Russia and Asia. This type of human more than any other people is impervious to panic normally felt when facing battle."[66]

But, still, Guderian says, we should not underestimate the Soviet Union economically, technologically, politically, or militarily.

This is all connected with the issue of a renewed German military. The defense of Europe can only be accomplished, Guderian contends, if Germany is restored as a full and independent partner.[67] The Western powers must defend Germany from the outset vigorously; they cannot allow the Russians to overrun Europe and then hope to come back and liberate the area. The subtext is that all remaining German officers in incarceration be freed, their rights – above all, pensions – be restored and that high command positions in any future German military be reserved for them. Guderian worked with a number of former comrades to achieve this goal, as American military intelligence agents spying on him discovered.[68]

From the beginning, the Americans were impressed with Guderian and sought out his advice. As we have noted, George Schuster, who interviewed Guderian just after the war, was quite taken by him and suggested that he be brought to Washington to advise our military.

Guderian also embarked on a quest to get German officers released from prison as a quid pro quo for future German military contributions to Western defense. He was particularly active in fighting for Jochen Peiper, the Waffen-SS commander who had ordered the shooting of American prisoners in 1944 at Malmedy. As he wrote to his former subordinate Geyr: "At the moment I am negotiating with General Handy (Heidelberg) because this honorable gentleman wants to hang the unfortunate Peiper. McCloy is powerless, because the Malmedy trial is being handled by Eucom, and it is not subordinate to McCloy. As a result I have decided to cable President Truman and ask him if he is familiar with this idiocy."[69] Interestingly enough, Peiper is one of the heroes of the Americans who romanticize the Wehrmacht, and especially the Waffen-SS, as we shall see.

Another classic memoir is that of former Major General F. W. von Mellenthin, *Panzer Battles*, which went through six printings in the United States between 1956 and 1976 and continues to be very popular among the romancers of the Wehrmacht.[70] While noting that the Germans were "faced by a ruthless enemy, possessed of immense and seemingly inexhaustible resources," an argument also used by the romancers of the Confederacy, Mellenthin is no admirer of the Russian soldier, whom he consistently depicts in racial terms. "The stoicism of the majority of Russian soldiers and their mental sluggishness make them quite insensible to losses. The Russian soldier values his own life no more than those of his comrades . . . Life is not precious to him. He is immune to the most incredible hardships, and does not even appear to notice them; he seems equally indifferent to bombs and shells." This is owing to the fact that many of the Russian soldiers were "Asiatics dragged from the deepest recesses of the Soviet empire." The Russian soldier "is essentially a primitive being, innately courageous, and dominated by emotions and instincts . . . He lacks any true religious or moral balance, and his moods alter between bestial cruelty and genuine kindness." He is marked by "dullness, mental rigidity, and a natural tendency toward indolence."[71]

Why then did the technically proficient and presumably racially superior Germans lose to the subhuman Russians? Again the answer lies in the mass manpower and material bulk of the Russian forces. "The achievements of the German soldier in Russia clearly prove that the Russians are not invincible . . . Even in the critical years of 1944–45 our soldiers never had the feeling of being inferior to the Russians – but the weak German forces were like rocks in the ocean, surrounded by endless waves of men and tanks which surged around and finally submerged them."[72]

Much more so than in the case of the generals, a truly mass readership devoured Hans Ulrich Rudel's memoirs, translated as *Stuka Pilot*. There is very little here of strategy and operations; no efforts to distance himself from Hitler. This is pure action from cover to cover. It is Rudel's own account of endless missions, mostly to dive-bomb and destroy Russian tanks. It is the story of much destruction, fanatic devotion to duty, sentimental comradeship, and narrow escapes. It begins with the opening of the Russian war, but most of the book deals with the long retreat from Stalingrad to Berlin and Rudel's determination to do anything in his power to stave off the Russians.

Rudel was the most decorated German soldier of World War Two: he won five medals for heroism, starting with the Knight's Cross. In the end, his exploits were such that Hitler had to dream up a new medal for him: the Knight's Cross with Golden Oak Leaves, Swords and Diamonds, only one of which was awarded during the war. Several times Rudel received his decoration directly from Hitler. He compiled 2,530 missions in his Stuka dive bomber (JU-87), destroying more than 500 tanks, 700 trucks, 150 flak positions, and a Soviet battleship. He was shot down thirty-two times. During the last months of the war he flew with a prosthetic leg. Stalin allegedly posted a 100,000 ruble reward for his capture.[73] He was called "The Eagle of the Eastern Front"[74] (he fought almost exclusively on the Eastern Front) and Field Marshal Ferdinand Schörner said of him "Rudel is worth an entire division."[75] His most famous quotation was, "Lost are only those who abandon themselves."

Rudel's book went through five printings just between 1958 and 1966, the last in a mass circulating Ballantine paperback (Bal-Hi series). It was translated into many languages and "total publication abroad reached more than a million copies."[76]

As was the case with generals such as Manstein and Guderian, Rudel's memoirs also earn a kind of legitimization from former enemies. *Stuka Pilot* is introduced in favorable terms by an English pilot/hero [who also flew after losing his leg] – Douglas Bader. Bader had been a prisoner in Germany during the war and had heard of Rudel's exploits. After the war, while Rudel was for a brief time in England as a prisoner himself, Bader helped him get a new prosthesis. In the foreword to Rudel's memoirs, Bader wrote: "I am happy to write this short forward to Rudel's book, since although I only met him for a couple of days he is, by any standards, a gallant chap and I wish him luck."[77] Similarly, Rudel's biography by Guenther Just (1975) is introduced by another Allied pilot – Pierre Clostermann. Clostermann was the most successful French pilot in the war and says of Rudel: "The story of Rudel's achievements is that of a man who continually displayed the noblest human virtues in the midst of a terrible drama, a struggle for life and death." The cover art for the biography features a Stuka diving toward a target while in the upper left-hand corner is a picture of smiling and smartly uniformed Rudel.[78]

In some respects, Rudel shares the outlook of much higher ranking German officers who wrote memoirs. He believes the war against Russia was a preventive one. "It looks as if the Soviets meant to build all those preparations up as a base for invasion against us. Whom else in the West could Russia have wanted to attack?"[79] He also shares their low estimation of Russian culture, underscoring the primitive nature of Russian civilization. Quartered in a mud hut, he wrote: "When you enter them you can imagine you have been translated to some primitive country three centuries ago . . . Once you have got used to it you can make out the best piece of furniture, a huge stone stove three feet high and painted a dubious white. Huddled around it three generations live, eat, cry, procreate and die."[80] He also uses scapegoats to help explain German defeats. The Russian winter was partly responsible: an "irresistibly advancing army...had been forced into dug-outs and trenches by the pitiless fist of an inconceivably hard winter." The huge spaces of Russia also played a role. "The vastness of the country is Russia's most valuable ally. With his inexhaustible man power he can easily pour his masses into any such weakly defended vacuum." And there is the standard reference to Russian superiority only in material, much of it from America. "The German soldier...has not been beaten on his merits, but has simply been crushed by overwhelming masses of material."[81]

But Rudel is also more honest than the generals, who emphasize their contempt for Hitler as commander and underscore the differences that separated them from the dictator. Rudel makes no secret of his admiration for Hitler and is critical of the generals who have misled him, particularly in their tendency to underestimate the strength of the Russians.[82] After the awarding of his first medal by Hitler, he remarked "All of us who were there at the front are amazed at his unerring grasp of detail . . . . He is full of ideas and plans and absolutely confident. . . . He radiates a calmness which infects us all. Each of us goes away to his task revitalized." On another occasion he writes: "I am impressed by his warmth and almost tender cordiality." And yet again: "He discusses the minutest details in the field of ballistics, Physics and chemistry with an ease which impresses me who am a critical observer in this department."[83]

Rudel is self-confident to the point of arrogance: "I am only able to straighten up for a fraction of a second and hit the tank accurately in its vulnerable parts thanks to my manifold experience and somnambulistic assurance." He presents himself as fearless and life affirming. "I want to live. I love life. I feel it in every deep drawn breath, in every pore of my skin, in every fibre of my body. I am not afraid of death; I have looked him in the eye for a matter of seconds and have never been the first to lower my gaze, but each time after such an encounter I have also rejoiced in my heart and sometimes cried out with a whoop of jubilation trying to overshout [sic] the roar of the engine."[84]

He is absolutely fanatic about leading his squadron in combat. He refuses all leave. Hospitalized with a case of hepatitis, he checks himself out against doctor's orders. He flies with a crude prosthesis shortly after losing a leg. He even on several occasions makes his acceptance of a medal from Hitler contingent upon Hitler's reversing his order that Rudel not fly.[85] Defending the Fatherland from the Bolshevik hordes becomes his obsession. "Up to this moment I had not been depressed because of my wound, but now I feel that I am again out of everything, condemned to inactivity when every able bodied man is needed."

"In spite of having been wounded five times, some of them seriously, I have always had the luck to make a quick recovery and to be able soon afterwards to pilot my aircraft again day after day, year in, year out, up and down the Eastern Front . . . I know the Russian front inside out. Therefore I feel an unremitting obligation to go on flying and fighting until the guns are silent and our country's liberty is assured." "I am seized with an uncontrolled fury at the thought that this horde from the Steppes is driving into the very heart of Europe."[86]

He already addresses the fact that the Western Allies, who are foolishly supporting the Russians, will eventually pay when the Russians turn against them. "The devil is now gambling for Germany, for all Europe. Invaluable forces are bleeding to death, the last bastion of the world is crumbling under the assault of Red Asia." "Cannot the Western Powers be made to see that Bolshevism is their greatest enemy and that after an eventual victory over Germany it will be the same menace to them as to us, and that alone they will no longer be able to get rid of it?" And in the end, he takes some satisfaction in the fact that his captors – the Americans and British – are slowly coming to see the Russian enemy for what they are. "They are talking about mass expulsions, rape and murder . . . now their views are an exact reflection of our own often enough proclaimed thesis, and expressed in language which is frequently copied from us."[87] Finally, Rudel's world is a man's world. He only mentions his wife twice in the entire book: once to note that he married her, then to mention toward the end of the book that she was sitting next to his hospital bed.[88] There is no attempt here, as, for example, was the case in von Stahlberg's memoirs, to make himself look more human, to soften the edges of his life, by writing at length about family.

One American interrogator noted that Rudel was a "typical Nazi officer."[89] He wasn't far from the truth. After the war, Rudel made no secret of his Nazi leanings and belonged to a number of radical right-wing organizations for the rest of his life. Right after the war he went to Argentina and made friends with the dictator Juan Peron, who made Rudel his air force adviser. While in Latin America, Rudel activated a rescue agency for escaped Nazis named the "Eichmann-Runde" and aided, among others, Josef Mengele. In Germany, he joined the "Socialist Reich Party," a right-wing neo-Nazi organization, and, when that party was forbidden, he became an unsuccessful candidate for office in its successor, the "Deutsche Reichspartei". Most members of both parties had belonged to the Nazi party prior to the end of the war. Rudel died in 1982. Even in death he could not escape his Nazi identity. Two Bundeswehr Phantom jets flew low over his grave, while a number of mourners bade him farewell with the Nazi salute. This caused a scandal. Though his biographer mentions his friendship with Peron, he is silent on Rudel's political activities.[90]

Popular histories, especially illustrated ones, reinforce the testimony of the generals' memoirs. Probably the best known and most widely read of these histories are those by Paul Carell, among which the most popular are *Hitler Moves East 1941–1943* and *Scorched Earth. Hitler Moves East.*[91] These and other books by Carell, some lavishly illustrated, have sold millions of copies in Germany and in the United States.[92]

Carell takes his message from the exculpatory accounts of the generals. In his books, Carell presents the Wehrmacht as heroes fighting for a lost cause. The German soldier fought a clean war imposed on him by an evil dictator. There is no mention of the war of aggression and racial annihilation, which the war in the East really was. The SS appear as soldiers just like all the rest. In the end, the overwhelming material and human resources of the enemy, partly bolstered by U.S. Lend Lease, defeat the Germans. In a kind of "what-if" history, Carell presents turning points such as Stalingrad or Kursk in a way that suggest they could have easily gone the other way – but unfortunately did not. If there is a villain – apart from the Asiatic hordes of Communism – it is the German dictator, who, by his feckless and irresponsible meddling, deprived Germany of the victory that the capable and professional soldiers might have delivered.

Carell was not a military man during the war, but he did actively serve the Nazi regime. As Paul Karl Schmidt, his real name, "Carell" was a press spokesman for Joachim von Ribbentrop's Foreign Ministry, where he formulated propaganda for the foreign press. In doing so he maintained close ties with the Wehrmacht, from whom he ultimately also learned a great deal about how the war was to be interpreted to Germans and foreigners alike. One of his specialties as propagandist was the Jewish question and on several occasions he remarked on the Jews as a "political pathogen, ferment for the decay and death of any national organism."[93] He began publishing war histories in the 1950s and continued his stream of publications well into the 1990s until his death in 1997.

Another stream that feeds the romanticization of the Wehrmacht is the popular war novel – which also complements the memoirs of ordinary soldiers. One of the most successful of this genre is the writing of Sven Hassel. Hassel, born in 1917, was an ethnic German of Danish and Austrian descent. He claimed to have been living in Denmark before the war, but wanted to serve in uniform, so that in 1937 he stowed away on a boat and went to Germany. There, after some delay, he was able to join the Wehrmacht and was soon part of the force marching into Poland. A year later he deserted, was apprehended, and was placed in a penal battalion – one made up of deserters, criminals, political dissidents, and anyone else the regime chose to label asocial. These units carried out the most dangerous work at the front, including clearing mine fields, and their casualty rates were horrendous. Hassel fought on all the fronts except North Africa and was wounded seven times. Most of the time he spent on the Eastern Front. Captured in Berlin in 1945, he spent the next four years in prison camps. Married in 1951, he began writing, encouraged by his wife. His first novel was *Legion of the Damned*, published in 1957, followed by *Wheels of Terror* (1959) and *Comrades of War* (1963). Eventually Hassel wrote fourteen novels, which have been translated into sixteen languages and published in fifty countries, with fifty-two million copies selling to date.

The first book is allegedly the tale of Hassel's own experience in the East; the others, fictional spinoffs. The books were best sellers in the 1950s, '60s, and '70s, then went out of print for several decades. Four of them, including *Legion of the Damned* and *Wheels of Terror* and *SS General*, have recently (2003) been reissued by Cassel Military Paperbacks and more are planned. Cassel's book cover designers provided readers with sensational displays of the German soldiers in action. The cover art for *Legion of the Damned*, for example, depicts a crazed and angry German soldier holding a potato masher grenade. Clearly, he is about to throw the grenade at the enemy. In the bright red and yellow background, fire consumes a building and enhances the shocking visual character of the book cover.

The books are really "grunt" novels. The characters represent a lost band of brothers; the German soldier as beleaguered figures fighting a war in which they do not believe for a regime they hate. They are experienced, expert killers and have a fatalistic sense of their own chances for survival. When time permits, they are also crude boozehounds always in search of good food and female companionship. Mostly they are filthy, smelly, and cold. Typical of the characters that run through Hassel's novels are: "Porta," a Berliner asocial with a foul, fast mouth; an expert sniper and a tank driver; musician; epicure, loudly flatulent; wears a yellow top hat into battle with his cat, Stalin, in his pocket. "Tiny," a former criminal; a giant of a man topping seven feet and weighing 260 pounds; puts on a stupid demeanor; explosive expert; valued by his comrades for his extraordinary sense of hearing, which detects the enemy sneaking up. "Legionair," a diminutive man, but deadly fighter, particularly with a knife; served with the French Foreign Legion, spins erotic sayings revolving around his post war ambition to open a brothel. "Ol 'un" – ten years older than the others, married with children. Imperturbable, he exerts a quiet leadership, always calm under fire.

These men hate Hitler and are contemptuous of the institutions of his regime – SS, Gestapo, and other political leaders like Himmler, Goebbels, and Goering; they don't like the generals much either. On one occasion, Hitler and several of his generals visit the unit. Field Marshal Manstein stepped out of one vehicle "followed by what seemed to be his entire staff. The number of medals on display was positively dazzling. Gold epaulettes were two a penny, monocles were so plentiful I thought people must be wearing one in each eye, and the rattling of spurs and sabers sounded like an entire cavalry charge."[94]

The SS is particularly hated. "Things reached the stage that no SS unit dared to move up during an attack if ordinary German soldiers were behind it. There would be a pause in the fighting to allow the Germans to mow down the SS. Once they had been dealt with the fighting would be resumed."[95] But Hassel is also inconsistent. The main theme of *SS-General* is the emergence of a tough SS general who led the penal battalion in an escape from Stalingrad and then several hundred miles back to German lines, a feat for which the general is shot for desertion at the end, having left Stalingrad against Hitler's specific orders. The soldiers at first view the SS general with hostility, but do nothing against him and accept his commands. One of them indicates why: "We started looking back at him, hating him, despising him, with murder in our hearts and our hands meekly by our sides. We had been too well trained. We had been Prussian slaves for too many years to break the habit of blind obedience. The idea of raising one's hand against a general was not one that came readily to mind."[96]

These soldiers do have one thing in common with the generals and their memoirs: both scapegoat the Russian winter, which allegedly affected the German soldier more than the Russian. "More soldiers died of frost and illness than by enemy fire. The Russian's best ally was nature, the Russian winter. Only the Siberian troops could withstand it. It seems as if the winter made these small soldiers with their high cheekbones more content and full of fight."[97] Or with respect to the snowstorms raging across the steppe: "The Russians were accustomed to it and equipped to deal with it, and the wind blew in their favor. We Germans were terrified by it. . . ."[98]

Occasionally the unit would fraternize with the Russians. On one occasion, men from both sides went skinny dipping in a river. "'This is the proper sort of war to have don't you think?' shouted a Russian NCO, and we agreed with him. They gave three cheers for Germany and we gave three cheers for Russia."[99] The characters regularly refer to the Russian soldiers as "colleagues." This would seem more fictional than not, although such incidents are not unknown. It reminds one a little bit of the famous Christmas truce between British and German soldiers in December 1914. But that war had just begun, and such a spontaneous truce would not happen again. In Hassel's book, the war has been underway for some time, and getting ever more barbaric. Hassel is perhaps trying, as he does elsewhere, to emphasize the common humanity of the "little people" on both sides. Unfortunately, he only strengthens the case of the

German generals that, except for the Nazi civilian administration, the Russian people and the German soldiers got along just fine.

Occasionally, a pale reflection of Nazi racism creeps in with terms like "Asiatic" or "Siberian" applied to troops who commit acts of barbarism against even their own countrymen; killing, looting, raping.[100] With respect to the Kalmuks, with whom the unit was sharing food and drink, one character observed: "They're all right at the moment, gentle as lambs . . . but you rub 'em up the wrong way and they'll be at your throat within seconds. . . ."[101]

Hassel is on the antifascist political left, but, certainly unwittingly, his writing does contribute to the myth of the heroic Wehrmacht – or at least of its common soldiers. These men fight viciously – but so do their opponents. They like Russian civilians, fraternize with them regularly, sharing what little food they have with them. The Russian peasants, in turn, are friendly and reciprocate. On one occasion, the Germans even function as midwives to a pregnant Russian woman.[102] Rarely does Hassel mention what the Wehrmacht was really doing or the extent that it was collaborating with the regime in its war crimes. In fact, you don't get the sense really that these men are part of an occupying force, never mind a genocidal one. They are in their own little local universe, fighting in isolation from the outside world. They are virtually de-contextualized. Moreover, these German soldiers are fully developed characters, attractive in a rough kind of way; the Russians, with few exceptions, remain shadowy figures.

Hassel's soldiers are like those of any army; the soldier as everyman. They would fit perfectly as characters in the "Dirty Dozen"; they are Bill Mauldin soldiers, so that a kind of relativization emerges, which disguises the fact that these regular guys fought, reluctantly to be sure, for one of the most criminal causes ever. Also, the NKVD, the Russian secret police, is seen as little different from the Gestapo. "Communist or Nazi, hammer and sickle or swastika, what difference did it make" says one character.[103] Finally, these men are only seen in the years of tragic retreat for the Germans. Most of Hassel's novels, which take place on the Eastern Front, are set in 1943 or thereafter, not during the years of triumphant advance. So, they fight on to their ultimate and tragic end; each novel ends in a sense with the survivors marching into the sunset – not unlike the famous *Landser* novels so popular in Germany in the 1950s and 1960s.

Hassel's novels have been translated into a number of languages in Europe, including English, French, Spanish, Dutch, Swedish, and Finnish. Only one of them, however, *Wheels of Terror*, has appeared in German, in Austria. It was also made into a film in 1988. The lack of German translations is perhaps a sign that the Germans themselves sense the inadvertent romanticization of the German army at the grass roots level.

Paralleling these popular war novels are memoirs published just recently by men who, like the characters in Hassel's novels, were just ordinary "grunts" during the war. They bear titles like *Blood Red Snow: The Memoirs of a German Soldier on the Eastern Front* by Günter Koschorrek, *In Deadly Combat: A German Soldier's Memoir of the Eastern Front* by Gottlob Biedermann, and *Adventures in My Youth: A German Soldier on the Eastern Front 1941–45* by Armin Scheiderbauer, which, as we shall see, sound remarkably similar to the war novels of men like Hassel.

Post-Vietnam

These memoirs, popular histories, and war novels had their greatest initial effect in the 1950s and 1960s. Their popularity never diminished completely, but moved into the background during the Vietnamese war. Military and intelligence circles at the top also tended to forget about the Wehrmacht during the war in Asia; the German performance in Russia had little to do with the jungle war in Southeast Asia. In the wake of our withdrawal from Vietnam in 1974, however, questions were raised about the reasons for our defeat, and especially about the disintegration of the U.S. Army, which, after all, won most of its engagements, even Tet, and had experienced no devastating defeats, as had the French at Dien Bien Phu. Why did the U.S. Army seem to lack cohesion? Why did discipline seem to collapse? Why were American soldiers in disproportionate numbers overindulging in drugs and alcohol, deserting, and fragging their officers?

As the Americans struggled to come to grips with these questions, they rediscovered the Wehrmacht. As one German observer put it: "In American military literature, taking recourse in the Wehrmacht experience appears to have become a kind of reflex in times of crisis."[104] In the late 1940s, the German generals managed to convince the Americans of the myth of the clean Wehrmacht, but the Americans, having been the winners in World War Two, did not seek to use the German army as a model. Now, in the wake of Vietnam, they did just that. What could the German army's experience, particularly in the East, but really on all fronts, teach the Americans about discipline, motivation, cohesion, perseverance, and fighting power? This was particularly important, because in the late 1970s and 1980s our attention once again was focused on Europe as the primary focus of the Cold War and the possibility of a conflict with Russia loomed large in our imagination. If that conflict were to break out, major reforms had to be put into place in the U.S. military.

As a result, U.S. agencies, particularly the Defense Department, commissioned a number of studies comparing the German and U.S. armies, or just examining the German army itself. Moreover, former German generals were once again consulted as to their opinions on both armies. As one scholar put it somewhat drolly, "At other times and places in the post world war, perplexed military reformers have looked to social science, game theory, high energy physics, or the nation's business schools for solutions to their quandaries. It may be another reflection of current perplexity that the quest has now returned to the peculiar history of the German army, whose experience in certain ways has unexpectedly come to seem not only relevant but exemplary."[105]

To begin, researchers looked back on similar studies commissioned right after World War Two. One was the famous report, published in 1948, by Edward A. Shils and Morris Janowitz, both of whom had served in U.S. Army Intelligence during the war, which examined the question of how the German soldier performed so effectively. The authors concluded that the German army had satisfied "certain *primary* personality demands" through the basic small or primary group – the platoon, or company. The army strove to maintain as much as possible the same personnel in a unit, even if it were restructured; to stress high levels of comradeship, including between officers and men; to assimilate replacements quickly, and to combine discipline and solicitude on the part of officers toward their men. The men were to view their unit as "one big family."[106]

Interestingly enough, this early study assigned little importance to Nazi ideology in the German army – as would the studies after 1974. Ironically, this would enable the authors and their readers – and the larger U.S. subculture – to continue to admire and "romanticize" the German army outside of any political, strategic, or ideological context.

Three studies in the late 1970s and early 1980s illustrate the results of American scrutiny of the World War Two German army. One by Richard A. Gabriel and Paul Savage essentially drew the same conclusion as had Shils and Janowitz three decades earlier. Their answer was: "German battlefield cohesion resulted directly from the individual soldier's personal reinforcement due to interactions through which he received esteem and respect from his primary group – squad, platoon and company – and to his perceptions of his immediate officers and NCOs as men of honor eminently deserving of respect and who cared for their men."[107] In other words, the Germans chose their officers very carefully, kept them close to their men, taking the same risks as their men and more. They also kept units together, sometimes rotating divisions out of the line and reconstituting them with buddies kept together, thus developing strong unit identification over time. The Germans also rewarded their men richly for success with medals, decorations, and commendations.[108] Again in this study ideology is seen as only peripherally important.

A second study praised the German army, even though the writer was an Israeli historian. Martin Creveld published his report in 1980 and largely reached conclusions similar to other studies: the German army, particular the officer corps, struggled to achieve quality, particularly by always sending the best men to the front and deliberately keeping the rear areas weak. His introduction to the problem of fighting power is an encomium of praise for the Germans.

> The historian is confronted with an army that . . . was outnumbered three, five or even seven to one. Yet it did not run. It did not disintegrate. It did not frag its officers. Instead, it fought doggedly on. It fought on even though Hitler's war was never at any time really popular in Germany. It fought on even though its homeland was being bombed to smithereens behind its back. It fought on even though many of its generals . . . regarded its commander in chief as little better than a raving lunatic . . . Yet for all this, its units, even when down to 20 percent of their original size, continued to exist and to resist – an unrivaled achievement for any army.

This is not only a virtually starry eyed characterization of the German army, but also an invidious comparison with the U.S. Army.[109] Interestingly enough, Creveld continued to make the most flattering comments on the Wehrmacht long after other historians had firmly tied the German army to Hitler's war of racial destruction in Eastern Europe. In an essay published in an anthology in 1999, Creveld still maintained that the Wehrmacht "combined initiative and discipline better than any modern army before or since" and that "the tactical and above all operational capabilities of this army were at the beginning so impressive, that they became nearly legendary."[110]

Finally, Col. T. N. DuPuy, an outspoken admirer of the Wehrmacht and determined military reformer, also published a book on the history of the German General Staff aptly entitled *A Genius for War*, in which he gives credit to the German General Staff for having given institutional form to military genius and excellence, by encouraging individual initiative, promoting the best to the top, and encouraging the best minds to study military history.

Even in 1944, he reports, the German army had a twenty percent combat effectiveness superiority and a three-to-two casualty-inflicting superiority over its enemies. Although he avails himself of complex mathematical models in his study, his prose leaves no doubt as to where he stands. "As to the German recovery from the disasters of mid-1944, it is difficult to find many other military accomplishments more worthy of being called a 'miracle' . . . But rarely have armies so totally defeated shown such amazing qualities of recuperation, once the opportunity was offered. No comparable historical example comes to mind."[111] Again, DuPuy tends to ignore ideological, political, and strategic factors.

The Americans did not simply rely on the documentation and on social science and psychological models for their assessment of reform in the U.S. Army, however. They also called in surviving German generals from the war – now thirty or forty years behind them. General William DePuy (not to be confused with Col. T. N. DuPuy), formerly a division commander in Vietnam, was called upon to organize and direct a Training and Doctrine Command, the office in charge of all training and continuing education in the U.S. Army as well as conceiving and writing its field manuals. As he reflected on where to get information, DePuy recalled the German army and its defensive battles toward the end of the war.

> More relevant, however, is the German experience against the Russians from Stalingrad to the end of World War II. For $2\frac{1}{2}$ years a German army of about three million men fought a strategic defensive battle against Russian armies of $5\frac{1}{2}$ million men . . . No western army but the Germans' has direct experience of such epic battles over such staggering distances. The performance of the German army in these circumstances was little short of miraculous.[112]

Now, DuPuy chose to bring over to the United States two former German commanders, General of Panzer Troops Hermann Balck, who was regarded by the Americans as a German George S. Patton, and his former Chief of Staff, F. W. von Mellenthin, author of *Panzer Battles* (1956), a favorite of the Americans, and more recently *German Generals of World War Two* (1977), in which he included a highly flattering portrait of his former superior Balck, whom he characterized as "Steadfast and Inflexibly Determined – A Highly Gifted Commander of Armored Forces."[113] The two Germans came to Washington in May, 1980, for high-level meetings in which they explained their World War Two tactics against the Russians, which they saw as potentially useful to NATO. Balck, commander of the 11th Panzer division, had been famous for his operations on the Chir river, where he turned back an enormous Soviet offensive in December 1942 with few losses by using flexible/mobile defense tactics. These he now tried to teach the Americans. Over four days, the Americans, who included DuPuy and a number of high ranking officers, listened deferentially, as illustrated by DuPuy's description of the two men: "General Balck tends to be a man of few words – somewhat brusque – almost laconic, but deeply thoughtful. He was, and is, clearly a man of iron will and iron nerves. He exudes a strong aura of confidence – confidence in himself, in the German army and in the German soldier. He has no doubt about the superiority of the German over the

Russian . . . " General von Mellenthin is a more gentle officer on the outside. However, his record and Balck's esteem tell us he is also a man of steel at the core."

The Germans passed on their old cultural prejudices to the Americans. Mellenthin: "The Russian is unpredictable. Today he is a hero attacking in great depth – tomorrow he is completely afraid and not willing to do anything. . . . Believe us, they are masses and we are individuals. That is the difference between the Russian soldier and the European soldier." Asked whether more education or exposure to western ideas would change the Russian soldier, Balck replied: "No, I don't believe so."

The two Germans were also quite persuasive in communicating to the Americans that their example in World War Two – particularly mobile defense and independence of lower level commanders – was one the Americans should emulate. At one point, on the last day of the seminar, it became apparent that invidious comparisons were being raised between the German army and the U.S. Army " . . . to the effect that the German leaders were uniformly superior in battlefield tactics." The Americans did not take issue. "The patent excellence and superb performance of Generals Balck and von Mellenthin at the discussion led the audience easily in that direction."[114]

Much of the advice was eventually incorporated into the new version of Field Manual 100–5 (1982).[115] The Americans were a bit slow on the uptake, however. In a rival war games session with the Americans against a Warsaw pact invasion force, the Americans met the Russian attack too far forward and were beaten. The two German generals retreated far into West Germany, then attacked the Russians on the flanks and won.[116] Mellenthin won additional American recognition four years later with an important publication on NATO defense prospects; needless to say, the book highlighted the German defensive tactics in Russia during World War Two.[117]

The results of these studies soon percolated down in the U.S. Army. A proliferation of articles appeared in popular military journals in the 1980s and 1990s. There was a tremendous revival of the famous German soldier/intellectual Carl von Clausewitz; courses on him were a must at U.S. Army Command and General Staff Colleges. Many articles on Clausewitz appeared in military journals, partly because his famous dictum, war is the extension of politics, was seen as a 150-year-old explanation of U.S. failure in Vietnam.[118]

Other articles celebrated great German soldiers, particularly chiefs of the German General Staff. Among the names that appeared frequently were Helmuth von Moltke, first chief of the imperial General Staff, and Hans von Seeckt, who revived and modernized Germany's military in the 1920s.[119] A number of articles appeared that compared German operational techniques to those of other armies – and in almost all of them the Germans emerged with their reputation intact.[120]

The positive view of the German army and what we might learn from it was not unanimous. Some argued that the Wehrmacht was not as good as we were imagining it to be: Its early victories were against weaker and ill-led armies; its intelligence was abysmal; its planning inadequate and based on false premises; its transport, mostly horse drawn, primitive; interservice rivalries abounded, and, in contrast to popular belief, the Wehrmacht was permeated by Nazis, particularly in the junior officer ranks.[121] Others argued that we had taken German concepts like *Auftragstaktik* (mission orders) completely out of context or failed to understand what they meant in the first place, thus suggesting that we perhaps had less to learn from the German experience than we thought. It was also suggested that the German successes early in the war did not rest on a superior body of doctrine, but precisely because of the lack of such a doctrine. The Germans stumbled into success to a degree, which surprised even them.[122]

These views, however, remained in the minority, and they were attacked strongly by those who maintained the view that the Wehrmacht was a superior fighting force from which we had much to learn. Creveld, for example, took on the critics, specifically Beaumont and Hughes, and averred: "For all its weaknesses at the top, the Wehrmacht, up to army level inclusive, was second to no fighting machine in history and better than any in the 20th century." Other writers referred specifically to the "forgotten war" of the Germans against the Russians and urged American officers to learn about the enemy through German experience.[123]

It was this view of the Wehrmacht that predominated in the 1980s and 1990s and that percolated down through the military ranks then out to a larger general public, consisting of war buffs, war gamers, and, increasingly, re-enactors, collectors, and Internet chatters. Indeed, the renewed interest in, and enthusiasm for, the Wehrmacht provided impetus to the larger culture to "romanticize" the German army as before. Despite the widespread knowledge of the Holocaust in the 1980s and 1990s, of which the romanticizers of the 1950s and 1960s were still largely ignorant, the parallel track of romanticizing the "clean" Wehrmacht continued and even grew in strength and intensity, partly thanks to the swiftly emerging Internet technology.

There are telling pieces of evidence that testify to the degree to which Americans held the German military and its leaders in high regard. One Lieutenant Colonel Verner R. Carlson became absolutely smitten with General von Mellenthin after reading his "masterfully written book," *Panzer Battles*, and went to South Africa to interview him. There, Mellenthin turns on the charm and wins Carlson over entirely, the result being a panegyric article which appeared in *Military Review*. "When he spoke of battles past, his pale blue eyes acquired a long-distant focus, as if he were at the forward edge of battle, still seeing the approaching Soviet tanks," Carlson wrote after listening to Mellenthin's tales of war in the East. Clearly, the sophisticated, charming Mellentin had cast a spell over Carlson just as effectively as had the German generals in the 1950s. Mellenthin was elegant, aristocratic, humble, and athletic and Carlson obviously took everything he said at face value, including his version of war, as well as his opinion of former comrades like Rommel, Guderian, and Balck. Carlson was reminded that more than one-third of the general officers in the German army had been killed in the war. "Despite these appalling losses and his imprisonment," Carlson concluded, "von Mellenthin's spirit is unbroken. He continues to ride his favorite horses 2 hours every morning, work at his writing desk 8 hours daily and act as an unpaid consultant to various charitable causes. Once a month, he presides over a formal dinner for his extended family of over 30 members. He goes on military maneuvers as often as possible and speaks at NATO and war colleges."[124]

These admiring interviews continue to the present day. The senior officers have all passed away, so that current interviews are essentially with former German grunts. One from 2005 has the title "Horse Soldier in Hitler's Army."[125]

A *Washington Post* article reprinted in the *Manchester Guardian Weekly* entitled "The Wehrmacht was the better army" highlights the studies by Crebeld and Col. DuPuy and repeats DuPuy's claim that the German army "inflicted casualties at about a 50% higher rate than they incurred from the opposing British and American troops *under all circumstances*."[126]

Lt. Col. Guenther Guderian, grandson of the World War Two Panzer leader, was assigned as Bundeswehr liaison officer at Fort Bragg in the mid-1990s. He said in an interview: "Sometimes, I get the impression that in the United States Army, even more officers know the name [Guderian] than in the German army." He went on to relate an incident, which happened while he was a liaison officer to the U.S. Army's 7th Corps. He entered the office of the operations officers and noted two large pictures on the wall. "One was Patton. One was my grandfather."[127]

Lt. Col. Alexander B. Roberts, U.S. Air Force, made a speech in 1994 entitled "Core Values in a Quality Air Force: The Leadership Challenge" in which he quoted former German General Guenther Blumentritt to the effect that knowledge is important, but character is indispensable.[128]

When the Kevlar helmets were introduced into the U.S. Army, they were very popular among the troops because of their resemblance to the World War Two German helmets.[129]

These stories are just the tip of the iceberg and demonstrate the extent to which a romanticization of the Wehrmacht had penetrated the U.S. military at all levels and would form the framework and supply much of the impetus for a continuation of the myth of the "clean" Wehrmacht in the larger American culture. The post-Vietnam revival of the Wehrmacht also provides the framework for popular histories, war gaming, Internet chatting, and re-enacting, which we will investigate in subsequent chapters.

5   Winning Hearts and Minds: The Germans Interpret the War for the United States Public

The German generals recognized the need to broadcast their message to broader audiences and their books, especially their memoirs, provided the main vehicle to achieve this end. In 1952, Heinz Guderian's *Panzer Leader* inaugurated a long line of German accounts of the war in Russia. Others soon followed, most notably Maj. Gen. F. W. Mellenthin's *Panzer Battles* in 1956 and Erich von Manstein's *Lost Victories* in 1957. Then, in the early 1960s, Paul Carell's popular history *Hitler Moves East* appeared and became a perennial favorite. Scores of publications followed over the next forty-plus years, among them the memoirs of Alexander Stahlberg, *Bounden Duty*. Stahlberg served as aide-de-camp (ADC) to Manstein and his work provided valuable insights into Manstein's behavior as well as that of the officer corps generally. As late as 1989, Hans von Luck's *Panzer Commander: The Memoirs of Colonel Hans von Luck* won an immediate audience in the United States. Released by Praeger Publishers in hardback, *Panzer Commander* went into mass distribution in 1991, when Dell Books published it in paperback. The book had already acquired an enormous reputation as a selection of the Military Book Club.

Since 2001, junior officers and German rank and file soldiers have also penned accounts of the Russo-German war. Gottlob Herbert Bidermann's *In Deadly Combat: A German Soldier's Memoir of the Eastern Front*, Armin Schei-derbauer's *Adventures in My Youth: A German Soldier on the Eastern Front 1914–1945* (Figure 7) and Günter K. Koschorrek's *Blood Red Snow: The Memoirs of a German Soldier on the Eastern Front* (Figure 8). Bidermann and Koschorrek enjoyed widespread readership through their repeated selections as featured books in the Military Book Club and/or the History Book Club, both with substantial memberships. Their perspectives grew out of the actual experiences of combat as infantrymen who faced the soldiers of the Red Army. They lacked the overall vision of higher-ranking officers, yet they related the feelings of young men who engaged in direct combat on the Eastern Front over the course of

Figure 7. Cover of *Adventures in My Youth: A German Soldier on the Eastern Front 1941–45*.

Figure 8. Cover of *Blood Red Snow: The Memoirs of a German Soldier on the Eastern Front.*

fours years of desperate fighting. Their works completed the long run of German accounts and gave readers a consistent narrative that reflects all levels of the Wehrmacht, from field marshals and lieutenants to corporals and privates, that spanned fifty-plus years.[1]

The audiences for these writings were varied, ranging from policy makers and military planners to a growing mass of people interested in popular military history. The scale of the titanic and increasingly desperate conflict in the East caught the imagination of many in the United States – and still does. In fact, publication of German memoirs and their selection by book clubs after 1991 suggest a continued active interest in the German military. Publishers, large and small, have recognized this avid interest and responded. A recent academic catalogue of the divisions of Random House, one of the major publishers in the United States, included Manstein's *Lost Victories*, Mellenthin's *Panzer Battles*, Luck's *Panzer Commander*, and Knappe's *Soldat*. Random House sent the catalogues to university faculty and librarians around the entire country and the proponents of the German version of the War in the East now moved into an educated audience. The Dell and Ballantine divisions of Random House rank as leading mass distributors of paperback books and cater to popular audiences. These two divisions released three of the memoirs in paperback. Presidio Press, one of the main publishers of military history, published the fourth. Readers can also purchase these books online at the Random House website. The 1996 spring catalogue of Schiffer Publishing Ltd. featured military histories. Of the 234 titles in military history, 204 dealt with the German military. In fact, a catalogue photo showed six Luftwaffe *a*ces standing together engaged in conversation. This photo illustrated Col. Raymond F. Toliver's [USAF (Ret.)] and Trevor J. Constable's *Fighter Aces of the Luftwaffe* listed on page 2. Much in keeping with the pathos of the "Lost Cause," "the great aces . . . could not win, yet they fought to the final hour in an unforgettable combat saga."[2]

A press dedicated solely to the German military, J. J. Federowicz, includes dozens of books that appear on the websites of the leading Internet booksellers, Amazon.com and Barnes and Noble. Ballantine, one of the large mass distributors under the Random House umbrella, has re-released several of the Federowicz books in inexpensive paperback editions. The Amazon listings also incorporate "Editorial Reviews" and readers' reactions, which provide brief analyses of the book and recommendations to other potential readers. The sites also include references to customers who purchased other books in addition to the featured book. In the case of Scheiderbauer's *Adventures in My Youth*, buyers also owned Bidermann's *In Deadly Combat* as well as five other memoirs on the German military experiences in World War Two. Buyers who selected Scheiderbauer's *Adventures of my Youth* for purchase would also find a list of five or six other East Front books purchased by other Amazon customers. This list typically included Bidermann's *In Deadly Combat*, Koschorrek's *Blood Red Snow*, and Knappe's *Soldat*. This listing represents a built-in reinforcement mechanism, which keeps a number of titles constantly before the eyes of an interested public.[3]

The frequency of programs on the History Channel featuring the Wehrmacht and World War Two underscores the popularity of the German military. The growth of websites dedicated to the Wehrmacht confirms the extent to which the German military is an icon in public life.[4] The Cold War made possible the success of the German accounts of the war. By the 1990s, as the Cold War was coming to an end, the narrative produced by these works had long since achieved canonical status and nourished the spate of books published since the early 1990s.

Legitimizing the Wehrmacht

One of the reasons that so many publishers put these memoirs on the market was not just their assessment of demand; the books, which might under other circumstances have been controversial, received legitimization through the comments, often on the dust jacket, of well-known scholars and popular writers of war history. The German officers and their supporters in the West also knew full well the necessity of enhancing the credibility of their books and their own reputations. With publication of each book, well-known military figures and military historians in the United States and Britain wrote prefaces that commended the authors for their valiant service. The authors also introduced anti-Communist rhetoric in their introductions in an attempt to capitalize on the almost universal fear in the United States and the West in general of the Communist "regime" that ruled the sprawling Russian empire and its satellites in Eastern Europe. Endorsements by noted military expert Martin Blumenson and British Army figure and military theoretician B. H. Liddell Hart (d. 1970) that appeared in earlier editions of Manstein's *Lost Victories* showed up again in the 1981 edition. Blumenson, in fact, won the 1995 Samuel Eliot Morison Prize awarded by the Society for Military History (publisher of the *Journal of Military History*) for "a body of contributions in the field of military history and reflecting a spectrum of scholarly activity contributing significantly to the field." Blumenson also worked in history programs of the U.S. Army and served on the faculty at "the National War College, the Army War College, and the Naval War College." He wrote that Manstein found himself in an untenable situation, yet one he could not abandon. As a Prussian officer, a field marshal, he had to uphold the sacred tradition of defending the German state. He owed "blind obedience" to a regime he and his fellow officers despised. Manstein responded as tradition and his training demanded: He served the political leadership and he fought for Germany. Blumenson praised Manstein for his integrity and moral leadership shown throughout his service in the Wehrmacht.[5]

Hart addressed the brilliance of Manstein's military command and his willingness to stand up to Hitler while head of Army Group South (AGS). Manstein spared no bluntness in arguing with the Fuehrer and in the end his frank arguments vigorously presented, very much in keeping with Prussian traditions, earned him a dismissal. His plan enabled German arms to crush the British and French forces in 1940; under his leadership, the 56th Panzer Corps on the Northern Front advanced an astounding 200 miles in the first few days of the war, and his leadership again led Germans arms to a brilliant victory in the Crimea in 1942. As Hart relates, Manstein's notion of strategic withdrawal as a prelude to a counterattack violated the Fuhrer's demand to hold fast on all ground seized.[6]

S. L. A. Marshall, one of the leading military advisors during World War Two and the doyen of military experts in the post-World War Two era, contributed his written endorsements of Manstein's first edition (repeated in every subsequent edition or reprinting through 2004) through his comments printed in the dust jacket. He wrote that *Lost Victories* was "an invaluable military book" that also will appeal to any reader "who enjoys the writing of a highly literate and articulate soldier, whose pen is as good as his sword." Marshall, famous for his classic analysis of the U.S. infantry, *Men Under Fire*, added the weight of his reputation to Manstein and his claims for the integrity of the German military. The dust jacket also included remarks by Hart, who praised *Lost Victories* as "one of the most important and illuminating contributions to the history of World War II." The dust jacket incorporated enthusiastic reviews from the prestigious *Foreign Affairs, Library Journal, San Francisco Chronicle, Yale Review*, and *Publishers' Weekly*. Such moral and professional authority gave the work, over the course of almost fifty years of publication and re-publication, a unique credibility. The comments of Blumenson, Hart, and Marshall also placed Manstein's piece in the center of the literature on the Eastern Front and military history in general.[7]

The same tension between duty and the criminal regime also appeared in the 1991 edition of *Bounden Duty*, by Alexander Stahlberg, who served as Manstein's aide de camp. The noted Sir John Hackett, whose many awards, long-term military service, and distinguished titles appear on the dust jacket, again addressed the difficult situation of a German officer. He faced the choice between his duty and obligation to his country and opposing the "criminal villain" Hitler. General Glenn K. Otis, former commander of the U.S. Army, Europe and former NATO commander of Central Army Group noted that Stahlberg provided a "fascinating account by one who was there." Stahlberg's work includes observations on what he perceives as Manstein's high moral character.[8]

Guderian's *Panzer Leader* won the favor of Liddell Hart, who wrote the forward to the first 1952 edition. Hart's comments appeared in the five printings issued by mass distributor, Ballantine Books, from 1957 to 1968 and the two Canadian printings in 1967 as well as the 1996 and fiftieth anniversary edition in 2002 by Da Capo Press. Hart describes at length Guderian's initial favorable impression of Hitler and the Fuehrer's enthusiasm for mobile warfare. This position certainly won over Guderian, the father of the German blitzkrieg. Hart goes on to write that increasing familiarity with Hitler disabused Guderian of his first impressions. Hart also explains why Guderian took up the profession of arms, namely to defend his country against its enemies. His genius accounted for the early victories in the war and was clearly the driving force on the battlefield. Hart labeled Guderian one of the "Great Captains of History."[9]

The 2002 anniversary of the first publication of Guderian's *Panzer Leader* included numerous praises from the respected and widely read *New York Times Book Review*, the *Christian Science Monitor*, *Time* Magazine, *Newsweek* Magazine, *The New Yorker*, and the *Times Literary Supplement*. The *New York Times Book Review* labeled *Panzer Leader* as the best among the memoirs written by German generals. The reviews clearly reinforce the separation between the professional soldiers and the political leadership, the fundamental argument the German officers desperately wanted to impress upon their new patrons, the U.S. military, and their new allies, the U.S. public.[10]

In the 1996 edition and in the 2002 reprinted edition, the press enlisted the support of noted military historian and World War tanker who served with the British army, Kenneth Macksey. Macksey brought the credentials of having published at least forty books on military history and served as editor of *The Penguin Encyclopedia of Modern War* and *Hitler's Options*. He also has written "biographies of Field Marshals Kesselring and Rommel." Above all, he authored the standard biography of Guderian. As such, his remarks carried substantial weight for a reader.[11]

Macksey described Guderian as a modest and proud officer who shied away from publicity. An inheritor of the Prussian tradition of military service, Guderian excelled in conceptualizing new armored tactics. Guderian desperately tried to frustrate Hitler's poor decision making and even fruitlessly pursued peace through diplomatic means, only to be disappointed by the Foreign Secretary, Von Ribbentrop. As Macksey concludes, Guderian survived "the monster" and then went to write his story "with dignity, honesty, and insight," which characterized his life.[12] Such remarks merely reinforce the arguments the German generals make in their own memoirs and contribute to their public image as politically naïve, courageous, loyal, and dedicated to their profession and their fellow countrymen.

The theme of ingenuousness and professional dedication appears in more recent publications. Historian and public figure, Stephen Ambrose, made Hans von Luck, author of *Panzer Commander*, into a freedom fighter and one completely innocent of politics. Ambrose writes:

> . . . for all his sophistication, in politics Hans is the simplest of men. It might even be said of him that he is apolitical. He is for freedom everywhere and against totalitarianism, whether it comes from the Left or the Right, but beyond that he just doesn't have any politics. I can't understand such an attitude, but there it is.[13]

In recounting an interview with Luck, Ambrose remarked that the Wehrmacht colonel came from an established Prussian family with deep roots in Prussian culture. In fact, Luck's ancestors fought with Frederick the Great. Luck fought for Germany and not for the Nazi party or its murderous ideology.[14]

In the 1992 publication of Siegfried Knappe's *Soldat*, the blurb on the inside of the dust jacket read:

> In Siegfried Knappe we find every-man – a dutiful soldier, a good and decent man. We recognize him as such – even though he unwittingly served a regime of unspeakable horror – because we see ourselves in him. And so we get a rare chance to understand how Hitler motivated a whole generation to carry out his monstrous schemes. And we learn at what cost, as we watch our man struggle to keep his bearings in life as Germany falls into rubble and his whole world collapses.[15]

The same sentiment that appeared in Guderian's and Manstein's works released in the 1950s still found expression in Knappe. Knappe expanded on the blurb comments early in the book when he related a conversation with his Russian captor, who asked him about Auschwitz. Knappe expressed total ignorance. He responded again with surprise when angry Russian guards questioned him about Bergen-Belsen and Buchenwald. Knappe wrote that he never grasped why or what the guards intended through these questions. He had no knowledge of the destruction of European Jewry or that the Nazi regime even planned such a horror. As a soldier he served his country and owed his loyalty to the German people and not the Nazi party. In fact, he showed little knowledge of the Nazis or their policies.[16]

The Moral Position of the German Officers

According to the German officers, the Nazis and Adolf Hitler also victimized the German people and the German soldiers. Hitler's frequent intrusions
into the conduct of military operations fatally compromised the campaign in
the East. The Nazis pursued a relentless campaign of terror in the rear areas
where the Wehrmacht had no control. The Nazis capitalized on the loyalty and
honor of an apolitical officer corps to realize their own nefarious ends. The soldiers themselves dutifully served the leaders of the German state and protected
the German people, observing a moral code with deep roots in the German
past. The German memoirs and accounts took on a "Lost Cause" aspect and
reminded the United States of the costs of defeat.

These books created and sustained the German officers' narration of the
war, the one many U.S. military people embraced and certainly the one known
best by the larger American public. Accounts such as Manstein's *Lost Victories*
embodied the essence of this Lost Cause, as do recent publications of ordinary
soldiers. The recent books reinforced the moral stance of German veterans
of the Eastern Front established in the decades before 1991. Paradoxically,
these post–Cold War books thrived despite two decades of German, Israeli,
and American scholarship that convincingly portrayed the Wehrmacht and the
Waffen-SS as part of the killing machine in the East.[17] Unfortunately, the scholarly writings remained confined to a small audience, whereas the readership of
the German authors (and their English-language spin-offs) was considerably
larger.

In keeping with the honorable character the veterans claim for the German
military, many of the German authors opened their accounts by stating they
would focus only on military operations. As military men unconnected with
the political world, a point all make early in their accounts, the authors see
no need to engage in the discussion of Nazi strategic aims. Manstein's opening
lines in *Lost Victories* immediately identifies the field marshal as a "*soldier*" who
will cover only the military part the war. To support his position, he quotes
internationally known British military figure, B. H. Liddell Hart, who wrote
that German generals lacked any political acumen; their talent emerged on the
battlefield. Clearly, Manstein was distancing himself from the crimes of the
regime, and at the same time elevating his professional image and safeguarding
his reputation.[18] Later Manstein wrote:

> I hope. . . . to have made it consistently clear that the decisive factor throughout
> [the war] was the self-sacrifice, valor and devotion to duty of the the German
> *fighting soldier*, combined with the ability of *commanders* at all levels . . . [19]

In this quote, Manstein reminded readers of the loyalty of the soldier and officers to Germany and their bravery in meeting their sacred obligation to defend the Fatherland. None should associate the field marshal with the crimes of the regime. Over four decades later, little had changed. The editor and translator of Bidermann's *In Deadly Combat* repeated the author's comments "in the original manuscript" that "it is of little value to restate many of the brutal historical occurrences that characterized and in some regard have come to represent World War II." The editor/translator recorded that Bidermann dealt only with frontline experiences. Similarly, in *Blood Red Snow*, Koschorrek rejected any need to open up the debate on whether soldiers in combat acted as heroes or murderers. He opted, instead, to "describe reality." As an ordinary soldier, he engaged that world and openly rejected any need to debate responsibility for the actions of others.[20]

These accounts dominated American thinking and knowledge of what has always seemed a distant yet, in some ways, fascinating conflict. Whereas the American public appropriately honors and commemorates the suffering of the six million European Jews killed by the Germans during World War Two, little if any sentiment has been or will be extended to the families of the eight million Red Army soldiers who died fighting the Wehrmacht and the Waffen-SS or the twenty-two million civilians killed by these military organizations and the killing squads, the Einsatzgruppen, that worked closely with the Wehrmacht.[21]

Only within the last decade have Russian-authored works or pieces that relied on Russian sources begun to appear. The end of the Cold War and the opening of Russian archives have led to more insight from the Soviet perspective.[22] Nevertheless, the German interpretation of the war still commands the attention of the U.S. public. With a forty-year head start and the persistent distrust of the Russians by Americans, conditioned by decades of anti-Soviet propaganda, the predominance of the German account hardly remains a mystery.

The German Narrative of the Eastern Front

In the course of fifty years of writing, the Germans placed the blame for the conflict and its defeat squarely upon the shoulders of Adolf Hitler and the Nazi party. The veterans and sympathetic authors wrote of the heroism of the German soldiers, the loyalty of the German military, and the honor these men earned. Their accounts consistently raised the issue of atrocities, but those committed by the Russians, not the Germans. Few could mistake the military for anything but an honorable institution staffed by brave and courageous men. Their actions could never be questioned and only the actions of their enemy in the East, the Russians, demanded closer scrutiny. The suffering of these men also created a pathos the U.S. public could admire and with which it could sympathize. The alliance between West Germany and the United States in defense of the West against their common enemy, the Soviet Union, made Americans sensitive to the claims in the German memoirs. In the eyes of the U.S. public, the Wehrmacht, its officers, and its men had achieved an almost unassailable status by the end of the Cold War.[23]

As we have seen, the former German generals created their own moral universe. By focusing almost exclusively on operational questions and avoiding any discussion of the political and strategic, they freed themselves from any responsibility to explain why they were serving a cause led by Adolf Hitler. Having done this, they proceeded to inject morality into their story by characterizing themselves and their subordinates as honorable men fighting for a Lost Cause in the East. They conjured up a black-and-white world, in which Hitler incorporated evil and they, virtue. However, even as they ascribed evil to the dictator, at the same time, they pictured him as bungling, inexperienced, often hesitant, and contrary. He embodied all that was infernal in the Nazi regime, but was at the same time blundering and ineffectual as a military commander.

Manstein, for example, contrasted the dictator, Hitler, who assumed all the vile characteristics of a tyrant, with the professionalism of officers, particularly those from the old honorable Prussian tradition, such as himself. Manstein wrote:

> On one side we had the conception of a dictator who believed in the power of his will not only to nail down his armies wherever they might be but even to hold the enemy at bay. The same dictator, however, who fought shy of risks because of their inherent threat to his prestige and who, for all his talents, lacked the groundwork of real military reality . . . On the other side stood the views of the military leaders who by virtue of their education and training still firmly believed that warfare was an art in which clarity of appreciation and boldness of decision constituted the essential elements. An art which could find success only in mobile operations, because it was only in these that the superiority of the German leadership and German fighting troops could attain full effect.[24]

The German officers used Hitler's interference and the seemingly inexhaustible supply of men and war materials on the Russian side to explain their defeat in the East. The consequences manifested themselves in the ruins of the German capital, Berlin, the bombed-out cities of Germany, the widespread suffering on the part of innocent civilians both in the bombing raids and in the expulsions that were carried out in the wake of the war as well as the inevitable Allied occupation of what remained of Germany by 1945.

Despite the valiant efforts of the professional officers, Hitler prevailed and Germany lost the war. The essence of this narrative has shaped the way those in the West have perceived the German military defeat in Russia. It enabled the German authors credibly to establish the innocence of the German army with regard to war crimes. It explained defeats in terms other than operative or tactical failure on the part of the professional officers. The political innocence of these German officers made them ideal pawns for the ruthless and criminal Nazi leaders. Their narrative of the war is thus more than just its history; it exculpates the military from any participation in a war of racial conquest and annihilation.

The more recent publications of the lower ranks of the officer corps and among the rank and file German soldiers in many respects reflect the views of their one-time superiors, although they mirror more the direct experience of combat, rather than the broader issues that faced the higher echelon officers. For example, in *Blood Red Snow* Günter K. Koschorrek commented on the intrusion of Hitler into the decision-making process of the Wehrmacht. Apprised of such situations by rumor rather than direct observation, Koschorrek wrote that Hitler's decision to force the 6th army to remain in the Stalingrad Pocket disillusioned many of the officers and soldiers who, in effect, faced a death sentence because of this command. Near the end of the war, Koschorrek and his fellow soldiers learn of Hitler's suicide. In a biting comment, he wrote, "We were shocked that the proud leader had decided to shirk his responsibilities in this cowardly way. But within a couple of hours he is forgotten: we have our own problems." At one point after a fall battle in 1944, Koschorrek also accused the Nazi leadership of cowardliness. The local party officials chose not to inform the civilian population of the need to leave their community, resulting in their having to wake up and face Red Army soldiers. Of course, the Nazis administrators, or "party bigwigs" as Koschorrek labeled them, had long since fled to safety.[25]

Bidermann argued that the German soldiers fought to defend their homeland and families and willingly gave up their lives to fulfill these tasks. None would take up arms for Hitler and his Nazi followers.[26] Carell enhances his account of the innocence and determination of the German soldiers with the photograph on the paperback edition of *Hitler Moves East* (Figure 9). It depicts two German soldiers in the heat of battle, both prone; one holding his rifle while the other is in the act of throwing his grenade at the enemy. As his book argues, the German soldiers fought with professionalism and dedication to their homeland and to the army. Koschorrek similarly argued that troopers

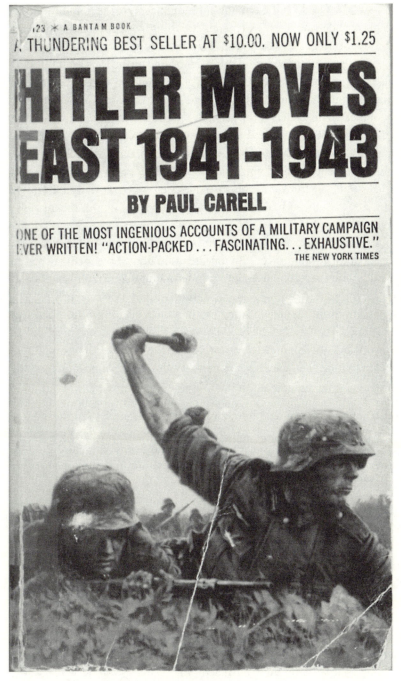

Figure 9. Cover of *Hitler Moves East 1941–1943*.

took up their arms to defend Germany and not to achieve the horrific aims of the Nazi party and its policies. The men in the frontlines opposed the Russians to protect themselves and their mates. A few men, notably his first lieutenant, fought for ideals above those sordid values embraced by the Nazi agents. Bidermann also wrote at great length on the death of his commanding officer, General Fritz Lindemann, for his involvement in the July 1944 assassination attempt on Adolf Hitler. In his sketch of the general, Bidermann reminded readers that the Nazis placed a 500,000 Reichsmark bounty for the capture of Lindemann, who was subsequently killed by the Gestapo. Bidermann praised Lindemann for his bravery, his battlefield ability, and his willingness to stand up against orders that needlessly threatened his men. He also severely criticized the political agents attached to German units and who earned the odious nickname of "politruk."[27]

At one point, Bidermann conflated the liquidation of the Jews, about which he claimed complete ignorance, with the fate of soldiers whose ideology placed them at odds with the National Socialists. Bidermann praised their bravery and deplored their mysterious disappearance at the hands of the Gestapo. Similarly, the slightest criticism of Hitler and the Nazis by a soldier could earn him a spot in the dreaded penal battalion if the pro-National Socialists officer were offended. Even bravery and ability would never overcome the offense. Koschorrek, too, commented that he had heard such rumors. With some disingenuousness, he wrote[28]

> I often got to hear that they have arrested someone and hauled them off to a concentration camp. People say that this is a labour camp, whose guards are SS men. They place dissidents and those who oppose the Third Reich in concentration camps. But no one knows anything for sure, as no one has ever come out.[29]

This narrative also provided the U.S. public with an account that made heroes of the German officers for their courage in challenging Hitler. It inflated their battlefield performance to the point where most citizens and even scholars argue that the German soldiers and armies stood far above their Allied counterparts. In fact, the general argument that the Russians won because of a superiority in numbers and material appeared in the United States in the work *Brute Force* by John Ellis.[30] Generals such as Guderian and Manstein still enjoy an immense readership, and books by Paul Carell continue to flood the market. Presses dedicated mostly or exclusively to the German military release book after book on the Wehrmacht, the Waffen-SS, and the Luftwaffe. These works embrace all aspects of the German narrative. In the post–Cold War, the narrative of the 1950s and 1960s still thrives.

Several of the men who penned memoirs expressed deep regret over the killing of the Jews. Yet, they all denied participation or even first-hand knowledge. Only Stahlberg raises the issue when he recounted his efforts to make Manstein aware of such activities. Stahlberg had learned that the SD and SS were killing Russian Jews. When informed, Manstein recoiled in shock and refused to believe that such actions were even possible. Stahlberg even claimed that his "great-grandfather Wilhelm Morris Hecksher had been a Jew." Of course Manstein knew well what was happening in his command area.[31]

These works also incorporated the theme of anti-Communism that appealed to an American public engaged in a Cold War with the Soviet Union. Manstein labeled the Communist rulers and their state as tyrannical and murderous. He betrayed his own true racial consciousness when he described the Soviet Union as an "Asiatic power" that ignored human life, a view seconded by Carell in *Hitler Moves East* and Mellenthin in *Panzer Battles*.[32]

Carell expanded on the theme of freedom in an intriguing story that has made its way through much of the literature. He related the tale of the German troops moving into the Caucasus Mountain range, where they encountered dispirited peoples full of hatred for their Communist rulers. They volunteered to join the German armies in their fight against the Communist state. As Carell characterized them:

> These freedom loving people believed that the hour of national independence had come for them. Stalin's wrath, when it struck them later, was terrible: all these tribes were expelled from their beautiful homeland and banished to Siberia.[33]

Such language cast the Soviet regime in an extremely hostile light and appealed to the U.S. public even into the 1990s.

Stahlberg, too, raised the theme of open rebellion. He characterized the Soviet rulers as bloodthirsty and tyrannical and suggested that the Russian people in states such Byelorussia would be easy to win over to the German side. This sentiment no doubt touched sympathetic cords in the United States, where many firmly believed that the Soviet rulers, through terror and use of arms, enslaved freedom-loving Russians.[34]

Anti-Communism also turned up in the writings of the men who fought in the trenches on the central front in Russia and on the steppe of Southern Russia. With respect to the battle for the Nikopol bridgehead in 1944, heavy machine gunner Koschorrek, in *Blood Red Snow*, commented that the six prisoners the Germans had captured in the search for information about Russian troop dispositions all exceeded fifty years of age, far too old for the battlefield. Only the fierce determination of the Communist commissar drove these men into battle. Bidermann explained at some length the role of the commissar. He wrote:

> ... spurred by threats, coercion, and patriotic appeals from the political commissar, the Russians threw themselves against us charging ranks. Motivated by abundant amounts of vodka and facing the angry muzzle of a commissar's pistol for any sign of hesitation, they threw themselves against us again and again.[35]

In his chapter, "The Enemy," Bidermann "observed mass numbers of desertions from the Soviet army early in the war." These deserters often joined the German army as laborers. Some came from the German POW camps far to the rear that Bidermann admitted were ghastly places. He, his men, and all in the Wehrmacht distinguished between the Russians who aided the Germans just for reasons of self-interest, namely survival, and those who "suffered starvation and forced labor under the regime of Stalin." These men detested the Bolsheviks and would do everything in their power to destroy them. Bidermann even picked up the Carell tale of "freedom-loving mountain peoples of the Caucasus" who fought for their Muslim religious beliefs against the atheistic Bolsheviks.[36]

Bidermann also reprinted letters to relatives from the Russians who joined the German side. These were among the personal items that belonged to General Lindemann that seemingly gave them credibility. In one, a Muslim wrote his family that they had endured years under "'the godless Soviets'" whom the Germans hopefully will vanquish and he asked Allah for the "strength" to achieve this goal. Another Hiwi (*Hilfswillige* or "volunteers"), as the Germans labeled them, praised the Germans for their "comradeship, equality and respect for one another, justice, and friendship." In one piece of correspondence Bidermann included, a wife roundly denounced her husband for reporting "for service." She and his children suffer for want of food and the local authorities ignore their plight.[37]

Bidermann recounted the decision of thousands of Russian prisoners to join the retreat of the German troops from Feodosia in the Crimea in 1942. In fact, these POWs marched away toward German lines without guards. Bidermann commented that the Russians knew too well they would suffer at the hands of Russian liberators for having surrendered to the Germans.[38] From such accounts, a reader could hardly tell that the Germans committed acts of aggression or that ordinary Russians expressed any sentiment except relief once the Wehrmacht occupied their communities.

Finally, Armin Scheiderbauer recounted the discovery of the Polish officers buried near Katyn in the Smolensk region. He encountered the International

Commission sent to investigate the uncovered bodies, apparently victims by the Soviet regime. He informed readers that the Nuremberg Trials of Nazi criminals ignored the slaughter of thousands of Polish officers and identified the Soviets as the responsible agent. In every sense of the word, the Soviet rulers were criminals. They killed Polish officers, oppressed their own people, and imprisoned them. These leaders even denied Russians freedom of religion. Few readers could sympathize with the Soviet government.[39]

Professionalism

The German officers also incorporated the theme of professionalism in their works. This theme is most apparent in the photographs that are used in almost all of these accounts. The photographs conveyed the sense of "being there" and the realistic portrayal of these men as they wished to be remembered. The visuals and their captions also gave the readers a quick and dramatic way to learn about these men and their actions in the Eastern Theater. Typically, the memoirs included photographs of the authors and fellow officers. The men always appeared in combat uniform and often in full dress outfits complete with medals, badges, and other insignia.[40]

In a typical example, the cover photo of Manstein's memoirs showed the field marshal in professional pose with the Knight's Iron Cross, a medal for exceptional service in combat, highlighted. Manstein, bereft of military cap, appeared with a serious and meditative demeanor. On the inside of the dust jacket, a profile of the field marshal, taken in 1944, showed a man with an air of confidence. These photos showed a man fully consistent with his own personal description in the memoirs and, of course, a truly dedicated professional. At one point in his personal recollections, Manstein wrote:

> The German generals of this war were the best-finished products of their pro-
> fession – anywhere. They could have been better if their outlook had been wider
> and their understanding deeper. *But if they had become philosophers they would
> have ceased to be soldiers.*[41]

The remarks reinforced the notion of political naiveté and dedication solely to the military tasks officers assume.

Several photographs following page 271 again addressed the theme of pro-
fessionalism. One shot depicts Manstein in deep concentration examining a situation map. The photo included several officers also concentrating on the details of the map and obviously sharing his concern over the disposition of forces. Behind them appeared a field tent that enhances the authenticity of the

shot while the caption read, "At H.Q. 50 Division in the Crimea." Clearly, the situation captured on the map grabbed the attention of Manstein. A subsequent photo showed the field marshal seated at a table in his command surrounded by his staff. All, including Manstein, were intent on the field map and the problems associated with the battlefield. Manstein fulfilled the expectation of his role as commander and one engaged in the demanding task of evaluating battlefield information.

In his tribute to Manstein, Stahlberg reinforced the man's professional character, one incapable of cruel, vindicative, or brutal acts. One of a series of photographs in Stahlberg's memoirs featured Manstein and his staff. They were studying maps in preparation for the last major German offensive of the war, Operation Zitadelle, the Kursk battle of July 1943. The conference occurred in a rail command car, which, Stahlberg reminded the readers, once belonged to Queen Victoria of Yugoslavia. Later in the book, Stahlberg commented on the professional demeanor of Manstein. Stahlberg wrote:

> The talk here was frank and open – the kind of talk we could not enjoy in Germany until the war was over. Freedom of speech at Manstein's table was a profoundly "Prussian" institution which held good that evening, too, . . .[42]

The quote illustrates Stahlberg's own admiration both for Manstein and the Prussian tradition he represented. It also divorced Manstein and his Prussian ethos from the Nazi party and its agents, who apparently deprived good Germans of the freedom of expression.

Siegfried Knappe went to great lengths to feature the professional character of the German soldier, one clearly at odds with the Nazi regime and the horror it inflicted on the Russian people. One photo of Knappe showed him in full dress uniform, including his medals. The caption listed these medals and the meritorious actions that justified the awards. In a more relaxed atmosphere, a series of photos depicted Knappe and his men at play and dining. These gave the reader a more human picture of Knappe and his buddies, men who were both officers and ordinary people with everyman's need for recreation and the fraternity of comrades breaking bread. Knappe returned to the professional ethos in a shot that captured him as part of the graduating class at the Kriegsschule *Potsdam* in 1942. The accompanying text informed the reader that Knappe and his fellow students carefully studied key battles and tactics from the glorious Prussian past, as they attempted to master the art of war and decision making. Knappe also noted that the General Staff, to which young officers aspired, was reserved for the best and the brightest in the Wehrmacht.[43]

Paul Carell, too, praised German officers for their professionalism. He wrote at some length on Guderian's operation that led to the seizure of Roslavl during

Barbarossa and on his challenge to Adolf Hitler on the decision to abandon the drive on Moscow and turn south toward Kiev. Guderian explained in forceful and professional terms why the thrust toward Moscow should continue. Carell inserted several pictures of Guderian that included one showing the colonel general about to board a command car. Guderian's confident smile matched the smart uniform with the attached Knight's Cross. Just as important, the picture was above one of ill-clad Soviet prisoners with grim looks and dirty uniforms. The contrast between the professionalism of the victorious Guderian and the defeatism of the Soviet POWs would immediately catch a reader's attention.[44]

Family, Christianity, and Sacrifice

The themes of family, Christianity, and sacrifice, often introduced in the memoirs of these German authors, create an entirely different image of these men. Their professional ethos always remained a primary focus, but more personal factors, such as humanity, morality, and personality, are also emphasized in their writings. This emphasis certainly makes the officers more attractive in the eyes of the reader and highlights the almost completely negative effect made when they describe the Russian enemy, who is cast in anonymous, racial terms. The German authors take pains to cast themselves in the role of ordinary people with concerns common to all men in war.

Shared experiences included personal loss of family members, always a painful experience. The death of Manstein's son, Gero, provides a prime example of family loss. He died on the Northern Front near Lake Ilmen, where he was serving with the 18th Infantry Division. Manstein goes into great length to describe his own suffering and that of his family over the death of their son. Manstein writes of his son's military aspirations in the context of the Prussian military traditions. For Gero, Manstein recalled, duty to fatherland stood out as the chief attraction of military life. The son clearly adopted the father's self-proclaimed political naiveté and his commitment to fight for Germany, not for any political party, including the Nazis. Manstein referred to his son as a "young aristocrat" and an honorable person whose qualities made him an anathema to the Nazi party.[45] For Manstein,

> It was his [Gero's] heritage to come from a long line of soldiers; built by the very fact of being an ardent German soldier. He was at once a gentleman in the truest sense of the word – a gentleman and a Christian.[46]

Manstein described his son as "particularly lovable – serious, thoughtful, but always happy." Manstein fully endorsed his son's military aspirations. For "it was in his blood to become a regular German officer – to be a trainer of German youth and to be at its head in times of stress." Manstein wrote of his son's funeral and the words of Pastor Kruger, who presided over the ceremony at the son's grave. Those present "laid his soul in God's hands." Manstein also noted that Gero joined many other sons of German mothers who died in the war, thereby linking the field marshal's personal tragedy with the nation as a whole.[47]

Knappe, like Manstein, also suffered personal loss because of the war. His brother died from wounds received in combat. Knappe commented that his brother, Fritz, died from a wound so severe that only massive doses of morphine would even slightly diminish the agony. In fact, the morphine left Fritz speechless. Knappe remembered that Fritz was "always proud of me and my accomplishments, and now he was going to die before he had real chance to achieve any on his own." The war had robbed Fritz of his life and his future. Knappe revealed his own bitterness toward a conflict that inflicted such suffering in young men and their families. In fact, the book cover for Knappe's work shows him in an innocent pose holding a dog, hardly the stuff of tough soldiers who participated in the deadliest war in history.[48]

Knappe included a 1942 photo of Fritz's Christian grave surrounded by flowers, commemorations sent by family and friends. The sight served as a reminder of the sacrifice made by all in war. Fritz's passing made his grieving mother even more worried over the fate of Knappe, her last son. Ultimately, the Nazi party was the source of this pain. In fact, the Nazis victimized Knappe, his brother, and his family as brutally as any participant in the war.[49]

Knappe captured another family moment in both text and photos of his wife, Lilo. She and Knappe, in civilian clothes, appeared in a community setting. In another shot, they enjoy a brief respite from a vigorous swim and in a third they posed for a photograph during their wedding reception. The text accompany this last shot reminded the reader that the two married in a "civilian ceremony and then in a church ceremony." Clearly, the authors wanted to stress their identity as committed Christians dedicated to the creed's sacred ideals. Knappe again raised the theme of religion as well as history and culture. He remarked that the church where the wedding took place served as the site for Martin Luther's first sermon, hosted Richard Wagner's baptism, and welcomed Johann Sebastian Bach as its organist. Knappe linked his wedding to Germany's glorious historic past rather than to the contemporary Germany of the 1940s, a very different and sinister place. One last picture caught Knappe flanked by his mother and new wife as he prepared to make the long journey back to the Eastern Front. Knappe commented that his loved ones experienced great sadness at this moment because they realized this parting could mark their last time together.[50]

Knappe wrote of the need to hide the horror he encountered on the Eastern Front from his beautiful wife. In no way did he want Lilo to learn of the "killing and dying" so common on the frontlines. In one poignant sentence, he declared:

> I did not want her to know about the dehumanizing things I had seen during the endless trek across a nation where people were forced to live almost as animals. Writing these letters also helped me to keep a balanced perspective: there is such a thing as beauty to be found in even the most gruesome of circumstances.[51]

Stahlberg, too, addressed the themes of family, Christianity, and sacrifice. One telling pre-war photo in his memoirs showed his four cousins, his grandmother, and his uncle, Hans von Wedermeyer. Together, the family represented the best of German society. The relatives had gathered for a confirmation ceremony of the four cousins. Stahlberg noted that the famous religious dissenter, Dietrich Bonhoeffer, whom the Nazis subsequently murdered, presided. The happiness of familial gathering, however, eventually vanished under the impact of the terrible war. The young men, shown in a photo, all died from combat wounds in various battles, while the uncle, Wedermeyer, fell at Stalingrad. Stahlberg's grandmother died "when the Russians overran her estate." The family buried the four cousins in the church cemetery that had served as the resting place for the Stahlbergs for 700 years. Even in death, the family ties to its traditional past persisted. The photo and its aftermath convey, as Stahlberg wanted, a picture of a close, traditional, religious family destroyed by the twin evils of Nazism and Communism in a brutal war into which they had been drawn as innocent protagonists.[52]

Stahlberg also presented the motherly and wifely side of the war experience. A photo of a kind, middle-aged woman, Stahlberg's mother, appeared in the photographic section of the *Bounden Duty*. She bore a sad look, as if she knew the terrible things that were to befall her family and friends because of the war. The caption read that she belonged to the Red Cross, one of the world's leading humanitarian organizations. The Red Cross stood in direct antithesis to the Nazi party. Stahlberg describes her as "truly, the daughter of a Pomeranian Pietist Prussian" and clearly identified her with a powerful religious tradition.[53]

Stahlberg also describes his mother's musical ability and, in the process, establishes a powerful tie with Germany's pre-Nazi past. He wrote glowingly of his mother's rendition of Beethoven's *Moonlight Sonata* and recalled her performing famous pieces by Brahms and Bach, including the St. Matthew/St. John Chorale. This musical theme appeared again when Stahlberg related his true aspiration to become a concert violinist as witnessed in a photo of Stahlberg holding his violin. Whether through his almost saintly mother or through his own longing for music, Stahlberg fashioned an image wholly at odds with the regime he served. The Nazis created a nightmare, while Stahlberg longed for the serenity of an artist's life, while his mother intended only to aid and heal the injured. In another ironic twist, the book cover shows the Nazi symbol broken by the subtitle of Stahlberg's book, suggesting his antipathy toward the regime, whereas the title, *Bounden Duty*, demonstrates his loyalty to Germany and the army.[54]

Armin Scheiderbauer and his family, too, dedicated much of their lives to good causes. The prologue to *Adventures in My Youth* (regrettably, the title seems to smack of boy scouting rather than the most destructive war in the history of the world) placed the author and his family firmly in the Christian tradition. The father served as a Protestant minister and continued to do so in the army of World War Two. Religion shaped every dimension of the son's life. He served the church in various capacities while growing up in Thuringia and fondly remembered the family celebrating specials events such as Reformation Day. As he wrote, Scheiderbauer learned from these experiences to use "Christian virtues" in his everyday life, hardly the stuff of an irresponsible man or soldier. Ironically, the book cover shows soldiers firing at the enemy from a trench with the obvious intent to kill, very much out of the Christian tradition (Figure 8).[55]

The father suffered because of his opposition to Nazi intrusion into religious beliefs. The Nazis and his congregation forced him out of the parish. Yet, the father still joined the Wehrmacht as an officer. "To him the life of an officer represented values similar to those of the church: duty to fatherland; a commitment to order and decency in society and responsibility for subordinates." The father apparently shared none of the ideas that animated Nazi party members and viewed his service in the military as a spiritually and patriotically fulfilling experience. In fact, the father took the family to Potsdam, the epicenter of the Prussian military tradition, while Scheiderbauer was still at home. The modest buildings and church and *Sans Souci*, the seasonal residence for Prussian monarchs, demonstrated to the family the sense of proportion that summed up the Prussian experience. The Nazi leadership, by contrast, had virtually no sense of proportion and entertained notions of world conquest that brought only misery to the German people.[56]

Later, while serving on the Eastern Front, he sent his parents a letter of grateful thanks for his Christian rearing. In the midst of such travail, Scheiderbauer wrote that he dearly appreciated the gift of the New Testament given to him by his father. The Psalm and verse the father used as dedication gave the son assurances that he would survive the many battles ahead of him.

Across decades, from one memoir to the next, the German authors depicted Christian principles as guidelines for many Wehrmacht soldiers and officers. If one only had access to these sources, then the charges accurately leveled against the Wehrmacht would be inconceivable.[57]

Civilian Encounters

German veterans frequently discussed their encounters with Russian civilians. To the alleged surprise of the German officers and rank and file, civilians rushed forward when Wehrmacht units marched through Russian villages "liberated" from Communist rule. Stahlberg recounted with pride that as his regiment moved closer to the Soviet capital, it encountered "small reception committees" from nearby villages. Often "young girls in white dresses, handed us flowers and presented bread and salt, the time honored symbols of good luck and welcome." A photo in Carell's *Hitler Moves East* depicts a young woman, plainly dressed with a scarf around her head, giving water to a thirsty German soldier. The man and his mates had stopped for a rest outside of Rzhev, just northwest of Moscow.[58]

In a poignant story, Koschorrek tells of the close friendship he and his mates had with a young Russian woman, Katya, while they were in the Ukrainian village of Dnyeprovka. The men thought of her as their "guardian angel." She and her mother "hosted" them while their unit was stationed in the area. Koschorrek flatly stated that Katya was "definitely off limits." She cleaned their rooms, made the beds, and always had a warm smile for the men. They, in turn, gave her chocolate, clothing, socks for her mother, and other needed items. She actually cried when the men went off on a mission, knowing well that the journey could mean their deaths. She placed small gifts on their beds and crosses for those who died in battle. Katya and her mother also prepared meals for the men upon their return from the front. Except for the gruesome fighting, the situation almost seemed idyllic! Paradoxically, the book cover shows a battle scene overwhelmed by destruction, hardly on keeping with such tranquil scenes (Figure 9). Of course, when Koschorrek and his men resumed their long retreat back to Germany, they worried over her fate once the Red Army moved into the village.[59]

Scheiderbauer provided the reader a case of similar compassion. Scheiderbauer and his men were following orders to raze the building on one side of a street for military purposes. For Scheiderbauer, the experience proved unsettling because he and his men had yet to engage in such destruction. As they prepared to burn the buildings, "an absolutely ancient man" approached the young officer and pleaded with him to spare one of the houses. As the "old man" explained, he had lived there his entire life and intended to die in his home. Scheiderbauer faced the choice of obeying orders or showing humanity to the old man. To the joy of his men, he left the house standing.[60]

Similarly, during a lull in the fighting, Scheiderbauer and his superior, *Hauptmann* Schneider, stopped to visit a Catholic church in a Lithuanian community. The priest invited them to lunch with him. Afterward, the *Hauptmann* was engaged in the charge of collecting the able men in the village for transport to the rear. The German command used this practice to prevent the Red Army from conscripting them into its ranks. The priest pleaded with the *Hauptmann* to release one of the young men who had served in the Red Army against his own wishes and had just married one of the local young women. Clearly outside the scope of his command, Schneider, with Scheiderbauer agreeing, allowed the groom to rejoin his wife. Scheiderbauer concluded the story with his discovery of a piano in the local chemist's house. As he related: "like a thirsty man coming to water, I sat down and played once again for the first time in months." According to these accounts, the German officers showed kindness to the Russian civilians whenever possible. The officers and soldiers came to Russia to fight the Bolsheviks, not to inflict suffering upon a civilian population that had endured the terror of communist rule for twenty or more years.[61]

Such kindness and compassion toward Russians seemed almost universal in these accounts. Bidermann told of his stay with a "Tartar family" in the Crimea. He and his men learned that the Tartars felt only bitterness toward the Soviets. The Germans exchanged foodstuffs with their host family and even celebrated the birth of a baby with the mother and friends. A German medic provided medical supplies and Bidermann's men gave her "sweets." Bidermann also commented on the frequent call to prayers made by the local Muslim Imam. Such incidents appeared throughout Bidermann's memoirs.[62] Tales such as Bidermann's, Scheiderbauer's, and others demonstrated to a reader that the German soldiers on the whole remained decent, honorable men concerned for the safety of the Russians as much as for their own mates. These depictions create an image of the Germans in Russia that contrasted sharply with portrayals of the SS and SD and other Nazi sympathizers. The Bolsheviks and their followers emerged as the cause of most of the suffering of the Russian people both before and during the war. The German officers and soldiers often attempted to alleviate their suffering and, where possible, restore religious freedom. The cover for Bidermann's work shows him in full dress uniform with a typical calm photographic look. In the background are German soldiers marching past a damaged building, suggesting the harshness of war but hardly the genocidal nature of the conflict. With Bidermann's professional poses above the battleground, a reader would never link him to the war's cruelty.

The religious theme is as important in occupied territory in these memoirs as it is on the home front. The Germans, as Christians, many of these officers wrote, held no animus toward the Russian Orthodox faith and often expressed dismay over the Communist banning of religious expression. Von Luck provided a rich description of Russians flocking to the cathedral in Smolensk after the Germans seized the city from the Red Army. The cathedral had escaped damage during the battle for the city and now acted as a beacon to former worshippers.[63] Luck related:

> I followed the women and the old men as I entered the cathedral and was deeply impressed by its beauty. It looked intact. The altar was adorned, burning candles and many icons richly embellished with gold bathed the interior in a festive light. As I went to the altar with my companions an old man, poorly dressed and with a flowing beard, spoke to me in a broken German.[64]

The holy man told Luck "you have liberated our city." He asked Luck, "May I say a first mass in this cathedral?" Of course, Luck urged him to go forward with the services. Upon returning to the Cathedral the next day, Luck saw a breathtaking sight: The city center was bursting with people, all proceeding at a slow pace toward the reclaimed church. Luck and his men remained inconspicuous and allowed the procession to move on its way.[65] Clearly moved by the experience, Luck wrote:

> The people fell on their knees and prayed. All had tears in their eyes. For them it was the first mass for more than twenty years. My companions and I were deeply moved. How deep must one's faith have been for these poor people, oppressed people, no ideology, no compulsion or terror had been able to take it from them. It was an experience I shall never forget.[66]

The Wehrmacht, it is suggested, not the Nazi regime, freed the Russians from their communist tyrants and restored their religious community. The army operated in a world distinct from the political sphere, and the culprits for the calamities that had befallen and would befall the Russian people ruled this political sphere, namely the Nazi and the Communist parties. The visuals in Luck's book, as in all such memoirs, complement the professional character of the German soldier. The cover includes two photos, one of German infantry marching to the front, whereas in another Field Marshal Rommel, the clean German commander who never served in the East, apparently is about to open a map while in the background is his staff vehicle. Inside, one photograph captures Luck holding a folder during the battle for Normandy, pensively looking ahead in a professional manner. Another photo depicts a contemporary von Luck in a business suit with a smile, every bit the cultured man, and hardly in class with Nazis such as Himmler. Such depictions never even hint at the ghastly nature of the war.

Carell, too, captured the Smolensk experience, emphasizing visuals rather than just text. He used a dramatic photo of what may have been the first mass in the Smolensk Cathedral. It showed overwhelmingly women with their traditional head covers and their children kneeling during the service. A very old woman, clutching a cane and holding the ornate railing to steady herself, stood near the altar. The audience conveyed a sense of relief at being in church after such a long absence. In the background of the church stood two Wehrmacht soldiers observing the worshippers. The caption read:

> The golden dome cathedral of Smolensk was packed when the German frontline-troops allowed an old Russian priest to hold the first divine service.[67]

Carell is always careful to distinguish the regular Wehrmacht troops from the rear area non-army units that conducted the atrocities. Stahlberg also emphasized that the SD and the SS had the sole responsibility for the murdering of civilians and Russian Jews. He declared that "while we, the soldiers, were permitted to get ourselves shot at the front, the SS went about its horrifying business behind our backs."[68] The Wehrmacht faced the dangers and liberated the Russian people, while the civilian administration ruthlessly exploited the Russians behind the frontlines.

The Battlefield

If the German accounts underscore benign and even generous behavior in victory, they stress the agony of defeat in such a way as to underscore the Lost Cause approach. One theme is the implacable courage of the German soldier even when faced with the seemingly inexhaustible supply of men and war materials possessed by the Red Army. German infantry fought against increasingly poor odds that made ultimate victory impossible. Still, they persisted in the trenches, even the cynical Koschorrek. Koschorrek and his buddies held defensive positions west of the Stalingrad Pocket. Well aware of the plight of the soldiers in the city, the men knew that they must keep the Russians from moving into German-held territory beyond the Don River. The Russians attack them with overwhelming numerical superiority. Koschorrek's group fired machine guns, carbines, anything that threw metal at the Russians. Russian soldiers died in large numbers and the Soviet charge came to a grinding halt.[69]

Bidermann recounted the successful defense of German positions in the Crimea in 1942. The Russians assaulted his unit "with overwhelming strength." Bidermann and his men persevered. Bidermann's unit also repeatedly faced overwhelming odds. In the winter of 1943, he and his men faced a massive Soviet attack on the Northern Front near Leningrad. The Bolsheviks frequently broke through the "thinly" defended German lines. Tanks, artillery, and hordes of "Bolsheviks" pressed down on the German troops. Eventually the Germans contained the attack at great sacrifice and in a frigid environment. As Bidermann wrote: Men "from East Prussia, the Rhineland, Bavaria, the Pfalz, Baden, and Würtlemberg" struggled against daunting odds. In the wake of the fighting, the men listened to the cries of the wounded and the dying. The German soldier faced superhuman challenges in what would become a losing, if valiantly fought, war. Such actions punctuated all the accounts of the Germans who spent the war in the front lines.[70]

The poor odds against the Germans only grew as the war progressed and the tide turned against the Wehrmacht. The men suffered severe shortages as the war moved away from Leningrad, Moscow, and Stalingrad and toward Central Europe. Bidermann and his men, retreating from Russia into Lithuania in the last few months of the war, turned to horsemeat to supplement their meager diet. Retreat replaced advance and despite heroic efforts on the part of the soldiers, Germany faced an impossible situation by 1945.[71]

Retreat brought its own agony. Along with the dangers of combat, the prospect of capture terrified the German soldier. Scheiderbauer, Koschorrek, and Bidermann all expressed great fear of captivity and the fate Russians dealt out to POWs. "Surrender" for someone such as Bidermann meant certain death. Koschorrek recorded his first-hand encounters with mutilated German bodies that convinced him that death was far preferable to capture. The suffering during retreat extended to each and every man. On the flight to the Bug River, Kosckorrek described the personal trauma he suffered. Ill-fitting boots turned his feet into bloody masses and the pain became almost unbearable. He had to stay on his feet since to abandon the retreat would have led to his capture. He wrote that he could still hear the Russian "Hurrah" as they came relentlessly on his heels. Those who failed to keep pace usually suffered death either by shootings or bayoneting. The few who asked the Russians "for mercy" instead were greeted with laughter before their slaughter. In fact, Koschorrek bitterly wrote that the Red Army soldiers "hacked to death" the "Russian women and children" who had helped the Germans merely to "survive."[72]

Agony awaited even those who actually survived capture. In June 1944, the Red Army launched a massive strike against the German Army Group center and virtually destroyed it. Hundreds of thousands of German soldiers died or went into captivity. As Bidermann informed his readers:

> Many died from thirst and exhaustion on the long journey or, unable to continue due to wounds or sickness, had been summarily shot where they collapsed during the endless march.[73]

Those who made it to the camps then faced a parade through Red Square before visiting Allied dignitaries and the Moscow population. In many cases, the German captives' digestive systems failed during the parade and "acute diarrhea . . . weaken[ed] them to an even greater extent."[74]

Death of comrades inevitably confronted these men. In the midst of the Russian *Bagration* offensive in June 1944, Scheiderbauer carried the dead body of Captain Muller to the regimental command post. Muller's face displayed total exhaustion. Then, Scheiderbauer and two regimental "runners" gave Muller a Christian burial near the command post. After saying the "Our Father," "the group stood in silence for a fallen comrade. In a visual demonstration of lost comrades, Bidermann included a photo of a staff meeting in the summer of 1943. Of the four men identified, three died in action and one at the hands of the Gestapo. At one point, the emotion of a comrade's death overwhelmed Bidermann, who, "for the first time" actually "wept at the loss of an especially close friend."[75]

In a grim description of the death of comrades on a "godforsaken bridgehead outside the Stalingrad Pocket," Koschorrek reminded readers of the true horror of dying on the battlefield. A Russian T-34 tank scored a hit on the men of a German anti-tank crew. Koschorrek told his readers that such deaths resulted in far more than a dead body bent over from a single wound. The Russian tanks had literally blown apart the German soldiers. The remnants of their bodies appeared "as individual lumps of flesh from arms, legs and buttocks, and in one instance, from a head. . . . "[76]

As disturbing for a reader were accounts of the wounded German soldiers. Bidermann described the hospital shelter for the men injured in combat. Their conditions ranged from broken bones to punctured lungs and cut arteries. They lie down:

> in filthy, torn uniforms, wrapped with blood-soaked bandages, as they filled the air with a confusing mixture of screams, groans, whimpers, and stony silence as they awaited their journey to an unknown destination.[77]

Certainly men ended up with a wooden cross rather than the prestigious Knight's Cross. Many lived on to endure the physical and mental consequences of their wounds.[78]

Koschorrek and Bidermann also showed pity and sympathy for the Russians. Koschorrek wrote that the dead bodies of Russian soldiers differed from their German counterparts only in the uniforms they wore. He went on to remark "Poor devils – most of them have faces as young as ours." Bidermann asked the question: "Must I kill today in order to save my own life and the lives of my comrades?" At another point, he pulled a severely wounded Russian soldier from "beneath layers of dirt and dust." Bidermann and his comrade carried the wounded Russian to a medical field facility for treatment. Despite the bitter fighting, German soldiers still showed kindness toward their enemy.[79]

These various depictions of the Eastern Front created and sustained a benign image of the Wehrmacht on the Eastern Front. Military genius could never overcome political power and certain victories slipped away in the hands of an amateur, Adolf Hitler. His policies led Germany into defeat and ruin. From field marshal to machine gunners, the German military could see the folly of Hitler's decisions and the policies of the Nazi party. Yet, they followed their calls to duty and loyalty to the German state and fought fiercely in a losing cause. They entered the war as professionals and conducted their battles and campaigns as professionals. Discipline and honor ruled their lives.

They expressed disdain for the Nazis and even utter indifference to Hitler's death near the end of the war. They concentrated their energies on the battlefields, saving their comrades and, when possible, defeating the Red Army. The political agents inserted into the Wehrmacht earned the contempt of the soldiers, especially after the tide turned against Germany. For these men, regardless of their rank, war commanded their attention and little else. They were shocked to learn of the Holocaust, a horror they never encountered on the frontlines. They apparently suspected poor treatment of civilians by the SD and SS and some knew of the fate awaiting POWs. Some clearly did not or argued the suffering of POWs resulted from the inadequately prepared camps, given that no one anticipated the numbers of Russians captured or who surrendered.

Just as importantly, these men, in their own accounts, remained true to their nobility of spirit. They followed their Christian principles, whether in restoring religious freedom to a people crushed by an atheistic, Bolshevik state, or living up to their principles in dealing with priests and civilians. They also showed a moral conscience in dealing with Russian soldiers and expressed sympathy with their Russian counterparts. When possible, the officers provided medical attention and shared their food. As Christians, moral men, and honorable soldiers they felt revulsion over the atrocities they claimed the Russians inflicted on Germans soldiers and the mutilation of dead German soldiers and officers.

They showed kindness toward civilians who "hosted" them during the military campaigns. They celebrated the birth of Russian children, gave the mothers chocolates, and provided medical supplies to ensure the health of mother and child. They shared food and supplies with the families in whose houses the Germans took up temporary residences. They developed warm personal relationships with their hosts and desperately worried about their fates once the Wehrmacht soldiers moved on and the Red Army men replaced them.

As fighting men, they endured much on the battlefields of Russia, Eastern Europe, and, finally, Germany proper. They saw comrades die ghastly deaths and suffer hideous wounds. They bore unimaginable conditions in Russian, from bitter cold to searing heat and knee-deep mud. They fought for days with no sleep, little food, and often with no chance of victory. They willingly sacrificed their lives to save their mates and struggled against overwhelming Soviet troops and war materiel in the vain hope of staving off defeat and saving the fatherland, their communities, and their families.

These accounts of the war and the actions of the German soldiers served as the main sources for understanding the war in the East. They influenced documentaries, gurus who built careers on writing of the German military for popular audiences, re-enactor groups that would flourish from the 1980s onward, and Internet participants who prospered on the new technologies of the 1990s. Of course, as the previous chapters made clear, the claims of these men conflicted with the realities of a war in which millions of Russian Jews died, as well as eight million Russian soldiers, and an appalling 22 million civilians, many of them women and children. The men who wrote these accounts remembered a war no Russian would recognize, yet the majority of Americans came to know almost first-hand. They prepared the way not only for the myth of the clean Wehrmacht, but also for a more recently emerging narrative of the Germans as victims.

6   The Gurus

Gurus are authors who are popular among the readers who romanticize the German army and, in particular, the Waffen-SS. Most of them have published a phenomenal number of books (although many are largely picture books). The gurus are authors who are most frequently mentioned in the Internet chatrooms, where romancers keep up a constant dialogue about their favorite German units or battles. They also appear in book catalogs, along with more mainstream scholars, and especially on the Internet websites of the giant booksellers such as Amazon.com or Barnes and Noble. Such sites also include praiseworthy comments about the books and their authors from visitors who provide brief reviews. This exposure raises their profile enormously and legitimizes them at the same time.

These authors combine a careful attention to detail and authenticity when it comes to battles, dates, uniforms, and decorations, with either a slanted or revisionist historical context – or none at all – imbedded in an heroic ethos. They also include in their texts large numbers of photos – of units, of combat scenes, and of many individuals, so that the illustrations have a kind of iconographic effect. The same is true for the terminology; German military ranks, vehicle names, and military decorations, which are always given in the original language and which also have a totemic value. The titles are often also romantically charged: *Lions of Flanders, Nordic Warriors, Knights of Steel, Riding East,* to name just a few. The striking cover art is invariably a romanticized view of men in heroic stances, which establishes for the reader at the outset the tone of the book, one that honors these men and never even engages the debate about the true horror that characterized the war in the East.

The gurus occupy a spectrum ranging from the racial, anti-Semitic revisionist right to the middle of the political spectrum, although in any given case there are shifts, depending on the type of publication. Many of them try to be apolitical, which helps them avoid an historical interpretive context for their books. But all of them give a heavy romantic emphasis to their writings, which accounts for their widespread appeal. In some cases, as their appeal grows, they graduate up the scale of publishing importance from self-publishing to the myriad small presses, which often seem to be concentrated in small towns in the eastern part of the United States, such as Schiffer, Bibliophile Legion Books, Merriam Press; to the top, particularly to the Fedorowicz publishing house in Winnipeg, Manitoba, which turns out scores of books dealing with the German army and related units during World War Two. To be published through Fedorowicz is to have arrived. Now and then, the work of one or another guru manages also to appear as a History Book Club selection or in the offerings of a mass distributor such as Ballantine or Bantam books. This ensures respectability, legitimacy, and a mass audience.

The gurus claim to be writing either "objective, factual" history or revisionist history. In reality, they are not writing history at all, for this would require an interpretive framework; rather, they are creating the basis for a fictional community, which they bid the reader to enter. It is a kind of historical community – but safe, because it lies in the past. In this sense, it resembles the world of the nineteenth-century romantic writers who conjured up the age of medieval chivalry to put the ruthless competition of their age in a safe context. In the gurus' community, the unit pictures are of *your* unit. The many photos of individuals with short bios are of *your* buddies. The uniforms and decorations are *your* accoutrements. The professional values of these men – courage, honor, loyalty, and patriotism – are *your* values.

The favorite outfit of the gurus is the Waffen-SS. The armed SS, which eventually consisted of thirty-seven divisions and nearly a million men, fought alongside the regular German army, yet operated under the control of Heinrich Himmler. They were better trained and armed than the regular army, subject to much more Nazi ideological training, and were used by Hitler as a kind of "fire brigade," especially in the East, to deal with crucial situations. This explains why the Waffen-SS had more dramatic victories, harrowing escapes, and a higher level of losses than the Wehrmacht itself – grist for the mill of the "romancers." What the romancers fail to mention, however, is the brutality of the Waffen-SS and that nearly 50,000 of its members functioned as concentration camp guards during the war. In fact, the Waffen-SS had its very origins in part in camp guard units. Theodore Eicke, who would command the Waffen-SS "Totenkopf" division, first commanded the Dachau camp and worked out the manual for guards on how to treat prisoners – a manual that became standard at all camps. Eicke was later inspector of the camp system. During the war, his units committed a number of war crimes, including the murder of 100 British prisoners of war in France in 1940. No wonder the gurus stay away from this information; it would dispel the aura of heroism, sacrifice, virtue, and ultimate tragedy that infuses their work.[1]

One important guru is Mark Yerger, a prolific writer – or at least publisher – of material on the Waffen-SS. He has published eleven books to date, most of them through Schiffer Publications, a house that specializes, among other things, in World War Two German military themes. The gurus, Yerger included, have tried over the years to cultivate ties – indeed friendships – with former Waffen-SS officers, while they were still alive, who inspired them and funneled material to them. His *Waffen-SS Commanders* volume II has a foreword by Otto Baum, former commander of "Das Reich," "Goetz von Berlichingen," and "Reichsfuehrer-SS" divisions and holder of the Knight's Cross with Oak Leaves and Swords. Baum has been friends with Yerger for many years and writes in the foreword: "As little as the German Wehrmacht was a criminal organization, as is partly maintained today, so little was also the Waffen-SS. Nothing will change this, neither the foolish and unfair treatment at Nuremberg nor the many false or enflamed representations from the time following the war that continue to the present."[2]

Yerger also has his heroes. One is Otto Kumm, about whom he has written a short biography and about whom he says: "Kumm's leadership of Regiment "Der Fuehrer" during the Rshew battles was both incredible as well as legendary."[3] Another is Otto Weidinger, also commander of the regiment "Der Fuehrer," about whom he says "Otto Weidinger was a much admired and trusted friend, possessing the most honorable character of anyone I've known."[4] These men also opened the door to Yerger to get material from many other Waffen-SS veterans, and influenced him clearly in a direction away from objectivity.

The relationship clearly works the other way around as well. Occasionally, American presses will bring out in English translation books written by former Waffen-SS commanders in German. Schiffer, for example, issued a translation of Otto Weidinger's *Comrades to the End*, the history of his own unit, the 4th SS Panzer-Grenadier Regiment "Der Fuehrer."[5] Weidinger is also one of Yerger's heroes. Weidinger, incidentally, was present during the war at the notorious massacre by the Waffen-SS at Oradour-sur-Glane in June 1944, and in 1985 wrote an article defending the conduct of the Waffen-SS and placing much of the blame on the Communist maquis resistance, whom he castigates for murdering German soldiers at nearby Tulle.[6]

The closest Yerger comes to being an historian is in his two volumes on Waffen-SS commanders. He has done assiduous research in archives in several countries, including the Bundesarchiv in Berlin, the Czech military archives in Prague (Vojensky Historicki Archiv), the Berlin Document Center, the Imperial War Museum in London, and the National Archives in Washington. Much of the biographical material that he uses comes from the SS personnel files in the Berlin Document Center. He has also had access to the private archives of a number of individuals, some writers like himself, and organizations, including several Waffen-SS veterans groups (*Truppenkameradschaften*). He also lists thirty-five names of people he interviewed, corresponded with, or whose papers he examined. In addition, he has consulted a wide range of secondary literature.

He is a stickler for detail and has mastered SS ranks, titles, decorations, and the short biographies of his subjects. Far from writing a prosopographical study with his extensive primary materials, he seems mainly interested in recording the military exploits of the Waffen-SS commanders and the medals they won for these exploits. Where available, he quotes at length from the letters of superiors nominating these men for their decorations. The book is full of pictures of these men, often being decorated by Hitler and, where available, pictures of the document signed by Hitler awarding them the medals or recording their promotions. These pictures and documents, as well as the commendations themselves, have an iconographical effect.

Only now and then does Yerger, somewhat reluctantly, one suspects, put these men in any political or ideological context. If his biographical sketches are to be complete, he must point out, for example, that one or another commander had his start in the SD, or Gestapo, or in the occupation forces during the war. Of Friedrich-Wilhelm Krüger, who was Higher SS and police leader in the General Government, Yerger says only that "His brutality and influence on the Polish people [!] resulted in an assassination attempt on his life while driving to his office on April 20, 1943."[7] In the case of Dr. Gustav Krukenberg, he notes that he led an anti-partisan detachment under Higher SS and Police Leader, Friedrich Jeckeln, but does not point out that Jeckeln was largely responsible for the massacre at Babi Yar outside of Kiev.[8] He also slips information into a more harmless setting, as with Kurt Meyer, who was "tried after the war for the killing of Canadian prisoners by his command during the Caen fighting. Meyer's death sentence was commuted and he was released . . . His memoirs, 'Grenadiers,' is a tribute to the soldiers of his various commands and reveals the dash, élan and bravery of their commander."[9]

As for his other publications, they are very long on pictures and very short on text. His "biography" of Otto Weidinger has only nineteen pages of text out of ninety-six pages total. Similar are his studies of Otto Kumm and Ernst August Krag. The makeup of these books, ranging from the many pictures to the hagiographic description of the men's careers to the titles and the cover art all create, in total, an iconographic package that imbeds the subject not in an interpretive historical framework but in a romanticized extra-historical world of bravery and sacrifice.

Yerger himself briefly addresses in poorly written statements what he thinks he is doing as an historian. He writes:

My interest in this period is historical, being born more than a decade after the conflict I have no emotional or social connection to the period. Personally considering politics and politicians of any period non-constructive time expenditure for discussion, I have no interest in either. Politics create the wars that soldiers fight while individuals have opinions arrived at by their own means. . . . As a biographical researcher I select topics for specific reasons. Logically, I am much more motivated to research admirable persons possessing positive characteristics."[10]

He disdains politicians and politics because they create the wars that good men have to fight. He ignores the political and strategic context of the war because they have no meaning for him. Instead, he is going to focus on the valiant deeds of "admirable" men, who are sent out to fight by much less admirable men.

Another, more radical guru is Richard Landwehr, who has published at least fourteen books, most of them having to do with the Waffen-SS and, especially, foreign volunteer units in the Waffen-SS, which he considers the greatest international army of all time. These include studies of Estonian, Danish, British, Romanian, French, Hungarian, Italian, Norwegian, Ukrainian, Wallonian, Flemish, and Dutch volunteers.[11] Like Yerger, he has developed friendships with survivors of the Waffen-SS and their families, especially those who immigrated to the United States after the war. As a result, he has earned their cooperation in writing his books and journal articles.

Some of the books are self-published, others appeared under the auspices of Bibliophile Legion Books of Silver Springs, Md., and others, usually reprints, in the so-called Stahlhelm Series, unit histories of the armed forces of the Third Reich issued in the United Kingdom through Shelf Books. Virtually all of the units he describes fought, at least until the last days of the war, on the Eastern Front. They are, thus, fodder for the "romancing" of that part of the war, of which Landwehr plays a conspicuous part. In all cases, the Brazilian illustrator Ramiro Bujeiro provides the front covers and some of the drawings inside the books. These drawings are very-much-romanticized renderings. Several examples illustrate the genre. One of the more popular, *Fighting for Freedom: the Ukrainian Volunteer Division of the Waffen-SS*,[12] is dedicated to "all former members of the international anti-communist army that was the Waffen-SS and to the soldiers of the 14th Waffen-Grenadier Division der SS in particular." This edition was timed to coincide with the fiftieth anniversary of the establishment of the 14th Waffen-Grenadier Division. The cover art shows an angry

Ukrainian SS soldier prepared to throw a grenade at the enemy, presumably Soviet Communist troops. The volume was made possible "to a large extent due to the efforts and support of Dr. Jaroslav Sawka (of the Ukrainian community in Sterling Heights, Mich., and contributor to the Ukrainian Weekly Press Fund). As for his sources: "Much of the material in this book was provided by individuals of Ukrainian descent who prefer not to be recognized." The book, says Landwehr, "has no pretensions about being a definitive history; it is merely a brief overview of the Ukrainian Volunteer Division of the Waffen-SS, designed to bring about a higher level of positive awareness about the subject."

This study, like all the others, is clearly revisionist. Landwehr obsessively argues that the Waffen-SS was not nearly as bad as alleged and that Allied soldiers – including Americans and Russians – have an equally bad record, which victor's justice has prevented from emerging. In fact, he puts the Waffen-SS itself into a very positive historical framework. It was "a unique experiment that fostered international unity, high ideals and valiant sacrifice against what can be termed the somewhat less than high-minded." Nowhere here does one find any mention of SS atrocities against civil populations or of the fact that tens of thousands of Waffen-SS men served as guards in concentration camps.

In his brief background sketch, Landwehr follows the same line as the German generals – that the Germans were welcomed as liberators until the atrocious behavior of the Nazi civil administration – Koch's regime – was put into place. "No paid agent could have done a better job for the Soviets than Erich Koch!"

Having established his historical context, Landwehr goes on to describe the formation, training, initial battlefield experience – at the battle of Brody – and then reformation and redeployment of the unit. He enhances the battlefield segment with short selections of diaries and remembrances of the participants. This portion of the book is a really rather prosaic prose description at which the author seems to be taking pains to be factually accurate. Again, however, his revisionist context always comes into play. This outfit helped to put down the Slovak national uprising, which Landwehr characterizes as a mutiny in which the "major culprits . . . were a treacherous clique of high-ranking Slovak Army officers and growing bands of leftist-communist-partisans." The Ukrainian Volunteer division ended the war fighting in Austria. Unlike so many other East European volunteers, they were saved forceful repatriation by the intervention of a Ukrainian cleric with Pope Pius XII, who urged the Allies not to forcibly turn the Ukrainians over to the Russians.[13]

As with all of his books, this one is replete with many pictures of the unit in action and in repose as well as photographs with short biographies of individual soldiers. These pictures – iconographical renderings really – can only serve the purpose of glorifying and often mourning these Waffen-SS soldiers.

Another similar volume is *Romanian Volunteers of the Waffen-SS 1944–45*.[14] This book is dedicated to Corneliu Zelea Codreanu and his successor, Horia Sima, leaders of the Legion of the Archangel Michael [the Iron Guard], a fascist organization in Romania, as well as to the Romanian Waffen-SS. He tells the story of the relatively few Romanian soldiers, about six thousand who served in the Waffen-SS toward the end of World War Two. Most of them were men who went over to the German side after King Michael, in August 1944, abandoned his German allies and invited the Russians into Romania. Landwehr regards this decision as an act of unparalleled perfidy. Hardly numerous enough to create a division, these men were formed into a combat regiment with attendant smaller units.

As with most of his works, Landwehr combines detailed description with personal reminiscences of survivors, many pictures, and the revisionist context. This short-lived unit, which was captured by the Americans in Austria at the end of the war, fared better than some. Given a choice between repatriation and staying in the West, most chose to stay. Many migrated to the United States after aiding American intelligence, although Landwehr avers "in recent years, the wretched offspring of the NKVD/KGB, the so-called 'Office of Special Investigations' in the U.S. Department of Justice has been turned loose to persecute many of the very same people who had generously contributed their skills and talents to the American side [during the Cold War]."

His conclusion: "The Romanian Waffen-SS troops were part of a great and noble attempt to dislodge the blanket of evil which threatened and indeed covered much of the world. Their efforts and deeds deserve to be preserved and remembered!"

Although his attitudes and revisionist interpretive framework come out clearly in his books, the depth of Landwehr's feelings about the Waffen-SS is exhibited most clearly in a journal he has been publishing since the late 1980s called *Siegrunen* (Runes of Victory), a reference to the SS lightning rod insignia, which itself had taken on totemic significance. This journal consists of short stories about various Waffen SS units; personal profiles of Waffen-SS soldiers and officers with many pictures, emphasizing heroic poses; diary entries of SS men; death notices; book reviews, and, always, editorial comments.

There appear to be a number of contributors; some of them close relatives of former Waffen-SS men of different nationalities. The issues appear irregularly in small numbers, seem sometimes to be thrown together carelessly, poorly edited, and with many typographical errors. Unlike Landwehr's books, this publication is aimed at a smaller group of initiates and is therefore more open in expressing Landwehr's prejudices.

Landwehr is not just anti-Communist; he has an animus against all the "Allies" (he always puts them in quotes) of World War Two. Clearly his heroes are the Waffen-SS and he identifies with these "Kameraden" entirely. He is also clearly alienated from his own time, which he sees as materialistic and secular. He romanticizes the Waffen-SS and sees embodied in its men the long-lost virtues of honor, loyalty, and integrity, all values that he misses in the modern world. The picture of a member of the Waffen-SS in issue 69, the 24th anniversary issue, shows a youthful SS soldier; above is a drawing of a determined SS soldier next to the title, *Siegrunen*. The soldier embodies the innocence of a warrior dedicated to his profession and not to realizing the ghastly aims of the "Final Solution."

Often, in his profiles, he pictures men who died valiantly in the service of a lost cause. He often portrays them in ways similar to the characters in Sven Hassel's novels. For example, he features Norwegian SS-*Rottenfuehrer* Martin Faugli, nicknamed "Lucky Shot" in one issue.[15] He also published a hagiographic article in the notorious *Journal of Historical Review* entitled "The European Volunteer Movement in World War II," in which he characterizes the "assault generation" from many European nations that had "risen up against the twin hydra of communism and big capitalism."[16] He dismisses the whole Holocaust theme as phony and instead draws attention to the atrocities of the "Allies," which remain hidden from the world.

He tries to unmask the so-called lies behind many of the well-known Nazi atrocities – Babi Yar, for example, or the infamous SS massacre at Oradour sur Glane, which he whitewashes by relying on the interpretation of Otto Weidinger, who was actually there and who, shortly after the massacre, took over the Waffen-SS regiment "Der Fuehrer." Weidinger himself became a kind of guru with his book *Kameraden bis zum Ende* [Comrades to the End], the history of his regiment, also published in English translation. [See Landwehr's letter to the editor of *Journal of Historical Review*, September 4, 1980]. Landwehr also redefines, in a revisionist way, the crushing of the Slovak uprising in the fall of 1944; he calls it the "Slovak military mutiny," which allegedly had no support from the general public.[17]

He also totemizes Nazi terms and objects. He gives all SS ranks in the original German; photographs of SS men's graves, uniform markings, and documents adorn the pages of *Siegrunen*. Pictures of SS men without any real context are featured throughout the journal and always on the front cover as well, as if the journal itself were a list of obsequies. Even the title – *Siegrunen* – has a totemic quality about it.

He clearly admires the surviving leaders of the fascist world. His personal favorite is Leon Degrelle, Belgian fascist leader, who organized a Walloon contingent for the Waffen-SS. Landwehr dedicates the September 1989 issue of *Siegrunen* to Degrelle, whom he characterizes as "the greatest living political and military leader of the 20th century."[18] On the front cover is a contemporary picture of Degrelle with handwritten greetings to Landwehr.

Five years later, upon the death of Degrelle at age 87, Landwehr writes an obituary: "This will undoubtedly be one of the saddest essays that I have ever had to write. Leon Degrelle died at 11:30 P.M. on 31 March, 1994. He was the inspiration for whatever I have done or accomplished in the writing/publishing field over the last couple of decades. . . . It goes without saying that Degrelle was a giant among men; perhaps the last and greatest hero that we will see for many a year to come."[19]

Landwehr also admires Horia Sima, the last Prime Minister of Romania during World War Two. He prints the text of a thank you note to Landwehr, after receiving and reading *Romanian Volunteers of the Waffen-SS*, "with surprise, emotion and gratitude. I have read this magnificent book . . . On another note, I thank you for your sacrifice in writing and publishing this book."[20]

Landwehr also printed approvingly the words of Florentine Rost van Tonningen, wife of Dutch finance minister and artillery officer in the 34th SS Division "Landstorm Nederland," written in 1945. Landwehr calls her "one of the truly great ladies of our time or any other era for that matter." Writing in 1945, she says: "But the present end phase signals the final cataclysm. The Third Reich is gone and past, they stood on the barricades. Now is the Fourth Reich: now *we* stand on the barricade." This "truly great lady" is better known as the "Black Widow," an unregenerate Nazi, married to a Belgian collaborator, a favorite of Hitler and Himmler, who later spread anti-Semitic/Holocaust denial literature. She caused an outcry in 1986 when it was discovered that she was using part of her pension to underwrite a neo-Nazi party in Holland. She has given a number of guest lectures at the Institute for Historical Review.[21]

Landwehr even tries the impossible – to rescue the reputation of one of the most notorious Waffen-SS leaders, Oskar Dirlewanger. Dirlewanger was an alcoholic outcast who committed sex offenses against minors, for which he went to jail on several occasions in the 1930s. Eventually, he was accepted into the SS in 1940 and set up a special detachment known as the Sonderkommando Dirlewanger. In 1941, his unit had expanded to a battalion (SS-Sonderbattalion Dirlewanger) and was used extensively to combat partisan units in Byelorussia. Here he was known for his brutal methods, including torture and rape. Even the SS investigated him but never brought him to trial. His unit earned further disgrace by its brutality in putting down the Warsaw uprising in August 1944 and the Slovak uprising in late 1944. Landwehr tries on a number of occasions in his *Siegrunen* to rescue Dirlewanger's reputation. Admitting that Dirlewanger was a "failed human being," Landwehr nevertheless asserts that Dilewanger's unit was "a very formidable and effective fighting unit. It may well have been the best anti-partisan troop to ever fight in any war at any time."

Dirlewanger's unit was very successful precisely because it was composed of poachers and criminals. Only after it began to admit "politicals" who had volunteered to get out of camps did the unit deteriorate. Landwehr believes that criminals make better fighting men than "politicals." Noting that Dirlewanger had been tortured and killed by Polish soldiers serving in the French army while he was being held at Althausen, Landwehr writes that "Dirlewanger's unit had dealt very effectively with the Soviet communist terrorist groups (pardon me, "partisan fighters"!), and since these tended to be led and supported by people of Jewish ethnic extraction (a fact that they continually like to brag about today), it is no wonder that the "Nazi hunters" had their fangs out for Dirlewanger."[22]

As to his motivation and inspiration, Landwehr writes that he was exposed to revisionist books as early as the 1960s: *Quisling: Prophet without Honor* and *The Last One Hundred Days* both gave a positive picture of the Waffen-SS. *The East Came West*, on the forced repatriation of the Cossacks, outraged him; a booklet on Deir Yassein, an alleged atrocity committed by the Israelis, did as well. Then came Paul Rassinier's book *The Drama of the European Jews*, which presumably exposed the "extermination fraud." Finally there appeared "good" Waffen-SS titles like those of Hugh Page Taylor. "But I was still not getting the information I needed, particularly about the European volunteers of the Waffen-SS, and "*Siegrunen*" was born, essentially as a conduit of material concerning both the Waffen-SS and, to some extent, the "unknown history" of the World War II era."[23] "This is why I started *Siegrunen* in the first place, because I wasn't getting the straight dope from the 'normal' sources and I wanted to provide a forum where the true facts about the Waffen-SS could be told without a heavy layer of 'establishment' propaganda to get in the way."[24]

Landwehr clearly feels alienated from his own age and time. He finds solace identifying with a heroic but doomed group of men who allegedly incorporated the values that Landwehr fears have disappeared in his world. This comes out subtly in his many books and blatantly in his journal. His own words underscore his alienation.

When the 'greatest generation' finished with their part in the 'good war', the international communists were able to enslave no less than one billion people and murder some additional tens of millions. None of who [sic] count as opposed to the so-called 'Nazi victims'! In the meantime we are left with squalid, debased, degraded, degenerate societies to live in (for as long as they continue to last), while such little things as truth, honor and decency are swept under the carpet.[25] . . . Like other contemporary regimes, the Dutch rulers have permitted every form of absolute degeneracy to prevail, but have cracked down hard on the "traditional values" represented by National Socialism and other related philosophies.[26]

Landwehr writes a blurb in an advertisement for his book *Fighting for Freedom*:

The war on the Eastern Front was witness to armed conflict between the most polarized ideologies that the world has ever seen: Europe against Anti-Europe. Ukraine was an integral part of Europe's shield in defense against the Communist enemy. The Waffen-SS was a unique experiment that fostered international unity, high ideals and valiant sacrifice against what can be termed the somewhat less than high-minded forces of Soviet Communism and its assorted international gangster allies.[27]

In an editorial, Landwehr notes that the revisionist Institute for Historical Review was taken over by disgruntled employees and its founder ousted. "What happened to the IHR may be commonplace in our present degenerate, materialist-capitalist dog-eat-dog culture, but it is certainly not appropriate in 'my' world. Integrity, idealism, honor and loyalty should be our watchwords at all times." He recommends now, since the *Journal of Historical Review* is tainted, that people instead turn to *The Barnes Review*.[28]

On the occasion of the D-Day commemoration in 1994, Landwehr wrote: "The importance that our rulers and media placed on 'D-Day' cannot be exaggerated; this was a turning point in the establishment of the current degenerate world order. Our beloved leader even flew his entire government, certainly the motliest collection of Marxist commissars, weird ethnic minorities and non-Christians since the glory days of Lenin and Stalin, in probably the largest travel boondoggle in U.S. history."[29]

One can perhaps best locate Landwehr in the shadowy radical right of revisionist history and moral confusion. One review noted recently the close similarity between the rapture novels so popular lately, like *Left Behind*, and the influential *Turner Diaries*, which allegedly, among other things, inspired Timothy McVeigh to bomb the federal building in Oklahoma City. Of both novels, the reviewer says: "Mainstream American public life and civic leaders are depicted as degenerate, irrelevant, useless, and ready to crumble."[30] This attitude seems closely to resemble that of Landwehr. One might just dismiss *Siegrunen* as the rhetoric of a socially marginalized man – were it not for the phenomenal success of his many books.

An important question arises out of the guru material. We have seen how the myth of the clean Wehrmacht was created and nourished. But the Waffen-SS is another entity entirely. Although, in the 1950s, Waffen-SS veterans tried to say that they were "soldiers like all the others," it was clear from the beginning that these units were particularly brutal, in training and in combat, were ideologically trained in National Socialist ideology, and, in part at least, functioned as concentration camp guards. Indeed, the origins of the Waffen-SS lay with the concentration camp system. Why then do the "romancers," to an extent even greater than in the case of the Wehrmacht, see these soldiers as romantic heroes? One clue may lie in one of the most popular of these men – the late Joachim Peiper.

On December 17, 1944, at the outset of the "Battle of the Bulge," Waffen-SS units shot and killed 120 unarmed American prisoners at Malmédy in Belgium. In the immediate area were elements of the Combat Group Peiper, led by the 29-year-old Waffen-SS officer Joachim (Jochen) Peiper. In 1946, after an investigation, seventy-four men were brought to trial for the murders. The central figure in this group was Peiper.

Beginning his career as an aide to Heinrich Himmler, Peiper rose to prominence on the Eastern Front with the Leibstandarte SS Adolf Hitler division in the initial invasion of Russia in 1941, then later as a regimental commander in the recapture of Kharkov in March 1943, an action for which he was awarded the Knight's Cross of the Iron Cross. He won more medals in other battles, both in Russia and later in Italy. In December 1944, he and the Leibstandarte were given a key role in initiating the Battle of the Bulge. It was in this context, as Peiper and his unit were dashing for the Meuse River, that the massacre occurred.

At the trial, Peiper was a central character, who stood out from the others as charismatic and charming. He took the responsibility of shielding his men. He was, as the leading scholar of this incident notes, "with piercing eyes, aquiline nose, and mouth whose corners sometimes turned down in a hint of cruelty... the Hollywood physical stereotype of the SS officer." He was also "characteristically courteous," carried himself with "dignity," and was highly intelligent and fluent in English. He also exhibited from time to time "flashes of good humor" – a distinctively non-German trait.[31]

In the end, most of the accused received sentences ranging from prison to death. Peiper was sentenced to die. By 1949, however, the context had changed completely with the advent of the Cold War and the prospect of needing German soldiers once again for Western defense. By then, the trial and sentences were being contested in the United States itself, as the details of pre-trial interrogation methods emerged. It turned out that violence, intimidation, mock trials, and other techniques had been used. The political right in the United States sensed a cause. There was also more than a hint of anti-Semitism involved because several of the interrogators, among them a Lieutenant William Perl, were Jewish; several, in fact, immigrants to the United States.

Investigations were opened in the early 1950s, including several Senate committees, on one of which was Joseph McCarthy, prepared to begin his sensationalist career. Receiving encouragement and information from right-wing and anti-Semitic elements as well as right-wing pro-German people in Wisconsin, McCarthy, catering to "anti-Semitic and isolationist sentiment in his home state,"[32] dominated the proceedings and grabbed headlines. He was also probably encouraged by a right-wing, anti-Semitic judge, LeRoy van Roden, who saw the trials as being a Jewish effort to take revenge on the Germans, and who also served on one of the investigating commissions.

A well-known right-wing pundit, Freda Utley, wrote an article in the *American Mercury* in November 1954 decrying the lack of justice for the Germans. She claimed that Colonel A. H. Rosenfeld, chief of the Dachau branch of the U.S. War Crimes Administration, admitted to using mock trials. "Yes, of course," he is supposed to have said at a press conference, "We couldn't have made those birds talk otherwise. It was a trick and it worked like a charm." Utley, appealing to the American innate sense of justice and referring to the Cold War, wrote: "For the sake of America's reputation for justice, no less than because we wish to enlist the German people as our allies against Communist tyranny, we should seek to right the injustice of the post-war period."[33]

Peiper became a folk hero in West Germany, as many groups tried to free the last of the World War Two imprisoned. Peiper's sentence was commuted to thirty-five years in 1954 and he was released in 1956, the last of the Malmédy condemned to be freed. Ironically, he then achieved some success as North American representative for the Porsche auto company, but lost this position when Italian workers demonstrated, reminding the world of some of his alleged atrocities committed while fighting partisans in northern Italy. He eventually moved to France, where he built a home and survived working as a translator. After an article on him appeared in the Communist newspaper, *L'Humanité*, pointing out his whereabouts, persons unknown fire bombed his home in 1976, killing him.[34]

This one case helps explain why Peiper, having been a folk hero in Germany during his trial, now became one for the romancers in the United States as well. Within the framework of the Cold War and the beginning of the McCarthy era, he was transformed from villain to hero. His behavior at trial, his personal characteristics, and his physical appearance all aided this process. His fluency in English also helped. Here in the flesh was the perfect mythical man – both a tragic and heroic figure.

Explaining why the "romancers" don't just admire individual Waffen-SS soldiers, but also the outfit itself, demands a look at certain parts of American popular culture. Landwehr himself offers one clue. According to him, the Waffen-SS "was probably the most 'democratic' armed force of modern times. Rigid formality and class structure between officers and other ranks was strictly forbidden. An officer held down his position only because he had proven himself a better soldier than his men, not because of any rank in society."[35] Obviously, this appeals to many Americans who resent or scoff at traditional elites and hate class hierarchies. The Waffen-SS was an elite, but earned, not inherited. The Waffen-SS also took on and gave command to men of lower social origin who could prove themselves on the battlefield. Americans appreciate this upward mobility as well. Moreover, there is something of the cowboy in the Waffen-SS; the men are rough and tough, their training consists more of field exercises than close order drill. Many of them were individualistic and nonconformist, enabling them to take full advantage of the German military's tendency to place responsibility in the hands of lower-ranking soldiers. They were seen as indifferent to danger and death, a collection of Rambos, and their casualty rates were much higher than those of the regular German army. They were also seen as idealistic, a result of lots of ideological training; comradely; and, most obviously, martyrs in a lost cause.

But not all of the heroes come from the ranks of the Waffen-SS. Other branches of the German military also provide shining lights. One comes from the Luftwaffe – Erich Hartmann. The title of his biography, written by Raymond F. Toliver and Trevor J. Constable, is *The Blond Knight of Germany*.[36] The cover of "Knight" already reveals much about what is inside and the historical framework into which the authors want to place their hero. The title conveys an aura that the Nazis themselves would have been pleased to see. "Blond" already suggests the image of the master race, whose main physiognomy consisted, of course, of blond hair, blue eyes, long narrow skull, and lean, powerful physique. "Knight" suggests the romantic feudal language the Nazis used constantly to describe not only their military, but also the very nature of the regime itself, where "vassals" swore allegiance and fealty to their "lord" – the Fuehrer. The term, applied to the military, is even more insidious because it suggests something of medieval chivalry with its generosity toward the enemy, magnanimity in victory, courtesy even in the face of hostility; in short, a whole range of behavior that not only fails to characterize the behavior of the German army in the East, but, indeed, marks its opposite. It is, conveniently, the language of romanticization – no era has been so romanticized as medieval

Europe, with its images of chivalry, of white knights jousting for the heart of fair lady.

Put the two words "blond"and "knight" together and you enter into the world not just of the German army manqué, but especially of the SS. Hartmann may have been an air force man and not Waffen-SS, but the stereotype is the same. Here we have a new aristocracy, a racial elite complete with dueling, courts of honor, and other trappings of nobility that only disguise the fact that to breed a new racial elite one has also to exterminate a lot of *Untermenschen*.

Then add to the cover a piece of romanticized art – a painting of a Messerschmitt 109 peeling out of the clouds to enter into a presumably gentlemanly jousting with the enemy, and you have the complete picture of the contents of the book. The picture, incidentally, was not a piece of captured German war art, but rather an illustration of the networking between Americans and former German veterans. An American artist, Harley Coptic, painted the picture and a photo inside the book shows an admiring Erich Hartmann autographing the lithograph.

Who was Erich Hartmann that he should be written about so admiringly by authors from states that opposed Germany in World War Two? He was the most successful German fighter ace of World War Two. Between November 1942 and May 1945, he shot down 352 confirmed enemy planes and won that most coveted of medals conferred by Hitler: the Knight's Cross with Oak Leaves, Swords and Diamonds.

But he was able to do something else as well, which illustrates the themes of this book: He was very easy to remake into an American hero. It is important to note that he spent his combat time exclusively on the Eastern Front. With one or two exceptions, all the planes he shot down were Russian planes. Moreover, he also survived years of Soviet captivity after the war. Then he returned to West Germany to be among the first to help establish the West German air force. In this capacity, he traveled far and wide and established a dense pattern of contacts and admirers in the U.S. military. And no wonder – Hartmann's postwar career is unthinkable without the Cold War. At a time when it seemed possible, indeed probable, that we might be locked in a land war with the Soviet Union, we found advice, some solicited, some gratuitous, from the Germans who had already fought the Russians. We received this advice from former high-level commanders like Halder and Manstein – but these were not combat heroes like Hartmann. We also found inspiration. Hartmann (and his like) took on a legendary dimension for Americans and provided a sense that the Russians could be beaten. And who could better suggest so than a pilot who had shot down more than 300 of their planes? Indeed, in 1957, Hartmann graduated from a USAF Fighter Course.

However, romanticizing the likes of Hartmann also meant taking on a load of the same ideological ballast, partly consciously, partly unconsciously, that had accompanied the war against the Russians that the Germans had already fought and lost, ballast that included many of the racial tenets of the Nazis, which could now be put into a safe context with Hitler and his main henchmen safely dead. "Blond knight," not a concept normally found in the traditional language of Americans or their soldiers, was part of this ballast and served the purpose of inspiring us to hang tough in the Cold War. It also allowed us to romanticize the Lost Cause of the Germans in the East, which, after all, had made our own enlistment in the effort to defeat Communism necessary.

The book is solidly encased in German approval. General Adolf Galland, former leader of the fighter arm of the Luftwaffe and himself a ubiquitous networker with Western militaries, provides the introduction. He expresses tremendous admiration for Hartmann as the "leading fighter pilot of all time," a man whose life is an "inspiring human drama," and calls the book "the most remarkable book ever written about a fighter pilot." He thanks the authors, whom "we of the German fighter pilot fraternity respect for their integrity and fairness," and adds, "we former fighter pilots of the Luftwaffe appreciate what you have done."[37]

Except for the Daily Operational History of Hartmann's unit (III/JU-52), which was allegedly smuggled out of East Germany by a former comrade, the authors fail to reveal the sources they consulted in their ten years of research, except to note that much of their material came from the documentation of the German Fighter Pilots' Association in Munich and from family members of Hartmann. The book is dedicated to "Usch. Who waited": i.e., the name of Hartmann's wife who waited for him during the years he spent in Russian captivity. This would suggest the lack of a critical interpretive framework for the resulting study.

If the book is not intended as a critical historical study, what do the authors intend? In their brief preface, they express the intent to add the name of Hartmann to the long list of chivalrous heroes of the air, including Eddie Rickenbacker and Oswald Boelke – an American and a German – but not primarily to enhance the military record. Rather, the authors clearly see their book as a contribution to the Cold War. By virtue of his ten years of Soviet confinement, Hartmann is "an unseen and unheralded hero of the . . . Cold War"; indeed, "his lonely struggle against the Russian secret police far eclipses anything he achieved as a fighter pilot." Finally, Hartmann's story, the writers assure the reader somewhat gratuitously, should be seen "as an indictment of war," which it certainly is not. But, one suspects, more importantly, "as a clear warning of what awaits the world should it ever fall under the sway of the NKVD-type mind."[38] What then, one is tempted to ask, was the Gestapo-type mind, which characterized the regime that Hartmann served willingly?

Three themes emerge in the first chapter: the natural leader, the romantic knight, and the depredations of the Cold War. Sketching Hartmann's character as it was revealed in Russian captivity, the authors describe characteristics that the Nazis themselves always admired in leadership: the born leader, the upstart, the cream that rises naturally to the top and transcends rank: "the best of German manhood in terms of character, will power and endurance"(p. 4). As described here, Hartmann could be a free corps leader in 1919, the leader recognized by his men and not determined by rank or institutional affiliation. The authors trace the source of that natural leadership to a romanticized combination of heritage and family. "Their source lay in his family background, free upbringing and native manhood, reinforced by the undying love of a beautiful woman" (p. 5).

There is also a strain of the Nazi antipathy to modernity as expressed by the authors in characterizing Hartmann. His values are traditional, not modern; he is an anachronism, "an incorrigible individualist in an age of mass effects and conformity." (5) [Landwehr would like this passage.] Nor is there missing an ingredient of the nonspecific religiosity favored by the Nazis (not Lutheran but *gottgläubig* or God-believing); Hartmann is not a religious man in the denominational sense, rather "his religion is one of conscience and is an extension of his fighting heart"(p. 6).

It is at the end of the book where the author's feudal romanticism really emerges most dramatically. The last paragraph of the first chapter (p. 14) reads:

> The battered shield of the Blond Knight is still carried with honor, and its escutcheons are still bright. More names of glory may yet be emblazoned on it [Auschwitz? Buchenwald?] for its fair-haired bearer is still a formidable participant in the tournament of life. The time has come to explore with him his story as a hero of the joust, the depth of his torment while in bondage, and his unforgettable romance with his beautiful lady.

One wants to take nothing away from Hartmann in terms of his skill and daring as a fighter pilot. However, to divorce his exploits from the regime, which he loyally served and from whose leader he accepted its second highest decoration, renders no service. Nor does placing him not in the historical context of a war of racial conquest and annihilation, but rather in a romanticized feudal joust between knights for the hand of fair a lady.

Among the more popular gurus, Franz Kurowski enjoys the unique advantage of being German and a Wehrmacht veteran. Unlike Yerger or Landwehr, Kurowski actually walked the "sacred ground" of German battlefields and endured the bitterness of defeat. He served in the Wehrmacht as a reporter, developing talents he later used in writing about the wartime exploits of the Wehrmacht, the Waffen-SS, Luftwaffe, and other German services. No one among the gurus can make as powerful a claim to authenticity as Kurowski.

His publications invite readers into a world that, without question in the minds of romancers, brings them the true experiences of war on the Eastern Front. As a veteran, Kurowski counts many of the men who served on the Eastern Front as his acquaintances, personal friends, and fellow brothers of the sword. His research often depends on access to the men and/or their families in addition to German wartime records. Often he uses extensive quotes from the diaries of the men who appear in his books. Kurowski, like all true gurus, ignores the charges of serious misdeeds leveled against the German military and, like the authors of the *Blond Knight*, provides an heroic context for the men he describes in his many works. These quotes greatly enhance the realism of his accounts and demonstrate Kurowski's own authenticity.

Over the years, Kurowski published scores of books on many dimensions of the German military in World War Two, which have enjoyed widespread popularity among German readers. Yet, without translations, Kurowski's books remained inaccessible to the vast majority of American readers. J. J. Fedorowicz Publishing resolved this problem when it released the first of Kurowski's popular works, *Panzer Aces*, in 1992, followed by his *Infantry Aces* in 1994. The cover art of these books, as in so many works on the German military, evokes the heroism, determination, and might of the German soldier and his weapons.

The largest distributor of reading material in the United States – Amazon.com – markets Kurowski's works as well. This distributor's website features some eighteen works for the North American market. These books have appeared almost annually from 1992 through 2005, including, most recently, *Panzerkrieg: An Overview of German Armored Operations in World War 2* in March 2005 and *Brandenburg Commandos*, released in August 2005. These books cover every aspect of the German military in World War Two.[39]

Among Kurowski's many works, two stand out: the classics *Panzer Aces* and *Infantry Aces*. Presses have released and reissued these books several times over the past decade. The books first enjoyed success while under the imprimatur of Fedorowicz. Apparently this success convinced Ballantine Books to reissue them as inexpensive paperback books aimed at a mass nationwide audience (Figure 10). The books appeared in 2002, some eight to ten years after Fedorowicz released them. They remain in print and easily available on Amazon.com. Subsequently, Stackpole Books, located in Mechanicsburg, Pa., published the two books for the third time. Under Stackpole's sponsorship, *Panzer Aces* and

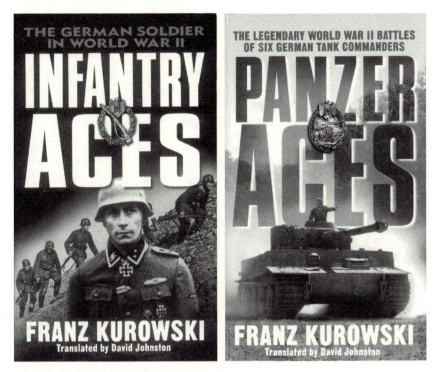

Figure 10. Cover art from *Infantry Aces* and *Panzer Aces*.

Infantry Aces fared well among buyers and romancers through Amazon.com. These works continue to enjoy a widespread and enthusiastic readership. Ballantine books also intended to issue *Panzer Aces* in audio CD form at an affordable price, thereby encouraging a substantial listeners' market.[40] Those readers who purchased either *Panzer Aces* or *Infantry Aces* also bought other books by Kurowski, including *Panzer Aces II* and *Luftwaffe Aces*.

The two books contain short accounts of German soldiers and their exploits in the European theater of World War Two. As in the case of the other gurus, the translation maintains the use of German ranks for army and Waffen-SS officers. Iconic terms such as *SS-Obersturmbannführer, Sturmbannführer, Obergruppenführer, Leibstandarte*, and *Generalfeldmarschall* appeal enormously to romancers. The translations also incorporate German names for weapons and vehicles. Kurowski includes many of the demigods of the Eastern Front in his stories, including the famous Kurt Meyer, known as *Panzermeyer* to his men; Joachim Peiper; Paul Hausser, general of the 2nd Panzer Corps; Field Marshal von Manstein; and others. These noted worthies of the romancer world commanded the men featured in Kurowski's tales of bravery on the Russian battlefields.

Kurowski's *Panzer Aces* and *Infantry Aces* paint an extraordinarily favorable portrait of the men who fought and died in battle against Germany's enemies. The stories move beyond mere tales of soldiers' exploits rendered in dramatic language. Kurowski gives the reader an almost heroic vision of the German soldier, guiltless of any war crimes, actually incapable of such behavior. In his accounts, the German soldier always demonstrates his loyalty to his comrades and to an army dedicated only to the defense of the Fatherland. The men depicted in Kurowski's books go beyond the call of duty for their comrades, whether it is rescuing them from certain death, exposing their person to lethal fire, or even rescuing a wounded comrade, although injured themselves.[41]

Sacrifice and humility are the hallmarks of the German soldiers. The actions of these soldiers often win them badges, medals, and/or promotions, yet the men remain indifferent to these awards. Instead, they demand to know if their comrades are recovering, are their wounds healing, or have they been taken to appropriate medical facilities. These powerful bonds of loyalty give the German formations their cohesiveness and account for their fierce determination, often in the face of certain defeat by their enemies.[42]

A classic example, as told by Kurowski, of the bonds of loyalty within the Wehrmacht occurred in February 1944, when Soviet armies trapped tens of thousands of men in the Cherkassy Pocket in southern Russia on the Dnepr River. Dr. Franz Bake led his heavy Panzer regiment to break into the pocket and open a corridor for the trapped units to escape. He and his men fought unit after unit of the Soviet Army. The Russian attack began in January and by February had inflicted severe losses on Bake's regiment. Re-equipped and even more determined, Bake led his regiment again toward the Pocket and by February 16 had opened the corridor. Bake and his men put up fierce resistance to Soviet counterattacks, enabling their fellow soldiers to reach safety. Their actions, even before the actual breakout, had already earned them the praise of Field Marshal Manstein. As Kurowski writes, "when the Soviets launched their expected attack, they were wiped out by the exhausted Panzer soldiers."[43]

Unselfish devotion to the men appears most prominently in the career of medic Franz Schmitz. Attached to the 95th Infantry Division operating in southern Russia, Schmitz and his team of medics moved into battle with the men. In this case, the division acted as a blocking force against Soviet troops breaking through German lines in the wake of the failed Kursk offensive. As casualties mounted, Schmitz and his men quickly moved to the area of fighting. He had already spent a long night rescuing wounded men from the front. Realizing the danger the troops faced, "there was no holding him back." He braved the fire of the combat zone to bring the injured troopers back to safety. His strength seemed inexhaustible. Every time he ventured onto the battlefield, he faced almost certain death, yet he persisted and ceased his Herculean effort only when no more wounded remained. By evening, through Schmitz' personal efforts, ninety-eight men who otherwise might have died on the battlefield had been rescued. As Kurowski remarks, "finally he could find no more wounded. He staggered back to the wood where he sank to the ground, exhausted."[44]

The men in Kurowski's accounts consistently showed their bonds of loyalty, especially in the face of death. Squad leader Josef Schreiber and his men exemplified this comradeship. Schreiber belonged to the 78th *Sturmdivision* battling an attempted Soviet breakthrough in the Orel area in the winter of 1943. Schreiber and his men dug in, determined to hold Hill 249.7. For days, they repulsed one Soviet attack after another and, though many men died or suffered wounds, they held their positions. Soviet attacks persisted. At one point, one of the men, Corporal Lemke, desperately called for more ammunition. Weighed down with ammunition, a grenadier raced toward the embattled Lemke. Despite being hit, the man "managed to crawl the last thirty yards" on hands and knees.[45] He knew that without the ammunition, his fellow soldiers would surely face certain death.

In the midst of the last of many assaults on Hill 249.7, Sergeant Schreiber walked past what he perceived as a dead Soviet soldier, who was in fact very much alive and waiting for an opportunity to strike. As Schreiber moved past him, the man stood up ready for an almost certain kill. One of Schreiber's men saw the danger and shot, just missing Schreiber, but killing the Russian.[46]

These terrifying yet poignant moments, where one man saves another, recurred throughout the long struggle to hold Hill 249.7. Day and night, the men fought with no relief and no replacements. "Twelve determined men, watching out for one other and depending on one another, were engaged in a desperate battle for survival."[47]

Then, at the first light of dawn, one of the men yelled, to everyone's immense relief, that support was coming. Schreiber immediately ordered the worn-out men to prepare for an attack.

> A moment of hesitation went through the twelve men who had looked death in the eye countless times that one night during fourteen pitiless hours. But, then they reached for their weapons, slung their reserve submachine guns, fed fresh belts of ammunition into the light machine guns, and followed the small Corporal who led the charge toward the Russian foxholes."[48]

Once the battle ended with a German victory, the men who made it through the maelstrom of battle gathered to honor their dead, those who had given their lives for their comrades. Colonel Kaether: "called the names of the fallen by company. The companies had been drawn up before the graves and stood in

deep silence. The men hardened by the daily fight for survival, saw the light of
the March sun on the white birch crosses. None of those [present] that day will
ever forget the song sung that spring morning: '*Ich hatt einen Kameraden.*'"[49]
In this context, the war did not seem to be about conquest and racial annihilation, but rather as a force to unite German soldiers as comrades in life and in
death.

As Kurowski views it, the war also reduced the social hierarchy that existed
in the civilian world. In fact, officers and men shared a common vision and
concern for each other. The officers always placed the welfare of their men above
their own. The son of Reich Foreign Minister, Joachim von Ribbentrop, Rudolf,
served in the SS division *Das Reich* 2nd as part of the 2nd SS-Panzer corps, under
the command of the celebrated General Paul Hausser. The younger Ribbentrop
had suffered wounds in battle and was still recuperating as Hausser ordered the
division to withdraw from the industrial city of Kharkov. Ribbentrop learned
that a small airplane had arrived specifically to fly him out of the battle zone.
He strenuously objected and demanded that ordinary soldiers be flown out,
with youngest going first. The medical doctor refused to listen to Ribbentrop's
protest and ordered him to board the awaiting plane. He quietly stood his
ground since the privilege of his father's position carried no weight for the son.
The youngest soldier among the wounded flew out of the Kharkov region as
Ribbentrop demanded.[50]

Kurowski also underscores the bravery of the German soldier and his
tremendous combat abilities. The men in both *Panzer Aces* and *Infantry Aces*
time and again showed outstanding capacities for leadership in the face of fire.
Their actions suggest daring beyond imagination and a determination to carry
on the fight no matter how insurmountable the odds. To these men, successful
battle meant victory over Germany's enemies and they used all their resources
to achieve that goal. In December of 1942, Major General Bake participated
in the attempt to relieve the Army trapped in Stalingrad. Conceived by Field
Marshal Manstein and led by Colonel General Hoth, the operation was intended
to punch a hole through the Soviet defenses and open up a corridor for the 6th
Army to retreat from certain destruction. Bake's Panzer company played an
important role in this desperate effort. He participated in a three-day tank battle from December 14 to 17. During the fight, he discovered that what seemed
to be German tanks were actually disguised Soviet tanks. Despite the odds,
Bake led his tanks into the fray and destroyed thirty-two of the some forty
disguised tanks and ended the threat to the relieving armor units at that point.
He then led his tanks forward to another encounter with Soviet tanks, which he
destroyed as well. His corps was actually within reach of the pocket, yet Soviet
forces proved too formidable. The action was in vain anyway, because Hitler

refused to allow the 6th army to break out. In the end, the Soviets deployed resources on such a scale that all the combat skills and bravery of Bake and his men proved fruitless. This tale fits into virtually all Lost Cause mythologies, which suggest that virtue lies with the losing side, and that the winners only prevail because of overwhelming superiority in material and manpower.[51]

German soldiers often demonstrated almost superhuman efforts on the battlefield yet were modest about their accomplishments. A classic example appears in the action conducted by Tiger tank officer Michael Wittman. Fighting near Kiev in November 1943, Wittman and his crew took out ten tanks and five anti-tank units in one morning. Later that afternoon, Wittman and his tanks destroyed another eleven Soviet tanks with the aid of reinforcements. In the course of the next few days, he and his crew accounted for some sixty tanks and nearly the same number of anti-tank guns. When his superior informed him that such an outstanding action merited the prestigious Knight's Cross, Wittman replied that his gunner deserved the medal, not him. Humility prevailed in spite of Wittman's achievement.[52]

As Kurowski tells it, the German soldiers fought a well-nigh chivalrous war with Soviet troops, showing concern for the Russian wounded, despite the atrocities many Soviet soldiers conducted against helpless captured or wounded Germans. German tank crews, for example, discovered the bodies of German soldiers at the Tatsinskaya airport, used by German supply planes to sustain the entrapped 6th Army in Stalingrad. Thrown into a ditch without the benefit of a proper burial, the bodies showed signs of torture.[53]

And yet, according to Kurowski, despite such reports, the German soldiers conducted themselves with respect and solicitation when dealing with Soviet soldiers. In an action in 1941, for example, SS Sergeant Michael Wittman fought his way to link up with a motorcycle battalion of the 25th Motorized Infantry Division to prevent its encirclement by Soviet forces. In the process, his assault gun took out eighteen Soviet tanks, an action that won him the Iron Cross, First Class. SS General Sepp Dietrich made the award and asked Wittman if he had a request. Without hesitation, Wittman told his commander that three wounded Russian soldiers on Hill 56, where they had fought, needed urgent medical attention. Dietrich assured Wittman that he would take care of the matter. The welfare of the Russian soldiers outweighed whatever importance he attached to the medal.[54]

This supposed concern for the Soviet soldiers emerged again among the troops in Army Group Center during the winter of 1941–42. In another incident, Sergeant Schreiber and his men had just turned back a Russian night assault. As he surveyed the battlefield, Schreiber noticed a wounded Russian lying just beyond his trench. The German pulled the man back to the safety of

the German defensive works and his wounds were attended to. Despite a ferocious battle, where no quarter was given or asked, the Germans again showed
their humanity vis-a-vis their enemy. Similarly, during this same winter in
southern Russia, medic Franz Schmitz and his men saved many lives in the
midst of fierce snowstorms and bitter cold temperatures. Russian and German
soldiers suffering from severe frostbite were treated medically without regard
for which side they fought on. Schmitz "and his comrades were aware that their
duties as medics superseded any differences in uniform."[55]

In Kurowski's world, honor, concern for the enemy, sacrifice for others, and
dedication to your comrades provided the moral scaffolding for the Wehrmacht
and the Waffen-SS. These virtues characterized the soldiers, their units, and
the military as a whole. The Germans struggled against tremendous odds, yet
always showed their humanity, even to their bitter enemies. The subjects of
Kurowski's books sometimes survived; often they perished. Michael Wittman,
despite his immense abilities as tank commander, met his end near the beaches
of Normandy in August 1944, when U.S. Sherman tanks, according to one
story, destroyed his Tiger. Others, like Josef Schreiber, fought bravely almost
to the end of the war, then, in February 1945, vanished like so many German
soldiers, a heroic fight ending in death and tragedy.[56]

Kurowski has created an image of the German soldier and officer without
flaws or character defects. He claims in the introduction that the stories were
taken from thousands of such cases and that these men and their exploits
represent the Wehrmacht and the Waffen-SS as a whole. "These men stand for
all those who returned wounded and broken, ashamed and beaten, bringing
the horror of their wartime experiences with them." Kurowski laments the fate
of veterans whose reputations suffered in the wake of German defeat in 1945.
They had endured hell in many forms and they had met the challenges of the
battlefields from one end of Europe to the other. Kurowski intends his books
to act an appropriate memorial to these men. They only served their country
and for that they suffered abuse.[57]

Kurowski's tales of heroism and sacrifice mirror the romancers' own vision
of the German soldiers. These men demonstrated immense capability and
fought selflessly for their comrades and for the Fatherland. Honor guided their
actions and kindness toward their enemies marked their true nobility. Kurowski
never once mentions the Nazi party, the Holocaust, or the barbaric exploitation
of the Russian people. He remains silent on the reasons why Germany invaded
the Soviet Union. The reality of the war in Russia, no doubted, included many
thrilling stories, if such an adjective were appropriate, of German bravery. Yet
the overwhelming documentation on the war in the East demonstrates that the
Germans behaved in ways just the opposite from the events in Kurowski's works.

Did German soldiers normally show concern for wounded Russian soldiers? Battlefields deaths, the ghastly treatment of POWs, and the systematic killing of large parts of the Soviet population suggest otherwise. Kurowski's place as a guru sustains the hoary myths about the German soldier that thrive into the twenty-first century.

Antonio Munoz specializes in publishing books and journals on the various non-German ethnic groups that fought with the Wehrmacht. He is a guru in at least two ways. First, he combines exhaustive research with an heroic description of his subjects. Next, Munoz is also a guru-impresario, who networks with other gurus, authors, and publishers in order to broaden the already wide audience of the romancers.

His motivation in specializing in units from Serbia, Croatia, Hungary, Romania, and the Baltic States may in part link to his personal history. Munoz is an émigré from Castro's Cuba; his grandfather hailed from Yugoslavia, where Tito's Communists eventually took power; and Munoz is a former U.S. Marine. His fierce anti-Communism might well have led him to tell the story of the anti-Communist fighters, who once fought with the Germans against the Bolshevik menace, and then, for most of Munoz's lifetime, were members of the "captive nations" the Communists had overrun.

Munoz demonstrates a profound admiration for the small powers allied with the Axis and their armed forces. Just as the romancers wanted a heroic rendition of the men in the German armed forces, Munoz firmly believed the men in Axis allied armies and small formations, too, needed their valiant tales of heroism retold to a public largely unaware of these men and their sacrifices. This zeal developed into a newsletter dedicated to Axis allied forces. Later, the newsletter became a full-blown magazine, *Axis Europa* (Figure 11). The symbol for *Axis Europa* echoed fascist art and showed a Nordic-type warrior fighting back a dark menacing figure (Figure 12). At the same time, Munoz began to publish books on the Axis military forces. Munoz used the newsletter, the journal, and the publishing business to promote the cause of the Axis allies and non-Germans who fought in the ranks of the Waffen-SS. Munoz's printed media also promoted organizational ties among the major guru outlets.[58]

In his rise to guru status, Munoz profited from his close relationship with the original guru, Richard Landwehr, and his journal, *Siegrunen*. This association began in the early 1980s, when Munoz worked with Landwehr in producing *Siegrunen*. Munoz reviewed books on the Waffen-SS, including those released in German and English and published by right-wing presses. He praised these works for their thoroughness and demonstrated his growing interest in Waffen-SS units, which found an outlet later in his expanded journal, *Axis Europa*. He served as contributing editor for Landwehr's *Siegrunen* in the mid- and late

Figure 11. A cover of the magazine *Axis Europa*.

1980s. In the 1980s and 1990s, Munoz occasionally wrote short pieces for Landwehr's journal.[59]

Munoz continued the association with Landwehr after his own publishing business began operations. Munoz's newsletter carried a "reader classified" section that occasionally featured calls for back issues of *Siegrunen*. Once Munoz's press began operation, he used *Siegrunen* to advertise his book service for pieces

Hitler's Eastern Legions

Volume - II
THE OSTTRUPPEN

Axis Europa, Inc. 53-20 207th Street, Bayside, N.Y. 11364 USA

Figure 12. A symbol used by Axis Europa Publications.

on the German military. Similarly, Landwehr placed advertisements for *Axis Europa* in *Siegrunen*.[60]

Munoz welcomed readers of *Siegrunen* and praised Landwehr's *Lion of Flanders: Flemish Volunteers of the Waffen-SS 1941–1945*, released by Shelf

Books. Munoz concluded, "No military historian studying the foreign volunteer movement should be without it [*Lions of Flanders*]." Munoz also used his personal ties with Landwehr in locating important sources. In researching *Forgotten Legions: Obscure Combat Formations of the Waffen-SS*, Munoz capitalized on Landwehr's expertise on the Waffen-SS and thanked him for having "selflessly donated or lent part of whole collections of photographs, documents, and other memorabilia for" *Forgotten Legions* (Figure 13. Cover Art from *Forgotten Legions: Obscure Combat Formations of the Waffen-SS*).[61]

Munoz's *Axis Europa* also served as an outlet for authors who worked on Axis auxiliary forces. Carlos Jurado, for example, built a reputation for his work on non-German units in the Wehrmacht and the Waffen-SS, interests similar to those of Munoz. He and Munoz followed a similar trajectory. Jurado earned his spurs as contributing editor to *Siegrunen*, where he served in that capacity at least through 2000. From 1985 through 1986, Jurado also served with another guru, Mark Yerger, and for some of this time with Ray Merriam, whose press, Merriam Press, later published *Siegrunen* monographs. Jurado also worked closely with Landwehr on the latter's *Romanian Volunteers of the Waffen-SS, 1944–1945*, released by *Siegrunen* in 1991. He enhanced his status as an expert on non-German units through publications on foreign volunteers in the Wehrmacht. In 1985, Osprey Publishing in the United Kingdom released his *Foreign Volunteers in the Wehrmacht, 1941–1945* and, in 1992, published his *Wehrmacht Auxiliary Forces*. Jurado also published articles in *Axis Europa* under the editorship of Munoz. As with so many gurus and romancers, including Munoz, Jurado demonstrates a fierce anti-Communism.[62]

In 1999, Munoz decided to shut down *Axis Europa*. It never returned sufficient profit to cover operating costs and the drain proved too much for his resources. Instead, Munoz decided to devote full time to his book publishing. Since then, his business has grown dramatically. He uses the company's sophisticated website to advertise and sell books dealing with the military forces of the Axis powers. At present Europa Books, the name for his enterprise, features more than twenty-five titles that deal with eight broad topics. These range from the German army and Waffen-SS to auxiliary forces from various southeastern and Eastern European countries. The books have a slick finish and each is packed with information from unit histories to original maps of various theaters.[63]

Europa Books also publishes lavishly done hardbacks. *Hitler's White Russians: Collaborators, Extermination and Anti-Partisan Warfare in Byelorussia, 1941–1944* is an expensive hard-cover volume done mostly in red and white. Glossy pages, scores of photographs and plain black-and-white maps and colored originals grace the pages of a 512-page book. Readers of these works are still drawn from the world of the romancers, but represent a smaller but dedicated subset of individuals with special interests in the lesser-known Axis forces. Reviews of the book by Amazon customers praised the work for thoroughness, "high-quality . . . production," and its "glossy stock." and for many new photos previously not available. The reviewer also appreciated the orders of battle; the charts and graphs; in short, the immense amount of detailed information. After years of struggling with different formats, Munoz now claims a major place among the romancers. Not surprisingly, buyers who purchased *Hitler's White Russians* also bought *Adventures in My Youth*, *Panzer Operations: The Eastern Front Memoirs of General Raus, 1941–1945*, and *Tigers in the Mud*, written by former Panzer commander, Otto Carius, and published by Fedorowicz Publishing. Readers of Munoz's works also showed a marked tendency to seek books on the Eastern Front.[64]

Munoz's *Forgotten Legions: Obscure Combat Formations of the Waffen-SS*, released by Axis Europa Books in 1991, shows the network of romancers at work. For the opening section, Munoz recruited Dr. Samuel W. Mitcham, Jr., a military historian on the faculty of Henderson State University in Arkadelphia, Ark., to write the forward. Mitcham wrote that he had been a fan of Munoz's since reading his work in *Siegrunen* in the 1980s. When asked to prepare an introduction to *Forgotten Warriors*, he readily agreed. *Forgotten Warriors*, Mitcham writes, "is the best English-language book on the armed SS that has been published in several years." He praises the research and the dramatic descriptions of the heroic actions of the SS. Mitcham tells the reader that he:[65]

> will find out what it was like to be surrounded with the SS fortress regiment in the doomed city of Breslau, fighting in the snow-covered ruins against odds of a dozen to one or more, or to be with a veteran SS infantry unit, fiercely resisting massive Soviet tank attacks with its last grenade as the Eastern Front crumbled.[66]

Mitcham paints a picture of desperate but heroic SS soldiers resisting an unstoppable force and in the end sacrificing their lives in a lost cause, a theme that echoes through much of the work on minor Axis powers and their national aspirations.

As if in vindication of these sentiments, Munoz's introduction to the book addresses the liberation of the Eastern European countries that lived under the yoke of what Munoz terms the "most detestable regimes." He describes the "freedom movements" that were sweeping throughout Eastern Europe. He also reminds readers that SS commanders such as Paul Hausser appealed to Eastern Europeans to join the "Pan European, anti-Communist crusade" being conducted against Stalin and his thugs. Yet, Hitler and his "henchmen" foiled all such efforts and extinguished the one opportunity to rid Europe of Stalin and his murderous followers.[67]

Interestingly enough, Munoz provides the romancer community with a somewhat different view of the war in the East than does, say, Kurowski. He acknowledges that the Germans behaved with brutality in the eastern war and that they did commit criminal acts not only against the Russian people, but the Jews as well, usually a taboo topic among the gurus. If he romances anyone, it is the many men who fought with the Germans, but with goals other than that of the Nazi regime – usually ethnic independence for their people. His one regret was that the Germans did not make earlier and much more extensive use of these volunteers.

Munoz's professional commitment in the quality and intensity of the research behind his books and his honesty in acknowledging the cruelty of the Germans separate him from other gurus and especially Richard Landwehr, whose unrivaled enthusiasm for the Waffen-SS persists to the present day.

7   Wargames, the Internet, and the Popular Culture of the Romancers

Romancing communities came together in two distinct eras. In the late 1960s and 1970s, wargaming won popularity among young people in their teens and twenties who were attracted by the challenge of games dealing with the complexities of war. Games that featured the Russo-German War helped fuel the growth of this burgeoning hobby, particularly in the 1970s, when the number of gamers expanded dramatically. Wargaming clubs, wargaming networks connected by mail, magazines, and national conventions soon followed the success of gaming companies. Romancers naturally saw wargames as the one opportunity to re-fight the battles of the Russo-German War with distinctly different outcomes. At the same time, demand for historical information on the German military also grew as hobbyists showed an unrivaled enthusiasm for more games on World War Two and specifically on the titanic battles that marked the life-and-death struggle on the Eastern Front. Magazines provided the medium for analysis of games, battles, and campaigns. Conventions periodically brought gamers together for three days of competition, lectures, and debates. Wargamers separated by significant distances developed schemes to play these complicated games via mail. As the industry expanded, Eastern Front games kept the reputation they enjoyed in the early days of the hobby.

By the 1990s, the Internet transformed and enlarged the romancer communities. Communications technology now brought romancers together on a constant basis. Web sites, chat rooms, various fora, and other formats greatly enhanced romancing communities and gave their members a new medium for their common interests. The romancer communities now crossed national boundaries and cultures. Information, news, debates, announcements, and any form of communication moved instantaneously to thousands of romancers. Specialty websites even invited German veterans, admittedly aged by the 1990s, to respond to questions from romancers eager for opinions of the men who actually fought at Stalingrad, Moscow, or Kursk. Websites also served as storehouses for a tremendous amount of historical information on the German military. Biographies of famous officers, accounts of key campaigns, descriptions of battles, and even day-by-day logs of events on the Eastern Front appeared on websites. The Internet and wargaming, then, provided romancers the means to construct long-lasting communities that joined enthusiasts who shared a passion for the Russo-German War.

The development of wargaming as an active hobby served as the basis for the first romancing communities that sprang up in regional centers such as New York City and Baltimore, Md., where the first major gaming companies appeared. Avalon Hill, headquartered in Baltimore, began releasing wargames in the late 1950s. One of its early best-selling games depicted the battle of Stalingrad and remained in print for many years after its publication in 1963. The company produced one of the best-selling wargames on the Eastern Front in 1970, *PanzerBlitz*. Avalon Hill also developed *The General*, a magazine that discussed the company's releases, answered questions from customers, and provided updates on future games.[1]

Simulations Publications Inc. (SPI), stationed in New York City, also made its mark on the industry. SPI dedicated its energies solely to wargaming, in contrast to Avalon, which catered to gamers in general, with one of several sections of the operation dedicated to wargames. Unlike Avalon Hill, which produced a few games annually, SPI consciously adopted a marketing strategy that depended on releasing multiple games every year. In the process, it successfully broadened the market for wargamers. The magazine *Strategy & Tactics* alone reached some 36,500 subscribers by the end of the 1970s. The company aggressively promoted its games through sophisticated artwork and packaging as it shifted from purely a mail-order business to retail operations. Its magazine, *Strategy & Tactics*, also changed its orientation. It still featured a historical simulation game with each of the six yearly issues, yet increasingly it "became more of a magazine of military history," historical information, and even contemporary warfare. The editor, James Dunnigan, and co-editor, Redmond Simonsen, started a new magazine, *Moves*, to debate and promote SPI's games, much as the *General* dealt exclusively with Avalon Hill's wargames.[2]

By the 1990s, more companies and wargaming magazines made their way into the market. Game Designers Workshop, The Gamers, Clash of Arms, and other companies joined an increasingly competitive market. *Command: Military History, Strategy & Analysis*, a glossy and smartly produced magazine, won the attention of wargamers with its lavishly done games and graphics. Each issue included a major article on the topic covered in the game and several shorter pieces.

As *Command Magazine, Strategy & Tactics*, and SPI suggest, wargames and wargaming magazines satisfied both the curiosity of romancers for vicariously experiencing the battles on the Eastern Front and their insatiable appetite for historical information on all aspects of this "mother" of all campaigns. Wargames incorporated tremendous amounts of detailed historical information about individuals, armies, weapons, battles, campaigns, planning, terrain, and many other aspects of the German armies and their opponents. Through the gaming magazines, many participants aired their interpretations of the war in Russia and debated many aspects of the conflict.

The games enabled the romancer to master this detail and then to re-create the battles that formed a central part of his/her world. One could read Paul Carell's description of Stalingrad, yet by 1979, a romancer could engage an opponent in the wargame, *Streets of Stalingrad*, with its detailed map of the city and the various buildings and factories that formed the heart of the battle. The cover art showed a group of embattled German soldiers in the midst of a destroyed Stalingrad, reduced to ruins by the fighting.

How did the Soviets resist the German attack and how can one reverse that outcome? What combination of arms would enable the 6th army to seize the tractor works or the grain elevator? These and other questions that romancers may have asked now could be answered.

Romancers could also study a close analysis of *Streets of Stalingrad* in the September-October issue of *Fire & Movement: The Forum of Conflict Simulation*, one of a number of wargame magazines that appeared in the 1970s and 1980s. The article carefully reviewed the mechanics of the game, the role of terrain, the assets of different types of weapons systems, and many other issues.[3]

The release of *PanzerBlitz* in 1970 fueled the growth of an infant industry. It proved an immensely popular game and attracted a large national audience and served as the catalyst for the flood of Eastern Front games in the 1970s and 1980s. It acted as a trendsetter from the moment of its publication. Its box cover art immediately caught the attention of romancers. It showed what appeared to be two German armored vehicles. German Panzer officers in the traditional black uniform, surveying the terrain to the front, stood ready for action. *PanzerBlitz* brought all the elements of tactical combat directly to the romancers. As a tactical level game, it incorporated features such as shortages of ammunition, advantages of infantry assaults on armored vehicles minus their infantry defense, the impact of superior German optics on artillery barrages, and the comparative advantages of German and Soviet tactics, among many items relevant to tactical combat. The game also deployed a full range of

German and Soviet weapons from mortars and tanks to self-propelled guns and motorcycle units.[4]

Players faced the challenges of battlefield commanders in Russia regarding which combination of weapons should be used in an attack. A romancer also had to deal with the role of terrain as he/she planned an assault. The counters that stood for different branches such as armor or infantry carried numerical values that indicated range, offensive/defensive capacities, and mobility. Counters for tanks, trucks and halftracks had images of these vehicles imprinted in the front. The iconic value of these images added to the power of the game. *PanzerBlitz* also gave the romancers a series of situation cards that were taken from actual combat on the Eastern Front. Situation #1 featured a Soviet raid on German rear areas. Situation # 3 depicted a German armor column moving toward the Russian city of Vyazma in the fall of 1941. The column drove into the remnants of Russian forces that survived the destruction of their unit by an earlier German attack. These scenarios depended on historical situations and enhanced the realism of the game for romancers.[5]

In 1974, Simulations Publications released *War in the East: The Russo-German Conflict 1941–1945*. Unlike the tactical *PanzerBlitz*, the long-awaited *War in the East* depicted the entire titanic struggle using division-sized units and large multi-maps. *War in the East* marked one of the first "monster" games in the industry and its scale greatly enhanced the appeal of Eastern Front games for romancers. The game covered all aspects of war, from production to rear areas. For the German player, rail construction assumed a major role because of the vast distances supplies and reinforcements had to travel before reaching the battlefields. As in the actual campaign, once the Wehrmacht advanced deep into Russia, it would faced a perilous situation as men, ammunition, food, and other necessities diminished significantly. Players had to calculate these conditions, much as the German High Command did in 1941. The game even incorporated the notion raised in almost every memoir about the baleful intrusion of Hitler into battlefield decision making. A standing rule prevented German troops from retreating, reflecting Hitler's refusal to surrender captured territory to the Russians. For the romancers who see Hitler as the source of many of the defeats in the war, the rule appropriately matched their own understanding of the conflict.[6]

SPI subsequently featured a profile of *War in the East* in *Strategy & Tactics*. The issue gave readers an in-depth look at orders of battle, strategies for the Russian player, and tactical options for the scenario on Stalingrad. For romancers, these insides gave a greater understanding of the game and its components. As these examples have suggested, these wargames and analyses focus intensely on the battles and campaigns.[7]

In the fall of 1976, *Strategy & Tactics* released *Panzergruppe Guderian: The Battle of Smolensk July 1941* as the featured magazine game. Unlike the tactical *PanzerBlitz* or the grandiose *War in the East*, *Panzergruppe Guderian* fell in the middle in terms of scale. It also incorporated one the of icons of romancers, Guderian, as its chief selling point. The cover art also featured Guderian and German armor. A photo of Colonel-General Guderian sat to the bottom right of the magazine cover (Figure 13). In full dress, his Knight's Cross was clearly visible and a pair of binoculars hung around his neck, suggesting his commander's role. His look exuded confidence, almost arrogance. The top of the magazine cover shows German armor advancing across the Russian landscape with a wrecked Soviet tank smoldering to the flank of the German tanks. The piece also claims Guderian's *Panzer Leader* remains the "best analysis of Blitzkrieg warfare." His abilities and theories made German successes possible. The use of *Panzergruppe*, an authentic German word, also appeals to romancers.[8]

The article included a sidebar on Guderian's World War Two career. It opened with Guderian's contribution to the notion of *Blitzkrieg* and identifies him as the author of this style of warfare. The piece describes in glowing terms his actions in the Polish campaign and the May 1940 invasion of France. The sidebar praises his actions on the Eastern Front and includes Guderian's own explanation for his dismissal by Hitler at the end of 1941. Guderian's order for his men to retreat in the face of Hitler's demand that all soldiers of the Wehrmacht stand their ground earned Guderian his removal. Later, the piece argued that the Panzer colonel general "was a specialist and a technician, the type of tool that can function in any political climate and be unaffected by it. His loyalty was to his army and to his country." The sidebar noted that although Hitler later appointed Guderian chief of the Eastern Front, the Fuhrer effectively exercised command even to the tactical level. Guderian's abilities operated under great constraint. For romancers, these remarks perfectly characterize Guderian, a man of principle and dedication to his martial duties and to defending his country. Guderian stood above the morass of politics and, certainly, the ugly swamp of Nazi crime.[9]

This German orientation appeared in many subsequent East Front games. *The Last Victory: Von Manstein's Backhand Blow, February and March 1943* (1987) captured the battle to retake the Ukrainian city of Kharkov by German forces. Manstein organized and led this effort in the wake of the near collapse of the southern front following the Stalingrad disaster. The box cover art shows a Wehrmacht Panzer officer with earphones, binoculars, and stern-looking face (Figure 14). He is standing up, in an open hatch. Behind him is a line of 55-ton Tiger tanks stretching along a city street. In the background, in blue

Figure 13. Cover Art from *Panzergruppe Guderian: The Battle of Smolensk, July 1941.*

with mist and smoke rising, stands Kharkov. The Nazi swastika sits in a lit circle to the top left of the cover. The accompanying historical commentary praises Manstein for his brilliance and his ability to recognize the assets of extremely able commanders under him, notably Paul Hausser, who led the 3rd SS Totenkopf Division.[10]

Figure 14. Cover Art from *The Last Victory: Von Manstein's Backhand Blow, February and March 1943*.

Manstein and Hausser figure prominently in the romancer's world. Manstein epitomized the Prussian officer who remained outside politics and fought for the Fatherland. He demonstrated courage, heroic behavior, and a commitment to the welfare of his men. Hausser's abilities and his repeated battlefield triumphs, even in defensive actions, elevate him to the circle of honored men in the German military. His membership in the elite Waffen-SS, a favorite of the romancers, only enhanced his status. The analysis presented both men as extraordinary battlefield commanders concerned only with achieving their objectives, using their men wisely, and always living up to their professional codes of behavior and performance. Both commanders disagreed with Hitler and his meddling in military affairs, a losing proposition by 1943. Manstein, like Guderian, suffered dismissal for disagreeing with the Fuhrer. This description matches in every way the expectation of romancers for an icon such as Manstein.[11]

Pro-German artwork games appeared frequently in wargames and wargaming magazines. The September 1988 issue of *Strategy & Tactics* dramatically illustrates the point. It depicts a German soldier on the front with a large red,

Figure 15. Cover Art from *Strategy & Tactics: The Fatalistic German Soldier.*

white, and back Nazi flag as background (Figure 15). The title of the featured
game, *Fortress Stalingrad: The Russian Winter Offensive 1942–1943*, appears
near the bottom of the cover. The artwork is taken from a Nazi propaganda
piece entitled *Der Sieg Wird Unser Sein*. The commentary in the main article on the campaign praises Manstein's incredible abilities as a commander
while denigrating Hitler and his intrusion in decision making. Such reasoning

Figure 16. *Planning an Advance.*

accommodated the romancers' vision of the military divorced from the Nazi regime yet suffering the catastrophic consequences of its decisions. The art and the argument again both fit perfectly into the romancers' understanding of the war in Russia and its heroes and villains.[12]

The article also incorporated artwork that gives a flattering or heroic image of the German officers and rank and file. The first, *At 49th Mountain Corps UQ: Planning the Advance into the Caucasus* (Figure 16), showed senior officers gathered around a table covered with maps. One held a large map and pointed to a specific location that suggested battle decisions facing the commanders. The majority of the officers stared intently at the standing officer's map. Many have thoughtful looks. The sketch conveyed a sense of professionalism. The second image, *The Heady Days of Summer: 6th Army Breaks into Stalingrad*, depicted three Nordic looking men fully armed and determined (Figure 17). One gripped the famous 42 machine gun while the other two looked into the distance. The last etching captured the desperate efforts of the German soldiers defending their positions; one man's head was wrapped in bandages and was partially covered with a long blanket. Other men in his trench have sunk to the ground in exhaustion while another *Landser* sat atop the trench and peered into the distance (Figure 18). The men gave the impression of defending against all odds and the will to keep the fight going no matter what the personal cost. These images and the impression they convey reaffirmed the romancers' idealized view of the German rank and file and their officers.[13]

Figure 17. Facing the Enemy.

This same sympathetic portrait of suffering German soldiers appeared on the cover of *Enemy At the Gates: The Stalingrad Pocket to Manstein's Counter-attack Army Group South–19 Nov 42 to 14 March 43*. Released by the Gamers Company, the game box featured exhausted and wounded German soldiers in a trench, clearly near the end of their endurance (Figure 19). One man, his head wrapped in a bandage, with a look of utter fatigue, leans against the trench wall with his rifle on the ground to front of him. Another man is sitting down with shovel in hand, staring up toward the standing *Landser*. Trapped in a doomed pocket, the end is all too apparent for these courageous young men. Only Manstein's creative mind saves the entire southern front from the "Red Tide." The image conveyed the impression of lost youth defending an indefensible position. Such heroism fulfills the romancers' notions of the men who served in the Wehrmacht.[14]

The artwork in the 1996 *Hube's Pocket*, released by the Gamers Company, provides a powerful example of this bias. It portrayed the breakout attempt of *Generaloberst* Hans Hube to lead his 1st Panzer army out of packet near the Dnestr River in the southern front. The game focused on the Manstein-led effort to free the 1st Panzer army from the Russian entrapment. The box

Figure 18. Germans Trapped.

art captured the essence of the game and portrayed the German soldier in a dramatic fashion (Figure 20). Moving into battle, determined German soldiers rode on a Panther tank or ran alongside the armored vehicle. They moved into the teeth of strong winds and a fierce snowstorm. The outline of another Panther on the flank suggested the tanks and men formed part of a larger battle group seeking escape from certain doom. The historic commentary stressed the tension between Hitler and Manstein over the field marshal's plan for the 1st Panzer army to break out of the pocket and re-establish better defensive positions to the west.[15]

The bibliography included Carell's *Scorched Earth* and Manstein's memoirs, *Lost Victories*, which provide dramatic accounts of the tension between Hitler and Manstein. For romancers, the game incorporated many of their ideals. A brave and courageous field marshal challenged Hitler. This was an often-repeated theme, and the source of most of the Wehrmacht's difficulties. Manstein's resolve grew out of his concern for his men and the fate of the Wehrmacht. The German troops faced dramatically greater numbers of enemy

Figure 19. Cover Art from *Enemy at the Gate: The Stalingrad Pocket to Manstein's Counter-attack Army Group South – 19 Nov 42 to 14 March 43.*

troops but engaged the Russians in a fight for the very existence of the 1st Panzer army. The game also includes black counters for the 2nd SS Panzer corps, an important icon for what romancers see as the elite formation in the German military.[16] Yet changes were about to happen that would alter the world of the

Figure 20. Cover Art from *Hube's Pocket*.

romancers. The games, magazines, and conventions would still enjoy a healthy life, yet dazzling technology would displace these traditional media outlets as the main source of information regarding the Eastern Front.

By the 1990s, wargaming magazines, new gaming companies, national wargaming, and regional wargaming conventions brought romancers together via print or face-to-face meetings. Games continued to feed the romancers' appetite for historical detail and for the interpretations that accommodate their understanding of the German military in the Eastern Front. The technology that mediated these encounters was essentially developed in the nineteenth century, with modifications in the last hundred years. These did create the basis for romancer communities and information outlets that informed romancers on a periodic basis of news in the industry. The games and the magazines had certainly created a sound foundation, yet the technology to enable romancers to come together remained primitive. The 1990s would see a dramatic break in the way people interacted.

The technological changes of the 1990s transformed the popular culture of the romancers. Until the arrival of the Internet, the exchange of information remained slow and cumbersome, unmediated by any significant technology. The Internet changed forever communications. Distance and time lost all meaning as electronic impulses moved information at incredible speeds at almost no cost. The Internet also created the vast potential for websites where huge amounts of information could be stored and accessed with relative ease. Monitors who handled websites could also update information almost daily if the need arose.

With amazing speed, those involved in the romancing embraced the new technology with all its possibilities. New romancing communities emerged in the decade of the 1990s, often identified by specific interests. Romancers showed a broad range of concerns. Some showed great enthusiasm for the Waffen-SS, a favorite of romancers because of the special bonds that united men in the Waffen-SS and the absence of hierarchy. Other sites also specialized in German weapons, elite forces, and even combat uniforms. Several major websites incorporated historical information, narratives of the war in the east, unit histories, biographies of noted commanders, and substantial discussion where romancers engaged in conversations and debates. One enterprising artist created portraits of the more famous, or "infamous, as the case may be," leading German officers. Stars of the Third Reich, such as SS officers Joachim Peiper, Paul Hauser, and Kurt Meyer, and well-known Army officers, including von Manstein, appeared on his website. These paintings depict the distinguished heroes that so enthrall romancers. Last, one company – Militaryreenactment, Inc. – recently advertised military coffee mugs with images of Wehrmacht and SS heroes on the mugs. The faces of Manstein, Guderian, Rundstedt, and Peiper grace these large cups. The famous tank commander, Michael Wittmann, the infamous Theodore Eicke, who led the Death's Head Division and designed Dachau, the model for the death camps, and Josef "Sepp" Dietrich, commander of the Leibstandarte and later the 1 SS Panzer corps and a war criminal, also appear on the mugs.[17]

These websites and the Internet promoted exchanges bound by neither time nor distance. Romancers in the United States searched for the addresses of German veteran organizations in the newly united German Republic. In some cases, veterans eagerly joined romancer chat groups, giving members access to men who served and fought in what romancers perceived as the heroic and courageous Wehrmacht and Waffen-SS. Romancers also explore the websites dedicated to the technical details such as weapons, vehicles, and other equipment. The authenticity of these sites makes the world of the German military come alive. The Internet has greatly empowered the romancers, expanded their numbers, and enhanced their capacity to acquire a great variety of new information.

A specialty site and one of the longest running websites, *Achtung Panzer*, deals with German armored vehicles. It came online in the mid-1990s and continues to enjoy substantial numbers of visitors every month. Its popularity and long life, at least for the Internet, where sites come and go with great speed, make it an appropriate site to examine. Its graphics immediately catch the eye of a romancer. *Achtung Panzer* features armored vehicle icons and a three-dimensional color picture of either a Tiger tank or Mark IV tank. The site provides romancers with the historical and technical detail they crave. The site includes numerous tanks from as early as World War I to the *Panzerkampfwagen* IV, the heart of the German armored forces in Operation Barbarossa. Each profile contains a visual of the vehicle and a substantive analysis of its key features. The list of vehicles includes tank killers and self-propelled guns. If one needs any type of information on a German armored vehicle, this site provides those data.[18]

Under the rubric "Additional Information," the site incorporates biographies of famous officers who commanded armor formations. The owners of the website state their nonpolitical position and reject any ties with fascist or neofascist organizations. As romancers, those who sponsor the website and those who participate in the website show their own biases for the Wehrmacht and the Waffen-SS. These appear most vividly in the biographies of noted commanders and tankers such as Erich von Manstein, Heinz Guderian, Otto Carius, and Michael Wittman. Of course, Manstein and Guderian are standard fare. Carius won the attention of romancers based upon both his battlefield exploits in Eastern Front battles and his publications through J. J. Fedorowicz. Wittman stands out as probably the most decorated and noted tank commander on the Eastern Front and even in the entire Panzer arm. His untimely death, at least for romancers, in the battles during the Allied efforts to break out of the pocket at the Normandy beach heads enhances his heroic and iconic status.[19]

The sketches of these men reinforce the perceptions of the romancers in many ways. The profile of Manstein's account clearly fits the romancers' notions of leading German officers. The biographical description recounts the distinguished family history of Manstein. It also includes a discussion of his medals and awards for bravery and astute leadership that add the heroic dimension to a figure more noted for his command abilities than battle exploits. The sketch lavishly praises Manstein as an exemplar of the ideal battlefield commander – able, creative, and demanding. In the biography, Manstein stands out as a hero dedicated to his men and their welfare. In 1943, he ignored Hitler's demands to stand fast and ordered German troops to break out of the encirclement known as the Cherkassy Pocket. His action saved the lives of thousands of men who otherwise would have died if Manstein had obeyed the demands of Hitler. He risked removal, yet his concern for the men under his command overrode any other consideration. Eventually his disagreements with Hitler earned him a dismissal. The sketch notes that Manstein was aware of the plot to kill Hitler, although he never played a role in the failed attempt.[20]

The sketch actually opens up a difficult issue for romancers – namely, war crimes. Of course Manstein faced charges and was convicted of criminal actions. The sketch avoids any discussion of his trial or his culpability. Instead, the account notes, seemingly with pride, that Manstein "successfully defended" German officers accused of crimes during the war. The sketch then moves quickly to Manstein's postwar record. Here it focuses on his role in creating the new German military, the one designed to defend the West against the new menace, the Soviet Union, also Manstein's old nemesis. As the sketch notes, he used his formidable powers as a former field marshal to advise the Bundeswehr in its role as part of an Allied coalition tailored to fight the Red Army. Overall, the sketch gives the impression of an honorable man dedicated to his men and his country. The conclusion drawn from this short narrative of Manstein simply repeats what had appeared in so many early works.[21]

In the biography of Heinz Guderian, the sketch attempts to place Guderian at odds with the German High Command and ultimately with Hitler. The description includes his early career as a cadet and junior officer, his service in World War One, and his role in creating the Panzer arm. The sketch praises Guderian for his battlefield exploits in France and Russia. The account stresses the tension that resulted from disagreements with the High Command on the urgency of high-risk advances against the enemy, Guderian's forte. His commanding officer in the 1941 campaign, General von Kluge, frequently clashed with Guderian, who chafed under Kluge's restraint. Ironically, Guderian's calls for a strategic retreat in December 1941 when facing a superior Russian force and his men were exhausted and depleted by the combat led to his dismissal.

Hitler returned Guderian to command in 1944 as chief of staff. Again, his violent disagreements with Hitler led to a second dismissal.[22]

Guderian's character also won him generous praise in the account. His loyalty to his men and their admiration for him marked the colonel general as an outstanding officer. Inevitably, Guderian won praise because of his mastery of armor warfare, an ability the German High Command never fully understood.[23]

In *The Verdict*, the piece confronts the issue of war crimes. As in the case of Manstein, the account skirts the issue of Guderian's participation in any such actions. It argues that Guderian never embraced anti-Semitism nor even showed an awareness of the Nazi program for their destruction. He simply never took account of European Jews. As General Inspector, he apparently never considered the fate of the millions of POWs and Eastern Europeans who ended up in German factories that he visited in tours. Of course, neither Guderian nor any other German officer raises the fate of these workers in their memoirs.[24]

The website's biographical array of famous German officers included the life of Hans Rudel, a "Stuka Ace" and a notorious Nazi acolyte. As in the other accounts, the sketch traces Rudel's career in the Luftwaffe. The account describes his many heroic battlefield actions and notes with pride the medals awarded him for these exploits. In one instance, Rudel risked his life to rescue a downed aircrew. They made an emergency landing and were stranded on the ground. They faced an enemy determined to kill or capture them. Rudel landed his plane and joined the men as they attempted to escape on foot. His legendary heroism persisted even when the war was clearly lost. He volunteered to fly a suicide mission at the end of the war in a desperate effort to stave off the inevitable Soviet advance. Rudel made contributions to the German war effort in other ways. He developed effective air tactics for the Stuka that became doctrine for the Luftwaffe air fleets. Last, the account includes statistics on his career as a pilot, from number of missions to the weight of all bombs dropped, largely on the Russians. These summed up his battlefield heroics.[25]

The sketch acknowledges his ties with the Nazis. Given Rudel's own words, the account could hardly ignore these associations. In published works, Rudel openly condemned the failed effort to kill Hitler, because, as the account stresses, the attempted assassination created chaos at a time when Germany's defenses were being compromised, especially by the Western Allied invasion. He also blames the German High Command because it worked against Hitler and his genius for war. His diary, released in print in 1953, identified him as a Nazi follower but, as the account notes, "it was no longer that bad to be a Nazi." Shortly after Rudel's death in 1982, two famous Allied pilots, Douglas Bader and Pierre Closterman, wrote a warm and praising foreword to the second edition of Rudel's diary. Again, the site downplays the Nazi sympathies of one of Germany's military heroes.[26]

Interspersed with such serious accounts are sections devoted to what are hobby-like activities. *Achtung Panzer* features a Panzer of the month contest in which participants submit their favorite Panzer and explain why. At the end of the month, the website monitors collect and evaluate the submissions, calculate the voters from website users and announce the winner. The winner for October 2001 was the Panther Tank, with 231 out of 1,130 votes cast. According to the announcement on page two of the November site, the next poll intended to identify the "favourite armored car" among armored vehicle enthusiasts. This activity fits perfectly with the armor emphasis and the romancers' detailed knowledge of the Wehrmacht.[27]

The November 11, 2001 site included an advertisement for Heinz Gunther Guderian's book, *From Normandy to the Ruhr: With the 116th Panzer Division in WWII*, along with the book cover. Aberjona Press in southeast Pennsylvania, one of several operations dedicated World War Two pieces and specifically pro-German works, released the younger Guderian's book. Heinz Gunther Guderian, of course, was the inspector general's son. The appeal of the name Guderian for romancers carries considerable clout in the marketplace of books and the publisher instinctively knew that the *Achtung Panzer* website provided the company with a potentially large clientele for the book. Last, the November 2001 website incorporated one of Guderian's famous quotes, "If the tanks succeed, the victory follows."[28]

The site also included a monthly Panzer quiz that asked questions such as "what version of the 88 mm gun was Tiger II's main armament?" Or "In 1944/45 Otto Carius commanded the 2nd company of schwere Panzerjager Abteilung 512. Yes or No?" Typical of sites that appeal to romancers, the questionnaire includes an iconic picture of a Panzer vehicle with an officer attired in the black Panzer uniform and sunglasses standing in the open hatch. The face of a Panzer officer imposed to the side stands above the Panzer quiz title. The page also featured a black-and-white photo that depicted German infantry firing from atop a self-propelled gun with smoke rising in the foreground. These pictures keep images of battle before the romancers and add a touch of realism to the site. From 1996 until 1999, *Achtung Panzer* attracted some 567,772 visitors, demonstrating the consistent appeal of *Achtung Panzer*.[29]

The owners of *Achtung Panzer* also show sensitivity about the possible identification of their pro-Wehrmacht sentiments with the Nazi ideology. They openly disavow any affiliation, sympathy, or belief in Nazi doctrines or current neo-Nazi organizations. The owners repeatedly emphasize the nonpartisan attachment of the *Achtung Panzer*. This position in many ways masks the inability of the participants to engage the revelations about the complicity of the Wehrmacht and the Waffen-SS in the crimes committed against civilians, POWs, and European Jews. The owners, for example, do admit an awareness of German policies that forced millions of Russian POWs and civilians into virtual slave-labor worksites in Germany where vast numbers died under harsh work regimes. Yet the website ignores any possible connection between these policies and the Wehrmacht or Waffen-SS officers. Their reputations remain intact, bolstered by the site's positive descriptions of these men and their heroic actions on the battlefields of Russia. These sustain the romancer's notion of the war and battle as distinct from responsibility for the actions of the Nazi regime. One must conclude that a certain degree of ingenuousness accounts for these omissions. The glowing descriptions of the Panzer officers and formations powerfully remind visitors to *Achtung Panzer* of the strength of the romancing ethos and myths more than fifty years after the war ended.[30]

Aware of the importance of the narrative of World War Two in understanding the role of the *Panzer* arm, the website incorporates a substantial bibliography dealing with German armor in World War Two. The link creates an immediate readings list for newcomers to the world of German armor and provides useful reference works for later consultation. The books listed include technically detailed pieces such as *Panzerkampfwagen I & II* and *Sturmartillerie – Self-Propelled Guns and Flak Tanks* to *Captured Tanks in German Service – Small Tanks and Armored Tractors*. The list also includes pieces by James Lucas, an author very sympathetic to the romancer view, of the German solider and his role in World War Two, and Gordon Williamson and Bruce Quarrie, both of whom popularize the German military in World War Two. Last, the file also lists videos available to the general public and that deal with the German war machine in several theaters of World War Two.[31]

The site features a forum for those interested in armor vehicles. It appears with a "Code of Conduct" that rejects any discussion of Nazi political ideology or revisionist history. It also asks that all participants demonstrate civility in their exchanges with other participants or their posting access will be removed. The site monitor holds the right to remove any message considered offensive. The conversations vary but usually focus on narrow topics such as the capacity of a 105 artillery piece to destroy a Panther or Tiger tank on the very first round fired or the problems with the self-propelled gun, the Ferdinand, in its inaugural battle at Kursk in 1943. The guestbook section includes the name of the participant, his/her residence, and the way in which she/he learned about *Achtung Panzer*.[32]

Finally, the site provides the reader with links to other sites featuring books and magazines. It praises the Military Book Club as the best source for works on military history. It also lists J. J. Fedorowicz and describes it as a specialty publisher dealing with materials on the German armed forces in World War Two. If a viewer follows the link, he/she moves into the heart of the romancing ethos when arriving at J. J. Fedorowicz.[33]

Fedorowicz's attitudes toward the German army appear most dramatically in a series of remarks by Otto Carius. He served as the commander of Heavy Panzer Company on the Eastern Front and appears in Kurowski's *Panzer Aces*. Most notably for romancers, this veteran wrote the popular *Tigers in the Mud*, a Fedorowicz book. It recounts the fierce armor battles in the East involving German 55-ton Tiger tanks, a topic that generates a great deal of enthusiasm among the romancers.[34] Carius' foreword to the Fedorowicz translation reminds readers of the sympathies of both Carius and the Fedorowicz Publishing Company for the German military. Carius thanks J. J. Fedorowicz for enabling German authors who write on World War Two to reach a broader market. Carius writes in direct reference to Fedorowicz Publishing:

> Through these publications, the defamation of the German soldier in film, television and the press has been countered and the picture of the *Wehrmacht* has been a more objective one by means of the help offered by many sources.[35]

Carius clearly expresses his dissatisfaction over the criticisms endured by the former members of the German military and his applause for Fedorowicz for helping to restore the image of the men who served Germany during World War Two. He then lambastes the memorials to German deserters and condemns those who dedicated these false memorials. For Carius, deserters constituted a tiny proportion of the twenty million who filled the ranks of the German military in World War Two while the lies about the German army fueled the damning claims about the German soldier. Carius declares that collaborators who once worked for the Third Reich sustain these perfidies. He concludes, and, we assume, so does Fedorowicz, given that it sponsored the book and cleared the foreword, that the German soldier only fulfilled his obligation to the state. Politicians choose the enemies, a refrain echoed by all veterans. Fedorowicz obviously agrees wholeheartedly with Carius.[36] The Fedorowicz link provides romancers with a reaffirmation of their sentiments toward the German soldiers and their field commanders.

Unlike *Achtung Panzer*, the *German Armed Forces in WWII* covers the whole range of the German military in World War Two. It remains one of the oldest romancer websites dedicated to the German military. By 2002, Jason Pipes had changed the name to *Feldgrau* and by 2005 the site had drawn more than a million visitors since its opening in 1996 as the *German Armed Forces in WWII*. Even more important, Pipes has long been a prominent member of the romancer community. He worked with Antonio Munoz as contributors to Richard Landwehr's *Siegrunen* during the 1980s and in the 1990s as editor for Munoz's *Axis Europa*.[37] Pipes also posted an essay by Munoz on Russian Volunteers in the German Army. Munoz had originally prepared the piece for a book by Lt. Gen. Wladyslaw Anders released by *Europa Books*.[38]

Pipes also works with an Internet guru, Marc Rikmenspoel, who developed a reputation for his work on the Waffen-SS. In fact, Pipes and Rikmenspoel co-authored a piece on the Norwegian Volunteers who served in the Wehrmacht that appeared in the *German Army in World War II* website. Rikmenspoel's own personal disposition toward the Waffen-SS appeared most vividly in his introduction to Richard's Landwehr's hostile review of Max Hastings' book, *Das Reich*. He agreed completely with the review of the Hastings book by guru Richard Landwehr that first appeared in *Siegrunen* in 1983. Landwehr criticized Hasting for misrepresentations, lies, and distortions. He downplayed the number of casualties suffered at the hands of Das Reich in the French village of Oradour-sur-Glane and accused Hastings of ignoring the numerous atrocities committed by the Red Army in Eastern Europe and Germany. He also expressed fear over the wide circulation of the book via book clubs and public and private libraries. Rikmenspoel revealed a deep-seated animosity toward those who write critically of the Waffen-SS, the very group he studied. His piece also suggested some common notions of the German army shared between Rikmenspoel and Pipes. In essence, Rikmenspoel defends the romanticized version of the Waffen-SS, one that praises its members' bravery and ignores their crimes.[39]

The dedication of Pipes to the German military shows most vividly in the wide range of information he has collected and made available to romancers and other interested parties. The site includes nine major areas of interest to those fascinated with the German military in World War Two. These sections cover "campaigns and battles," "medals and awards," the Waffen-SS, the German army, the allies of Germany, and other related topics. Visitors can also participate in the continuing online discussions of issues surrounding the German military. The site uses icons such as a Waffen-SS soldier to guide visitors to the relevant information on topics of their choice. For romancers, *German Armed Forces* provides a gold mine of data, opinion, and debate. In fact, the Pipes site had more than 1,000 histories of German military units and "1,200 pages of information" as of November 1999. Such sites sustain the romancer's world and create public fora available twenty-four hours a day. In many ways, they have become the meeting place for romancers throughout the United States and Europe.[40]

The *German Armed Forces* site includes polling on issues of great interest to romancers. In fact, it hosts regular opinion polls that solicit responses from participants. These polls ask for reader responses on matters such as, "Which

Division do you think was the most elite?" "Which arm of services interests you the most?" and "Which personality interests you the most?" These questions presume a substantial knowledge of the German military, usually quite detailed. Hundreds of readers give their responses. Interestingly, the respondents chose Waffen-SS and the army as their favorite and the *Leibstandarte* and the *Grossdeutschland* as their favorite units.[41]

Pipes' site contains numerous files on German combat divisions of all types, from infantry to armor and mountain. The files incorporate a short history of each division, its regiments, and its commanders. The file also contains a chart indicating area and date of service throughout the war. Sometimes, as in the case of the SS Charlemagne division and the Spanish volunteer division, the accounts praise the bravery and vigor of a unit in its battles against Soviet troops. The essays also describe the fierce weather conditions German troops faced in Russia and the demanding terrain they had to navigate. These descriptions obviously emphasize the struggles German soldiers confronted in the Soviet Union and their determination and sacrifice in meeting these demands of the battlefields. The section on German units also reviews smaller formations such as Schwere Panzer Abteilung 501 or specialized units, notably the Eisenbahn-Panzerzug 6, or an armored train. Some files included analyses of the assets and liabilities of weapons used by the Germans. The analyses even discuss modifications made to improve the performance of German weapons.[42]

For the enthusiasts, the Pipes site featured a reprint of a German manual for Panzers. It stressed the "thirty basic lessons" for Panzer officers leading armor and armored formations in Russia. Similarly, the site contains a glossary of German terms, from *Befehlshaber* to *Totenkopf*. These give romancers access to the iconic language so popular in this group, and it gives them clear definitions of important words. The search for detail and rarity, so common among the romancers, emerges in these files of the Pipes site.[43]

The site incorporates an extensive bibliography that includes technical works that detail weapons, badges, insignias, regalia, and other items of the Wehrmacht and Waffen-SS. These pieces provide the authenticity and the nuts and bolts held in such high regard by romancers in their efforts to recreate the lost world of the German military.

The bibliography hardly neglects the gurus. The works of Yerger, Munoz, Landwehr, and Kurowski account for twenty-six volumes of the listed books. For example, Landwehr's *Narva 1944: The Waffen-SS and the Battle For Europe* and *Lions of Flanders: Flemish Volunteers of the Waffen-SS, 1941–1945* appears in the bibliography. The *Narva* title covers the battles to contain the Soviet offensive to break out of the Leningrad siege and suggests the fate of the entire continent rested on the outcome of this battle. A German victory would save

Europe from the onslaught of the Communist forces. The men dedicated to defeating the Communists in the East also fought with the elite Waffen-SS. In *Lions of Flanders*, Landwehr portrays the struggles of the heroic Flemish volunteers who joined German forces on the Eastern Front in November 1941 and gave their lives to defeating the barbaric forces of Communism. These were men willing to make the ultimate sacrifice to save their homelands and men who stood the challenges to earn a spot in the ranks of the Waffen-SS, a privileged formation that selected only the toughest and most dedicated volunteers. The Flemish volunteers clearly demonstrated their commitment and their toughness. Such characterization appeals to the romancers and their vision of brave men fighting against the Soviet menace in the East. The bibliography also lists fifty-three volumes of Landwehr's *Siegrunen* magazine that carry dense information packets about the German military as well as incorporate the romancers' noble vision of German soldiers and their officers.[44]

Munoz's books also appear in the *German Armed Forces* Bibliography. His popular *Forgotten Legions: Obscure Combat Formations of the Waffen-SS* appears on the recommended readings list (Figure 21). Munoz packed the book with information of every conceivable kind about formations little known and ignored in the standard works on the Waffen-SS. For romancers attempting to master every detail of even the smallest Waffen-SS formation, this work is indispensable. Munoz's thoroughness included unit strength, casualties, orders of battle, unit organization, and countless maps locating Waffen-SS formations. His *Hitler's Eastern Legions, Volume I, The Baltic Schutzmannschaft* and *Hitler's Eastern Legions, Volume II, The Osttruppen* also appear in the bibliography. These, again, incorporate the highly detailed information so important to romancers.[45]

A bibliography intending to give direction for readers interested in the German military inevitably includes the works of guru Mark Yerger. His works on the Waffen-SS remain indispensable for romancers. These books provide the historical detail all romancers crave. Typical of a guru, Yerger's accounts praise the Waffen-SS officers for their abilities and daring in combat. For instance, Artur Phleps began his military career in the service of the Austro-Hungarian forces in World War One. From the beginning, he distinguished himself in combat. He acquired Romanian citizenship in 1919 and then in 1941 joined the Waffen-SS, where he led the Westland regiment in the SS Wiking Division. In combat, he regularly performed heroic acts, leading his men often against overwhelming odds, and consistently demonstrated his "bravery and boldness." The biographic sketches regaled readers with stories of combat action that won Phleps medals and promotions for leadership and victories. The sketch included twelve black-and-white pictures of Phleps in various situations such

Figure 21. Cover art from *Forgotten Legions: Obscure Combat Formations of the Waffen-SS.*

as discussions with other officers. In some cases, the photographs captured Phleps posing with fellow SS officers. He also commanded Otto Kumm, J. J. Fedorowicz author and, obviously, veteran of the Eastern Front. The inclusion of Yerger's works in the bibliography demonstrates the importance of these websites in sustaining the romancers' world.[46]

The website's bibliography also features many authors extremely agreeable to the romancers' notions of the war and German soldiers. James Lucas' *War on the Eastern Front: The German Soldier in Russia 1941–1945* gives a very sympathetic portrait of the *Landser* struggling against the odds and the weather on the Eastern Front. Lucas' works cover many topics, including the last year of the war. He generally describes the German officers and men in very positive terms. Lucas also developed a special relationship with guru Mark Yerger and SS veteran and author Otto Wiedinger. The latter served in the Das Reich division during the war and, as a result, knew first-hand many veterans of the Russo-German conflict. He personally introduced Lucas to many veterans at the frequent reunions veterans held over the years since the end of the World War Two. These men assisted Lucas in writing the volume on Das Reich. Such an approach perfectly accommodates the need of romancers for authenticity in writings on the Eastern Front. Lucas also makes available the personal stories of German heroism inaccessible from any other source, a perception at the heart of the romancers' world. Lucas, Weidinger, and others all served well the inclinations of the romancers.[47]

The Pipes site features a wide-ranging online forum, "The German Armed Forces in WWII Online Message Forum." It draws readers from all over the United States, Europe, and Australasia and covers a multitude of topics relevant to the German armed forces. The Waffen-SS stands out as a favorite topic among participants in the forum. For instance, in the winter of 2000, one participant queried about a good history of the Seventh SS Freiwilligen-Division "Prince Eugen." The visitor showed a particular interest in photographs of officers who held the ranks "of *Haupsturmfuhrer through Oberststurmbannfuhrer*" in the SS Prince Eugen Division. He asked if veteran magazines would have such photos. Translator of the German Munn Verlag edition for J. J. Fedorowicz, Marc Rikmenspoel, recommended Otto Kumm's piece, *The History of the 7 SS Mountain Division "Prinz Eugen"* published by J. J. Fedorowicz, one of the leading romancer presses. He, of course, worked with Landwehr and Munoz and published a book on the Waffen-SS through Fedorowicz. In this one exchange, a prominent figure in the romancing ethos recommended a major work written by a Wehrmacht veteran, published by a right-wing German press and then published in English through one of the leading romancer presses.[48]

Rikmenspoel's book on the Waffen-SS won him notoriety among the Romancers. He later published his *Waffen-SS Encyclopedia* through the Military Book Club, further enhancing his reputation. His participation in the many online discussions of the Waffen-SS won him a status as an Internet guru. His reputation as an expert on the Waffen-SS often facilitated his frequent participation in online discussions hosted by the Pipe's Forum. Rikmenspoel presumed visitors to the site knew of his work, where he asked for their advice on the title of his next book on the Waffen-SS Knight's Cross winners. His own suggestion was pure romancing, "Victories in Defeat." He clearly saw these men as heroic and their ultimate defeat not of their own making.[49]

Participants responded with enthusiasm to his query. Many commended him on his first work and expressed admiration for the brave and courageous men whose stories will make up the heart of Rikmenspoel's second book. One wrote: "I think you are writing about the extraordinary deeds of these brave soldiers." Several members of the group actually took issue with the word "victories," given the ultimate defeat of the Waffen-SS. Jason Pipes, Rikmenspoel's friend and associate, disagreed when he argued "there were many victories at the hands of these brave men and honorable men in the ranks of the Waffen-SS." Pipes, the founder of the site and monitor of the Forum, demonstrated his own sympathies for Rikmenspoel's romancing vision of the Waffen-SS when he recommended the title *Honor in Defeat: The Knight's Cross Holders of the Waffen-SS and Their Battles*. Rikmenspoel wholeheartedly endorsed Pipes' sentiment and pointed to the many victories of the Waffen-SS throughout the war. The men who won the Knights Cross all experienced victories in a war that ended in defeat. Rikmenspoel thanked all the contributors and writes that he will probably have "Victories in Defeat" as his main title.

He also openly praised the work of guru Mark Yerger's *Waffen-SS Commanders*, which serves as model for the Knight's Cross work.[50]

In the end, the discussion revealed the romancing attitudes in the context of the "Lost Cause." In the romancers' world, the Waffen-SS epitomizes honor and fought their battles free of the horror that was so much a part of the Nazi regime. For romancers, the Waffen-SS stood as the premier military formation on the Eastern Front. In the hands of Internet guru Rikmenspoel, the romancing ethos enjoys a spirited life via the Internet.

The Waffen-SS drew many other romancers into these online discussions. In a series of exchanges moderated on the Pipes' Online Forum, participants engaged the stories of valiant non-Germans who served in the Waffen-SS. The participants sympathetically describe what they considered the grotesque fate of these brave and honorable men who served in the Waffen-SS as foreign volunteers. One contributor protested the hypocrisy of the French resistance fighters who committed violent excesses against those who collaborated with the Germans. These "fighters" (i.e., those in the resistance) were visibly absent until 1944, when the tide began to turn against the Germans. Few showed the bravery so common among the Waffen-SS volunteers, who paid a steep price for their sacrifices. In Belgium, the men who served in Degrelle's SS Brigade ended up in the Brussels Zoo, kept in cages for a spitting session by Belgian citizens, many of who enjoyed a pleasant existence under German occupation. The contributor wrote: "Aah, those valiant Belgian resistance fighters" mocking their alleged bravery. Others suffered grievously in Russian camps where very few ever came out alive. In one startling case, a member of the Walloon Division ended up in a "Belgian-run concentration camp." He managed to escape and made his way to his fiancée's home, where authorities apprehended the two of them. As a former member of the Rexist Movement in Belgium, the fiancée served a year in a concentration camp while the Walloon veteran, originally sentenced to death, ended up serving five years in prison. Marginalized, he endured prolonged economic privation after his release but retained the "ethos" of the SS, "*Meine Ehre Heisst Treue.*" Such devotion to a cause and the honor inherent in this devotion generates the enthusiasm romancers have for the Waffen-SS. It embodies the very characteristics expected of honorable men in the service for their country. These actions fulfilled the romancers' expectations for the battle organizations that fought for Germany and not for the Nazis.[51]

Non-German members of the Waffen-SS suffered many privations, as the Internet exchanges make clear. Many died in virtual massacres administered by the merciless Red Army. In southeastern Europe, Serbian resistance fighters and their Soviet allies tortured and then virtually slaughtered volunteers in Waffen-SS units. In the Baltic states, many of the men who survived the war found refuge in the guerrilla movement that sought independence from forcibly imposed Soviet rule. The movement lasted into the 1950s before the Soviets brutally suppressed it. For those who wanted more information on the non-German volunteers, one of the participants in these exchanges recommended a forthcoming article in Antonio Munoz's *Axis Europa* that would treat the non-German members of the SS elite battlefield formations. These descriptions portray honorable men cruelly treated for their loyalty and bravery by cowards or, worse, murderers acting in the name of a hideous regime. Men spit upon because they lived by a code of honor stayed true to their oaths. These sentiments perfectly match the values and perceptions of the romancer.[52]

The Pipes site also contains considerable discussion of the literature of the German armed forces. In one exchange, a newcomer to the Pipes sites expressed curiosity over the best German memoirs. One respondent suggested two pieces, well known to romancers, *Stuka Pilot* by Hans Ulrich Rudel and Guy Sajer's

Forgotten Soldier. A German veteran wrote of Guderian's *Panzer Leader* as "one of the most truthful memoirs as well as one of the most interesting one of the WWII writings," a sentiment widely shared by romancers. Another posting praised Hans von Luck's *Panzer Commander* and characterized it as a mature piece of writing on the war. Von Luck's piece showed the authenticity that is so critical for romancers. Participants also endorsed Mellenthin's *Panzer's Battles*, for them an insightful account of the war. These works reinforce the romancers' understanding of the German military and in particular its role on the Eastern Front.[53]

As important, recommendations also incorporated the works of the gurus. In a 1998 exchange, one visitor expressed concern over the "historical accuracy" of Richard Landwehr's work. In response, a veteran of the Pipes site informed the newcomer that Landwehr's works are solid. He wrote that Landwehr "researches and tries to put more accurate information on the Waffen-SS Units than other authors." He further added that Landwehr personally knows many former members of the Waffen-SS, with whom he often corresponds. In demonstrating Landwehr's thoroughness in researching, the participant commented that his journal, *Siegrunen*, incorporates photos generally rarely available in any source. In essence, these remarks remind romancers that Landwehr brings the detailed historical information they desperately want to re-create the world of the Waffen-SS. Landwehr's own commitment to what he perceives as accuracy fulfills this demand and sustains the romancers' engagement with this lost world of the early 1940s.[54]

Guru Franz Kurowski's works also command attention on the Pipes site. One visitor asked about the quality of Kurowski's *Last Battalion* and if the translation were solid. One participant responded that Kurowski's book was thorough and includes actions large and small in the defense of the Reich against the Western Allies and the Soviets. He also wrote that Kurowski included an account of the massacre of German civilians in Nemmerschar in East Prussia by the men of the Red Army. Kurowski did provide readers with the grisly details of this slaughter of what he termed innocent women, children, and old men. As Kurowski relates. the Soviet raped and murdered the women, including girls as young as eight years. Soldiers even mutilated many of these innocents. Such descriptions make the Germans the victims and the German soldiers saviors. The Red Army fulfilled all the romancers' expectation of uncontrollable brutality.[55]

Several days after this exchange, Internet guru Marc Rikmenspoel sent information on Kurowski to another party. He advised the individual who made the inquiry that Kurowski was available though J. J. Fedorowicz, one of the romancers' presses. Rikmenspoel also commented that Kurowski wrote books covering broad areas of World War Two and used pseudonyms for many of these pieces. Subsequent exchanges recommended other Kurowski works, *Panzer Aces* and *Infantry Aces*.[56]

Pipes' online forum features many other exchanges that refer to romancer-type book and presses. Discussions of works that covered the Waffen-SS include works by German authors Rolf Hinz, *East Front Drama – 1944*, and George Nipe, *Decision in the Ukraine, Summer 1943, II, SS and III. Panzerkorps*, both published by J. J. Fedorowicz. James Lucas's *Last Year of the German Army* appeared in an exchange that focused on the II. Panzer division, Das Reich, and its attempt to rescue German units in Prague in May 1945. One visitor asked if anyone could comment on Hans von Luck's *Panzer Commander*. One respondent wrote, "von Luck tells it like it is." Other remarks praised the book, although one individual complained that von Luck never voiced his opinion on the war. In a separate exchange on von Luck's "whereabouts," one participant stated that *Panzer Commander* "deeply touched" him and he wanted to write and tell von Luck about the impact of the book.[57]

The paucity of works from the Russian position drew attention in the online discussions. In 1999, a visitor announced the imminent reissuing of John Erickson's long out-of-print *The Road to Stalingrad* and *The Road to Berlin*. These works marked an important milestone in the literature of the Eastern Front. In preparing these massive volumes, Erickson used countless Soviet documents, interviews with veterans of the Great Patriotic War, as the Russians labeled it, German sources, and materials from East European archives. He presents the war from the Soviet position and provides romancers with a very different perspective on the conflict.[58]

Despite their importance, the volumes remained out of print for years after their first publication. One participant showed little awareness of these magisterial pieces. Most agreed that the volumes were "informative." Despite this general opinion, one participant warned readers that Erickson "to some extent reflects the Soviet official history of the war" and "some of the facts and figures are in error in the same way as in the memoirs of the Soviet generals." Another participant accused Erickson of being the "ultimate Soviet apologist" but drew a sharp rebuke from another participant in the debate. These reactions demonstrate that works such as Erickson's book provoke strong reactions from those sympathetic to the romancers' interpretation of the war in Russia. The rarity of these pieces also stands in sharp contrast to the huge volume of works based on German sources and in agreement with the romancers' understanding of the Russo-German war.[59]

Romancers also engaged issues of moral salience. In November of 1998, a discussion occurred over the matter of whether the Waffen-SS took prisoners, the main point being the accepted notion they killed everyone they captured. One reader very sympathetic to the Waffen-SS argued that in the case of the commissars, the Waffen-SS refused to take prisoners, certainly justifiable in the mind of the reader, given the enmity of the Communists toward Germany. Similarly, in the case of Russian NKVD units, Waffen-SS operated under identical orders. The NKVD, "a special division of the secret police," stood as the ideological and terrorist edge of the Soviet regime. On some occasions, the Waffen-SS refused to take men into captivity because of the ferocity of the battle or some personal incident that outraged the Germans. The participant pointed out soldiers in every army on occasion refused to take prisoners. He referred to the Israeli defense force and its leading general, Moshe Dayan, who reported that his men took no prisoners in their 1967 race through Sinai Desert. The same participant also noted that the Waffen-SS acted nobly in the defense of innocents. He referred to the French-recruited Waffen-SS Charlemagne Division that deployed its men in Pomerania in 1945 to save civilians from the rapacious Red Army. During that struggle, the men of the Charlemagne Division encountered many Waffen-SS soldiers from other units who had suffered torture at the hands of the Soviet Commissars.[60]

Respondents also took issue with the notion that the Waffen-SS never took prisoners. Waffen-SS, another visitor argued, acquired its ignoble and unjustified reputation as result of action taken by the SS Totenkopf Division when its men went on a rampage in the wake of the death of Theodor Eicke, their commander, who was shot down by Russian anti-aircraft in 1943. In general, the reader claimed, the Waffen-SS did not kill their captives, despite the assertions of "Allied propaganda." Another participant in the discussion claimed orders for killing captives existed but in the context of retaliation, particularly in the case of partisan assaults. He also pointed out the Red Army operated on the standing order of executing German soldiers who belonged to "units that were too good for their liking." Romancers even asserted that the U.S. Army unfairly committed atrocities against the Waffen-SS. One participant claimed that the U.S. Army followed standing orders to kill all Waffen-SS soldiers. According to the participant, these orders assumed the baseless rumors that Waffen-SS men "executed" soldiers of the U.S. Army.

For romancers to believe that the Waffen-SS consisted of murderers who killed prisoners without provocation would represent a repudiation of their entire belief system about the German military and, in particular, of the most valued organization in that system, the Waffen-SS. The men who embodied the spirit of honor and bravery simply could never fall into the morass of unjustified killing.[61]

This issue of war crimes appeared in the spring of 1998. A visitor to Pipes' site asked if the 5th SS-Panzer division, Wiking, committed crimes against Russian Jews. A video on the unit claimed its men slaughtered several hundred Jews during its actions in the Russian campaign. A romancer very sympathetic to the Waffen-SS sent an extended response rejecting this claim. He argued the Wiking remained one of a handful of units against which the Soviets never lodged accusations of war crimes. In fact, the Russian literature on the war demonstrated a profound respect for the Wiking, a high opinion that persisted after the war. The respondent then described the experiences of the Wiking men discovering the remains of thousands of murdered Ukrainians in Lemberg and Tarnopol during the 1941 drive into the Ukraine, clearly the work of the Soviets. Civilians who welcomed the Wiking as a liberator took its men to the sites where the dead bodies were rotting. The participant did admit the Einsatzgruppen may have killed the local Jewish population but the Wiking remained guiltless. He concluded:

> In today's current climate of self-hatred and self-flagellation that the Germans seem to be going through, this accusation is yet another nail in the Coffin of the German military tradition, which many in that country feel should be erased from Germany's collective memory.[62]

The participant then responded to a suggestion that Jason Pipes should establish a website for war crimes. He recommended those with an interest in such topics should use the websites of Simon Wiesenthal or Beate Klarsfeld, noting, "yes, they have them." He then argued that the time spent in such an activity would better be used uncovering Soviet acts of brutality, for "they murdered far more people than the Germans ever did."[63]

These expressions of hostility reflect the romancer's unhappiness over what he/she perceives as unfounded criticism of an honorable and noble organization. For this romancer, Wiesenthal and Klarsfeld were, apparently, pursing the wrong individuals for war crimes. As these remarks suggested, he embraced the anti-Communist ethos that so many Germans adopted after the racial war against the Russians failed. The Waffen-SS remained above such violent acts and fought to protect Germany and not to destroy peoples the Nazi regime earmarked for destruction.[64]

Much like the *Achtung Panzer* website, the Pipes site includes many discussions of historical detail, a topic of great interest to romancers. In November 1999, an exchange occurred over whether tank commanders in the Grossdeutschland Panzer Division had tiger stripes on their helmets. In another exchange, the participants argued over the type of camera carried by journalists who accompanied the troops to the front. In a third series of communications, one visitor asked about the technical details on a specific piece of equipment used on the Fw 190F-8 German fighter plane. He knew the information likely appeared in an issue of *Waffen Revue* and asked if someone had a run of the magazine. A reader who owned issues 1–100 sent a reply indicating he would help. These minor points occupy many of the exchanges in the Pipes site as romancers search for the authenticity that brings them as close as possible to the German military of World War Two.[65]

Pipes' online forum features conversations on other websites that deal with the German armed forces. In fact, announcements about sites suggest the ethos of the romancer culture. In December 1999, a posting asked "What has happened with *Achtung Panzer.com*?" The visitor queried, why does *Achtung Panzer* now demand "a username and password?" He wrote, "Have the tanks turned commercial?" "Where is the military history research essence?" The person apparently saw these sites as free because of the mutual interest in the German armed forces and presumed commercialism corrupted the spirit of the romancers' world. The monitor of the *Achtung Panzer* responded that the site will remain free and he had no intentions of charging for use. The password and username were simply devices to control the flow of visitors that overwhelmed the capacity of the website.[66]

Jason Pipes then joined the exchange and sent his greetings to the *Achtung Panzer* host, George Prada, by his first name. The host then invited Pipes to visit *Achtung Panzer* and urged him to participate in its online forum. With his vast knowledge, the host wrote, Pipes would make an important contribution to those who used *Achtung Panzer*.[67]

The Pipes website was only one of many that covered the German military. *Axis Biographical Research*, for example, developed resources to provide a complete guide to Axis personalities throughout Europe. Avowedly nonpolitical, typical of all these sites, the *Axis Biographical* site provides information on many topics, from the Reich government to various military branches of the regime. Individuals who assisted the organizers of the site in research included guru Mark Yerger, Waffen-SS "expert" Marc Rikmenspoel, Fedorowicz author George Nipe, and *Axis Europa* associate Andris Kursietis and his brother Valdis Kursietis, as well as U.S. military officers. The organizers came from many different backgrounds. Some were independent writers, video directors, and even a submariner in the U.S. Navy. The founding members were all professionals or in the process of finishing graduate degrees. The site includes a book review and online forum sections. As of August 1999, it attracted some 167,839 visitors after three months in operation. Other sites that focus on the Axis forces include the massive *Axis History Factbook, The Elite Forces of the Third Reich*

1933–1945, The Arsenal of Dictatorship, World War II Online Message Forum, and *Panzerdiesel.*[68]

The Internet also facilitates an exploration of the attitudes, opinions, reading materials, and activities of those engaged in imagining and recreating the world of the German soldier, his commanders, and his enemies. Such a tool allows us to answer, in a limited way, the persistent and looming question: What draws an audience to the topic of the Wehrmacht and the Eastern Front? We caution that our evidence in no way represents the complete picture. Still, the evidence gives us some hard evidence about what attracted young men, and these are all men, to the war in Russia.

For many, the attachment developed early and persisted into their adult lives. Often, fathers and uncles were veterans of World War Two. Even grandfathers participated and, in some cases, German relatives actually fought with the Wehrmacht in Russia and could relate what seemed to be true accounts of the battlefield. Such a source would prove irresistible to boys or young men learning of war for the first time. In one case, the participant declared that his family was "proudly represented in the German Wehrmacht." In all cases, the stories told by their fathers, uncles, and grandfathers captivated these men as young boys and began a life-long attachment to the Wehrmacht and its struggles on the Eastern Front. In some cases, the participants were European and grew up surrounded by the very battlefields where the fate of the Wehrmacht was decided.[69]

In other cases, books, comics, films, and television shows sparked an interest in World War Two that led these men to the German military. The books ranged from the familiar Paul Carell's *Hitler Moves East* to Peter Neumann's *Black March* and Hans Rudel's *Stuka Pilot.* The scale and the magnitude of the struggle enthralled our participants and hooked them on the German military. One young man commented that the easy availability of Carell's volumes in cheap paperback form, courtesy of Ballantine and later Bantam Books, sparked his insatiable appetite for accounts of the Eastern Front. Similarly, Sven Hassel's fictional tales of the Eastern Front caught the imagination of these young men and led them into the literature on the war in Russia. Powerful descriptions of battle from the German side, even if fictional, captivated the readers and led them to seek more tales of the fighting in Russia. In one case, the participant read a biography of Herman Goring, *The Third Reich Marshal,* which so captivated the reader that he "brought Swastika bedecked books to school" and, needless to say, incurred the enmity of many of his classmates. In many cases, the daunting odds that faced the Wehrmacht and the immensely difficult time opponents had defeating the German armies intensified their appeal to readers.[70]

The media, too, played a role in creating an interest in the German military. In some cases, movies such as *The Longest Day* or the television series, *Hogan's Heroes*, with its constant threats of sending the characters portraying German soldiers to the Eastern Front, caught the attention of viewers. Sunday afternoons spent watching war movies also provided a beacon for the participants to seek more and more information about World War Two and German arms. Depictions of reality or even actual comedy proved sufficient to hook some on the Eastern Front and war itself. In one case, the participant complained that American movies never really gave him much understanding of the Germans or even fair treatment. For this participant, the victors clearly wrote the history from their perspective and the media only reproduced the sentiments of these accounts. In some cases, the participants read stirring German narratives. Hans Rudel's *Stuka Pilot* provides one example. Its action scenes and heroic stories led one participant to scour his father's books for wartime tales and finally to search the television for visual portrayals of the Wehrmacht, which he may have perceived as a closer representation of combat. In this case, the participant's father and grandfather had fought in the Wehrmacht, so the stories he encountered in the American context often proved at odds with his family's recounting. In all these examples, combinations of books, visual media, and, often, commando comics introduced the participants to German arms while they were young. Many embraced the German perspective at an early age, which only fed their imaginations and eagerness for more readings and experiences with the Eastern Front and the Wehrmacht.[71]

These imaginings also relied on other representations of the German Wehrmacht and the Eastern Front. Models of weapons, soldiers, and battles drew many to the hobby of collecting. World War Two memorabilia led others into the world of German medals, uniforms, and German militaria in general. Wargames attracted another audience, the members of which are able to replay the events of World War Two with dramatically different outcomes – namely, German victories in various battles. Often these habits developed at an early age and reinforced tendencies generated by reading or viewing more material on the German army. Even Sergeant Rock comics and models played a role for some.[72]

Inevitably, such encounters produced romanticized visions of the German military and the Eastern Front. The postwar World War Two generation of young men in the United States grew up in a Cold War America that prepped them for military service. The vast majority of American male youth saw the military as a patriotic duty necessary to defend America against Communism embodied in the USSR. They also found themselves surrounded by veterans who fought a "Good War" and defeated murderous opponents, oddly the very

Germans whom the United States would recruit in its Cold War efforts and whom these young men would embrace for decades to come.

Books and visual media on World War Two also play an important role in creating the romanticized world of the Wehrmacht. These abound from 1950s onward. Given the pressures of the Cold War, accounts of the Eastern Front, usually written by Germans, featured heroic efforts of the Wehrmacht in its battle against the Russians. Following the lead of the German memoirs and accounts, postwar American youth interested in this theater apparently saw the war in the East as a combat theater where soldiers and generals fought for victory on the harsh battlefield while ideological aims of the state remained unarticulated for these men. Sven Hassel's books, an important source for many, hardly painted a sanitized image of war on the Eastern Front and their readers certainly appreciated and even admired what Hassel's characters endured and withstood. Few could have imagined the true nature of the war in Russia or found a hostile view of the Germans in the Eastern Front given the preeminent status of Germany in the American alliance system of the era. None realize the horror of a theater where women and children proved the chief victims. Nor do they seem to grasp that scores of cities and thousands of towns and villages were razed by the fighting or the scorched earth practices pursued by both the Germans and Russians. Moreover, urban and rural places, when they came under attack, almost always counted civilians present, despite the best efforts of the Soviets to evacuate them. They suffered accordingly. The complexity of the war and the German responsibility for these horrors, however measured and assigned, eludes those engaged in the Eastern Front as a recreation or hobby. Even now such interpretations prove rare and are always fiercely disputed.

The attitudes some of the participants expressed, then, suggest a favorable and idealized vision of the conflict in Russia and the roles of the Wehrmacht and the Waffen-SS in that campaign. Comments by the participants certainly reveal their attitudes and biases toward the German military as well as an absence of a critical understanding of the complexity of that institution and its role in World War Two. One enthusiast proclaimed: "Man for man, unit for unit, army for army, they (i.e., the Germans) were unbeatable." He went on to write, "they were incredible warriors who accomplished prodigious feats whether on the defensive or the offensive." Such a statement in no way connected the military to the Nazi regime and its goals, which all participants roundly condemn. The soldiers appear as "warriors," politically ingenuous, yet martially brave and fierce.

Other participants stated they were "caught up in the romantic images of those days" and developed "life-long addiction to the Wehrmacht." One even joined the U.S. Marines for the real experience. Ironically, he ended up as a curator in a Marine Museum where, he did note, there was "lots of German stuff." Another participant also signed up for the military and quickly learned that his romantic vision proved just that, a fantasy. Still, he argued, his experiences brought him closer to the Herr Landser who fought in "those long, gone, simpler times. . . . " He expressed "respect and admiration" for his Eastern Front counterparts. The participant's attachment to the German soldier only strengthened because of his own experiences in war and substituted a new romanticism that filled his imagination. At its most extreme, the romanticism led another participant literally to "dream [of being] in [the] Stalingrad Battle" where he "threw a Potato masher over the side of a SdKF2Z 232 [German Halftrack] . . . " at the enemy. The dream endowed the fantasy with a substance reality kept from him. In no way did the experiences and imaginings of these men bring them any closer to the complexity and the horror of the Eastern Front.[73]

The romancer's world expanded dramatically with the introduction of the Internet. It created communities separated by huge distances joined through common interests and mediated by the new electronic communications. The new websites incorporated information on a scale unanticipated under more traditional storage means. It remains accessible to those romancers who engage in an endless search for a better understanding of the heroic world of the German military. The Internet also created an environment in which debate and exchanges occur on a twenty-four-hour basis and span the globe. The romancers' culture now flourishes in the new technological environment.

8 Romancing the War: Reenactors, and "What If History"

The appeal of the myth of the "clean Wehrmacht" in American popular culture emerges most vividly in reenactment associations, which seek to re-create the battles of the war in Russia and the units that fought them. The reenactments extend beyond the world of armchair generals, avid readers, and collectors of Eastern Front memorabilia. The reenactors actively re-fight the battles and actions of the Eastern Front with an insistence on absolute authenticity in uniforms, equipment, and terrain. They all hope that the actions they undertake result in a German triumph, something that detracts from historical authenticity, but does serve the romancers' purpose of reversing the "Lost Cause." A genre of books one might call "what if" history books greatly enhances the alternate history approach of the reenactors. These books describe how the outcome of the war in the East might have been different if only the Germans had proceeded differently, if only Hitler had not intervened, if only the generals had been able to carry out their own plans.

To prepare for their participation in reenactment events, romancers rely on a variety of sources. They can avail themselves of the vast literature, including memoirs, on the German army to understand the men who fought in Russia. Quite often they use collectors' books that feature the paraphernalia of war, including actual equipment, uniforms, and weapons of the era as references. A wide array of manufacturers and distributors of facsimiles exist to make available the necessities of reenacting to romancers. The readings, combined with first-hand experiences and observations, give reenactors a good deal of information on the nuts and bolts of well-known formations such as the Grossdeutschland and heralded Waffen-SS divisions. Few seem to acknowledge the absolute dedication of the Wehrmacht divisions and especially the Waffen-SS to Hitler, the Nazi state, and its goals.[1]

History of Reenacting

As an active hobby, reenactment traces its origins to the encampments Union Civil War veterans held in the decades after 1865. Slowly the encampments expanded to reenactments as veterans sought to relive their exploits on the very battlefields where they had fought and suffered. Unexpectedly, Confederate veterans joined these events and soon the harshness of the war that once so bitterly divided these men evolved into a camaraderie based on their shared experiences of being in combat. As the Civil War generation died out, such events faded, to be replaced by competitive events set up and run by new generation of Civil War enthusiasts. These men established the National Muzzle Rifle Association in the early 1930s, which hosted shooting contests using Civil War weapons. A member of the National Muzzle group founded the North-South Skirmish Association in 1950. The men who joined this new group engaged in small-scale reenactments taken from larger Civil War battles. Members of this group dominated the ranks of the reenactors who commemorated the centennial of Civil War during the first half of the 1960s. These reenactments included the major battles from Bull Run or First Manassas to Gettysburg.[2]

The reenacting of twentieth-century wars grew out of the Civil War groups. Civil War reenacting expanded dramatically in the 1980s and 1990s as tens of thousands of enthusiasts participated in small and large events. This group of reenactors contributed many of those who formed the first units of twentieth-century reenacting units.[3]

The actual origins of German reenactment groups stretched back to the decade of the 1970s. In the mid-1970s, Fred Poddig and his Missouri friends established World War Two reenacting. For Poddig, his father's angry reaction to the portrayal of German soldiers in the television series *Hogan's Heroes* as incompetents and buffoons spurred the young Poddig to set the record straight. He understood his father's distress because Germans as clowns clearly diminished the U.S. Army's victory over the Third Reich. As a veteran of that war, the father saw such depictions as a breach of honor. The son realized, as the father knew, that the German soldiers brought professionalism and toughness to the battlefield and those qualities the young Poddig hoped to demonstrate in his reenactment unit, 1SS Leibstandarte. Poddig began the journey to the romancer world.[4]

In May of 1975, he and his associates staged the first World War Two reenactment at Weldon Springs, Mo. A $10 fee gave a participant food, ammunition, and a smoke grenade. By October, Poddig had formed the 1SS Leibstandarte (St. Louis-based) and acquired two "*Kübelwagons*" (German staff car*)*, a Zundapp motorcycle/sidecar, and a 1940 Ford truck. The event caught the attention of SS veterans' organizations in Germany, which volunteered to give advice and help Poddig's small band. Already under scrutiny by the Jewish Anti-Defamation League and the media, Poddig refused the aid proffered by the SS groups.[5]

Within a few years, Poddig was engaged in manufacturing equipment, uniforms, and related materials for reenactors, anticipating the lively market for reenacting gear. At the same time, his unit, the 1SS Leibstandarte, assumed a public face when it joined the parades and other public events sponsored by groups such as Veterans of Foreign Wars and the American Legion. Poddig and others who joined the hobby in these early years endured a marginal status because of their short hair and army fatigues in an era when fashion called for radically different looks. Indeed, just the effort to sustain the early units proved challenging.[6]

By 1985, the fledgling 1SS Leibstandarte (LAH) had grown to 100 men. Changes accompanied this expansion. Poddig standardized the uniforms the men wore and dramatically increased the number of the unit's military vehicles. Members also forged connections with the U.S. Army in an effort to secure sites for their reenactments. The military offered installations including Fort Knox and Fort Campbell in Ky. and Fort McCoy in Wis. for reenactment events. The LAH also used Boy Scout reservations that had the space and appropriate terrain necessary for battlefields. At the beginning of the 1990s, the number of reenactors in the LAH (the iconographic acronym) reached 150, allowing the group to set up a headquarters section beyond the "Kompanie" (often those who construct the websites for these groups use the German spelling for terms such as company). Within the year 1991, 200 members now staffed the unit. Equipped with a formal headquarters, the LAH added a second complement of a standing vehicle park. In keeping with the intentions of the organizers, the LAH also formed a *Feldgendarmerie* [military police] platoon, seen as a necessity for a fully functioning headquarters. By 1999, the LAH exceeded 250 members at a time when reenacting began to flourish in large part because of the availability of the Internet. The LAH published a newsletter twice every month and operated an online discussion group available to all members. Last, LAH also maintained a website with current information on the unit's activities. These enabled reenactors to keep in daily contact across significant distances, informed members of upcoming events, and provided them with substantial amounts of information useful for reenacting. The site drew some 354,000 from 1998 through early January 2006.[7]

Recruits receive a welcome newsletter that includes the *Kompaniefuehrer* to whom they would report. The recruit's application moves to the *Kompanie Stabscharfuehrer*, who reviews the information and approves admission to the

LAH. The *Kompanie Stabscharfuehrer* then mails to the recruit his SS Combat Identification Card and the recruit formally joins the LAH. The *Kandidate* (the website always uses German iconographic words when possible) will serve a probationary period before he gains full status as a member of the LAH. Realism infiltrates every aspect of reenacting and showed the seriousness of the first generation of German reenactors.[8]

The robust nature of reenacting appears in the numbers of new groups in existence by the end of the 1990s. Some forty German reenactment groups, including six Luftwaffe parachute units, had made their appearance, far outnumbering their nearest rival, the American reenactment units (twenty-one). Among the German units, the Waffen-SS, with twenty reenactment units, proved the most popular. For example, enthusiasts organized a second 1SS Leibstandarte in California. Their counterparts in Colorado established the 2SS Das Reich, while the 11SS Division Nordland began operations in Kansas. Wehrmacht units appeared on the east coast, where the 7 Kompanie, "Grossdeutchland," and the 3.Panzergrenadier Division, among others, held reenactment events. By 2006, romancers ran some 124 German reenacting units, naval and battle groups among them.[9]

These units usually affiliated with larger reenactment societies that covered a state or a region. For instance, the 1SS Leibstandarte in California registered with the California Historical Group lodged in Anaheim. The Northwest Historical Association is based in Portland, Ore., whereas the Texas Military Historical Society in Bellarie, Texas, covers the southwest United States. These societies dedicate their efforts to preserving the memory of World War Two "by organizing public show battles, . . . educational programs, and displays for state, community, and school events." Book dealers, video companies, magazine series, and a growing number of war material manufacturers and distributors of war memorabilia have also joined the busy landscape of reenacting. Firms such as Bill Bureau's Militaria, Lost Battalions, 1944 Militaria, Third Reich Documents (produces award certificates and related paper materials), and International Historic Films, which sells war films, provide a few examples of this rapidly expanding section of the hobby. By 2006, reenacting, in general, had matured to the point that the hobby held its first national convention in the Chicago metropolitan area.[10]

Reenactors and Their World

Reenactors come from a broad array of occupational backgrounds. Many pursue professions in their daily careers. Chemists and computer programmers shed their professional garb to don the outfits of German soldiers or the black uniforms of SS units on weekends. Telephone operators and car mechanics also leave their offices or shops for the battlefields on many weekends throughout the year. Even affluent investment bankers flee from their stressful business pursuits to join their fellow reenactors. Once with their units, the daytime distinctions in occupations, income, or status vanish and new signifiers such as authenticity or military rank take hold as the battles begin.[11]

When the events end and the men celebrate their labors, equality prevails where neither civilian positions nor wealth play a role. Friendship and the bonds created by their common interests, some might call it obsession with reenacting, bind them. Drinking from steins, they sing German songs dedicated to the Fatherland. On one occasion, reenactors commemorated the fabled Grossdeutschland Unit by decorating their barracks with the division's flag and flags bearing the Nazi swastika. Posters taken from the war lined the walls. The men gathered to honor those who often made the ultimate sacrifice for their country and to keep their memory alive. A Grossdeutschland veteran even joined the reenactment unit for their weekend event, enhancing the realism these men so eagerly sought.[12]

The men who join German reenactment units often fear that discovery of their off-duty preoccupation would hinder their careers. As result, they often choose to keep their reenactment persona secret. They know full well the frightening images Nazi regalia and German uniforms bring to the minds of many Americans. Still, many admit they came to reenactment because of their fascination with some aspect of war. For some, their encounters with Civil War reenactments in the 1960s triggered their desires to become reenactors. For others, they simply loved the German uniforms. They even expressed admiration for the SS uniforms and subsequently joined SS reenactment units. One even admitted, "they [the Germans] were sort of the bad guys."[13]

The rough equality ensured by common uniforms, an enduring interest in war, and commitment to the common soldier of World War Two, fanatical at times, explains their involvement in reenacting. These sentiments separate them from the occasional dilettante who may read a book on some famous battle and even show up for a reenactment. The rough camaraderie arising out their fascination both with war and with the army and SS create in these men bonds impossible in their day-to-day existence. The German reenactors use *Kameradschaft* (comradeship) to describe these intense relationships. The common interest also led to friendships between professionals and workers whose social worlds would rarely, or more than likely never, overlap in real life. The mutual pursuit of these men creates ties as strong, if not stronger, than the normal social relationships produced by their class and occupational positions.

A few German reenactors meet at a German restaurant in dress uniforms to celebrate their participation in reenacting and the German soldiers they emulate. Often, reenactors express the feeling that the public fails to understand these bonds, so rare in the society, and, yet, so important.[14]

The Reenactors as Amateur Historians

Reenactors engage in both private and public events, the latter obviously being the most visible. The public venue features "air shows, encampments," reenactments designed for civilian spectators. Reenactors call these events "*touronz*" (reenactor term for "tourist events") and are often part of an elaborate show sponsored by major patrons. Federal agencies such as the Department of Defense; private organizations, notably the Military Vehicle Preservation Association; and municipal authorities can participate in hosting such proceedings.[15]

Websites frequently announce that the goal of reenactment units is to educate the public. Reenactors use public events to give talks about World War Two. For example, the German reenactment unit, 10SS Panzer division, Frundsberg, declared on its homepage, "We consider ourselves to be amateur historians. We try to further our knowledge of World War II through public and tactical reenactments. . . . " The statement stressed that the members of this reenactment group attempted to portray with the utmost authenticity the German soldier, the Waffen-SS soldier, and their everyday lives. The reenactors accomplish this goal "by wearing the uniform and gear" of these men. The declaration underscored the incredible amounts of historical information necessary to engage in reenacting.[16]

Similarly, the World War Two Historical Preservation Group (W2HPG) declared, "our purpose is to promote a better understanding of the role of the common soldier in the historically significant events that shaped the twentieth century." Members of this group intend "to educate the public about the daily routines, living conditions, equipment, and uniforms of the combatants of the Second World War." W2HPG members "represent hundreds of individual volunteers in more than a dozen separate reenactment groups. . . . " These volunteers hosted numerous exhibitions in which the W2HPG demanded that the volunteers "remain in a 'First Person' impression for the duration of the event." Of course, those engaged must demonstrate absolute historical accuracy because the events amount to a teaching mechanism for the public and an occasion for "photo opportunities." The W2HPG saw reenactments as providing an "educational environment that fosters a better understanding and appreciation of the experiences of the soldiers of the Second World War."[17] The California Historical Group, an umbrella organization for California reenactors, similarly conducted " . . . public displays [to] better educate the public on the daily rigors of the common soldiers," which demanded that the reenactors acquire a keen sense of the material culture of the German soldier and the members of the Waffen-SS units they attempted to emulate. Those who conduct such events, including reenactments, must show a good deal of historical knowledge because these affairs involve question-and-answer sessions and constant interaction with spectators.[18]

In their talks, the reenactors rarely move beyond the details of the war or the dress and weapons of individual soldiers. These concerns reflect their dedication to emulating the common soldier and commemorating his memory. The larger issues of morality, culpability, and economic and social forces at play remain noticeably absent in these discussions. After all, the reenactors pursue their avocation because of their commitment to the common soldier, regardless of nationality or reputation. In interacting with the public, the reenactors even avoid labeling themselves as reenactors. Some prefer to use terms such as "'living historian'" and label their appearances in public events as performing rather than reenacting. Reenactors often see public events as part of their obligation because civilians expect these public performances.[19]

Some spectators respond favorably to the displays of the German reenactors who win praise for their exacting drills and command attention from the audience as they "barked out orders in German." The men even sing German war songs that arouse the crowds. Veterans of the U.S. Army, too, lauded the SS reenactors. Surprisingly, audiences often include Wehrmacht veterans who applaud the commemoration and sincerely appreciate the efforts of reenactors to keep alive the memory of the German soldier. The Germans even occasionally express surprise at the American reenactors because at home the German veterans often face harsh criticisms because of the policies of the Nazi regime. There is no record of German veterans or reenactors engaging in discussions over the crimes committed by the army and SS against civilians.[20]

Reenactors and the Internet

Private events are the heart of reenacting. These usually last an entire weekend and can involve hundreds of participants. Smaller affairs range from fifteen to a hundred reenactors. Often, these are outdoor events and participants expect to spend nights in the field. Fridays are usually devoted to organizational matters and socializing, with occasional night fighting. The actual tactical fighting occurs on Saturdays, followed by a social gathering unless a night event is scheduled. On Sundays, reenactors clean their weapons and depart for home. Reenactors see these private events as the moment when they face the challenges of the battlefield and can experience the feelings and emotions the men of the World War Two knew firsthand. As one reenactor explained, he can "imagine history by looking at the scene from the perspective of 1942." These "revelations" never move beyond the personal and the larger issues that precipitate the war and raise serious moral concerns remain visibly absent.[21]

Reenactors rely on the Internet to maintain contact. In effect, the website has developed into their main line of communications. For example, the 1st SS Leibstandarte incorporated a glossary of Waffen-SS ranks and brief descriptions of the duties and roles of each rank. This page described the mechanisms for promotion that all recruits should know. The page also identified the grade officer, who made decisions on promotion. Such information was vital for reenactment groups, which employed promotion as an important means to reward their members for battlefield actions and performances. To achieve the rank of *Unterscharführer* (SS-Staff Sergeant) in the 1st SS Leibstandarte, a candidate "must have met the requirements for *SS-Rottenführer* [team leader and equivalent to senior lance corporal in the Wehrmacht, Obergefreiter] and displayed above-average dedication and leadership qualities." The *Kampanieführer* forwarded the nominations and the "Chief Council" "approves" the promotion. For the 1st SS, an *SS-Kandidat* (*SS*-recruit) needed to have participated in and finished "three recognized events." These regulations posted to the website provided the realism so actively sought by reenactors.[22]

Websites include guides to identifying rank. Labeled, "Rank, Military Courtesy, and Organization of the Army: *Dienstgrad* and *Gliederung des Heeres*," the 1st SS Leibstandarte's page incorporates visuals of insignias. Reenactors learned that "the German Army was very formal and 'correct' – almost to an extreme." Recognizing rank remained a vital necessity. The chief means for recognition appeared in the *Schulterklappen* or shoulder strap. The short text describes the straps for commissioned and noncommissioned officers and explains the difference between the two categories. Sketches of shoulder straps for various ranks from *Unteroffizier* (corporal) to *Oberleutenant* (first lieutenant) accompanied the text. Again, this page called for a good deal of research by the author to meet the current demands for authenticity. Exactness both in the visuals and in the description proved a must. Armed with such information, the reenactor would be able to participate with confidence gained through reading and study.[23]

The sites often display photographs of reenactors fully equipped for combat. The 1st SS Leibstandarte posted a photo of a reenactor standing alongside his armed vehicle, fully geared with weapons, SS uniform, and helmet. The text accompanying the photo described the vehicles found in a Waffen-SS combat unit and gave the potential recruit a realistic snapshot.[24] For those interested in a closer view of specific weapons, the same website provides snapshots. The common "Karabiner 98K Mauser with *Gewehrsprenggranaten* (rifle grenade) and the Mauser with the *Seitengewehr* (bayonet)" appeared in one photograph. The caption below this visual briefly explained the history of the 98K, the volume produced during the war, and how it operated. It also included its range, weight, and length. Other photos presented the "*maschiner* pistol" [sic] 43/44 (MP43/44) and the 81 mm (8cm) mortar.[25]

The demands of reenactment units move beyond the artifacts of war to the physical appearances of the German soldier. One site asked the question: "But what did the actual person inside the uniform look like?" Following the question was a series of subheadings from facial hair to tattoos and weight. The discussion of facial hair provided insight into the preoccupation with exactness. The text reviewed the specifics of facial hair allowed in German regulations. Mustaches were permissible, but only within limits. The page on physical appearances incorporated etchings to show the recruit the limits and style of mustaches. As a codicil, the page added for those weary of shaving or trimming the statement, "think of it this way, it's not like you are being asked to cut part of your anatomy, facial hair will grow back, we promise you." They also cautioned that facial hair simply was not stylish and rarely appeared on a German soldier. Beards and sideburns were declared out of bounds in no uncertain terms. Only the mountain troops, the *Gebirgsjäger*, were actually allowed to have beards and then exclusively at certain altitudes. As the text stated, "We are portraying German soldiers in WWII, not one of Stonewall Jackson's troopers in the American Civil War." The page went on to suggest a specific hairstyle, "shaved from the neck and tapered up to the top of the ear all the way around and slicked straight back . . . " An etching of this hairstyle also accompanied the text to provide the recruit with a visual. The page also warned recruits "we realize that this [hair style] is a little extreme, especially if we don't want to scare our families or the people we work with!"[26]

Still, the search for realism demanded that hairstyles approximate the "Prussian" haircut and reenactors were warned that failure to meet these standards would keep one out of an event because organizers enforced "strict rules on haircuts." In one case, a reenactor actually discovered a Finnish barber who cut hair for the Finnish and German troops during World War Two. He gave the reenactor the ultimate realistic haircut, what the veteran barber labeled the "*Wehrmachtschnitt*" (Wehrmacht cut). The reenactor simply declares "*Wehrmachtschnitt*" and the barber knows exactly what the romancer wants. Failing such exacting standards, the only option for reenactors was the "field barber," which often proved a dicey alternative. The effort to remake one's identity clearly emerges as the goal of such demands. The reenactors literally transformed themselves into German soldiers; nothing less was acceptable.[27]

Regulations allowed reenactors to wear only period eyeglasses and to carry 1940s eyeglass holders. Unit regulations demanded that reenactors must also meet weight requirements. Because German soldiers were thin, reenactors had to stay trim and in shape. Reenactment groups even asked actual German veterans of World War Two for their evaluation of the reenactors. The veterans stated bluntly that the reenactors were "too fat!" German veterans also complained that the reenactors slouched and chewed gum just like Americans. Germans stood upright and never chewed gum as if they were "cows!"[28]

These sites enable romancers to acquire artifacts and facsimiles from World War Two. One site gives readers a glimpse of the pieces available for collectors and reenactors. The section includes a brief discussion of Mausser rifles written by the editors of *American Rifles*, who comment that the thirty-two-page pamphlet is "a great reference for Mausser collectors." The review also states the piece is "a must for any WW2 German re-enactor." Another review comments on the book, *German Automatic Weapons of WW II*. The 128-page work includes the essential photos, so central to reenactors and collectors who want authenticity and realism. The review notes that the book includes " . . . detailed close-ups of markings. . . . " of great interest to re-enactors. At one point, the reviewer writes that the original German eyeglass case gives a reenactor an extremely useful tool for either display or using in the field. The piece was also "a must for any WW2 German reenactor."[29]

Authenticity and Reenactors

The dedication to realism compelled the World War Two Historical Preservation Group to produce a series of Authenticity Guidelines for the major participants in Europe: the British, the Germans, the Russians, and the Americans. The purpose of these guidelines was to establish agreed-upon conventions for the entire hobby. The author for the German standards belonged to the Grossdeutschland reenactment unit, an affiliation that legitimized his credentials. His regulations covered a wide range of objects, from dyes and uniforms to the pay book and helmet demanded of every reenactor. The standards also aimed directly at "unruly" actions that called for dismissal.[30] The author declared that "a lot of time was spent to produce this guide, all in order to enhance the field impression of the whole unit, and each individual impression is a key factor toward our success." The author further advised novices "to study individuals from other German reenacting units who have refined their impressions (ask your sponsor or NCO who we mean here)."[31]

For the die-hard reenactor, the 1935 German training manual, *Der Rekrut*, is available through one of the many manufacturers that now sustain the material needs of the hobby. *Der Rekrut* appears in English translation for the American audience and, because it is literally a reprint of the 1935 edition, provides the ultimate in authenticity. The website advertisement for *Der Rekrut* warns the reenactor, "If you don't know 'Der Rekrut,' then you're just dressing up as a German." Only the knowledge gained in *Der Rekrut*, the advertisement presumes, can *make you* a German. The advertisement stresses that *Der Rekrut* remains singular; no other translation exists of the 1935 manual or, for that matter, of any pre-war German manual. The advertisement for *Der Rekrut* gives the re-enactor a list of chapter titles such as "The duties of a German Soldier," "The Soldier's behavior in Public", and "Combat Duty," which cover every aspect of the martial world of the German soldier.[32]

The page incorporates links to other pages on the *Leibstandarte* website. The heading reads "An Online Resource for the German Re-enactor" followed by various page titles such as "So You Want to Be a German Soldier" to "*Die Grundausbilding* (basic training)" and "*Der SS Soldat*." These pieces are intended to provide reenactors with insights helpful to those new to the hobby. The author of "So You Want To Be A German Soldier" opens his two articles with an extremely short personal introduction. Reenactors learn that the author first engaged in reenacting in 1990, a time when the materials of the hobby such as quality reproduction of uniforms and equipment were rare. New to reenacting, the author quickly began his research to learn as much as possible about the German army. In the process, he discovered that the Waffen-SS consisted of elite units. Soon his research demonstrated that the uniform and other equipment he had purchased simply failed to meet the high standards that guided reenactors. Close inspection of period photographs of Waffen-SS personnel and their war uniforms convinced him that his own reproduction fell short. As the hobby matured and more realistic uniforms and equipment became available, the author was able to buy the most authentic materials that helped make him a Waffen-SS soldier. After some $5,000 in expenses, he finally made an impression that satisfied the standards of the hobby.[33]

The author then categorizes the types of reenactors he has encountered in the decade since 1990. These fall into three groups: the half-hearted, the moderates, and the die-hard. The half-hearted at best feign realism. They may have a K98 but they eat pizza, sleep in modern tents, and have little idea of what is expected of them on the battlefield. These types earn the special scorn of the author. He makes the point that "having an impeccable impression requires time, money and research." His description of the diehards stands in sharp contrast to the lackluster participants. The die-hards spare no expense to acquire the best equipment and uniforms. They meet all the standards expected of a German soldier, from proper haircuts to knowing German drill and commands. These men speak German in the field, sing German war songs, and even wear German underwear. They are German soldiers in every sense of the word. The author concludes with "*Gott Mit Uns*" or "God is with us." This short piece demonstrates the extent to which reenactors will go to transform their very civilian identities. From underwear to weapons, they want to *be* the Waffen-SS soldier or the Wehrmacht soldier who marched across the battlefields of Europe. The bitter irony of the concluding remark that God stood on the side of the Germans contrasts sharply with the horrors brought by the Germans in World War Two.[34]

A second page introduces reenactors and potential recruits to basic training and workshops intended to upgrade one's knowledge of the German military. In keeping with the demands for realism, the author introduces himself as *Truppenführer* of *1. Kompanie, 1.Zug* (platoon). He recounts that his unit had just completed their first "*Grundausbildung*" (basic training) and "*Unterführerschule*" "noncommissioned officers school." The events opened with the author recounting the history of the 1 SS Leibstandarte from its founding in 1975 until the present, which quite captivated him. He came away impressed that the founders "back then" had no access to quality reproductions and had to use originals. Still, they persevered. Following the history of the unit, "experts" then conducted a series of workshops on various aspects of reenacting and the need to maintain a first-rate impression. Reenactors also learned of the need never to wear their uniforms and gear while traveling to an event, because of the general hostility this practice provokes among "civilians" unaware of reenacting. These workshops also focused on the authenticity of the German manual of arms. Of course, the men inevitably marched to the German cadence as part of the actual training, and lunch consisted of *Spanner* stew. At the end of the day, awards were given, notably the *Ritterkreuz* ("Knight's Cross") and "*the Deutsch Kreuz im Gold*" (German Cross in Gold), which the author described as "awe inspiring." More training events were planned, the author noted. He closed with the comment that those in the unit are of the "highest caliber of men . . . who are willing to make a difference to others in our unit and to the hobby as a whole." He signed off with the SS motto, *Meine Ehre Heisst Treue*, "my honor is loyalty," and the German farewell, *uscha* [sic] and his unit's identification. Clearly, these experiences fulfilled his romanticized vision of the original Leibstandarte and confirmed his understanding of the intent and ideological disposition of the Waffen-SS as a fighting organization defending the Reich in an heroic fashion and untouched by ideology and practices of the Nazis.[35]

The extent to which authenticity dominates every aspect of reenacting appears in a short one-page advice sheet. The author runs through the various parts of a German uniform, admonishing reenactors on the mistakes often made in dress. He notes early in the essay that the "LAH [*Leibstandarte*] historically has been the frontrunner in the development of German reenactor standards" and that the unit's "overall standards are higher than any German WW Two reenactment unit in existence."

This advice proves extremely detailed, as one would expect in a group dedicated to authenticity. The author writes that although quality boots are now available, he cautions reenactors against purchasing the Swiss army boots merely because of their low cost and durability. The author notes with a discerning eye that Swiss boots have bright speed lacing hooks [sic] that, he claims, instantly expose the boots as "inaccurate," a failure that even a quick glance at the boot will reveal to an observer. Boots, he further advises, should include "leather soles, hobnails and heel irons." Enthusiasts, he urges, should also buy the toe irons. Such attention to detail ranges from caps and belts to chow and watches. Ultimately, the writer advises that the proper attitude and spirit of the reenactor remains as important as authentically reproduced uniforms, weapons, and other war materials. He declares that the reenactor should think and act as if he were a top-flight German soldier and this act, combined with authenticity, makes you the ultimate soldier. The men in your unit, the men in the opposing formations, and the many civilians who attend the re-enactments will recognize your commitment.[36]

This concern with authenticity has created the "Stitch Nazi," a variant of the hardcore reenactor, who demands exacting standards of authenticity. They post their complaints to websites or in reenactor newsletters. In one event, the presence of reenactors who donned "herring bone twill uniforms" rather than the expected woolen uniforms angered "Stitch Nazis." They strongly objected to such a blatant violation of realism. Moderates among reenactors take exception to what they see as harassment by these extremists. Yet both camps agree that "Farbs" (reenactors who do not dress or behave with the authenticity demanded by the guild) who arrive at reenactments inappropriately outfitted, wearing "digital watches," smoking "filtered cigarettes," or wearing "poor reproductions" of period uniforms should be chastised. To prevent such egregious errors, the Grossdeutschland reenactment unit connects new members with "Old Hands," who assist the recruit in securing proper uniforms and equipment.[37]

More obsessive reenactors yearly visit German veterans to develop a better understanding of the war and the men who participated in the fighting. Some even attempt to master German to make their battlefield performances more authentic. One reenactor flew to Germany, where he could study the photographs from the period lodged in the German Federal Archives. These, he hoped, would add to his knowledge of the details of German soldiers and the environment in which they fought. Some reenactors, admittedly atypical, decorate their homes with period pieces and furniture or dedicate one room to display their collector's items. A few even "live in the period." No doubt, reenactors may acquire such paraphernalia at the flea markets that regularly appear at reenactment events.[38]

Authenticity and Romancing

Visuals also play a major role for all reenactors. Reenactment units use websites to advertise videos dealing with the German military. German-made videos, for example, enable the reenactors to glimpse the material world of the German soldier, giving them pictures of actual weapons, uniforms, helmets, badges, and other martial accoutrements of World War Two. *Strafbataillon 999*, a film about a punishment battalion, touches the psychological aspects of the reenactor's identification with the German soldier. The reviewer poignantly writes that the battalion is far more than an ordinary unit, as the advertisement from International Historic Films claims. Battalion 999 is a punishment unit where men who broke German military codes are placed. Here, we see the common man connection and the quiet heroism valued so much by the reenactors.[39]

> These soldiers are being punished by the high command for "crimes" like ordering retreats to save men's lives or working too hard to discover an anti-gangrene serum. These men are abused by their commanders, made to dig useless trenches under fire, and sent into a final suicide mission. Their enemies are everywhere.[40]

The reviewer concludes that the film brings an unusual realism to the screen in its grim depiction of the Eastern Front. Clearly, this profile fits the reenactors' own self-image and provides strong justification for that perception.[41]

"What If History" on the Eastern Front

The fascination with alternate outcomes, which stem from the reenactor's psychological need to reverse the verdict of history in World War Two, appears most dramatically in the numerous "What If" accounts of the war in the East. In these accounts, fateful decisions are remade that enable the Germans to win particular battles, campaigns, and, ultimately, the war itself. For the Eastern Front, the "What Ifs" include a number of supposed events that alter the outcome of the war. In the more outlandish, the Germans develop and deploy atomic weapons against the Soviets with, needless to say, catastrophic consequences for Soviet armies. In other cases, Hitler suffers a serious injury that prevents him from directing the war in the East. In his absence, the generals conduct the war in a more professional manner and defeat the Soviets. Other works remain closer to the narrative of the war, the one constructed by German officers after the actual event. In most cases, the alternate solution incorporates a strong animus against Communism, suggesting that a German victory was justified to rid the world of the Red menace. Of course, to have plausibility, the authors suspend any discussion of the actual aims of the Third Reich in the East and the central role of the Wehrmacht in realizing those ends.

The authors of important works of alternate history often come from the ranks of the military, have been important contributors to the literature on the war in Russia, and occasionally work for consulting agencies that deal in military matters. Representative of these authors is R. H. S. Stolfi, who wrote *Hitler's Panzers East: World War II Reinterpreted*, published by the University of Oklahoma Press in 1991 (Figure 22).[42] The History Book Club and the Military Book Club both made it one of their featured selections and the work continues to enjoy widespread popularity. Typical of such works, the biographical and introductory materials provide the reader with evidence of the author's legitimacy in writing such an account. R. H. S. Stolfi, as the blurb on the dust jacket makes clear, served as a Professor of Modern European History at the Naval Postgraduate School in Monterey, Calif. In his what-if account, Stolfi portrays Operation Barbarossa not as it really was – a failed campaign – but as a brilliant undertaking that led to the defeat of the Soviet Union. The dust jacket and the opening pages emphasize that this reevaluation of the opening phase of the German assault on the USSR provided a "lesson" for NATO planners as they considered ways to combat a Soviet strike on Western Europe. The cover art shows a German armored vehicle advancing with soldiers atop and firing at the enemy, presumably the Russians (Figure 22. Cover Art from *Hitler's Panzers East; World War II Reinterpreted*). In bold letters above the combat scene, the cover read "But for one fateful decision, Germany could have won World War II in the summer of 1941." The target audience then was regular army officers as well as the general public.[43]

Stolfi's legitimacy in addressing the NATO issue derived from the book, *NATO Under Attack*, a work he co-authored with F. W. Mellenthin, a former member of the German General Staff who fought in several theaters, including

Figure 22. Cover Art from Stolfi's *Hitler's Panzers East: World War II Reinterpreted*.

the Eastern Front. Mellenthin lends considerable credibility to Stolfi, given that the German officer participated in many battles in the East and knew first hand many of the officers Stolfi refers to in his account of Barbarossa. Mellenthin also wrote the very popular *Panzer Battles: A Study of the Employment of Armor in the Second World War*, first published by the University of Oklahoma Press in 1956 and re-released by the mass publisher, Ballantine Books, in a paperback edition in 1971.[44]

Stolfi's book argues that, in real history, the Germans lost World War Two in the opening stages of Barbarossa. If the Germans had triumphed in Russia by the fall of 1941, they would have won the Second World War. The field commanders understood clearly how this victory could have been achieved.[45] For Stolfi, Hitler's decision to invade the USSR ranked as the most crucial decision of the entire war, made at a time when the Germans had the resources to win. The German military had just finished remaking the political map of Europe, had defeated all its opponents, and stood confident in its ability to win any campaign. Russia presented a formidable challenge, yet few commanders questioned the ability of the Wehrmacht to achieve victory in the East. Such a triumph would have opened to Germany the vast resources of the USSR and made the Third Reich invincible against assaults by other powers.[46]

Stolfi's argument hinges on the tactics of the Wehrmacht in conducting warfare. These tactics aimed at a quick victory and maneuvers fully capable of neutralizing the size of the Soviet forces. The speed of the German assaults, the impact of their superior weapons and the coordination of weapons systems of the German military gave the German army unrivalled assets. The German military also stressed initiative at all levels of command down to noncommissioned officers.[47]

The blitz style of attack enabled the Germans to penetrate into the rear of the Soviet armies, to sever links between command posts and front line units, and to disrupt rear areas in general. Soviet armies found themselves isolated and under constant assault from the Germans. Fortunately for the planners of the invasion of the Soviet Union, Russian troop formations remained in place when the Germans launched their attacks. Rather than retreating and giving up ground in order to regroup, the Russian armies held their ground and quickly suffered defeat as the German armored spearhead surrounded them. The speed and disruption caused by the German spearhead also made the huge scale of Soviet armies meaningless because they never effectively engaged German armor nor even proved capable of containing the armored thrusts. In the opening six weeks, the Russians suffered unparalleled losses as whole armies disintegrated and fronts vanished under the ceaseless assault of German arms.

From the start, the German generals drove their armored spearheads toward Leningrad in the North, Kiev in the South, and, most importantly, Moscow in the center. The military commanders understood that capturing Moscow was the key to victory. As Stolfi explains, the capital was of enormous significance politically, economically, and symbolically. It was a manufacturing center. It served as the central railhead for the entire Soviet transportation system; all lines converged on Moscow, a fact that enabled Soviet planners to move troops with dispatch from one front to another. Stalin and the Communist leadership governed the entire country from Moscow. As the campaign proceeded, Army Group Center (AGC), led by two Panzer groups, one commanded by the father of the blitzkrieg, Heinz Guderian, and the other by the able Herman Hoth, defeated the armies it faced and by the end of July stood at Smolensk, the last major city before Moscow. According to Stolfi, the Germans stood on the edge of victory.[48]

Stolfi then explains why, in reality, the campaign went awry. Hitler surfaces as the main cause of Barbarossa's failure. His intrusion into decision making and his failure to see Moscow as the main prize in the invasion in the end foiled the plans of the General Staff and canceled out the battlefield victories of the field commanders. Seeing Russia as a storehouse of raw materials, Hitler conceived of the campaign as a way of building up German resources to defend the German state against its enemies. Hitler also wanted to protect Germany from its enemies by surrounding it with conquered territories. In essence, he sought to create an impregnable fortress. His officers, such as Guderian, saw the campaign as the means of destroying an enemy, the Soviet regime. For them, the capture of Moscow would achieve that end. Hitler's orders to divert troops to Leningrad and to send Guderian's Panzer group south in early August to seal the huge encirclement at Kiev thwarted the entire plan for victory. At the moment Guderian moved his tanks south, AGC faced little opposition beyond Smolensk. AGC had the resources. Men and armored vehicles were in sufficient number and their previous victories had psychologically weakened the Russians.[49]

By the time AGC resumed its advance at the end of September, the moment for victory had slipped away. The Soviets had rebuilt their armies and defenses while Germans arms suffered from the wearisome march south to Kiev and back toward Moscow. Although AGC possessed sufficient men and arms to destroy several Russian armies in operation Typhoon, that victory yielded no strategic results. The fall rains again gave the Soviets recovery time and then a fierce winter literally froze German arms exhausted by months of campaigning. The Soviets held and, with reinforcements from the East, conducted a major counterstroke in December, throwing the Germans back a hundred miles west of Moscow. The delays in the German offensive and the breathing space they gave the Russians spelled defeat for the Germans not only in 1941 but ultimately as well. Stolfi then notes that subsequent battles such as Stalingrad and Kursk only confirmed the outcome of 1941.

Reading Stolfi's account, one would have no idea of the complicity of the German army in the crimes of the Nazi regime in Russia. He simply ignores the predatory behavior of German warfare and subsequent occupation. He fails to mention the "Commissar Order," mandating the shooting of Communist Party officials and other suspected people, like partisans and Jews; the "Jurisdictional Order," which pre-amnestied the German forces for any acts they committed against the Soviet population; and the "Hostage Order," which prescribed the shooting of fifty civilians for every German soldier killed by partisans. Nor does he mention the close collaboration between the German army and the Einsatzgruppen, the "operational groups" that followed the army into Russia, killing hundreds of thousands of people.[50] Stolfi is urging the U.S. Army to study the Wehrmacht only in its operational activities and, by implication, to take no notice of its role as an agent of genocide.[51]

Hitler's aims proved even more encompassing than the destruction of the Jewish population in the East and the subjugation of the Slavic peoples. The Nazi leader, his advisers, and the military hierarchy also agreed that the urban populations were scheduled for starvation and then, obviously, removal. Virtually no one disagreed with the Fuehrer on this point. Once his troops advanced deep into Russia by mid-July 1941, Hitler and his coterie determined that those who survived the German onslaught would live without any rights and, as implied, the privilege of owning weapons. The Wehrmacht paved the way for the reduction of local populations and then German settlement in these seized territories.[52]

The Germans never intended to liberate any of the peoples living in the Soviet Union. Even in areas where the population showed some enthusiasm for the Wehrmacht, the Germans fully intended to replace the local peoples with other Germans. Even in the Ukrainian and the Baltic States, where sympathies for the Germans ran high and the ethnic minorities in the region saw the Germans as a tool to realize their own nationalistic aspirations, the invading armies arrived as conquerors, not liberators. Hitler actually concluded that his regime would also recruit Germans from southeastern Europe and then, "presumably" move them into the soon-to-be-vacated lands in Russia. A careful reading of the master outline in "General Plan for the East" reveals the intentions of Hitler and the German leadership.[53]

The Germans also accelerated their killing of Russian Jews along with innocent civilians, the mentally retarded, party members, "and anybody who looked unpleasant." POWs suffered grievously in the hands of the Wehrmacht, which showed little mercy. Clearly, Germans relentlessly pursued Hitler's goals of removing and reorganizing millions of people in the East. To believe otherwise demands a detachment from the reality of the German regime and the almost universal support it received from the German people.[54]

Stolfi does discuss atrocities – those allegedly committed by the Russians against the Germans. He openly rejects the Germans as the responsible parties in acts of inhumanity. Instead, Stolfi vigorously argues that the Russians were the agents of such cruelty and the Germans were the victims. Stolfi writes:

> The accounts of murder, mutilation, and maiming come entirely from German sources but are so general, from so many different observers and commentators, and in so consistent a pattern as to be exempt from serious question.[55]

He argues that the Soviet leadership used terror as a way of controlling their troops and suggests that the atrocities may also have resulted directly from the harsh political and social realities of Soviet life and of the Russian national character.[56]

In the climate of post World War Two, when Nazi crimes dominated the headlines, none would dare reveal the Soviet crimes. Later, the rising tide of the Holocaust accounts made such revelations impossible. Last, Stolfi separates frontline units from rear-area security forces that have come under condemnation for violence against the Russian people.[57]

Stolfi borrows heavily from the arguments made by former German generals in the many memoirs and narratives of the war in the East published in the decades before Stolfi wrote his study. From the start, German generals, including Franz Halder, Heinz Guderian, and Erich von Manstein, advanced the most important of these arguments that Hitler bore responsibility for defeat. Hitler's arbitrary and amateurish interference lost the war that could have been won by the professionals. Stolfi goes to great lengths to praise the field commanders, in particular Guderian.[58] His decisive actions in France and on the Eastern Front embodied the essence of the German style of attack that proved so successful early in the war. He and other generals such as Herman Hoth, commander of Panzer Group 3 with AGC, provided the Wehrmacht with the leadership and talent, Stolfi argues, that made it unique in the period 1939–41. Such praises reflect what the officers wrote about their own participation on the Eastern Front. Virtually none engaged in self-criticism, least of all Manstein and Guderian.

Stolfi borrows other ideas from the Germans as well. His description of the Russian soldier and the role of the commissar also reflect what German officers related about the Eastern campaign. The Russian soldier, Stolfi writes, clearly had almost no capability to take the initiative, unlike his German counterpart.

He followed orders even if they threatened his life. Despite the determination and fierceness of the Russian soldier, the discipline in the Red Army usually depended on the political officers, the commissars. These men repeatedly shot their own troops if they showed cowardliness or attempted to desert, habits embraced by the military officers. Either the Russian soldier resisted the Germans or his own leaders would kill him. Officers also constantly reminded the troops that the Germans usually shot POWs. The average Russian soldier, Stolfi claims, lived in dread of both his own officers and the enemy. Manstein, Mellenthin, and others similarly described the Russian soldier.[59]

Stolfi also argues that the Germans used "surrender passes" with great success. German planes dropped these on Russian soldiers, urging them to give up and promising good treatment. Apparently Soviet soldiers responded in large numbers to this persuasion. Stolfi also claims that the men often executed their military and political officers before going over to the German lines, a plausible description if one accepts his earlier characterization of the Russian leadership. According to German sources, the Russian POWs seemed elated to escape the grasp of their officers and the regime in general. What Stolfi ignores is the German record on the treatment of POWs in the East. Fully three-and-a-half million POWs died in German custody, 57% of Soviet prisoners who fell into German hands. The resolve of Soviet soldiers to resist Wehrmacht assaults stiffened as they became aware of the fate that awaited POWs in German camps.[60]

Finally, Stolfi embraces the revisionist notion that the German attack on the Soviet Union actually was a preemptive strike. This myth was spread by German generals after the war and taken up anew by V. Rezun (or Suvorov, his pen name), who wrote in 1985 that Stalin actually planned a revolutionary war against Germany from 1939 on and had ordered the massing of troops near the frontiers along German or German-held lands. Instead of the German assault fulfilling Hitler's long-held ambition, first articulated in *Mein Kampf*, the June invasion actually amounted to a preemptive strike against an enemy preparing to destroy Germany and her allies. Stolfi makes precisely this point when he writes that the deployment of large Soviet forces along the western frontier culminated a planned assault against the Reich. The Soviets intended to launch their main forces against Romania and Eastern Europe, which accounts for the concentration of Soviet armies in the south. Given that the Soviets ultimately won, they imposed their view that the Germans were the aggressors and the Russian were the victims. For Stolfi, the troop disposition demonstrated an "opportunistic and aggressive policy on the part of the Soviets."[61]

David Glantz, one of the leading scholars on the Soviet Union in World War Two, points out the improbability of a preemptive strike by the Russians. True, intelligence reports convinced Stalin of a German buildup sufficiently menacing to order mobilization of his troops. He also ordered several of his armies into forward positions. At the same time, Zhukov submitted a plan for a strike against the Germans. Entitled "Report on the Plan of Strategic Deployment of Armed Forces of the Soviet Union to the Chairman of the Council of People's Commissars of 15 May 1941," the plan called for a counter blow before the Germans launched their own strike. Yet, the plan lacked any grounding in reality. Even to assemble the vast numbers of men and materials required for such a move would take at least two months, long after the Germans began their invasion. More importantly, Soviet armies simply lacked adequate weapons, training, and leadership to pull off such a gigantic preemptive strike. Their record in Poland and Finland hardly inspired confidence and only showed the desperate need to re-equip and retrain the Soviet military. Stalin certainly recognized the inadequacies of his military establishment and was not about to begin a preventive war against Germany.[62]

Stolfi recycles many of the myths that he inherited from former German generals as to the possibilities of German victory in the summer of 1941. Informed by a profound anti-Communism, he suggests both an alternative outcome of Operation Barbarossa, and that such an outcome would have been preferable to what actually happened. The anti-Communist sentiment that colored much of Stolfi's analysis appears again in Colonel Samuel Newland's essay re-creating the Eastern Front, in which the Germans again triumph. Newland also comes with impressive credentials; he is a National Guard colonel and, at the time of publication, professor in the Department of Advanced Studies at the U.S. Army War College. He is the author of several books on the Germany army and the Eastern Front. His essay appeared in the popular *What If? Strategic Alternatives of Word War II*. Newland's credentials as a scholar who has published on the Wehrmacht and the German campaign in the East lend credibility to his essay.[63] Prominent scholars from both the United States and Great Britain as well as veteran authors and retired military officers with their own publishing records also contributed to the edited volume. This larger context lends credibility to Newland's argument.[64]

Newland argues that if the Germans had treated the peoples under their occupation more humanely, they could have counted on mass support that would have enhanced their chances of victory. Newland opens the essay by pointing out the significant number of non-Russians who took up arms with the invading German armies against Stalin and his regime. He appropriately points out that the Soviet regime conducted brutal policies against many ethnic minorities who saw the Germans as a means to enact revenge. He then minimizes the impact of German atrocities by arguing that under Soviet leadership, the ethnic minorities endured decades of harsh policies whereas the Germans only had two years to inflict their brand of suffering on the Russian people. Newland also stresses the impact of Stalin's collectivization of farming on the Ukrainians, who initially saw the Germans as liberators. The peoples in the recently annexed Baltic States also sided with the Germans when they seized Latvia, Estonia, and Lithuania. In fact, the Germans raised SS divisions from the Ukrainian and Baltic populations.[65]

The Germans encountered more disgruntled ethnic populations in the summer of 1942, when they moved into the Caucasus Mountains. Turkish and Persian peoples in the region lived under Stalin's harsh regime and by 1942 had built up a good deal of anger over Soviet policies. These peoples, Newland argues, also viewed the Germans as liberators. Many Russians also deserted to the Germans, although this exodus dried up considerably once the Russian soldiers began to learn of the horrific treatment of POWs by the Germans (something Stolfi ignores).[66]

Newland goes on to suggest that a policy of autonomy under German rule provided another alternative to the actual policies the Germans developed for the East. Here, Newland points to the example of the Kaminsky Brigade, which operated in the Bryansk forest region west of Moscow. The Russians there were treated decently and did collaborate with the Germans. The Germans recruited Bronislav Kaminsky to their ranks in 1941 to assist in eliminating rear-area opposition to German occupation. Previously, he had served the Communist regime, which gave him substantial experience working with people in the Orel-Kursk area. Kaminsky succeeded beyond the Germans' wildest expectations and soon the forces resisting the Germans vanished. His men killed or wounded more than 2,000 partisans and moved out some 12,531 "civilians." The Germans then rewarded Kaminsky by allowing him to set up the Lotoky Self-Governing District under the umbrella of German administration. Kaminsky then renamed his force the Russian People's Army of Liberation.[67]

The Germans used this "successful" model in dealing with another unhappy ethnic minority, the Cossacks. The Germans used the same integrationist approach with these people who followed the Germans in their retreat out of Russia. For Newland, this strategy held great potential for the Germans, who could have combined the benign integrationist approach with their many battlefield victories. German armies did recruit (or dragoon) locals in large numbers to help them with many logistical and other supply and rear-area operations.[68]

The real Kaminsky Brigade, despite its anti-partisan success, scarcely provided a model for integrationist policy, as its actions in the Warsaw uprising in 1944 demonstrated. Accused of rape and pillage on a massive scale, Kaminsky had to face the German officers who expressed displeasure with the sordid actions of his men. The Brigade actually arrived in the Polish city with a fierce reputation for their actions in the rear areas of Kursk, where they worked closely with the Dirlewanger Brigade composed of thieves and ex-convicts. They fought a brutal war with partisans who engaged in fierce tactics themselves. The Kaminsky unit's reputation hardly recommended it as a model for a respectable occupation with collaborationists and, in reality, the unit was better designed for punitive purposes.[69] To presume that Kaminsky assisted the Germans in pacifying rear areas to create safe and loyal regions ignores the fundamental fact that his men earned an unwholesome reputation for rapine and pillaging.

At the conclusion of his essay, Newland argues that if the Germans had adopted a civilian-friendly policy from the first day of Barbarossa, then they would have won the hearts and minds of the Russian people. The German officers broadcasting that they came as liberators would have proven eminently successful and recruited hundreds of thousands of Soviet citizens to support the Germans. The Germans could also have returned the thousands of émigrés who had fled the Bolsheviks in the wake of the revolution. Their presence would have given the Germans some legitimacy. At the same time, if the Germans established liberation committees, their members would have added more to the integrity of the Germans. Of course, Newland admits such a possibility was unlikely. In fact, it was far more than unlikely. This strategy flew in the face of stated German aims in the East that openly intended to murder millions and did precisely that in what Newland terms a "brief occupation." Such an alternative has absolutely no basis in the reality of Nazi policy and Wehrmacht actions. The alternative suggests a German military and regime sympathetic to the Russian people when their only aim was to destroy much of the Russian population. The Newland piece seems to incorporate a common theme in the memoir literature and in the "What If" literature, namely the Communists embodied evil and the German military, in contrast to the Nazi civil administration, held out the hope of liberation to the oppressed peoples of the Soviet Union. The reality differed dramatically from these imaginary flights of fantasy and creates an image wholly at odds with the Nazi regime and its military forces.

Conclusion

In the fall of 1983, World War Two veteran Joseph Polowski died in his home city of Chicago. A seemingly anonymous death, Polowski's passing actually marked the end of a long tradition of advocating peaceful coexistence dating back to the late 1940s. He and the men in his unit were the very first American soldiers to encounter their Russian counterparts on the Elbe River in April 1945. They celebrated the end of a vicious conflict that claimed the lives of millions of human beings, including an appalling thirty million dead in the Soviet Union. Both groups of men clearly understood the profound meaning of their encounter; a monstrous enemy had been defeated through their joint struggle. To preserve peace, especially in an age of nuclear weapons, Polowski publicly called for disarmament and negotiations at a time when the United States and the Soviet engaged in an expensive and dangerous arms race.[1]

For Russia, that struggle began in June 1941, when German troops crossed into the Soviet Union and opened a war to the death. Alerted by newspapers, books, magazines, radio, and diplomatic and military exchanges, Americans followed the course of the war from the opening battles to the reduction of Berlin in 1945. With the Japanese attack on Pearl Harbor in December 1941 and Hitler's declaration of war on the United States, American and Russia became allies in the fight against Nazi Germany. The media released countless stories about Russian heroism and sacrifices to the American public. Citizens read about Russian soldiers giving up their lives to save their country. Russians also formed guerrilla bands to thwart German military efforts and complement the exertions of the Red Army to defeat German forces. The media portrayed the sacrifices of civilians and workers conscripted by the millions into the Soviet War economy to manufacture the weapons necessary to carry on the fight against the invaders.

Americans also discovered, to their horror, the atrocities inflicted on the Russian people by the German army, the Waffen-SS, and the murdering squads that accompanied the German forces. Russian families lost countless loved ones to the cruelty and barbarity of the German genocidal machine. Husbands, mothers, children all died at the hands of the German troops. Americans saw pictures of the physical destruction the Germans visited upon the Soviet Union. City after city suffered terribly under German aerial and land assault. Thousands of villages and towns simply vanished as the Germans waged a fierce campaign of scorched earth against Russia. Sympathy for the Russian people flourished among the American public, symbolized by the Russian War Relief Committee that organized donor drives among Americans to send needed materials, food, and medicine to the suffering Russian people.

Moving the calendar ahead to the 1990s, very different images of the Russo-German war exists in the minds of Americans. The Germans, and not the Russians, appear as the victims of that terrible conflict. Millions of Americans remember the rape of Berlin by the Red Army. Few could explain the Kharkov war crimes tribunal held in 1943 to try German soldiers for barbarities against innocent Russians and even fewer could recount the destruction wrought by German troops in Byelorussia (today Belarus) in the summer of 1942. The heroes of the Russo-German War were no longer brave young Russian men and women who gave up their lives by the millions to defeat Germany.

Instead, German soldiers in both the Army and Waffen-SS stand out as men who gave up their lives in an honorable fight against the Soviet armies intent on destroying the Fatherland. Countless memoirs, biographies, and autobiographies written by German veterans and translated into English in romantic prose describe the German efforts to save Germany and even Europe from the Red Army and hordes from the East. Names such as Manstein and Guderian are familiar to every Army officer and widespread among a reading public that buys books sympathetic to the Germans. Until very recently, few books telling the Russian side of the war circulated among the American reading public, and among those published, even fewer survived their initial release.

How, then, did the exhausted and fearless German soldier who fought in a losing cause replace the Red Army soldier as the symbol of the struggle in the East? The story began almost as soon as the war ended. The German officers faced a difficult task in the mid and late 1940s. How could they detach their war records from the Nazi regime, convince the Allies they suffered much at the hands of their political rulers and persuade the Allies of their value in rebuilding Germany? Preexisting ties between German and American military officers certainly helped predispose the U.S. military toward the German position.

Even more important, the outbreak of the Cold War provided the context that facilitated the German success in joining the Americans in the struggle against the Soviet Union, once the main ally of the United States and then its fiercest of enemies. The Berlin Airlift of 1948, the formation of NATO in 1949, and the start of the Korean War in 1950, among other events, transformed the wartime allies into deadly enemies. The Cold War blinded the Americans to crimes committed by the German military and proved a godsend for officers such as Heinz Guderian, Franz Halder, and Erich von Manstein, all now queuing up to give the Americans advice on how to fight the Soviet Army.

Facing a formidable Soviet Union, the Americans turned to the Germans for counsel in facing the Communist forces. The Americans first recruited former Wehrmacht officers to write their accounts of fighting the Russians; after all, who knew better how to kill Russians then the men who dispatched 30 million of them? Headed by former Chief of Staff Halder, several hundred officers churned out 2,500 reports, each several hundred pages long, on their experiences in combat against the new menace, the Red Army. Of course, in the process, Halder and his associates took the occasion to promote the "clean Wehrmacht," an organization dedicated solely to the battlefield and innocent of any war crimes. The growing association between the German veterans and the U.S. officers provided fertile ground to establish one of the strongest postwar alliances of the Cold War. Many of those who worked under Halder later became advisors to or prominent in the resurrected German Army, renamed the Bundeswehr. The Myth of the Eastern Front clearly enjoyed a promising start.

Manstein and Guderian proved tireless workers in fleshing out the "clean Wehrmacht." Manstein's service during the winter of 1942 and through much of 1943, when the Germans fought defensive battles against countless numbers of Russian troops, ideally met needs of the U.S. Army. Understrengthed, it faced the same inexhaustible mass of Russian troops and materials that confronted the Americans in the 1950s. U.S. Army officers welcomed Manstein's experiences and his endless streams of advice in written text and discussions on preparing for and fighting the formidable Soviets. Of course, Guderian, the supreme self-promoter, also offered his wisdom of conducting operations against the Russian forces. He wrote a short book explaining to NATO leaders the best ways to defend Europe against the eastern hordes, much as he and his men did in World War Two. Guderian and Manstein and, in fact, all senior officers knew perfectly well what Hitler planned for Russia's peoples, including its Jewish population.

American officers and diplomats ignored such details as the Cold War heated up during the 1950s. In fact, deals between the newly created West German republic and the United States exonerated German veterans of war crimes, including Waffen-SS members. The Bundeswehr joined NATO armies as stalwarts preparing for the final showdown with the Soviets.

From diplomats and military officers, the myth of the "clean Wehrmacht" made its way into a broader American public and soon became an enduring story in American popular culture. German memoirs, autobiographies, and accounts of the war in Russia flourished from the later 1950s onward and especially in the 1960s, when mass paperback distributors pedaled these accounts to an American audience predisposed to the German perspective by years of Cold War rhetoric. Inexpensive and readily available, works such as Carell's *Hitler Moves East* found willing consumers thrilled by the romanticized stories and prose that carefully promoted the "clean Wehrmacht." The themes of professionalism devoid of political or ideological content, duty-bound to the homeland, family men, and good Christians as well as self-sacrificing soldiers make these men the romanticized heroes that drew praise from the American public. Such accounts appeared year after year and enjoyed publishing successes demonstrated by their continuous reissuing over the course of a half-century.

By the 1980s and 1990s, junior-level officers and even rank-and-file soldiers penned their versions of the war in the East. These accounts differed little in spirit from the memoirs of the field marshals and colonel generals of the 1950s. The German soldier fought for the Fatherland and to defend his family and community from the Communist forces from the East. German soldiers suffered both from the Nazi regime indifferent to their plight and from the Communist one intent on destroying not only Germany but also Western civilization itself. Millions of German soldiers willingly gave up their lives to protect their loved ones. German soldiers fought bravely in Russia even to the point of aiding Russian soldiers and civilians, traits noticeably absent among the Red Army rank and file. German officers and enlisted men also showed disdain for their Nazi overlords, whose racial and political aims remained unknown to the military. Such accounts continued to flourish into the twenty-first century. Book clubs repeatedly featured these accounts as their main selections. For those enthralled by Manstein and Guderian in the 1950s and the 1960s, Bidermann and Koschorrek provided fresh accounts of German heroism and self-sacrifice.

For enthusiasts who relished every new German story of the Eastern Front, these accounts sustained their insatiable appetites. By the 1960s and 1970s, the German version of the titanic struggle in the East won the hearts and minds of millions in the United States. The publishing achievements of Manstein and Guderian and the failure of accounts sympathetic to the Russians demonstrate the long-term success of German veterans in re-creating themselves as heroes amidst villains.

Gurus such as Richard Landwehr and Frank Kurowski carried the messages of these veterans to an eager audience of enthusiasts or romancers who eagerly awaited each new account and embellishment of the "clean Wehrmacht" and its heroic soldiers. Gurus praised German soldiers, including, and often especially, Waffen-SS men, for their bravery on the battlefield. The gurus combine detailed knowledge and personal friendship with veterans to demonstrate their own authenticity, the premier trait for romancers. Their works include rare photographs and laudatory texts that cast the German soldiers in an extraordinarily favorable light. Dashing figures such as the renowned Jochen Piper appear in the works of gurus such as Mark Yerger. Gurus place German soldiers such as Piper in contradistinction to the Nazi Party members who attempted to realize the ghastly ends of Hitler and his henchmen.

As the cult of the romanticized German soldier grew in the reading public, it also enjoyed a new following among the tens of thousands of wargamers who appeared in increasing numbers during the 1960s and the 1970s. Games on the Eastern Front helped propel the hobby into countrywide prominence as national and regional conventions and nationally distributed magazines won a permanent following in the United States. Games such as *Panzerblitz* and *War in the East* depicted the German army as an institution dedicated solely to the battlefield. Gaming magazines repeated the themes promoted in the reading literature that provided many of the sources for these games. Few would suspect Guderian's Nazi sympathies or Manstein's participation in dividing up the spoils of murdered Russian Jews in reading these magazines or playing the wargames. They, like the gurus, assiduously avoided the racial and political dimensions of the Third Reich. German soldiers, after all, fought in defense of the Fatherland and not the Final Solution.

The Internet transformed the romancers' culture into one of twenty-four-hour participation and transnational base. Internet sites stored incredible amounts of information about the German military, its officers and men, and its battles and campaigns. Topics as diverse as weapons, medals, and military ranks appear on these sites. Online fora enable romancers to carry on discussions of the German military on a continuing basis and across continents and oceans. Manstein, Guderian, and the other luminaries of the German military often form the basis of these discussions. Discussions often deal with the Waffen-SS. In one case, participants went to great lengths to make it clear that the SS Wiking Division was guiltless of war crimes, a fact they claimed was supported by Soviet praise for the unit. Books by Mellenthin, Luck, Knappe, and others appear on Internet site reading lists for participants. These sites draw hundreds of thousands of visitors every year and demonstrate the popularity of the German military, one innocent of any war crimes or association with the Nazi regime and Hitler.

From the mid-1970s onward, reenacting also won favor among romancers. By the end of the 1990s, dozens of reenacting groups formed across the United States commemorating Wehrmacht and mostly Waffen-SS units. The men and a few women who joined these units desperately want to relive the German military world of the late 1930s and the early 1940s. Authenticity drives these individuals. From 1940s-style eyeglasses and haircuts to German uniforms and boots, reenactors want the most realistic war equipment and style; anything less warrants severe criticism, especially from hardcore reenactors. The reliving even extends to the use of German when possible and certainly German martial songs. Judges evaluate participants and award points in the actual reenacting battle. Bankers, clerks, and mechanics, from all economic classes and occupations, show up on weekends to relive the world of the Wehrmacht and Waffen-SS. For the reenactors, the men who served in the German military represent the highest ideals of courage and bravery. In public events, reenactors carry this message to the general public who come to see reenactments and listen to reenactors talk about their obsession. Readers, Internet participants, reenactors, military officers, diplomats, gurus, and book club members all keep the myth of the "clean Wehrmacht" alive and healthy.

Demonstration of the romancers' notions of the brave and heroic German soldier currently continues to appear with great frequency. Today, Soldat FHQ, a popular supplier of reenacting materials, provides an important channel for romancers literally to connect with the men whose memories they sustain. Soldat FHQ affords the recruit the opportunity to morph into a true German soldier. The manufacturer produces the *Soldbücher*, or paybook, that originally contained the personal information of a soldier in the Wehrmacht. In seeking to obtain the *Soldbücher*, the recruit fills out an application that first asks the recruit to write his actual name and address. Next, the application shifts to the actual historical impression. Here, the candidate lists his new German name and the actual enlistment date of the German soldier whose identity he assumes. He acquires his identification number (*Erkennungsmarke*) and lists his blood type and gasmask size. The newly morphed Wehrmacht soldier also lists his German birth date and place and his religious affiliation. The web page includes a photograph of two pages of a *Soldbücher* to demonstrate the product's realism.[2]

The realism of the *Soldbücher* appears in the comments of a German veteran of World War Two in an exchange that occurred in late 2006. He commends

Soldat FHQ for accurately reproducing his own "*Soldbücher*, Awards Documents & Awards." The veteran wrote:

> "I believe that you should seek employment in German intelligence service. You have performed a masterpiece of duplication. One suggestion would be that the documents should have been aged as well. Otherwise you did very well. I shall draft a letter to you which will highlight your understanding of German culture.... Please accept my thanks for your exceptional skills and understanding of what the Wehrmacht was all about, the ability of producing originality in what you do."[3]

The monitor of the site added that Soldat FHQ was fully capable of aging equipment. In fact, if one types in http://www.soldat.com/Aging, the page *Soldat Custom Aging* appears. It shows an officer's cap "that [Soldat]... aged for a customer." The site periodically posts items aged for its clients in order to persuade potential customers to use Soldat's services. On November 1, 2006, the site included a photo of a "Hitler war period cap" that a customer wanted because it resembled the cap worn by the actor [Bruno Ganz]who played Hitler in the movie *Downfall*. The owner of the site also noted that Soldat "use[d] the correct cord and cockade while the movie cap did not."

Customers praised the quality of the Soldat's products. One wrote, "Jim..., whose *Soldbuch* is on your web site, is a member of our unit. After his glowing testimonials, we are recommending" that all the members in our unit use your company. Purchasing an *Erkennungsmarke*, among other products, including *Reichsmarks* and color postcards, would exceed $300 and suggests the persistent commitment of the reenactors to achieve authenticity. The owner of the site informed readers that

> [D]uring the *Soldbucher* application process you will have decided on, and define, your first person impression's background. Add the matching *FHQ's Erkennungsmarke* and you become your impression... when asked who you are, you pull out your FHQ *Soldbuch* and *Erkennungsmarke* and say 'Ich bin...' End of story.[4]

Remembering the stresses of war, Soldat FHQ also provides a "pray request page." The website states, "put the whole armour of God! Website specifically for military prayer." The reenactor site leaves no stone unturned in its effort to give the customer the realism of the German soldier and his world.[5]

This dedication to reenacting in general has spawned the World War II Historical Re-enacting Society, Inc. It attempts to serve as umbrella organization for World War Two reenacting groups across the nation. It charters units that meet the expectations spelled out on its website. These range from

authenticity and relations officers to unit name and "list of authorized uniforms, weapons, equipment. And vehicles." The organization's authenticity
committee and its board of directors must approve all applications before
chartering a unit. Of course, all materials submitted must have adequate documentation. If approved, the president, vice president, and secretary of the
Society sign off on the application.[6]

Internet sites continue to feature many of the books included in the current study. *Feldgrau.net*, one of the largest and certainly most important of
these sites, recently published a list of "German World War II Memories and
Diaries." The list incorporated Knappe's *Soldat: Reflections of a German Soldier,
1936–1949*, Gottlob Herbert Bidermann's *In Deadly Combat: A German Soldier's Memoir of the Eastern Front*, Otto Carius' *Tigers in the Mud: the Combat
Career of German Panzer Commander Otto Carius* (a J. J. Fedorowicz release),
Heinz Guderian's *Panzer Leader* (listed in German as *Erinnerungen Eines Soldaten*), Erich von Manstein's *Lost Victories* (listed in German as *Verlorene Siege*),
Gunther K. Koschorrek's *Blood Red Snow* (listed in German as *Vergis' die Zeit
der Dornen nicht*), Hans von Luck's *Panzer Commander: The Memoirs of Colonel
Hans von Luck*, Friedrich Wilhelm von Mellenthin's *Panzer Battles: A Study of
the Employment of Armor in the Second World War*, among other pieces covered
in the study. The descriptions also reflect the pro-German bias so common in
such reviews. The short paragraph on Knappe's book stresses his service record
and his years in captivity under the Soviets. The description of von Luck highlighted his gallantry, his awards, and his achieving the rank of full colonel at an
early age. It also notes his capture by the Soviets and his years in a Soviet labor
camp. The opening sentence under Manstein's name declares that he ranked as
"one of Hitler's most brilliant generals in World War II." The sentence comes
directly from the cover of Manstein's memoirs.[7]

In October 2006, the same website, *Feldgrau*, also included favorable comments on works such as Bidermann's *In Deadly Combat*, Korschorrek's *Blood
Red Snow*, and Carius' *Tigers in the Mud*, as well as glowing descriptions of
Guderian and Mellenthin in its forum. One participant wrote of Bidermann's
piece, "that I think I lent it to someone and they liked it so much they forgot to return it." In responding to an Internet inquiry asking for a review
of the book, a participant declared, "I highly recommended it. His unit was
decimated at Stalingrad, it was only thru luck that he wasn't in the Kessel
[encircled area]." A second participant commented that "the actual narrative
is first rate." A third asserted, "reads fast, doesn't wallow in blood and guts. You
can feel the fear and adrenalin." Another wrote, "I especially loved his focus
more on camaraderie instead of thumping some political agenda. I loved his
down to earth writing style." An extended review of *Tigers in the Mud* opens

with "I was really impressed with the author's candid descriptions of his peers and superiors. . . . You could get the feel of how the soldiers' qualities over the war years changed from excellent to those that did not want to fight." The reviewer praises the book for its originality, its visuals, and its focus on detail. The reviewer concludes: "All in all an excellent memoir, in my opinion, worth getting." Last, in a debate over the superior book, Guderian's *Erinnerungen eines Soldaten* or Mellenthin's *Panzer Battles*, respondents lavish praise on both works and authors. One chose Guderian's book because he exercised command over a broader part of the army as Inspector General. Another concludes that both works deserve praise and one should read them "in tandem." The focus in these works always remains the military dimension and never broaches the more controversial topics of atrocities, Nazi indoctrination, or the commitment of the soldiers in the Wehrmacht to Hitler and his regime.[8]

Gurus also still keep their presence felt throughout the ranks of pro-Wehrmacht and Waffen-SS acolytes. Mark Yerger acts a moderator on the "SS/Waffen-SS Forum Parameters." His noted expertise among romancers makes him an ideal choice to handle the many discussions that occur in this forum. Yerger declares the forum "is NOT a political debate area" and promises to censure all racists or "zealous political attacks. . . . " He answers questions on the Waffen-SS and comments that "I've done research and writing on SS topics so will be glad to assist anyone in my specific areas if I can." The favorable sentiment toward the Waffen-SS continues to enjoy a healthy existence. In the exchanges listed for this date, Yerger wrote forty-seven replies.[9]

The media and mass distribution magazines feature programs and articles that incorporate themes raised in our study. The History Channel also promotes the romancers' fantasies about the Eastern Front in its widely viewed documentaries on the Russo-German War. The Channel reaches millions of viewers nightly, many of whom see the documentary with its actual footage and sound as an accurate portrayal of the brutal conflict in the East. Media companies use the latest technologies to transform guru books into audio format readily available on *Amazon.com*. These bring the most extreme form of the romancer myths of the Eastern Front to a broad consumer audience.

Military History Quarterly (*MHQ*) and *Military History*, both available on newsstands and in the ubiquitous Barnes and Noble bookstores, often carry interviews or stories about heroic Germans who fought in Russia during World War Two. With catchy titles such as "Tank Busting Stuka Pilot" and "Besieged Outside Stalingrad," these magazines attract a large audience from the general public. The "Besieged" article appeared in *MHQ* in the winter of 2003. Written by a veteran of Stalingrad, the piece described the experiences of a young tank driver, Fritz Bartelmann, who escaped the Soviet encirclement of the 6th

Army. Typical of stories Germans related in their accounts of the war in Russia, Bartelmann wrote of a crude Russian village where men had to cope with lice-infested bedding and huts plagued by rodents searching for food and warmth. He described the Russian women for the most part as "mundane." As so often told by German veterans, Bartelmann treated Russian POWs with respect and, as a result, they enjoyed working for him. Even a Russian Jewish POW, a ballet master in peacetime, willingly labored under Bartelmann's direction. Of course, Bartelmann incorporated a tale of German suffering when he related the painful death of a young soldier hit by a Russian mortar. He made sure the pictures the young man carried with him were sent to his family members. Bartelmann embodies the decent, respectful, and courageous German soldier whose thoughts were always of others. His story benefited from the quality reputation of *MHQ* and the well-known historians, Victor David Hanson and John Lynn, of Fresno State University and the University of Illinois, respectively, whose articles appeared in the same issue of *MHQ*.[10]

Military History also features pieces on the Eastern Front. In "Tank Busting Stuka Pilot," Ed McCaul interviewed Herman Neumann, who flew the Ju-87 during the Russo-German War. McCaul opened with questions on Neumann's background and early history. The veteran recounted that the Sudetenland Germans of his Czechoslovakian hometown suffered grievously under the policies of the national government. Secret police appeared in the 1930s and soon Germans disappeared or ended up in camps from which they never returned. In fact, Czech guards needlessly beat to death a German professor whose only crime was making frequent trips to the latrine because of an intestinal problem. Only the arrival of the German army saved Neumann and his family from such actions. Neumann also endured the loss of his brother, who died in combat on the Russian front. The German as victim, a common theme in the literature, enjoys currency in the popular magazines of the United States.[11]

Neumann showed all the characteristics of the good German officer. He told of his admiration for the great Hans Rudel, who enjoyed legendary status among Stuka pilots. His exploits inspired men such as Neumann. In true self-sacrificing manner, Neumann, after being wounded and placed in a hospital for treatment and recovery, gave up his bed to a more seriously injured soldier. Neumann also showed a lack of awareness of Hitler's plan for the extermination of European Jews. He admitted his knowledge of the camps, yet he believed these housed only people who threatened Germans. He never even suspected the camps were designed to kill Jews. Pictured in a Stuka cockpit, Neumann comes across, as so many German veterans did, as a young man dedicated to the defense of his country with little understanding of the horrors the Nazis inflicted on millions of innocent people. In fact, he commented that the July 20th attempted assassination on Hitler baffled him. Why, he asked, would anyone want to kill Germany's leader in the time of war? Innocence, determination, courage, and suffering all characterized Neumann.[12]

In the winter of 2005, another piece on the Eastern Front appeared in *Military History*. The article, entitled "German Horse Soldier on the Eastern Front," featured an interview with veteran Jürgen Drogmuller, who served with a cavalry unit in Army Group North. Like so many veterans who published their stories about the Eastern Front, Drogmuller professed utter ignorance of the extermination of European Jews or the campaigns against gypsies and other beleaguered minorities. Similarly, he told of oppressed Russians greeting German troops with flowers and relief at being freed from their Communist rulers. The German troops showed immense civility toward civilians when the soldiers provided the Russians with medical care, so difficult to come by in war zones. Drogmuller also told the interviewer of the fear of the Communist Party that existed in the early 1940s. This anti-Communist theme appears frequently in the memoir literature. Of course, showing his goodwill, he set free a Russian POW, actually a onetime civilian with whom Drogmuller once shared dinner. Ultimately, the German veteran made his way to the American sector where he surrendered, a fate far better that of entering Russian captivity.[13] These themes still thrive in mass popular culture today.

The History Channel, too, features pieces that promote the romancers' mythical views of the German military. During the week of May 2, 2005, the History Channel commemorated the sixtieth anniversary of the Allied victory in World War Two with a twelve-part documentary, *Hitler's War*. The first six segments examine in detail the conflict in the East. The documentary intended to give viewers a first-hand account that incorporated footage from wartime cameras, testimony from participants, and a narration that provided the context for understanding the war in the East. Despite the actual cruelty of the war and our knowledge of the Wehrmacht's complicity in this horror, the series embraces the myths of the good German soldier, a German army unaware of crimes against the Russian people, and German soldiers as victims.

Several examples illustrate this point. Early on, the Commissar Order is mentioned, almost in passing. There follows an interview with a German veteran who stressed his humanity and who claimed to have let go a commissar whom he had captured and was supposed to shoot. On another occasion, after a passing mention of the SD and *Einsatzgruppen*, the main perpetrators of mass murder, an elderly Jew, Urichem-Fischl Rabinoff, is interviewed. He was the sole survivor in his whole family of the Holocaust. He survived only because a German soldier stationed in Pinsk – Günther Gruel – saved him by giving him false identity papers. On another occasion, fleeting mention is made to the shooting and terrorizing of civilians and to the mass starvation of the population. But again, an interview follows in which the former German soldier, remembering his puzzlement at the sight of Russian women scraping meat from the bones of a dead horse, admits to ignorance of the predatory policies that were a daily affair in German-occupied areas. Mention is briefly made of orders to shoot civilians, but immediately a German soldier, Martin Wunderlich, is interviewed telling how he refused to shoot a Russian civilian and, in fact, released him. The pattern is obvious: a minimal reference on the part of the narrator of German crimes followed by an interview with a real person, who comes across credibly and humanely and who denies he ever committed or heard of such crimes, leaving the viewer with the impression that German soldiers were mostly all decent people, while some unseen perpetrators committed the crimes that have barely been alluded to. This amounts to a whitewash of the Wehrmacht. Often when the German soldier as depicted did encounter war crimes, he was outraged and tried unsuccessfully to stop them. On one occasion, Hans-Guenther Stark of the 23rd Infantry Division is attacked by a Russian women's battalion. With great reluctance, he gives the order to fire on them with machine guns and they fall en masse. This incident gives Stark the opportunity to discourse on the madness of war. Generally, the German soldier is depicted as being both anti-war and anti-regime, which, in the face of the very heavy political indoctrination received by the German soldier, is not credible. One Russian woman is interviewed, telling how a German soldier shared his food with her.

The film also puts the German soldier against the background of home, family, loved ones, and religion to an extent that is denied the Russians. This is human interest material that makes the German more interesting, three dimensional, and attractive, whereas the Russians just seem to be about taking care of business. The film interviews the former fiancée of Alfons Metzger, with old snapshots in the background showing them planning their wedding. Then he is called to go the Eastern Front and Stalingrad, from which he never returns. This kind of story appears several times in the film. The Germans are also shown singing Christmas carols in a familiar, familial setting, praying for their men in battle. Much is made of the popular song "Lili Marlene," a romantic love song. The only singing on the part of the Russians consists of martial songs as Russian soldiers march through Moscow on the way to the front.

These repeated tales drown out whatever brief references the documentary makes to German culpability. In short, the German soldiers and their families suffer as much and maybe even more than the thirty million Russians who died in the conflict. For romancers, this depiction perfectly mirrors their own understanding of the war and the place of the German military in the Russo-German struggle. The German version of the war first promoted in 1946 continues to thrive in the twenty-first century.[14] The persistence and the power of this myth prevent any substantial engagement of the American public with the true horror of the Eastern Front and the incredible suffering the Germans inflicted on tens of millions of Russians. The "good German" seems to be destined for an eternal life.

Notes

1. Americans Experience the War in Russia

1. Helene Keyssar and Vladimir Pozner, *Remembering the War: A U.S.-Soviet Dialogue* (New York, Oxford University Press, 1990), see Preface, pp. vii–xviii, for a discussion of the American and Soviet soldiers who first met on Elbe River on April 25, 1945 and for efforts to keep alive the dialogue. See also pp. 189–95. The book provides an account of World War Two from the Soviet and the American perspectives through narrative and biographical accounts.
2. For a general history of the Third Reich, see Michael Burleigh, *The Third Reich: A New History* (New York, Hill & Wang, 2001); for the best biographical account of Hitler, see Ian Kershaw, *Hitler 1889–1936 Hubris* (New York, W.W. Norton & Company, 2000) and *Hitler 1936–1945 Nemesis* (New York, W.W. Norton & Company, 2000).
3. On this question, see George C. Herring, Jr, *Aid to Russia 1941–1946. Strategy, Diplomacy and the Origins of the Cold War* (New York, Columbia University Press, 1973); for contemporary U.S. aid to the Soviet Union, see Donald M. Nelson, "American Production – Russian Front," *Survey Graphics* February 1944, pp. 56, 59, 99, 134–37. For Russian evaluation of United States military aid, see Richard Lauterbach, *These Are the Russians* (New York, Harper, 1944), pp. 62–63. See also *Wall Street Journal*, 24 June 1941, p. 3, 26 June 1941, p. 4, 28 June 1951, p. 4, 30 August 1941, p. 2; *Time*, 13 April 1942, pp. 22–23, 15 March 1943, p. 24; "Lend-Lease to Russia," *Life*, 29 March 1943, pp. 13–19.
4. For examples of the voluminous reporting of the *New York Times*, see *The New York Times Index* (New York, The New York Times Company, 1945), pp. 1722–40 on the Eastern Front.
5. Ralph Levering, *American Public Opinion and the Russian Alliance, 1939–1945* (Chapel Hill, The University of North Carolina Press, 1976), p. 54.
6. For one example of an account of German inhumane policies in action, see Pierre van Paaseen, "Hitler's Butchers," *Look*, 8 September 1942, pp. 38–39. For an example of the awareness of German policies toward the Jews, see "All Jews' Aid Asked for Russian Battle," *New York Times*, 6 November 1945, p. 8.

7. For contemporary accounts of Russia's past experiences with invaders, see *New Republic*, 21 July 1941, pp. 79–81; *Time*, 14 July 1941, pp. 20–21, 4 August 1941, p. 18, 22 September 1941, p. 18, 10 November 1941, p. 26.

8. For accounts of the war from the Russian perspective, see the two-volume work by John Erickson, *The Road to Stalingrad, Stalin's War with Germany, volume 1* (New York, Harper & Row, Publishers, 1975) and *The Road to Berlin, Continuing the History of Stalin's War with Germany* (Boulder, Colo., Westview Press, 1983). For an extensive analysis of the development of the Soviet military up to 1941, see John Erickson, *The Soviet High Command: A Military-Political History 1918–1941* (Boulder, Colo., Westview Press, 1984). For a general history of World War Two, including the Eastern Front, see Gerhard L. Weinberg, *A World At Arms: A Global History of World War II* (New York, Cambridge University Press, 1994). For examples of contemporary reporting, see *Time*, 21 December 1942, pp. 25–26; 28 December 1942, pp. 17–18; 4 January 1943, pp. 28–29; 11 January 1943, pp. 23–25; 25 January 1943, pp. 28–29; 1 February 1943, pp. 30–34; 12 February 1945, p. 22; 19 February 1945, pp. 27–28; 9 April 1945, p. 36; 23 April 1945, p. 33; "Round Two in Russia," *Fortune*, May 1942, pp. 80–82, 130–41.

9. Levering, *American Public Opinion and the Russian Alliance*; for polling data, see pp. 43, 128, 130, and 142–43.

10. For a discussion of the purges and their impact, see Erickson, *The Road to Stalingrad*, chapter 1.

11. *Time* 27 July 1942, pp. 22–24; 22 February 1943, pp. 20–21; William Henry Chamberlin, *The Russian Enigma* (New York, C. Scribner's Sons, 1943), pp. 227, 229–30; *Look*, 19 May 1942, pp. 16–18, 20 October 1942, pp. 18–21; Lauterbach, *These Are the Russians*, pp. 122–27, 129–33, 135–36, 138; *Life*, 29 March 1943, pp. 98–105; *Look*, 1 June 1943, pp. 40, 42. For visuals of Timoshenko addressing Russian officers, see *Look*, 19 May 1942, pp. 17–19. See also Mark Gayn, "Russia's Five Best Generals," *Look*, 1 June 1943, p. 40.

12. Wallace Carroll, *We're in this with Russia* (Boston, Houghton Mifflin, 1942), p. 100.

13. *Ibid*., pp. 109–10; *Time*, 5 July 1943, p. 26.

14. Walter Kerr, *The Russian Army: Its Men, Its Leaders and Its Battles* (New York, Garden City, 1942), pp. 92–93, 100.

15. *Time*, 22 February 1943, pp. 20–21; Alexander Poliakov, *The Russians Don't Surrender* (New York, E. P. Dutton, 1942), pp. 52–53, 60 for visuals of medical treatment in the field; Carroll, *We're in This with Russia*, pp. 110–11.

16. *Life*, 29 March 1943, p. 103; *Time*, 5 July 1943, p. 28; Poliakov, *The Russians*, p. 176; Walter Graebner, *Round Trip to Russia* (Philadelphia, J. B. Lippincott, 1943), cover page next to title page.

17. Kerr, *The Russian Army*, p. 6.

18. *Ibid*., pp. 92–93, 100; Chamberlin, *The Russian Enigma*, p. 254.

19. Kerr, *The Russian Army*, pp. 127–28.

20. *Time*, 3 April 1944, p. 28.

21. *Ibid*., 31 January 1944, p. 33, 14 February 1944, pp. 29–30, 13 March 1944, p. 20, 3 April 1944, pp. 27–28, 10 July 1944, p. 24, 3 July 1944, p. 26.

22. *Time*, 20 March 1944, pp. 26–28; Graebner, *Round Trip to Russia*, pp. 136–37; Carroll, *We're in This*, pp. 125–26.

23. *Look*, 11 August 1942, pp. 16–19.

24. *Look*, 19 May 1942 p. 20; *Time*, 31 July 1944, p. 17–19; Carroll, *We're in This*, pp. 97–99, 101; Edmund Stevens, *Russia is No Riddle* (New York, Greenberg Publisher, 1945), pp. 274–75.

25. See exhibit, "World War Two through Russian Eyes," San Diego, Calif., 2001, author's notes. For a description of Alexander Pokryshkin's exploits in the war, see Lauterbach, *These Are the Russians*, Book 5, pp. 157–79.

26. *Time*, 31 July 1944, pp. 17–18; Carroll, *We're in This*, pp. 98–100.

27. *Fortune*, July 1942, "Soviet Industry", pp. 61–68, 84, 88, 90.

28. *Life*, 29 March 1943, pp. 64–65.

29. *Ibid*.

30. *Fortune*, December 1942, "Part I: The Job Before Us," pp. 93–109; *Time*, 17 November 1941, pp. 22, 24–25; 27 July 1942, pp. 80, 82; 4 May 1942; 24 July 1944; *Life* 29 March 1943, pp. 64–65; *Reader's Digest*, "Stalin's Ural Stronghold," February 1942, pp. 29–34; Andrew J. Steiger, "The Soviet Middle East," *Survey Graphic*, 1944, pp. 72–75.

31. Steiger, "The Soviet Middle East," pp. 72–75; Graebner, *Round Trip to Russia*, pp. 96, 97; *Life*, 29 March 1943, pp. 64–65.

32. *Fortune*, December 1942, "Part I: The Job Before Us," pp. 93–109; *Time*, 17 November 1941, pp. 22, 24–25; 27 July 1942, pp. 80, 82; 4 May 1942, p. 29; 24 July 1944; *Life*, 29 March 1943, p. 20; *Reader's Digest*, "Stalin's Ural Stronghold," February 1942, pp. 29–34; Steiger, "The Soviet Middle East," pp. 72–75; Lauterbach, *These Are the Russians*, pp. 202–03.

33. *Time*, "Miracle in the East," 24 July 1944, pp. 33–34; Lauterbach, *These Are the Russians*, p. 203.

34. *Time*, "Miracle in the East," 24 July 1944, p. 33; Chamberlin, *Russian Enigma*, p. 241.

35. Levering, *American Opinion and the Russian Alliance*, p. 37.

36. *Look*, 27 June 1944, p. 74. For a detailed, contemporary account of Stalin, see Lauterbach, *These Are the Russians*, pp. 99–121.

37. *Time*, 4 January 1943, p. 22.

38. Levering, *American Opinion and the Russian Alliance*, p. 114.

39. Wendell Willkie, "Stalin: 'Glad to See You Mr. Willkie,'" *Life*, 5 October 1942, p. 35.

40. Eric Johnston, "My Talk with Joseph Stalin," *Reader's Digest*, October 1944, p. 10.

41. *Time*, 25 January 1943, p. 8.

42. For examples of studies of World War Two films, see Robert Fyne, *The Hollywood Propaganda of World War II* (Metuchen, NJ, & London, The Scarecrow Press, Inc., 1994); K. R. M. Short, ed., *Film & Radio Propaganda in World War II* (Knoxville, The University of Tennessee Press, 1983); Thomas William Bohn, *An Historical And Descriptive Analysis of the "Why We Fight" Series* (New York, Arno Press, 1977); Jeanne Basinger, *The World War II Combat Film: Anatomy of a Genre* (New York, Columbia University Press, 1986), Roger Manvell, *Films and the Second World War* (New York, A.S. Barnes and Company, 1974).

43. *Life*, March 29, 1943, p. 20.

44. *Time*, 28 June 1941, p. 23.

45. *Time*, 29 September 1941, p. 18.

46. *Time*, 9 July 1942, pp. 44–45.

47. *Time*, 17 November 1941, p. 25.

48. *Life*, 29 March 1943, pp. 80–81.

49. Maurice Hindus, *Mother Russia* (Garden City, NY, Garden City Publishing, 1942), p. 273.

50. *Time*, 1 July 1942, p. 43.

51. Graebner, *Round Trip to Russia*, pp. 32, 41. For a description and pictures of Soviet Ballerina Marianne Bogulubskya, see Graebner, *Round Trip to Russia*, pp. 112–13 and photographs following.

52. For examples of women engaged in wartime industry, see also Graebner, *Round Trip to Russia*, photographs following pages 96–97. For a story in a popular American magazine on the role in Soviet women in wartime jobs including combat, see also Anna L. Strong "Soviet Women in War," *Look*, 21 October 1941, pp. 16–32. See also *Time*, 20 April 1942, p. 27 for a short account of Major Valentina Grizodubova and her role in leading women fighter and bomber pilots.

53. Rose Maurer, "Those Russian Women," *Survey Graphics*, February 1944, pp. 109, 152, 155, 157.

54. Hindus, *Mother Russia*, p. 316.

55. Margaret Bourke-White, *Shooting the Russian War* (New York, Simon and Schuster, 1942), pp. 64, 163.

56. Hindus, *Mother Russia*, p. 324.

57. Albert Rhys, "Meet the Russian People," *Survey Graphic*, February 1944, p. 42–45, 130–33, 130.

58. *Ibid*.

59. *Time*, 4 January 1943, p. 23.

60. *Look*, 22 August 1944, p. 51.

61. Hindus, *Mother Russia*, p. 72.

62. Graebner, *Round Trip to Russia*, p. 72.

63. Bourke-White, *Shooting*, p. 177.

64. R. J. Overy, *Russia's War* (New York, Penguin, 1998), p. 162.

65. Johnston, "My Talk with Joseph Stalin," p. 3.

66. Helen Iswolsky, "Spiritual Resurgence in Soviet Russia," *Survey Graphic*, February 1944, pp. 112–15.

67. Hindus, *Mother Russia*, p. 261.

68. *Time*, 17 January 1944, p. 38.

69. Bourke-White, *Shooting*, pp. 138, 149, 157.

70. For examples of maps in popular magazines, see *Life*, 9 September 1942, p. 32; *Time*, 11 September 1942, pp. 23–24, 36, several maps following the course of the German invasion; *Time*, 12 July, 1942; *Time*, 1 November 1943, pp. 23–35; "One Sixth of the Earth," *Life*, 29 March 1943, pp. 61–62, 7 September 1941, p. 32; Paul Schubert, "How did the Russians Do It?" *Look*, 21 March 1944, pp. 34, 36, 38, 41; for maps on the battle for Stalingrad, see *Time*, 9 November 1942, pp. 23–24, 36.

71. *Look*, 19 March 1946, pp. 42–51.

72. Levering, *American Opinion and the Russian Alliance*, pp. 57–57.

73. *New York Times*, 7 November 1942, p. 7.

74. *New York Times* 7 November 1942, pp. 7, 8, 08 November 1942, p. 37; Levering, *American Opinion and the Russian Alliance*, pp. 100–01.

75. Levering, *American Opinion and the Russian Alliance*, p. 100.

76. *Ibid.*, pp. 71–72.

77. November 6, 1942, p. 8. For other examples of well-known Americans writing or speaking on the war in Russia, see Joseph E. Davies, "What We Didn't Know About Russia," *Readers' Digest*, March 1942, pp. 45–50; C. L. Sulzberger, "The Russian Battlefront," *Reader's Digest*, September 1942, pp. 75–78. *Survey Graphic* ran a nine-part series, "Calling America," that sold several hundred thousand copies on events in Russia. Well-known pro-Soviet writer, Albert Rhys Williams, edited the February 1944 issue, entitled "American-Russian Frontiers." It featured writers and public figures from Lewis Gannett and Walker Duranty to Edward C. Carter of the RWR and Edgar Snow. See also Levering, *American Opinion and the Russian Alliance*, pp. 58–60; for those who remained critical of the Soviet Union and its leadership, see also, Levering, *American Opinion and the Russian Alliance*, p. 37.

78. *Time* 14 June 1943, p. 25.

79. *Ibid.*

80. Lois Mattox Miller, "From John Doe to the Russian Front," *Reader's Digest* May 1942, pp. 122–24. The Russian War Relief Committee was first known as the American Committee for Medical Aid to Russia before the name change in September 1941.

81. Levering, *American Opinion and the Russian Alliance*, pp. 81; Miller, "From John Doe," pp. 122–24.

82. Belulah Weldon Burhoe, "Russian War Relief at its Source," *Survey Graphics*, February 1944, p. 53; Miller, "From John Doe," p. 124.

83. Edward C. Carter, "Our War Relief Gets Through," *Survey Graphic*, February 1944, pp. 54–55.

84. *Ibid.*

85. *New York Times*, 23 June 1942, pp. 1, 11–12.

86. *Ibid.*

87. *Time*, 20 July 1942; David Schiff, "Fruit of the Poison Tree," *Times Literary Supplement*, 6 May 2005, p. 3; Levering, *American Opinion and the Russian Alliance*, p. 82.

88. Walter S. Hixson, *Parting the Curtain: Propaganda, Culture, and the Cold War, 1945–1961* (New York, St. Martin's Press. 1997), pp. ix–xii, 2–9; *New York Times*, 21 & 22 June 1942, E5 and E6.

89. Bertram Wolfe, "Silent Revolution," *Reader's Digest*, July 1941, pp. 87–90; Jan Vatlin, "Academy of High Treason," *Reader's Digest*, August 1941, pp. 52–56.

90. Alexander Polyakov [sic], "The Red Guerrillas," *Reader's Digest* January 1942, pp. 128–32; John Scott, "Stalin's Ural Stronghold," *Reader's Digest* February 1942, pp. 29–34.

91. Max Eastman, "Stalin's American Power," *Reader's Digest*, December 1941, pp. 39–48.

92. *Ibid.*

93. Levering, *American Opinion the Russian Alliance*, p. 54.

94. *Ibid.*, p. 60; *Time*, 1 March 1943, p. 14.

95. Miller, "From John Doe," pp. 122–24; C. L. Sulzberger, "The Russian Battlefront," *Reader's Digest*, September 1942, pp. 75–78; Maurice Hindus, "Report on Russia," *Reader's Digest*, November 1942, pp. 90–92 and "The Price Russia is Paying," *Reader's Digest*, April 1942, pp. 47–50.

96. Joseph Davies, "*Mission to Moscow,*" *Reader's Digest*, March 1942, pp. 45–50; Milton Mayer, "Little Papa Litvinov," *Reader's Digest*, April 1942, pp. 81–84.

97. Wendel Wilkie, "Life on the Russian Frontier," *Reader's Digest*, March 1943, pp. 1–7.

98. Max Eastman, "We Must Face the Facts About Russia," *Reader's Digest*, July 1943, pp. 1–14; quotes are from pp. 6–7.

99. Boris Voyetkov, "The Last Days of Sevastopol," *Reader's Digest*, August 1943, pp. 74–81; Johnston, "My Talk with Joseph Stalin," pp. 1–10; William White, "Report on Russia, Part II," *Reader's Digest*, December 1944, pp. 101–22 and "Report on Russia, Part II," *Reader's Digest*, January 1945, pp. 106–28.

100. Richard Lauterbach, "Russia's Number One Soldier," *Reader's Digest*, May 1945, pp. 71–74; Leigh White, "The Soviet Iron Fist in Rumania," *Reader's Digest*, August 1945, pp. 95–99.

2. The Cold War and the Emergence of a Lost Cause Mythology

1. See Gerd Überschär (ed), *Der Nationalsozialismus vor Gericht. Die alliierten Prozesse gegen Kriegsverbrecher und Soldaten, 1943–1952* (Frankfurt, Fischer Verlag, 1999), p. 243.

2. *Ibid.*, pp. 245–47.

3. *New York Times*, 30 August 1944; also Michael Marrus, "History and the Holocaust in the Courtroom" in Ronald Smelser (ed), *The Holocaust and Justice* (Evanston, Ill., Northwestern University Press, 2002), fn. 13.

4. See Telford Taylor, *The Anatomy of the Nuremberg Trials* (New York, Little, Brown and Co., 1992), p. 108.

5. Cited in Arnold Krammer, "American Treatment of German Generals During World War II" in *Journal of Military History*, 54 (January 1990), p. 42.

6. Taylor, *Anatomy*, p. 239.

7. See William J. Bosch, *Judgment on Nuremberg: American Attitudes toward the Major German War-Crimes Trials* (Chapel Hill, University of North Carolina Press, 1970), p. 167.

8. *Ibid.*, p. 171.

9. Taylor, *Anatomy*, p. 520.

10. Quoted in Ulrich Herbert, *Hitler's Foreign Workers: Enforced Foreign Labor in Germany under the Third Reich* (Cambridge, Cambridge University Press, 1997), p. 140.

11. See Whitney Harris, *Tyranny on Trial. The Evidence at Nuremberg* (Dallas, Tex., Southern Methodist University Press, 1954), p. 186.

12. See Bradley Smith, *Reaching Judgment at Nuremberg* (New York, New American Library, 1979), p. 166.

13. Harris, *Tyranny*, p. 185.

14. Smith, *Reaching Judgment*, pp. 185–86, 209–13.

15. *Trial of the Major War Criminals before the International Military Tribunal* [hereafter IMT] (Nuremberg, *Secretariat of the Tribunal*, 1947–1949), Vol. 4, 28th day.

16. *Ibid.*, pp. 316–18, 321. Contrast this testimony with the statement of Manstein's ADC Alexander Stahlberg, *Bounden Duty. The Memoirs of a German Officer, 1932–1945.* Trans. Patricia Crampton (New York, Brassey, 1990), pp. 312ff; also on Manstein and the watches incident see Jörg Friedrich, *Das Gesetz des Krieges. Das deutsche Heer in Russland 1941 bis 1945. Der Prozess gegen das Oberkommando der Wehrmacht* (Munich, Piper, 1993), pp. 668–70.

17. *IMT*, Vol. 4, 29th day, pp. 476–84.

18. *Ibid.*, Vol. 4, 28th day, pp. 373–75; also Taylor, *Anatomy*, pp. 246–49.

19. *Ibid.*, Vol. 4, 28th day, p. 254.

20. *Ibid.*, Vol. 4, 28th day, pp. 469–71.

21. Taylor, *Anatomy*, p. 241.

22. Author's translation. The statement is dated December 12, 1945. See Bundesarchiv/Militärarchiv Freiburg. N422 Nachlass Röttiger, p. 4.

23. See Beate Ihme-Tuchel, "Fall 7: Der Prozess gegen die Südost-Generale (gegen Wilhelm List und andere," in Überschär (ed.), *Nationalsozialismus vor Gericht*, pp. 144–54.

24. See Wolfram Wette, "Fall 12: Der OKW-Prozess" (gegen Wilhelm Ritter von List und andere), in *ibid.*, pp. 199–212.

25. *Ibid.*, p. 208.

26. See Helene Keyssar and Vladimir Pozner, *Remembering War. A US-Soviet Dialogue* (New York, Oxford University Press, 1990), pp. 191 and 208–12.

27. *Ibid.*, xi.

28. *Military Government Journal. Normandy to Berlin* (Cambridge, University of Massachusetts Press, 1971), p. 269.

29. *Changing Enemies. The Defeat and Regeneration of Germany* (New York, Norton, 1995), p. 143.

30. See Kenneth Hechler, "The Enemy Side of the Hill: The 1945 Background on Interrogation of German Commanders" in Donald Detwiler (ed), *World War II German Military Studies. A Collection of 213 special reports on the Second World War prepared by former officers of the Wehrmacht for the United States Army* (New York, Garland Publishing, 1979), Vol. 1, pp. 77–78.

31. Vincent Sheean, "How did Russia get that way?" *Look*, 4 September 1945, p. 62.

32. Captain Lucienne Marchand, *Look*, 30 October 1945, pp. 28ff.

33. Pages 5–8; on this issue see also Robert Abzug, *Inside the Vicious Heart: Americans and the Liberation of Nazi Concentration Camps* (New York, Oxford University Press, 1985), pp. 152ff.; also Dewey Browder, *Americans in Post-World War Two Germany* (Lewiston, NY, Edwin Mellen, 1998), pp. 4–5; and Earl Ziemke, *The U.S. Army in the Occupation of Germany, 1944–1946* (Washington, DC, Center of Military History, Department of Defense, 1975), p. 327.

34. Joseph Bendersky, *The 'Jewish Threat'. Anti-Semitic Politics of the U.S. Army* (New York, Basic Books, 2000), p. 351.

35. See Browder, *Americans*, pp. 4–5, 17–20.

36. On the whole question of Russian behavior and policy in their zone of occupation, see Norman Naimark, *The Russians in Germany. A History of the Soviet Zone of Occupation, 1945–1949* (Cambridge, Harvard University Press, 1995). See especially Chapter Two on rape.

37. See Bosch, *Judgment*, pp. 90, 75, 80 resp.

38. See Dietrich Orlow, *A History of Modern Germany, 1871 to Present*, Fourth Edition (Upper Saddle River, NJ, Prentice Hall, 1999), p. 203.

39. United States Senate, Committee on Foreign Relations, *Documents on Germany, 1944–1970* (Washington, DC, 1971), p. 42.

40. See Kai Bird, *The Chairman: John J. McCloy and the Making of the American Establishment* (New York, Simon & Shuster, 1992), p. 310.

41. *Ibid.*, p. 315.

42. *Ibid.*, pp. 338–39; also John Mendelsohn, "War Crimes and Clemency" in Robert Wolfe (ed), *Americans as Proconsuls: United States Military Government in Germany and Japan, 1944–1952* (Carbondale, Ill., Southern Illinois University Press, 1984), pp. 227–59.

43. Bird, *Chairman*, p. 361.

44. See Frank Buscher, *The U.S. War Crimes Trial Program, 1946–1955* (New York, Greenwood Press, 1989), pp. 166f.

45. Bird, *Chairman*, p. 368.

46. See Thomas Schwartz, *America's Germany: John J. McCloy and the Federal Republic of Germany* (Cambridge, Harvard University Press, 1991), p. 268.

47. *Ibid.*, p. 165.

48. *Ibid.*, p. 175.

49. See *Chicago Tribune* article by Hal Faust of 23 February 1948, pp. 1–2.

50. Buscher, *War Crimes*, pp. 43, 165f.

51. *Ibid.*, p. 37.

52. Americans were well aware of Halder during the war. Just as the Nazis were about to launch their 1942 offensive against the Russians, *Time* magazine devoted a cover story to Halder, entitled "Hitler's Halder. Thunderbolts Should Strike on Time," 29 June 1942, pp. 21–24.

53. With regard to Hitler and the campaign in the East, see pp. 35–57. In this context, see Jürgen Förster, "Hitler als Kriegsherr" in S. Förster, M. Pöhlmann, and D. Walter (eds), *Kriegsherren in der Weltgeschichte. Von Xerxes bis Nixon* (Munich, Münchener Dom-Verlag, 2006).

54. Quote is in Christian Hartmann, *Halder. Generalstabschef Hitlers 1938–1942* (Paderborn, Ferdinand Schoeningh, 1991), p. 125.

55. See Affidavit H of Halder, November 22, 1945 (www.ess.uwe.ac/genocide/Halder.htm), p. 2.

56. This is the opinion of one of Halder's biographers. See Gerd Überschär, *Generaloberst Franz Halder. Generalstabschef, Gegner und Gefangener Hitlers* (Göttingen, Muster-Schmidt, 1991), pp. 45f.

57. See Christian Streit, *Keine Kameraden. Die Wehrmacht und die sowietischen Kriegsgefangenen 1941–1945* (Bonn, Dietz, 1991), pp. 33, 52f.

58. *Ibid.*, pp. 31ff.

59. See Carl Dirks and Karl-Heinz Janßen, *Der Krieg der Generäle. Hitler als Werkzeug der Wehrmacht* (Berlin, Propyläen, 1999), p. 28.

60. Olaf Kroehler, "Goals and Reasons: Hitler and the German Military" in Joseph Wieczynski (ed.), *Operation Barbarossa: the German Attack on the Soviet Union, June 22, 1941* (Salt Lake City, Utah, C. Schlacks, 1993), p. 59.

61. See Hartmann, *Halder*, p. 125; Überschär, *Halder*, p. 59f.

62. See Arnold Lissance (ed), *The Halder Diaries. The Private War Journals of Colonel General Franz Halder* (Boulder, Colo., Westview Press, 1976), entry of 3 July 1940; also Dirks/Janßen, *Krieg*, p. 132.

63. See Jürgen Förster, "Das Unternehmen 'Barbarossa' als Eroberungs-und Vernichtungskrieg" in Militärgeschichtliches Forschungsamt, *Das Deutsche Reich und der Zweite Weltkrieg*, vol. IV, *Der Angriff auf die Sowietunion* (Stuttgart, DVA, 1999), p. 429.

64. Überschär, *Halder*, p. 61; Jürgen Förster, "Hitler Turns East-German War Policy in 1940 and 1941" in Bernd Wegner (ed), *From Peace to War. Germany, Soviet Russia and the World, 1939–1941* (Providence, RI, Berghahn Books, 1997), p. 120; Bernard Kroener, "The 'Frozen Blitzkrieg': German Strategic Planning against the Soviet Union and the Causes of Its Failure," in *Ibid.*, p. 140.

65. Dirks/Janßen, *Krieg*, pp. 133–34.

66. *Halder Diaries*, entry of 4 April 1941; and Hartmann, *Halder*, p. 240.

67. *Halder Diaries*, entry of 6 April 1941.

68. *Halder Diaries*, entry for 30 March 1941; also Hartmann, *Halder*, p. 241; Überschär, *Halder*, p. 59; and Streit, *Keine Kameraden*, p. 34.

69. Überschär, *Halder*, p. 63.

70. Bernd Boll/Hans Safrian, "On the Way to Stalingrad: The 6th Army in 1941–42", in Hannes Heer/Klaus Naumann (eds), *War of Extermination. The German Military in World War II* (New York, Oxford, Berghahn Books, 2000), pp. 237–71; on the "criminal orders" see also Manfred Messerschmidt, *Die Wehrmacht im NS-Staat. Zeit der Indokrination* (Hamburg, Publisher 1969), pp. 396ff.; also Helmuth Krausnick, "Kommissarbefehl" in *Vierteljahreshefte für Zeitgeschichte*, #25 (1977), pp. 682–738.

71. Gerhard Hass, "Zum Russlandbild der SS" in Hans-Erich Volkmann (ed), *Das Russlandbild im Dritten Reich* (Köln, Weimar, Böhlau Verlag, 1994), pp. 201–24.

72. Christian Streit, "Soviet Prisoners of War in the Hands of the Wehrmacht," in Heer/Naumann, *War of Extermination*, p. 82.

73. *Halder Diaries*, entry of 14 November 1941.

74. Streit, "Prisoners" in Heer/Naumann, *War of Extermination*, p. 85.

75. See Kroehler in Wieczynski, *Operation Barbarossa*, p. 61; see also Gerhard Weinberg, *Germany, Hitler and World War Two. Essays in Modern German and World History* (Cambridge, Cambridge University Press, 1995), p. 289, where he argues that from the invasion of Poland forward the German generals were largely in accord with Hitler; also Andreas Hillgruber, "*Das* Russlandbild der führenden deutschen Militärs vor Beginn des Angriffs auf die Sowietunion" in Hans-Erich Volkmann, *Das Russlandbild im Dritten Reich* (Cologne, Böhlau, 1994), pp. 125–40.

76. Streit, *Keine Kameraden*, p. 299.

77. *Halder Diaries*, Entry of 22 July 1940.

78. See Geoff Megargee, *Inside Hitler's High Command* (Lawrence, University of Kansas Press, 2000), p. 124.

79. Walter Schellenberg, *The Labyrinth; Memoirs of Walter Schellenberg* (New York, Harper, 1956) p. 204, 223.

80. Streit, *Keine Kameraden*, pp. 80 and 333, fn. 92.

81. See Norman Goda, "Black Marks: Hitler's Bribery of His Senior Officers during World War Two, in *Journal of Modern History*, 72 (June 2000), pp. 413–52.
82. See Überschär, *Halder*, pp. 81–84.

3. The German Generals Talk, Write, and Network

1. See Ronald Smelser, "The Myth of the 'Clean' Wehrmacht in Cold War America" in Doris Bergen (ed), *Lessons and Legacies VIII. From Generation to Generation*, (forthcoming from Northwestern University Press).
2. See Gerd Überschär, *Generaloberst Franz Halder. Generalstabschef, Gegner und Gefangener Hitlers* (Göttingen, Muster-Schmidt, 1991), pp. 87–91 for the following narrative.
3. For a copy of the verdict see BA/MA Freiburg, N220/65 Nachlass Halder. 44 pages, issued October 26, 1948.
4. On the activities of the Halder mission, see: Charles Burdick, "Vom Schwert zur Feder. Deutsche Kriegsgefangene im Dienst der Vorbereitung der amerikanischen Kriegsgeschichtsschreibung über den Zweiten Weltkrieg. Die organisatorische Entwicklung der Operational History (German) Section," in *Militärgeschichtliche Mitteilungen*, Vol. 10 (1971), pp. 69–80; by same author, "Deutschland und die Entwicklung der amtlichen amerikanischen Militärgeschichtsforschung (1920–1960)," in K. D. Bracher (ed), *Deutschland zwischen Krieg und Frieden* (Düsseldorf, Droste Verlag, 1991), p. 99–107; also Christian Greiner, "'Operational History (German) Section' und 'Naval Historical Team.' Deutsches militärstrategisches Denken im Dienst der amerikanischen Streitkräfte von 1946 bis 1950," in Manfred Messerschmidt, et al. (eds), *Militärgeschichte. Probleme-Thesen-Wege* (Stuttgart, Deutsche Verlags-Anstalt, 1982), pp. 409–35; also Bernd Wegner, "Erschriebene Siege. Franz Halder, die 'Historical Division' und die Rekonstruktion des Zweiten Weltkrieges im Geiste des deutschen Generalstabes," in Ernst Willi Hansen, et al. (eds.), *Politischer Wandel, organisierte Gewalt und nationale Sicherheit. Beiträge zur neueren Geschichte Deutschlands und Frankreich* (Munich, R. Oldenbourg, 1995), pp. 287–302.
5. Burdick, "Schwert," p. 73.
6. That the German officers working with Halder took the anti-Bolshevik struggle very seriously is revealed in their correspondence with one another. See, e.g., Major General Erich Dethleffsen to Colonel General Zeitzler, 23 April 1951, BA/MA Freiburg, Nachlass Zeitzler N63/3, pp. 179–81; and Alfred Toppe to Halder, 9 May 1951, *Ibid.*, pp. 35–36.
7. See undated memo to Col. Amen in NARA, M1270, Roll 6, Page 307.
8. Leo Freiherr Geyr von Schweppenburg, one of the writers, later said that one or another incriminating document would disappear while being examined by the German officers, and that the Americans occasionally helped out. See Überschär, *Halder*, p. 95.
9. They included General Hans von Greiffenberg, Lieutenant General Oldwig von Natzmer, Major General Alfred Toppe, Major General Burkhard

Müller-Hildebrand, Major General Hellmuth Reinhard, Colonel Alfred Zerbel, and Major Herbert Büchs. Burdick, "Schwert," p. 77.

10. See *zu Frage 14* in Institut für Zeitgeschichte, Munich. ED 91, Nachlass Geyr, Vol. 10, no page number.

11. A good example is his correspondence with former general Gotthard Heinrici, who was writing a lengthy manuscript on the war in the East. See BA/MA Freiburg, Heinrici Nachlass, N265/71, pp. 90–93, letter of November 27, 1952 and Heinrici's response of January 20, 1953, p. 97; see also Halder to Zeitzler, who was composing a manuscript on the 1st Panzer army, January 30 and April 15, 1958, BA/MA Freiburg, Nachlass Zeitzler, N63/9; Colonel Kenneth Lay, Chief of the Historical Division, thanked Zeitzler for his work, characterizing it as "something of extraordinary value," 21 July 1958, *Ibid.*

12. See Wegner, "Erschriebene Siege," p. 293, fn. 24.

13. On Heusinger's career, see *Spiegel* cover story, "The Tragic Career," of February 29, 1956, pp. 24–31; that he was aware of cooperation between the army and the SS in the East comes out in a Nuremberg deposition by Ernst Rode, former Chief of the Command Staff of the Reichsfuhrer-SS, who names Heusinger as well as Warlimont, Zeitzler, and Guderian as men with whom he had discussions during the war on anti-partisan strategies. See Affidavid #17, Exhibit USA-562, Document # 3715-PS; that some Americans were suspicious of Heusinger's background come out in a query from Senator Jack Miller (Iowa) to John McCone, CIA Director on 11 January 1962, requesting a response to a constituent query based on a 15 September 1961 article in the *Christian Century* called "Henchman Heusinger," which emphasized Heusinger's Nazi past. NARA, CIA-RDP80B01676R002800230011-7.

14. Detwiler, *German Military Studies*, has published 213 of more than 2,500 German reports and studies in twenty-four volumes. Fifteen through nineteen, in particular, focus on the Eastern Front.

15. See "Small Unit Actions" in *ibid.*, 18, p. 2. The manuscript became Department of the Army pamphlet no. 20–269 (July 1953).

16. See "Russian Combat Methods in World War Two" in *ibid.*, pp. 3–4. The manuscript became Department of the Army pamphlet no. 20–230 (September 1950).

17. *Ibid.*, Vol. 19, pp. 1, 3.

18. "The Peoples of the Soviet Union," in *ibid.*, 19, p. 9. MS # C-035.

19. See "The Army Historical Program in the European Theater and Command. 8 May 1945–31 December 1950," compiled in 1951 for the Historical Division by Theodore Bauer, et al. in *ibid.*, I, p. 98. A complete list of all manuscripts (Series A,B,C,D,P,T) written from 1945 to 1959 in the Foreign Military Studies series is given in Vol. I.

20. See Kevin Souter, "To Stem the Red Tide: The German Report Series and Its Effect on American Defense Doctrine, 1948–1954," *Journal of Modern History* 57 (October 1993), pp. 653–88.

21. *Ibid.*, pp. 676–77.

22. Letter of April 19, 1952 in BA/MA Freiburg, Nachlass Blumentritt N252/8. Halder asked, in addition to Blumentritt, Georg von Sodenstern, Kurt Brennecke, Friedrich Fangohr, Edgar Roehricht, and Gustav Bechtolsheim to join the team. All were former infantry generals.

23. See Souter, "Stem," pp. 682–83.
24. In Halder's Nachlass in the BA/MAS Freiburg, N220/202, see Captain Frank Mahin to Halder, 22 June 1949, p. 242–43; Major General Orlando Ward to Halder, 14 July 1950, p. 3; Lieutenant General M. S. Eddy to Halder, 23 October 1950, p. 203; Lieutenant Colonel Louis Nawrocky to Halder, 7 March, 1952, p. 79; N220/203 Brig. General P. N. Robinett, former head of the Historical Division and now head of the Office of Military History to Halder, 9 December 1953, p. 138.
25. Resp. N220/111, Tagesnotizen: 17 September 1954, p. 54; 21 February 1955, p. 17; 29 March 1955, p. 29; Tagesnotizen, November 20 1956, N220/112, p. 8–9; Tagesnotizen: 10 March 1960, N220/111, p. 30.
26. See "Ansprache des Generaloberst Franz Halder vor OCMH am 6.12.55" in BA/MA Nachlass Halder, N220/118, pp. 27–28; see also Taylor's letter of appreciation to Halder, 27 January 1956, *ibid.*, p 55. Halder also liberally distributed military literature to his audience.
27. See Kent Roberts Greenfield to Halder, 8 February 1956 in *ibid.*, p. 51.
28. See Frank F. Rathbun to Halder, 7 October 1958, *ibid.*, N220/82, p. 68.
29. See General H. I. Hodes to Halder, 18 March 1959, *ibid.*, N220/90, p. 59.
30. Letter of 20 June 1961, *ibid.*, N220/84, p. 176.
31. See document of December 11, 1958; Halder thanks to Naval Institute of 28 February 1959; and Halder to Anselm, 27 February 1959 in *ibid.*, N220/204, pp. 16–17.
32. See Überschär, *Halder*, p. 100.
33. See Williamson Murray, then a senior at Yale, later a prominent military historian, to Halder, March 20, 1963, and Halder reply n.d. in *ibid.*, N220/84, pp. 41–42 and 38–39 resp.; also Ingeborg Bauer of Hope College to Halder, 26 November 1963, *ibid.*, N220/85, p. 143.
34. Letter of 21 September 1963, *ibid.*, p. 163.
35. On the Himmerod meeting, see Donald Abenheim, *Reforging the Iron Cross: the Search for Tradition in the West German Armed Forces* (Princeton, Princeton University Press, 1988) pp. 60ff; also David Clay Large, *Germans to the Front. West German Rearmament in the Adenauer Era* (Chapel Hill, University of North Carolina Press, 1996), pp. 97–102.
36. See Alfred Streim, "Saubere Wehrmacht? Die Verfolgung von Kriegs-und NS-Vrbrechen in der Bundesrepublik und der DDR," in Heer/Naumann, *Vernichtungskrieg*, p. 575.
37. From McCloy to Secretary of State Acheson, January 24, 1951, in U.S. State Department, *Foreign Relations of the United States* (hereafter FRUS), 1951, Vol. 3, part 1, pp. 446–47; on this important event see also Abenheim, *Reforging*, pp. 69–70; Klaus von Schubert, *Wiederbewaffnung und Westintegration* (Stuttgart, DVA, 1970), pp. 82–84; Gerhard Wettig, *Entmilitarisierung und Wiederbewaffnung in Deutschland, 1943–1955. Internationale Auseinandersetzungen um die Rolle der Deutschen in Europa* (Munich, Oldenbourg, 1957), pp. 400–01.
38. See Bendersky, *Jewish Threat*, p. 368.
39. "Notes on a Meeting at the White House," January 31, 1951, FRUS, *ibid.*, p. 449.
40. See Large, *Germans to the Front*, p. 117.
41. Report of December 3, 1952, in BA/MA Freiburg, Nachlass Munzel, N447/32, no page number.

42. See Walter H. Nelson, *Germany Rearmed* (New York, Simon and Shuster, 1972), p. 75.

43. This author attended one such function where the guests were former Luftwaffe General Adolf Galland and Wing Commander Tuck of England. These men became close friends after the war and were godfathers for each other's sons. A German air force veterans association (*Fliegergemeinschaft*) regularly touted contact between German and Allied airmen of World War Two. See "Renowned personalities" in http://www.fliegergemeinschaft.de/main.english/main/page5_9_e.

44. Many of these letters are in BA/MA Freiburg, Nachlass Munzel, N447/101.

45. This album is in *ibid.*, N447/81.

46. See esp. letter from Colonel C. G. Simenson, U.S. Military Attaché in Bonn to Munzel, 12 January 1961, asking Munzel to comment on Simenson's analysis of a maneuver, "Hold Fast." A draft is included. Simenson also intends to consult with Munzel after the next maneuver, "Wintershield," *Ibid.*, N447/101.

47. Retired Colonel Anton-Detlev von Plato to Munzel, 5 April 1960, *ibid.*, N447/101.

48. See draft of letter from Munzel to Dutchak, n.d., *ibid.*, N447/101. There is also a letter from a retired U.S. officer announcing proudly at his advanced age the birth of a new little "Panzergrader," n.d. but 1962, *ibid.*, N447/101.

49. James Jones to Munzel, 1 June 1976, *ibid.*, N447/101.

50. See article, presumably in *New York Times*, n.d., "At Anzio All of Us Knew Kesselring," NARA, CIA-RDP75-00001R000400410013-5.

51. For a good background on the reform movement in the Bundeswehr, see Large, *Germans to the Front*, chapter 8.

52. *Ibid.*, p. 199.

53. Klaus Naumann, "Godfathers of Innere Führung? German-American Interaction During the Early Years of the Bundeswehr," unpublished manuscript in authors' possession, pp. 10–11.

54. See report of December 15, 1963, "Estimate of the Combat Value of the German Army" in HHPL, Truman Smith Papers, Subject File Box 2, Germany-Army Development 1963–1964.

55. U.S. News and World Report, 8 September 1950, pp. 24–26.

56. See *Spiegel*, #49, 3 December 1952, p. 14; the plan met resistance, especially from Secretary of the Air Force, Thomas K. Finletter, and was eventually dropped. See *Spiegel*, #22, 27 May 1953, p. 33.

57. Eleven-page report of 25 November 1955 (quote on page 11), in BA/MA Freiburg, MSg1/2454.

58. See eleven-page report of January 1958, pp. 1, 2, 5, 7. BA/MA Freiburg, Nachlass Büschleb, N596/12.

59. See Kern to Geyr, 3 August 1952; Haeger to Geyr, 19 February 1953; Kern to Geyr, 21 March 1953; Kern to Geyr, 15 January 1954; the article was entitled "The Return of the German Officer Corps . . . Will It Help or Hinder Western Defense?" 21 July 1952, pp. 48–49. In Institut für Zeitgeschichte, Munich, Nachlass Geyr, ED 91, Vol. 39.

60. See Souter, *Stem*, p. 679, fn. 120.

61. David Thelan, (ed.), *Memory and American History* (Bloomington, Indiana University Press, 1989), p. xv.

62. Cambridge, Cambridge University Press, 1985, p. 206.
63. *Race and Reunion: The Civil War in American Memory* (Boston, Belknap Press, 2001), p. 3.
64. See Norbert Frei, *Vergangenheitspolitik. Die Anfänge der Bundesrepublik und die NS-Vergangenheit* (Munich, C. H. Beck, 1996).
65. See introduction by Alan Dershowitz to N. P. Chipman, *The Andersonville Prison Trial. The Trial of Captain Henry Wirz* (Birmingham, AL, Notable Trials Library, 1990).
66. *The True Story of Andersonville Prison: A Defense of Major [sic] Henry Wirz* (reprinted by Iberian Publ. Co, Athens, GA, 1991), pp. 246–48.
67. Chipman, *Andersonville*, p. 375.
68. For the continuing struggle today, see Gary Waltrip, "Andersonville: A Legacy of Shame . . . But Whose?" in www.pointssouth.com/csanet/andersonville.htm.
69. Blight, *Race and Reunion*, p. 9.
70. Quotes are from *Ibid.*, pp. 256 and 265, respectively.
71. *Ibid.*, p. 257.
72. *Ibid.*, p. 215.
73. On Early, see Gary W. Gallagher, *Lee and His Generals in War and Memory* (Baton Rouge, Louisiana State University Press, 2000), p. 51.
74. Blight, *Race and Reunion*, p. 260.
75. *Ibid.*, p. 274.
76. Gallagher, *Lee*, p. 215.
77. *Ibid.*, pp. 218–21.
78. See Carol Reardon, *Pickett's Charge in History and Memory* (Chapel Hill, The North Carolina University Press, 1997).
79. On Rommel, see Ralf Georg Reuth, "Erwin Rommel – Die Propagandaschöpfung," in Ronald Smelser/Enrico Syring (eds), *Die Militärelite des Dritten Reiches/27 Biographische Skizzen* (Berlin, Ullstein Verlag, 1995), pp. 460–75.
80. See Tony Horwitz, *Confederates in the Attic. Dispatches from the Unfinished Civil War* (New York, Pantheon Books, 1998), p. 187.

4. Memoirs, Novels, and Popular Histories

1. St. Paul, Zenith Press, 2004.
2. Cambridge, Mass., DaCapo Press, 2002.
3. See Enrico Syring, "Erich von Manstein – das Operative Genie," in Ronald Smelser/Enrico Syring (eds), *Die Militärelite des Dritten Reiches. 27 Biographische Skizzen* (Berlin, Ullstein, 1995), p. 343. Syring's essay on Manstein provides the best overview of the man's career.
4. New York, William Morrow & Co. 1948, p. 66.
5. *Ibid.*, pp. 330f.
6. See *Lost Victories* (St. Paul, Zenith Press, 2004). The subtitle of this edition of Manstein's memoirs attests to the longevity of his myth: "The War Memoirs of Hitler's Most Brilliant General." Oliver von Wrochem's *Vernichtungskrieg und Erinnerungspolitik: Erich von Manstein – Akteur und Symbol* (Paderborn, Schöningh, 2006) appeared too late to be included in this study.

7. *Ibid.*, p. 63.

8. See Richard Overy, *Russia's War. A History of the Soviet War Effort: 1941–1945* (Middlesex, Penguin, 1997), p. 219.

9. Manstein, *Lost Victories*, p. 275.

10. *Ibid.*, p. 278.

11. See *Der Spiegel*, 14 January 1959, p. 28.

12. Manstein, *Lost Victories*, p. 88.

13. *Ibid.*, p. 93.

14. *Ibid.*, p. 109.

15. *Ibid.*, p. 124.

16. *Ibid.*, p. 198.

17. Quote from Oliver von Wrochen, "Die Auseinandersetzung mit Wehrmachtverbrechen im Prozess gegen den Generalfeldmarschall Erich von Manstein 1949," in *Zeitschrift für Geschichtswissenschaft*, Vol. 46 (1998), p. 329.

18. Original speech reprinted in Roland Kopp, "Die Wehrmacht feiert. Kommanders-Reden zu Hitlers 50. Geburtstag am 20. April 1039," in *Militärgeschichtliche Mitteilungen*, Vol. 60 (2003), p. 512.

19. Stein, *Manstein*, pp. 62–65.

20. *Ibid.*, p. 180.

21. *Ibid.*, p. 202–05.

22. The text of the order and cross-examination are printed in *The Trial of German Major War Criminals. Proceedings of the International Military Tribunal Sitting at Nuremberg, Germany, Part 20, 29 July-21 August, 1946* (London, HM Stationery Office, 1949), pp. 71–73.

23. See Guido Knopp, *Hitlers Krieger* (Munich, Bertelsmann, 2001), p. 191.

24. On the Simferopol incident and its aftermath, see Stein, *Manstein*, pp. 271–81; also Jörg Friedrich, *Das Gesetz des Krieges. Das deutsche Heer in Russland 1941 bis 1945. Der Prozess gegen das Oberkommando der Wehrmacht* (Munich, Peiper, 1993), pp. 649–71; on Simferopol and the watch incident, p. 658–71; also Michael Schröders, "Erich von Manstein – ein unpolitischer Soldat?" in Forum "Barbarossa": Beitrag 3-2004.

25. Wrochen, "Auseinandersetzung," p. 343; see also Andrej Angrick, "Im Windschatten der 11. Armee. Die Einsatzgruppe D," in Gerhard Paul/Klaus-Michael Mallmann (eds), *Die Gestapo im Zweiten Weltkrieg. Heimatfront und besetzten Europa* (Darmstadt, Wissenschaftliche Buchgesellshaft, 2000), pp. 481–502.

26. *Ibid.*, p. 347.

27. Alexander Stahlberg, *Bounden Duty. The Memoirs of a German Officer 1932–45* (London, Brassey's, 1990), pp. 312–15.

28. Manstein, *Lost Victories*, p. 471.

29. See Oliver von Wrochen, "Rehabilitation oder Strafverfolgung. Kriegsverbrecherprozess gegen Generalfeldmarschall Erich von Manstein im Widerstreit britischer Interessen," in *Mittelweg 36*, vol. 3 (1997), p. 29.

30. *Spiegel*, 2 April 1952, vol. VI, no. 14, p. 14.

31. A good overview of the trial – prosecution and defence – is provided by Wrochen, "Auseinandersetzung," pp. 329–53; see also Tom Bower, *Blind Eye to Murder. Britain, America and the Purging of Nazi Germany – a Pledge Betrayed* (London, Andre Deutsch, 1981), pp. 241–67.

32. Stein, *Manstein*, p. 202.
33. Taken from Reginald Paget's subsequent book, *Manstein. His Campaigns and His Trial* (London, Collins, 1951), pp. 190–91.
34. Wrochen, "Auseinandersetzung", p. 352.
35. *Spiegel*, 2 April 1952, vol. VI, no. 14, p. 8.
36. Schröders, "unpolitischer Soldat?" p. 6.
37. Review by Stefan Possony, Georgetown University and Foreign Policy Research Institute, in *Military Affairs*, 23 (spring 1959), p. 41.
38. Vol. XIII, No. 2.
39. Heinz Guderian, *Panzer Leader* (New York, DaCapo Press, 2002) p. 92.
40. *Ibid.*, p. 26.
41. *Ibid.*, pp. 136–37, 142, 185, and 259 respectively.
42. *Ibid.*, p. 247.
43. See Heinz Magenheimer, *Hitler's War. Germany's Key Strategic Decisions 1940–1945 Could Germany Have Won World War Two?* (London, Cassell, 1997).
44. Guderian, *Panzer Leader*, p. 150.
45. *Ibid.*, p. 152.
46. *Ibid.*, p. 249.
47. For the Wehrmacht's real policy, for example, in the area outside Leningrad during precisely the period Guderian mentions here, see Johannes Hürter, "Die Wehrmacht vor Leningrad. Krieg und Besatzungspolitik der 18. Armee im Herbst und Winter 1941/42," in *Vierteljahrshefte für Zeitgeschichte*, 49 (2001), pp. 377–439.
48. Guderian, *Panzer Leader*, p. 180.
49. *Ibid.*, p. 257.
50. *Ibid.*, p. 159.
51. *Ibid.*, p. 289.
52. See Christian Streit, "Die Kontroverse um die 'Wehrmachtausstellung'" in *Aufbau*, No. 26, 24 December 1999, p. 3; on Rode, see Rode Affidavit, No. 17, Exhibit USA-562, Document Number 3715-PS, International Military Tribunal. *The Trial of the German Major War Criminals. Proceedings of the International Military Tribunal Sitting at Nuremberg, Germany* (London, His Majesty's Stationery Office, 1946), January 7, 1946, part 4, pp. 370–71.
53. Guderian, *Panzer Leader*, p. 274.
54. See Gerd Überschär/Winfried Vogel, *Dienen und Verdienen. Hitler's Geschenke an seine Eliten* (Frankfurt, S. Fischer, 1999), pp. 168–74; also Frank Bajohr, *Parvenüs und Profiteure. Korruption in der NS-Zeit* (Frankfurt, S. Fischer, 2001), p. 36.
55. Guderian, *Panzer Leader*, p. 346.
56. See Bryan Fugate, *Operation Barbarossa. Strategy and Tactics on the Eastern Front, 1941* (Novato, Calif., Presidio Press, 1984), p. 110.
57. Quoted in Geoffrey Megargee, *Inside Hitler's High Command* (Lawrence, University of Kansas Press, 2000), p. 214.
58. *Ibid.*, p. 223.
59. See Heinrich Schwendemann, "Strategie der Selbstvernichtung: Die Wehrmachtführung im 'Endkampf' um das 'Dritte Reich,'" in Rolf-Dieter Müller/Hans-Erich Volkmann, *Die Wehrmacht. Mythos und Realität* (Munich, Oldenbourg, 1999), p. 224.

60. Entries of March 6 and 9, 1943, in Louis Lochner (ed, trans.), *The Goebbels Diaries* (New York, Eagle Books, 1948), p. 318, 328.

61. Helmuth Heiber/Peter Glantz (eds), *Hitler and His Generals. Military Conferences 1942–1945* (New York, Enigma Books, 2003), p. 483.

62. NARA, RG319, Box 71A, Vol. 5, folder 3.

63. The German title was: *Kann Westeuropa verteitigt werden?* (Göttingen, Plesse-Verlag, 1950).

64. Ibid., pp. 23, 28–29. (authors' translation).

65. *Ibid.*, p. 30.

66. *Ibid.*, p. 35.

67. *Ibid.*, p. 54.

68. See CIC agent report of 5 June 1950 in NARA, RG319, Box 71A, Vol. 4, Folder 1.

69. Guderian to Geyr, January 2, 1951, in Institut für Zeitgeschichte, Munich, Geyr Papers, ED 91, Vol. 18.

70. *A Study of the Employment of Armor in the Second World War* (New York, Ballantine, 1976 edition).

71. *Ibid.*, for these quotes see pp. 259, 281, 319, 350, and 352 resp.

72. *Ibid.*, p. 365.

73. See Hans-Ulrich Rudel in http:/en.wikipedia.org/wiki/Hans-Ulrich_Rudel; also Hans-Ulrich Rudel (July, 1916–1982) in http://www.achtungpanzer.com/gen9 .htm. Some information from Jörg Muth. Also Hans-Ulrich Rudel, http://members .aol.com/ab763/rudel.htm.

74. For an adulatory picture/biography of Rudel, see Günther Just, *Stuka-Pilot Hans-Ulrich Rudel: His Life Story in Words and Photographs* (West Chester, Pa., Schiffer, 1990), p. 9.

75. *Ibid.*, p. 39.

76. *Ibid.*, p. 36.

77. Rudel, *Stuka Pilot* (New York, Ballantine Bal-Hi printing, June 1966) p. 8; subsequent editions of the memoirs were published, including in The Noontide Presses' "War and Warriors Series" with two printings, in 1987 and 1990.

78. Just, *Stuka-Pilot*, p. 7.

79. Rudel, *Stuka Pilot*, pp. 21–22.

80. *Ibid.*, p. 47.

81. *Ibid.*, for the quotes, pp. 49, 113–14, and 233 respectively.

82. *Ibid.*, pp. 161, 188.

83. For quotes on Hitler, see *Ibid.*, pp. 80, 136, 189 respectively.

84. For the two quotes, see *Ibid.*, pp. 206–07, 55 respectively.

85. See *Ibid.*, pp. 136, 187, 196.

86. For the three quotes, see *Ibid.*, pp. 176, 184, 193 respectively.

87. For the three quotes, see *Ibid.*, pp. 200, 212, 238.

88. *Ibid.*, pp. 53 and 210 for the two mentions of his wife.

89. *Ibid.*, p. 234.

90. See Informationsdienst gegen Rechtsextremismus: (http://lexikon.idgr.de/r/r_u/ rudel-hans-ulrich/rudel-hans-ulrich.php.

91. New York, Bantam, 1965 and New York, Ballantine, 1966 respectively.

92. These two books went through five printings between February 1965 and January 1967.

93. On Carell, see Ronald Smelser, "The Holocaust in Popular Culture: Master-Narrative and Counter-Narrative in the Gray Zone," in Jonathan Petropoulos and John K. Roth (eds) *Gray Zones. Ambiguity and Compromise in the Holocaust and Its Aftermath* (New York, Berghahn Books, 2005), pp. 275–77, quote is on p. 276; most recently on Carell, see the biography by Wigbert Benz, *Paul Carell. Ribbentrop's Pressechef Paul Karl Schmidt vor und nach 1945* (Berlin, Wissenschaftlicher Verlag, 2005).

94. *SS General*, p. 290.

95. *Legion*, p. 227.

96. *SS General*, p. 182.

97. *Wheels*, p. 130.

98. *SS General*, p. 172.

99. *Legion*, p. 179.

100. *Wheels*, pp. 280–81.

101. *SS General*, p. 236.

102. *Wheels*, p. 260–63.

103. *SS General*, p. 265.

104. See Klaus Naumann, "Godfathers of the *Innere Führung*? German-American Interaction during the Early Years of the Bundeswehr," unpublished manuscript courtesy of the author, p. 13.

105. See David Schoenbaum, "The Wehrmacht and G. I. Joe: Learning *what* from History?" in *International Security* 8 (1983), p. 202.

106. "Cohesion and Disintegration in the Wehrmacht in World War Two," in *Public Opinion Quarterly*, XII (1948), pp. 202, 285, 298.

107. *Crisis in Command. The Mismanagement in the Army* (New York, Hill and Wang, 1978), p. 34.

108. *Ibid.*, pp. 34–36.

109. *Fighting Power. Germans and U.S. Army Performance, 1939–1945* (Westport, Conn., Greenwood Books, 1982), p. 5.

110. "Die deutsche Wehrmacht: eine militärische Beurteilung," in Rolf-Dieter Müller/Hans-Erich Volkmann (eds), *Die Wehrmacht. Mythos und Realität* (Munich, Oldenbourg, 1999), pp. 333–38.

111. *A Genius for War. The German Army and General Staff, 1807–1945* (Englewood Cliffs, NJ, Prentice-Hall, 1977), pp. 5, 295.

112. See Uwe Heuer, *Reichswehr-Wehrmacht-Bundeswehr. Zum Image deutscher Streitkräfte in den Vereinigten Staaten von America. Kontinuität und Wandel im Urteil amerikanischer Experten* (Frankfurt, Peter Lang, 1990). This is a valuable study of changing attitudes toward various German armies from the 1920s through the 1960s, using extensive U.S. sources. Here, see p. 352 for DuPuy's quote. Also pp. 341–44; DePuy's respect for the Germans in part derives from his World War Two experiences. He served with the 90th division from Normandy on to the end of the war. He especially appreciated the Germans' carefully constructed positions, their zone defense, their use of vehicles as assault guns, their fire suppression, and their weapons positioning. See William DePuy, Romie Brownlee, and William Mullen, *Changing an Army: An Oral History of General William E. DePuy, USA Retired* (Carlisle Barracks, PA and Washington, DC, U.S. Military Institute and Army Center of Military History, 1986).

113. F. W. von Mellenthin, *German Generals of World War II: As I Saw Them* (Norman, University of Oklahoma Press, 1977), p. 189.

114. See the final report written by DuPuy, *Generals Balck and von Mellenthin on Tactics: Implications for NATO Military Doctrine* (Maclean, Va., BDM Corporation, 1980), pp. 10–13 and 21 for quotes; the BDM Corporation, which sponsored the meeting and provided the technology for wargaming, is a CIA engineering contractor.

115. See Heuer, pp. 341–44, 352ff, and especially p. 75, fn. 103.

116. Anecdote to author from William S. Lind.

117. With R. H. S. Stolfi, *Nato Under Attack. Why the Western Alliance Can Fight Outnumbered and Win in Central Europe Without Nuclear Weapons* (Durham, NC, Duke University Press, 1984).

118. Heuer, pp. 379–80; see, for example, William B. Pickett, "Eisenhower as a Student of Clausewitz" *Military Review* 65 (July 1985), pp. 22–27; and Steven J. Argersinger, "Karl von Clausewitz: Analysis of FM 100–5," *Military Review* 66 (February 1986), pp. 68–75.

119. See Col. Michael D. Krause, "Moltke and the Origins of Operational Art" in *Military Review* 70 (September 1990), pp. 28–44; and Lieutenant Col. Laurence R. Sadoff, "Hans von Seeckt. One Man Who Made a Difference," *Military Review* 67 (December 1987), pp. 76–81.

120. See, for example, Major George A. Higgins, "German and US Operational Art: A Contrast in Maneuver" in *Military Review* 65 (October 1985), pp. 22–29; Lieutenant Colonel Paul Tiberi, "German versus Soviet Blitzkrieg", *Military Review* 65 (September 1985), pp. 63–71; Major Stephen T. Rippe, "Leadership, Firepower and Maneuver: The British and the Germans," *Military Review* 65 (October 1985), pp. 30–36; Major Glen L. Scott, "British and German Operational Styles in World War II," *Military Review* 65 (October 1985), pp. 37–41; Captain Peter R. Mansoor, "The Second Battle of Sedan May 1940," *Military Review* 68 (June 1988), pp. 65–75.

121. See, in particular, the articles by Roger A. Beaumont in *Military Review*: "On the *Wehrmacht* Mystique" 66 (July 1986), pp. 44–56; and "'Wehrmacht Mystique' Revisited" 70 (February 1990), pp. 64–75.

122. See Daniel J. Hughes, "Abuses of German Military History," *Military Review* 66 (December 1986), pp. 66–75; and Captain Antulio J. Echevarria II, "Auftragstaktik: In Its Proper Perspective," *Military Review* 66 (October 1986), pp. 50–56.

123. "On Learning From the Wehrmacht and Other Things," *Military Review* 68 (January 1988), p. 69; Captain Michael Phipps, "A Forgotten War," *Infantry* (November-December 1984), pp. 38–40.

124. "Portrait of a German General Staff Officer," *Military Review* 70, no. 4 (April 1990), pp. 70 and 81 respectively.

125. Roger Steinway in *Military History*, February 2005, pp. 34–41. Steinway is a high school teacher in Texas. He recommends for further reading Stephen Fritz' *Frontsoldaten* and Guy Sajer's *The Forgotten Soldier*.

126. May 19, 1985, p. 15.

127. *Fayettville Observer-Times*, 14 December 1995, "#1950," no page.

128. *Aerospace Power Journal*, Summer 1994, no page.

129. Anecdote to author from Bruce H. Siemon, Command Historian, USAREUR.

5. Winning Hearts and Minds: The Germans Interpret the War for the United States Public

1. Gottlob Herbert Bidermann, *In Deadly Combat: A German Soldier's Memoir of the Eastern Front* (Lawrence, University of Kansas Press, 2000); Günter K. Koschorrek, *Blood Red Snow: The Memoirs of a German Soldier on the Eastern Front* (London, Greenhill Books, 2002); Armin Scheiderbauer, *Adventures in My Youth: A German Soldier on the Eastern Front, 1941–1945* (West Midlands, England, 2003); Hans von Luck, *Panzer Commander: The Memoirs of Colonel Hans Von Luck* (New York, Dell, 1989); Siegfried Knappe and Ted Brusaw, *Soldat: Reflections of a German Soldier, 1936–1949* (New York, Orion Books, 1992). The first edition was issued the same year by Praeger; see *Panzer Commander: The Memoirs of Colonel Hans Von Luck* (New York, Praeger, 1989); for book club selections see, *History Book Club Review* June 2001, p. 27 and *Warfare: The Magazine of the Military Book Club* (August 2001), p. 4 for Bidermann's *In Deadly Combat*; *Warfare: The Magazine of the Military Book Club* (October 2002), p. 15 and *Warfare: The Magazine of the Military Book Club* (Holiday 2001); and for Koschorrek's *Blood Red Snow*, *Warfare: The Magazine of the Military Book Club* (October 2003), p. 15 and (Veteran's Day 2002), p. 5. In 2002 *Blood Red Snow* was the main selection of the Military Book Club.

2. See *Military History Titles 2003: Titles for Course Adoption* (New York: Random House, Inc. 2003), cover and p. 2 and *www.randomhouse.com/academic*.

3. *Adventures in My Youth: A German Soldier on the Eastern Front 1941–1945* on amazon.com. http://www.amazon.com/exec/obidos/ASIN/187462206X/qid= 1115141337/sr=2-1/ref=pd_bbs_b_2_2_1/103-8958436-7746218, pp. 1–6. For list see, http://www.amazon.com/exec/obidos/tg/listmania/list-browse/-/ 8ZR5YQOFTHH2/qid=1115140053/sr=5-1/ref=sr_5_1/103-8958436-7746218, pp. 1–9.

4. *Hitler's War: The Eastern Front* (six part series on the History Channel shown during the week of May 2–6, 2005; *D-Day to Berlin* (shown during May 2–6, 2005 on the History Channel) and *The Last Week of World War II* (shown during the week of May2–6, 2005 on the History Channel).

5. Field Marshal Erich von Manstein, *Lost Victories*, Trans. Anthony C. Powell (Novato, CA, Presidio Press, 1982), pp. 9–11, 13–18, dust jacket; See also "1995 Society for Military History Awards," *Newsletter of the Society for Military History* (1995), p. 3.

6. Manstein, *Lost Victories*, pp. 9–11, 13–18, dust jacket; for the 1957 edition, see *Lost Victories*, see dust jacket.

7. Manstein, *Lost Victories*, dust jacket for the 1957 and 1981 editions.

8. Stahlberg, *Bounden Duty: The Memoirs of a German Officer 193–45*. Trans. Patricia Crampton (London, Brassey's, 1987), dust jacket.

9. Heinz Guderian, *Panzer Leader* (Cambridge, MA, DeCapo Press, 2002), pp. 1–5.

10. Guderian, *Panzer Leader*, dust jacket, first inside page.

11. Guderian, *Panzer Leader*, pp. vii–xii.

12. *Ibid.*

13. Luck, *Panzer Commander*, p. xxxiii. Ambrose also notes that Luck admired Rommel more than any other general. Rommel, of all the German commanders, stands

out as subject of many biographies and a feature character in several Hollywood movies. He is also the clean general who fought in theaters where mass killing played a small or nonexistent role. See Ralf Georg Reuth, "Erwin Rommel – Die Propagandaschuopfung" in Ronald Smelser/Enrico Syring (eds.), *Die Militärelite des Dritten Reiches* (Berlin, Ullstein, 1995), pp. 460–475.

14. Luck, *Panzer Commander*, p. xxii.
15. Knappe, *Soldat*, inside dust jacket.
16. Knappe, *Soldat*, pp. 61. Knappe expressed repulsion for the anti-Semitism of Hitler and the Nazis. See Knappe, *Soldat*, p. 122.
17. For an account critical of this literature see Gerhard Weinberg, *A World At Arms: A Global History* (New York, Cambridge University Press, 1994); see sections on the Eastern Front. For a scathing indictment of the German military in the barbarity of the Eastern Front, see Omer Bartov, *The Eastern Front 1941–1945: The German Troops and the Barbarisatiion of Warfare* (New York, St. Martin's Press, 1986) and *Hitler's Army: Soldiers, Nazis, and War in the Third Reich* (New York, Oxford University Press, 1992).
18. Manstein, *Lost Victories*, pp. 17–18.
19. *Ibid.*
20. Bidermann, *In Deadly Combat*, p. ix–xii, 1–9; Koschorrek, *Blood Red Snow*, p. 9–13; Manstein, *Lost Victories*, p. 18.
21. For accounts of the war from the Russian side, see Helene Keyssar and Vladimir Posner, *Remembering War: A U.S.-Soviet Dialogue* (New York, Oxford University Press, 1990), which recounts the moment of cooperation between the soldiers of the Soviet Union and the United States Army. See also Vladimir Karpov, *Russia at War* (New York, Vendome Press, 1987), John Erickson, *Road to Stalingrad: Stalin's War with Germany* (New York, Harper & Row, 1975), and *Road To Berlin: Continuing the History of Stalin's War with Germany* (Boulder, Colorado, Westview Press, 1983). These two works represent the most thorough scholarly accounts of the war that rely primarily on Russian sources and interviews with Russian participants. *Road to Stalingrad* was first published in 1975 and *Road to Berlin* in 1983. Both went out of print and reappeared only in 1999 when Yale University Press, an academic, not a commercial publisher, released them in paperback. Alexander Werth's monumental *Russia At War* first appeared in 1965. Werth was actually present in Russia during the war and had access to those who endured its horrors. The book went out of print after its first publication and only re-appeared in 1986 in hardback and at the end of the 1990s in paperback.
22. See footnote 8 for citations.
23. History channel programs of May 2005 and the material in chapter 8 demonstrate the currency of these views.
24. See previous footnote.
25. Koschorrek, *Blood Red Snow*, pp. 73, 294, 311.
26. Bidermann, *In Deadly Combat*, pp. 152–153.
27. *Ibid.*, photo following p. 212, pp. 226–231.
28. *Ibid.*, pp. 105–106, 153.
29. Koschorrek, *Blood Red Snow*, p. 264.
30. John Ellis, *Brute Force: Allied Strategy and Tactics in the Second World War* (New York, Viking, 1999).

31. Stahlberg, *Bounden Duty*, pp. 312–315, 286.
32. See Paul Carell, *Hitler Moves East 1941–1943*, trans. Ewald Osers (New York, Bantam, 1966), pp. 35–38, for what Carell states was the cruel way the Soviet state ignored the sacrifices of the Soviet soldiers who defended the Fortress of Brest-Litovsk in June 1941. The regime clearly showed no appreciation for their sacrifice. See, pp. 93–95 for the relentless nature of Soviet attacks, often suicidal, on German lines; in this case, the effort by Marshall Timoshenko to hold the Germans at the Smolensk-Yelenya Bend. Carell also claims that the individual holds no value in the East, unlike the West, where the individual is sacred. Mellenthin, *Panzer Battles*, p. 197.
33. Carell, *Hitler Moves East*, p. 554.
34. Stahlberg, *Bounden Duty*, p. 198.
35. Koschorrek's *Blood Red Snow*, p. 160 and Bidermann, *In Deadly Combat*, p. 58.
36. Bidermann, *In Deadly Combat*, pp. 117–119.
37. *Ibid.*, pp. 119–121.
38. *Ibid.*, p. 121.
39. Scheiderbauer, *Adventures in My Youth*, p. 51.
40. For an account of wartime photography, see Susan D. Moeller, *Shooting War: Photography and the American Experience of Combat* (New York, Basic Books, Inc., 1989). For a discussion of photography and its complexity see, Catherine Lutz and Jane L. Collins, *Reading National Geographic* (Chicago, Ill.: The University of Chicago Press, 1993). Chapter one provides an introduction to photography, readings photos and representation in photography. For a discussion of German military photography on the Eastern Front, see Peter MacPherson, "The Photographers of Barbarossa," *Military Historical Quarterly* 2 (Winter 1990), pp. 60–69. The cover photo at the beginning of the article included a shot of hundreds of Russians marching to prison camps where, according to Gerhard Weinberg in *World At Arms*, their chances of survival remained slim to none. MacPherson attempts to remove the focus of his article, Hans Hubermann, from any association with the horrors of the Eastern Front. According to MacPherson, Hubermann was a professional to the last day of the war. Hubermann never belonged to the Nazi Party and regularly rebuked German soldiers for killing innocent civilians. He tried to stop such killings when possible. The piece also contains an honest description of the some of the suffering the Russian people endured at the hands of the German war machine. Despite this openness the author includes a photo of a large number of Russian civilians (many were young people and children) rushing toward a German war vehicle waving their hands and smiling, no doubt a rare occurrence. Another shot captures Hubermann in full uniform standing next to two young Russian women in Smolensk. The picture suggested an amicable exchange between Hubermann and the Russian women. See p. 62. The shot with the civilians is in keeping with photos of Russian civilians and German soldiers in the memoirs and accounts.
41. Manstein, *Lost Victories*, p. 17.
42. Stahlberg, *Bounden Duty*, p. 232.
43. Knappe and Brusaw, *Soldat*, pp. 105, 109, 215 and photos following pages 144 and 224.

44. Paul Carell, *Hitler Moves East 1941–1943*. Trans. Ewald Osers (New York: Little, Brown and Company, 1964), pp. 101 and Part One, chapter 5 for the battle for Rosslavl. For visuals, see following p. 64.

45. Manstein, *Lost Victories*, p. 271.

46. *Ibid.*

47. *Ibid.*, pp. 270–271. The story of the younger Manstein's death appeared in Stahlberg's work. The ADC described the suffering and grief of Manstein. He also links the Christian burial with the anti-Nazi sentiment of Manstein. See Stahlberg, *Bounden Duty*, p. 232.

48. Knappe and Brusaw, *Soldat*, pp. 215, 218–219.

49. Knappe, *Soldat*, pp. 215, 218–219 and picture following p. 224.

50. *Ibid.*, p. 231 and photographs following page 224.

51. Knappe, *Soldat*, p. 156 and photographs following p. 224.

52. Stahlberg, *Bounden Duty*, p. 193 & photos following p. 173.

53. *Ibid.*, pp. 191–193 plus photos following page 173.

54. *Ibid.*

55. Scheiderbauer, *Adventures in My Youth*, Prologue, p. 35.

56. See citation in fn. 65.

57. Scheiderbauer, *Adventures in My Youth*, p. 42. Later in the text, Scheiderbauer commented that he worried over the next rotation to the Russian front and only by placing his "trust in God" would he feel some sense of relief. See, p. 77.

58. Stahlberg, *Bounden Duty*, p. 165 and Carell, *Hitler Moves East*, photos following page 96.

59. Koschorrek, *Blood Red Snow*, pp. 154–162, 170–171, 184–186, 213–217.

60. Scheiderbauer, *Adventures in My Youth*, pp. 67–68.

61. Scheiderbauer, *Adventures in My Youth*, p. 102. For Scheiderbauer's own personal loss, the death of his brother who served with the elite Panzer division, Herman Goring, in Italy, see pp. 127–128.

62. Bidermann, *In Deadly Combat*, p. 65. For other examples, see pp. 38, 80, 89–91, 103–105.

63. Luck, *Panzer Commander*, pp. 69–73.

64. *Ibid.*, p. 72.

65. *Ibid.*, pp. 72–73.

66. *Ibid.*, p. 73.

67. Carell, *Hitler Moves East*, photos following page 96.

68. Stahlberg, *Bounden Duty*, p. 202.

69. Koschorrek, *Blood Red Snow*, see chapter though for battles around Stalingrad.

70. Koschorrek, *Blood Red Snow*, pp. 64–65; Bidermann, *In Deadly Combat*, pp. 159–166. For additional examples of the Germans facing overwhelming odds, see Koschorrek, *Blood Red Snow*, pp. 40–41, 51–2, 220; Bidermann, *In Deadly Combat*, pp. 96, 159–166.

71. Bidermann, *In Deadly Combat*, pp. 247–248, 269–270.

72. Scheiderbauer, *Adventures in My Youth*, p. 137; Bidermann, *In Deadly Combat*, p. 94, 236. Koschorrek, *Blood Red Snow*, pp. 230, 234–236. Ironically, Red Army soldiers shared the same fear of German captivity and a real fear. But Koschorrek wrote that he encountered a Russian captive from Kiev who learned from Russian

soldiers that escaped Russian captivity that the Germans actually treated them humanely. See Koschorrek, *Blood Red Snow*, p. 229. Bidermann commented that the frontline troops treated the Russians with care. Yet, these men betrayed no knowledge of the rear-area policies of the Nazi party and the "*Sonderkommando*" excesses. These excesses led to "atrocities" on frontline troops who suffered in some ways as the victims of the Nazi agents. See Bidermann, *In Deadly Combat*, p. 43.

73. Bidermann, *In Deadly Combat*, p. 235.
74. *Ibid.*, pp. 235–236.
75. Scheiderbauer, *Adventures in My Youth*, p. 90; Bidermann, *In Deadly Combat*, photos following p. 212 and p. 33.
76. Koschorrek, *Blood Red Snow*, p. 97.
77. Bidermann, *In Deadly Combat*, p. 59.
78. For other examples of death and suffering on the battlefield, see Koschorrek, *Blood Red Snow*, pp. 84, 100, 105–107, 149–150, 260, 300; Bidermann, *In Deadly Combat*, pp. 124, 130–131, 195, 208; Scheiderbauer, *Adventures in My Youth*, p. 109.
79. Koschorrek, *Blood Red Snow*, p. 176; Bidermann, *In Deadly Combat*, pp. 18, 34.

6. The Gurus

1. See Charles Syndor, *Soldiers of Destruction: The SS Death's Head Division, 1933–1945* (Princeton, NJ, Princeton University Press, 1977).
2. *Waffen-SS Commanders. The Army, Corps and Divisional Leaders of a Legend* (Atgen, Pa., Schiffer Military History, 1999).
3. *Ibid.*, p. 11.
4. *Otto Weidinger* (Winnipeg, Fedorowicz, 1987) p. 19; *Otto Kumm* (Winnipeg, Fedorowicz, 1987); *Ernst August Krag* (Atgen, Pa., Schiffer, 1996).
5. A translation of the original *Kameraden bis zum Ende* (Atgen, Pa., Schiffer Military History, 1998).
6. He mentions the incident also in his book, *Ibid.*, pp. 278–301; "Tulle and Oradour: A Franco-German Tragedy" (privately published, 1985). One of the gurus, Marc Rikmenspoel, summarizes the German case in an article "Tulle and Oradour: The German View" on www.dasreich.ca/ger_oradour.html.
7. Vol. II, p. 14.
8. *Ibid.*, p. 44.
9. *Ibid.*, p. 111.
10. Weidinger, Introduction, n.p.
11. The full publishing information is: for examples of Landwehr's work on the Axis minorities in the Waffen-SS, see Richard Landwehr, *Lions of Flanders: Flemish Volunteers of the Waffen-SS, 1941–1945* (Bradford, U.K., Shelf Books, 1996), *Nordic Warriors: SS-Panzergrenadier Regiment 24 Danmark, Eastern Front, 1943–1945* (Bradford, U.K., Shelf Books, 1999), *Romanian Volunteers of the Waffen-SS, 1944–1945* (Silver Spring, Md., Bibliophile Legion Books, 1991), *The "Wallonien": The History of the 5th SS-Sturmbrigade and 28th SS Volunteer Panzergrenadier Division* (Brookings, Ore., Siegrunen Magazine, 1984).

12. (Silver Spring, Md., Bibliophile Legion Books, 1985) 3rd edition in 1993, pp. 202 and 205.

13. *Ibid.*, pp. 14, 17, 141.

14. Landwehr, *Romanian Volunteers*, pp. 126, 128, 10. Materials in this paragraph and the following two paragraphs that deal with the Romanians come from this source.

15. #59, Vol. X, No. 3 (Summer 1995), pp. 13–17. His volumes are somewhat erratically numbered.

16. The article is entitled: "The European Volunteer Movement in World War II," *Journal of Historical Review 2* (Spring 1981); see Web site www.vho.org/GB/Journals/JHR/2/1/Landwehr59-84.html.

17. No. 3 (1993), pp. 18–25.

18. Nos. 5 and 6, Vol. 8.

19. X, No. 1 (Fall 1994), p. 3.

20. IX, No. 54 (March 1993), p. 3.

21. Shofar FTP Archive File: orgs/american/wiesenthal.center/swc.oprep.

22. X (Fall 1994), p. 33; see also article in No. 42, 1987, "The Evolution of the Waffen-Grenadier Division der SS," pp. 4–14. On Dirlewanger, see Richard Rhodes, *Masters of Death. The SS-Einsatzgruppen and the Invention of the Holocaust* (New York, Alfred Knopf, 2002), pp. 248–50.

23. See No. 55 (January 1994), pp. 3–4.

24. Vol. X, No. 3 (Summer 1995), p. 3.

25. No. 69 (Summer 2000) p. 4.

26. *Ibid.*, p. 6.

27. No. 5 (January 1994), p. 72.

28. No. 57 (Fall 1994), p. 5.

29. *Ibid.*, p. 6.

30. Edmund D. Cohen, "Review of the 'Left Behind' Tribulation Novels: Turner Diaries Light" in *Council for Secular Humanism*. See http://www.secularhumanism.org/library/fi/cohen_21_2.html.

31. See James Weingartner, *Crossroads of Death. The Story of the Malmédy Massacre and Trial* (Berkeley, University of California Press, 1979), p. 261; also by same author, *A Peculiar Crusade. William M. Everett and the Malmédy Massacre* (New York, New York University Press, 2000).

32. Weingartner, *Crossroads*, p. 218; also 200–01.

33. Article entitled: "Malmédy and McCarthy" printed on www.fredautley.com/malmedy.htm.

34. See Weingartner, *Crossroads*, p. 264. See also his chapter "McCarthy and Freedom."

35. See footnote 5, p. 1.

36. (Blue Ridge Summit, Pa., Tab Aero, Division of McGraw Hill, 1970). The two authors, separately or together, have written seven other books on the Luftwaffe.

37. Introduction; no page number.

38. From authors' preface, xiii to xv. Following quotes are from pp. 4, 5, 6, 14 resp.

39. For the Amazon websites that feature Kurowski's publications, see http://www.amazon.com/exec//obidos/search-handle-url/ref=br_ss_hs/002-4064754-8088802?platform=gurupa&url=index%3Dstripbooks%3Arelevance; http://www.amazon.com/exec//obidos/search-handle-url/ix=stripbooks&rank=%2Brelevanc2rank&fqp=relevance%01281000-%02keywords%01franz%25. Franz Kurowski,

Brandenburg Commandos: Germany's Elite Warrior Spies In WWII (Mechanicsburg, Pa.: Stackpole Books, 2004).

40. Franz Kurowski, *Panzer Aces* (New York, Ballantine Books, 2002) and *Infantry Aces* (New York, Ballantine Books, 2002); *Panzer Aces* Audio CD (abridged) (as advertised on Amazon.com). For the Amazon ranking, see http://www. amazon.com/exec/obidos/tg/deatail/-/0811731731/qid=1121022524/sr=1-111/ ref=sr111/002-4964754-8088802?v=glance&s=books.

41. Kurowski, *Infantry Aces*; for example, see accounts of Sepp, Lanier, Fran Schmitz, and Josef Schreiber. Kurowski, *Panzer Aces*, see accounts of *Generalmajor* Dr. Franz Bake, Rudolf von Ribbentrop, and Michael Wittman. For similar tales of courage and heroism, see Kurowski, *Panzer Aces II*, Sepp Brandner, one of the soldiers described by Kurowski.

42. See stories cited earlier.

43. Kurowski, *Panzer Aces*, pp. 70–71.

44. *Ibid.*, pp. 299–302.

45. *Ibid.*, pp. 366–76.

46. *Ibid.*, p. 377.

47. *Ibid.*, pp. 377–78.

48. *Ibid.*, p. 378.

49. *Ibid.*, p. 378.

50. Kurowski, *Panzer Aces*, pp. 163–65.

51. *Ibid.*, pp. 32–44.

52. Kurowski, *Panzer Aces*, pp. 348–55. For other examples of German leadership abilities and actions, see Kurowski, *Infantry Aces*, pp.163–65, 174–75, 366–70, 382–91; *Panzer Aces*, pp. 39–42, 48–51, 57–61, 65–69, 74–75, 194–201.

53. Kurowski, *Panzer Aces*, pp. 44–48.

54. *Ibid.*, pp. 310–15.

55. Kurowski, *Infantry Aces*, pp. 370–71, 284–85.

56. For other examples of comradeship, see Kurowski, *Panzer Aces*, pp. 178–83, 192–93, 228–29,323–25, 334–36; Kurowski, *Infantry Aces*, pp. 256–63, 280–81, 288–91, 294–96, 304–05, 362–65, 378–81.

57. Kurowski, *Infantry Aces*, pp. 1–2.

58. See his biographical statement on Europa Books' website: "From Hobby to Magazine to Books: The Birth of Europa Books," pp. 1–3; http://www. axiseurpa.com/about.php. For examples of the focus on minor Axis powers in the Journal, see Jason Pipes, "SLOVAKIA! A History of the Slovak Units on the Eastern Front in WWII," *Axis Europa: The Journal of the Axis Forces 1939–1945* (Summer 1998), pp. 18–22; "The Serbian State and Frontier Guard, 1941–1945 (part one)," *Axis Europa: The Newsletter of the Axis Allied Forces, 1939–1945* I (January-February, 1995), pp. 1, 3–9 and "'Za Hrvatsku I Krista': For Croatia & Christ: The Croatian Army, 1941–1945," *Axis Europa: The Newsletter of the Axis Allied Forces, 1939– 1945* I (January-February, 1995), pp. 1, 10–22; "For King and Fatherland: The History of the Montenegro Volunteer Corps. 1943–1945 (part III)," *Axis Europa Magazine: The Magazine of the Axis Allied Forces, 1939–1945* II (January-February 1996), pp. 9–13. Henry L. DeZong IV, "The Moslem Militia and Legion of the Sandjak," *Axis Europa Magazine; The Journal of the Axis Allied Forces, 1939–1945* II

(June-July-August 1996), pp. 3–14; "Wasted efforts: The History of the SS 'Kama' Division," *Axis Europa Magazine: The Magazine of the Axis Allied Forces, 1939–1945* 1 (July-August 1995), pp. 1, 3–4. "From the editor," *Axis Europa Newsletter of the Axis Allied Forces, 1939–1945* (January-February, 1995), p. 23. Note that titles varied and are used as noted in each issue.

59. "Readers Classifieds + Odds and Ends," *Axis Europa Newsletter*, issue 4 (July-August 1995), p. 26. "Readers Classified Section," *Axis Europa Newsletter*, issue 5 (September-October 1995), p. 26. Antonio Munoz, "*Waffen-SS* Books," *Siegrunen* 43(1987), pp. 5–6, "*SS* and Police Leader 'Outer Alps' Schematic," and "*SS* police Leader 'Upper Italy West' Schematic," *Siegrunen* 57 (Fall 1994); "Achtung! Axis Europa," *Siegrunen* 59 (Summer 1995), p. 6, for advertisement. "Soon to be available," *Siegrunen* 40 (1986), p. 4; "*Waffen-SS* Books – Photo Histories," *Siegrunen* 39(1985), p. 35; Antonio J. Munoz, R. T. R., "Parachute Battalion: The History of the SS-Fallschrimjaegar-Battalion 500/600," *Siegrunen* 8 (September 1989), pp. 29–70.

60. "Readers Classifieds + Odds and Ends," *Axis Europa Newsletter*, issue 4 (July-August 1995), p. 26. "Readers Classified Section," *Axis Europa Newsletter*, issue 5 (September-October 1995), p. 26. Antonio Munoz, "*Waffen-SS* Books," *Siegrunen* 43 (1987), pp. 5–6; "*SS* and Police Leader 'Outer Alps' Schematic," and "*SS* police Leader 'Upper Italy West' Schematic" *Siegrunen* 57 (Fall 1994) and "Achtung! Axis Europa," *Siegrunen* 59 (Summer 1995), p. 6 for advertisement. "Soon to be available" *Siegrunen* 40 (1986), p. 4 and "*Waffen-SS* Books – Photo Histories," *Siegrunen* 39 (1985), p. 35.

61. "From the editor," *Axis Europa Newsletter*, issue 2 (March-April 1995), p. 23. See editorial page *Siegrunen* 44 (1987), p. 2 and *Siegrunen* 43 (April-June 1987), p. 2. Munoz also praises first-rate academic books, see his review of Gerald Kleinfeld and Lewis A. Tambs, *Hitler's Spanish Legion: The Blue Division in Russia*, in "New Book Releases," *Axis Europa* (Jan-March, 1996), p. 15 and Dr. Valdis O. Lumans, *Himmler's Auxiliaries: The Volkdeutsche Mittelstelle and the German National Minorities of Europe, 1933–1945* in "Book Reviews," *Axis Europa Magazine* (May-June-July-August 1997), p. 32.

62. For a list of Jurado's books, see Amazon website: http://www.amazon.com/exec/obidos/search-handle-url/index=books&field-author-exact=Carlos%20 Caballero%20Jurado/002-4064754-8088802. For a description of *Foreign Volunteers of the Wehrmacht, 1941–1945*, see Amazon website: http://amazon.com/exec/obidos/tg/detail/-/0850455243/qid=1122048844/sr=8-3/ref=sr 8 xs ap i3 xg114/002-4064754-8088802?v=glance&s=books&n=507486; For *Wehrmacht Auxiliary*, see http://amazon.com/gp/product/1855322579/002-4064754-8088802?5 Fencoding-UTF8&s=books&v=glance. For a description of *Breaking the Chains*, see Amazon website: http://www.amazon.com/gp/product/1855322579/002-4064754-8088802?%5Fencoding=UTF8&s=books&v=glance. For citations of these works, see Carlos Caballero Jurado, *Foreign Volunteers, 1941–45* (London, Osprey Publishing, 1985), *Wehrmacht Auxiliary Forces* (London, Osprey, 1992), *Breaking the Chains* (Halifax, West Yorkshire, UK: Shelf Books, 1998); see editorial or opening pages in *Siegrunen* issue, 39 (July-September 1985), 40 (October 1985-September 1986), 42 (January-March 1987), 43 (April-June 1987), 44 (1987),

Inside page *Siegrunen* 5&6 (September 1989), Inside page *Siegrunen* 54 (March 1993), Inside page *Siegrunen* 55 (January 1994), Inside page *Siegrunen* 55 (Fall 1994), Inside page *Siegrunen* 59 (Summer 1995), Inside page *Siegrunen* 66 (Fall 1998), Inside page *Siegrunen* 68 (Winter 2000), Inside page *Siegrunen* (Summer 2000). For Merriam Press, see Richard Landwehr, *Steadfast Hussars: The Last Cavalry Divisions of the Waffen-SS* (Brookings, Ore., *Siegrunen*, 1997); Richard Landwehr, *Budapest: The Stalingrad of the Waffen-SS* (Brookings, Ore., *Siegrunen*, 1999). Merriam Press actually "designed, produced and printed" these works for Landwehr. See p. 2 of each work. For articles in *Axis Europa*, see C. C. Jurado, "Against Stalin and Stalinism, Count Grigori von Lambsdorff, 1936–1945," *Axis Europa* 14 (Summer 1998), pp. 8–11 and "Against Stalin and Stalinism, Count Grigori von Lambsdorff, 1936–1945," *Axis Europa* 15 (Fall 1998), pp. 15–18. For another example of the anti-Communist theme, see Dr. Perry Perik, "August 1942: The Bloody Prelude of the Dutch *Waffen-SS* on the Russian Front," *Axis Europa* 15 (Fall 1998), pp. 6–7.

63. Antonio J. Munoz, *Hitler's Eastern Legions, Volume-II; The Osttruppen* (Bayside, N.Y., Axis Europa, Inc., 1997), pp. 3–5; Munoz, *The Baltic Schutzmannschaft*, pp. 8, 10.

64. http://www.amazon.com/exec/obidos/tg/detail/-/1891227424/ref=ord_cart_shr/102-1047711-2940166?%5Fencoding=UTF8, pp. 1–2.

65. "Readers Classifieds + Odds and Ends," *Axis Europa Newsletter*, issue 4 (July-August 1995), p. 26. "Readers Classified Section," *Axis Europa Newsletter*, issue 5 (September-October 1995), p. 26. Antonio Munoz, "*Waffen-SS* Books" *Siegrunen* 43 (1987), pp. 5–6; "SS and Police Leader 'Outer Alps' Schematic," and "SS police Leader 'Upper Italy West' Schematic," *Siegrunen* 57 (Fall 1994) and "Achtung! Axis Europa," *Siegrunen* 59 (Summer 1995), p. 6 for advertisement. "Soon to be available," *Siegrunen* 40 (1986), p. 4 and "*Waffen-SS* Books – Photo Histories," *Siegrunen* 39 (1985), p. 35.

66. Anthony J. Munoz, *Forgotten Legions: Obscure Combat Formations of the Waffen-SS* (Bayside, N.Y., Axis Europa Books, 1991), p. xiii. Samuel W. Mitcham, Jr., *Hitler's Field Marshals and Their Battles* (Lanham, Md.: Scarborough House, 1994), Acknowledgments. Mitcham has published fourteen books on the German military in World War II, see http://www.amazon.com/exec/obidos/search-handle-url/index=books&field-author-exact=Samuel1%20W.%20Mitcham/002-4064754-8088802.

67. Munoz, *Forgotten Warriors*, p. xvii. Munoz's works contain a storehouse of detailed and useful information lavishly displayed and intensely studied. Few have his mastery of such detail and few dedicated such efforts to retrieving and publishing this vast amount of information as Munoz. For other examples of his works, see Antonio J. Munoz, *Hitler's Green Army: The German Order of Police and their European Auxiliaries 1933–1945, Volume II, Eastern Europe and the Balkans* (Bayside, N.Y., Europa Books, Inc., 2005) and Antonio J. Munoz, *Hitler's Green Army: The German Order of Police and their European Auxiliaries 1933–1945, Volume I, Western Europe and Scandinavia* (Bayside, N.Y., Europa Books, Inc., 2005).

7. Wargames, the Internet, and the Popular Culture of the Romancers

1. For a brief early history of contemporary wargaming, as well as a description of Panzerblitz, see: the Editors of *Consumer Guide, The Complete Book of Wargaming* (New York, Fireside Books, Simon and Schuster, 1980), pp. 13–21, 178–79.

2. The Editors of *Consumer Guide, The Complete Book of Wargaming*, pp. 18–20; see *Strategy & Tactics* 72 (January-February 1979) and *Strategy & Tactics* 86 (May–June 1981) as examples. For *Moves: Conflict Simulation Theory and Technique*, see Bill Dunne, Mike Gunson, David Paris, "Panzergruppe Guderian, A Dissenting Approach" *Moves: Conflict Simulation Theory and Technique* 33 (June–July 1977), pp. 8–10.

3. Dan Lombardy, designer, and David Parham, researcher, *Streets of Stalingrad, Sept-Nov, 1942*, Phoenix Games, 1979; Gary Charbonneau, "Streets of Stalingrad," *Fire & Movement* 23 (September–October 1980), pp. 27–39. The article includes "Close-Up" analysis, organization and charts, errata for mistakes, and a response by designer, Dan Lombardy.

4. *PanzerBlitz: The Game of Armored Warfare on the Eastern Front 1941–1945* (Baltimore, Md., Avalon Hill Game Company, 1970). *Designer's Notes & Campaign Analysis*, pp. 3–7. Booklet is part of the gaming materials. The Editors of *Consumer Guide, The Complete Book of Wargaming*, pp. 178–79.

5. *PanzerBlitz: The Game of Armored Warfare on the Eastern Front 1941–1945*, see scenario packet, part of game materials.

6. *War in the East: The Russo-German Conflict 1941–1945* (New York, Simulations Publications, Inc., 1974). For another example of the "monster" game, see John M. Astell, Paul R. Banner, Frank Chadwick, and Marc Miller, designers, *Fire in the East: The Russian Front, 1941–1942* (Bloomington, Ill.s, Game Designers' Workshop, 1984). For a review of the game, see John T. Schuler, "Close-Up: Fire in the East," *Fire & Movement: The Forum of Conflict Simulation* 44 (September/October 1985), pp. 30–47, and see a series of articles on *Fire in the East* in the *The Grenadier* 25 (March–April 1985), pp. 7–33; for a large-scale game on the Eastern Front released as a magazine format, see "Proud Monster: The Barbarossa Campaign 1941," *Command: Military History, Strategy & Analysis* 27 (March–April 1994), game-enclosed article by Ty Bomba, "Proud Monster" pp. 12–26. The cover art for the magazine is in red with a landser in green swinging his rifle butt against the Soviet Hammer and Sickle, which is disintegrating under the blows of the rifle. For a review of wargames in general up to 1980, see the Editors of *Consumer Guide, The Complete Book of Wargaming*.

7. Stephen Patrick, "Battle for Germany: The Destruction of the Reich Dec. 1944–May 1945," *Strategy & Tactics (S & T)* 50 (May/June 1975), wargames that accompanied each issue of *S&T*. For examples of articles on the Eastern Front, see Sterling Harris, "Airpower in the Stalingrad Campaign Part 1," *Strategy & Tactics* 169 (July/August 1994), pp. 23–33; Joseph Miranda, "Air War on the Eastern Front, 1941–1945," *Strategy & Tactics* 214 (January/February 2003), pp. 38–51.

8. Victor Madej and Shelby Stanton, "The Smolensk Campaign 11 July–5 August 1941," *Strategy & Tactics* 57 (July–August 1976), pp. 4–19 plus the game

Panzergruppe Guderian: The Battle of Smolensk July 1941. Stanton served in the U.S. Army in Vietnam, where battlefield wounds forced his retirement. He has written extensively on Southeast Asia as well as other topics in military history. See http://www.randonhouse.com/rhpg/authors/results.pperl?authorid-29510; Guderian is often in gaming titles and his battlefield actions command the attention of wargame designers. For example, see Dean N. Essig, game and series designer, *Guderian's Blitzkrieg: The Panzer Leader's Last Drive, The Drive on Moscow September 21th to December 20th, 1941* (Homer, Ill., The Gamers, 1992). Note the 21th error was copied directly from the wargame box. Apparently the proofreader missed the error.

9. Victor Madej and Shelby Stanton, "The Smolensk Campaign 11 July–5August 1941," p. 12.

10. *The Last Victory: Von Manstein's Backhand Blow* (King of Prussia, PA, Clash of Arms Games, 1987).

11. *Ibid.* The historical commentary did speak highly of the improving Soviet capacities to wage offensives against the Germans. The commentary pointed out that the main weakness of the Soviets resided with the lower-level officers. The piece blamed the purges of the 1930s and the losses suffered in the 1941 battles for this weakness.

12. Ty Bomba, "The Fuhrer's Will: Hitler and the Stalingrad Pocket," *Strategy & Tactics* 124 (December 1988), pp. 14–19. For the German version, see http://cc.msnscache.com/cache.aspx?q=8132199432148&lang=en-US&mkt=en-US&FORM=CVRE8. Scroll to Films-original Nazi War Movies.

13. Bomba, "The Fuhrer's Will," pp. 14, 17. Note the article includes Soviet stamps at the end celebrating the Russian victory. However, they pale in insignificance when compared to the dramatic pro-German posters. For the German version of the cover art, see http://www.nazi-lauck-nsdapao.com/ p. 3.

14. Dean N. Essig, game & series designer, *Enemy At the Gates: The Stalingrad Pocket to Manstein's Counterattack Army Group South – 19 Nov 42 to 14 March 1943* (Homer, Ill., The Gamers, 1994).

15. Dave Fredericks, game designer, and Dean N. Essig, series designer, *Hube's Pocket* (Homer, Ill., The Gamers, 1996), and in the game the booklet, "Operational Combat Series," pp. 15–19. For material on Hube, see Earl Ziemke, *Stalingrad to Berlin: The German Defeat in the East* (Washington, D.C., Center for Military History, U.S. Army, 1968), pp. 188, 280–82.

16. Fredericks and Essig, *Hube's Pocket*, and in the game the booklet, "Operational Combat Series," pp. 15–19. For material on Hube, see Ziemke, *Stalingrad to Berlin*, pp. 188, 280–82.

17. See *Achtung Panzer* for German armored vehicles, http://www.achtungpanzer.com/panzer.htm. For the Eastern Front, see Eastern Front Web Ring, http://eastfront.virtualave.net/. For wargamer sites, see http://www.geocities.com/Pentagon/Quarters/8662/links.htm and http://www.wargamer.com/contest/tank.asp. For uniforms, see http://www.soldat.com/. For books, see http://www.11thpanzer.com/index11.htm. For portraits, see http://www.ortelli-art.com/military/mr11.htm, and also mr12 and mr 06. And http://www.ortelli-art.com/militar.milit-e.htm;

http://www.ortelli-art.com/military/ and http://www.ortelli-art.com/military/
unit-e.htm. For mugs, see http://www.hstrial-derickson.homestead.com/Mugs~
ns4.html. The company now operates as an eBay store; see http://stores.ebay.com/
Military-Mugs-and-Models and http://feedback.ebay.com/ws/eBayISAPI.dll?
ViewFeedback&userid=sssteiner&frm=1742.

18. http://www.achtungpanzer.com/panzer.htm.
19. http://members.tripod.com/George_Parada/gen8.htm; on same site, see also gen2,
    gen4, gen5 gen9, gen10. Note, *Achtung Panzer* as of January 2006 was temporar-
    ily out of operation. The owner, George Parada, was looking for sources of
    money to handle the costs of maintaining such a large website. Typing in *Achtung
    Panzer* on a search engine will take one to the notice. The website is presently in
    operation.
20. For Manstein, see http://members.tripod.com/George_Parada/gen8.htm.
21. http://members.tripod.com/George_Parada/gen8.htm.
22. http://members.tripod.com/George_Parada/gen2.htm; http://members.tripod
    .com/George_Parada/gen9.htm.
23. http://members.tripod.com/George_Parada/gen2.htm; http://members.tripod
    .com/George_Parada/gen9.htm.
24. http://members.tripod.com/George_Parada/gen2.htm.
25. http://members.tripod.com/George_Parada/gen9.htm.
26. *Ibid*.
27. http://members.tripod.com/George_Parada/whatsnew.htm; http://www.
    achtungpanzer.com/vote.htm; http://www.achtungpanzer.com/panzer.htm.
28. http://members.tripod.com/George_Parada/whatsnew.htm; http://www.
    achtungpanzer.com/vote.htm; http://www.achtungpanzer.com/panzer.htm.
29. http://www.achtungpanzer.com/qiz.htm; http://members.tripod.com/George_
    Parada/whatsnew.htm.
30. For a statement declaring a nonpolitical position, see http://www.achtung.com/
    panzer.htm. This is taken from *Achtung Panzer* in August 2005.
31. http://members.tripod.com/George_parada/book.htm#videos; http://members.
    tripod.com/George_Parada.htm. For a listing of topics covered in the site, see
    http://members.tripod.com/George_Parada/map.htm.
32. http://www.InsideTheWeb.com/messageboard/mbs.cgi/mb47087.
33. http://www.achtungpanzer.com/bolk.htm.
34. See http://www.amazon.com/exec/obidos/tg/deatail/-/0811731731/qid=
    1121022524/sr=1-111/ref=sr 1 11/002-4964754-8088802?v=glance&s=books;
    http://www.amazon.com/exec/obidos/tg/detail/-/0345451945/qid=1121024070/
    sr=1-4/refsr_1_4/002-4064754-80888027?v=glance&s=books.
35. Otto Carius, *Tigers in the Mud* (Winnipeg, J. J. Fedorowicz, Inc. 1992), p. 1.
36. *Ibid.*, pp. 1–2.
37. http://www.uwm.edu/-jpipes/start.html; http://www.uwm.edu/-jpipes/jason.htm.
    See also discussion of Antonio Munoz in chapter 6 of this book, Gurus.
38. http://www.uwm.edu/-jpipes/rvol.html; http://www.uwm.edu/-jpipes/wssb.html;
    http://www.oradour.info/appendix/landwehr.htm; http://www.uwm.edu/-jpipes/
    norway.htm; for Feldgrau, see http://feldgrau.com/.

39. http://www.uwm.edu/-jpipes/rvol.html; http://www.uwm.edu/-jpipes/wssb.html; http://www.oradour.info/appendix/landwehr.htm; http://www.uwm.edu/-jpipes/norway.htm.

40. http://www.uwm.edu/-jpipes/start.html.

41. http://www.uwm.edu/cgi-bin/jpipes/poll_lt_v2.0.cgi; http://www.uwm.edu/-jpipes/poll1.html; http://www.uwm.edu/cgi-binjpipes/poll_lt_v2.0.cgi?load=lastpoll.

42. http://www.uwm.edu/-jpipes/spain.html;http://www.uwm.edu/-jpipes/eisb6.html; http://www.uwm.edu/jpipes/spa501.html.

43. http://www.uwm.edu/people/jpipespnzfwd.html; http://www.uwm.edu/-jpipes/glossay.html; http://www.amazon.com/exec/obidos/tg/detail/-/0918184045/qid=1128137778/sr=1-6/ref=sr_1_6/002-4064754-8088802?v=glance&s=books. Shelf Books reprinted the original Landwehr released by Bibliophile Legion Books in 1982 as part of the new Stahlhelm Series. Typical of a guru, Landwehr writes early that the volunteers for the Flemish Legion met the highest standards whereas those men of questionable character often ended up in the resistance movement against the Germans. Later he writes that the Latvians had suffered grievously at the hand of the Soviets and their Jewish collaborators, who helped identify Latvians to be murdered or sent to camps in the Soviet Union. For Landwehr, the German soldiers ended up protecting Latvian Jews from a Latvian population justifiably, in Landwehr's mind, angered with these collaborators. The Germans even safeguarded Jewish synagogues. The Latvians who struck at their fellow Jewish nationals were completely justified and only the kindness and humanity of the Germans provided some measure of protection for these collaborators. So, in an odd twist, the Germans, perpetrators of the Holocaust, ended up defending the very people against whom they conducted a systematic extermination. And the persons who assaulted the local Jewish population, the non-Jewish Latvians, were actually justified in their actions. One can easily see why Landwehr embraced the Deniers' position and even published in their journal. See Richard Landwehr, *Lions of Flanders: Flemish Volunteers of the Waffen-SS-Eastern Front, 1941–1945* (Bradford, West Yorkshire, U.K., 1996), pp. 10, 24–25 and chapter 6.

44. http://www.uwm.edu/-jpipes/book.html.

45. http://www.uwm.edu/-jpipes/book.html.

46. Mark C. Yerger, *Waffen-SS Commanders. The Army, Corps and Division Leaders of Legend: Kruger to Zimmermann* (Atglen, Pa., Schiffer Military History, 1999), pp. 146–63. See also Mark Schmedes, pp. 194–99; Fritz von Scholz, pp. 204–07, Kurt Meyer, pp. 107–14.

47. See James Lucas, *War on the Eastern Front, the German Slider in Russia, 1941–1945* (London, the Military Book Club, 1991); *The Last Year of the German Army, May 1944–May 1945* (London, Arms and Armor, 1994); *Das Reich: The Military Role of 2nd S Division* (London, Arms and Armor Press, 1991), see Acknowledgment for thanks to Weidinger and Yerger, *Hitler's Commanders: German Bravery in the Field 1939–1945* (London, Cassell & Co., 2000). The men covered in this book all won the prestigious Knight's Cross, see Preface, pp. 7–11, and as an account that praises German battlefield performance, it demonstrates the sympathies of Lucas for the Wehrmacht and Waffen-SS. See also Werner Haupt, *Army Group North The Wehrmacht in Russia, 1941–1945* (Atglen, Pa., Schiffer Publishing Ltd., 1997), *Army*

Group South: The Wehrmacht in Russia, 1941–1945 (Atglen, Schiffer Publishing Ltd., 1998); *Army Group Center: The Wehrmacht in Russia, 1941–1945* (Atglen, Schiffer Publishing Ltd., 1997). These are translations of German editions. Haupt served in the Wehrmacht in the Northern theater; Alex Bruchner, *The German Defensive Battles in the Eastern Front 1944* (Atglen, Schiffer Publishing Ltd., 1991). See http://www.uwm.edu/-jpipes/book.html, pp. 1–10.

48. http://www.uwm.edu/-jpipes/wwboard/messagesnew/3052.html; see on same address, 3056, 3059, 3067, 3069; for bibliographical data on Rikmenspoel's books, see http://www.amazon.com/exec/obidos/tg/detail/-/0971765081/ref=pd_bxgy_text_1/002-4064754-80888027?v=glance$s=books&st=*; http://www.amazon .com/exec/obidos/ASIN/0921991428/qid=1123803227/sr=2-1/ref=pd. The title of the Rikmenspoel book is *Soldiers of the Waffen-SS: Many Nations, One Motto* (Winnipeg, J. J. Fedorowicz, 1999).

49. http://www.uwm.edu/-jpipes/wwboard/messagesnew4/128.html; with the same website address, see also 333, 339, 253, 223, 192, 175, 213, 156, 214, 150, 155, 161, 162, 217, 134, 133, 138, 221, 131, 146, 145, 148, 222, 129, 130, 218.

50. http://www.uwm.edu/-jpipes/wwboard/messagesnew4/128.html; with the same website address, see also 333, 339, 253, 223, 192, 175, 213, 156, 214, 150, 155, 161, 162, 217, 134, 133, 138, 221, 131, 146, 145, 148, 222, 129, 130, 218.

51. http://www.uwm.edu/-jpipes/wwboard/messages/1356.html. See 1361, 1381, 1359 at this same site.

52. http://ww.uwm.edu/-jpipes/wwboard/messages/1367.html; and at the same site, see 1367, 1383, 1385, 1386. For exchanges on the Waffen-SS, see http://www. uwm.edu/-jpipes/message/510.html and 511, 529, 975 for the Prinz Eugen Division; http://uwm.edu/-jpipes/wwboard/messages/477.html and 665, 484, 485 for Dutch Waffen-SS Officers; http://www.uwm.edu/-jpipes/wwboard/ messages/432.html and 434 and http://www.uwm.edu/-jpipes/wwboard/ messagesnew4/25588.html and 25575, 25543, 25553, and 25593 for SS rank.

53. http://www.uwm.edu/-jpipes/wwboard/messagesmew4/31978.html; see also in same exchanges, 135, 50, 41, 19, 16, 11, 31994, 9, 31925, 31931.

54. http://www.uwm.edu/-jpipies/wwboard/messagesnew2/4590.html and 4548; see also http://www.uwm.edu/~jpipes/wwboard/messagesnew1/3346.html for Landwehr piece on "British Members of the Waffen-SS in WWII." Marc Rikmenspoel, who posted the recommendation, also gave Landwehr's *Siegrunen* address, as well as the price for the booklet on the topic. For further discussion in this exchange, see 3390, 3379, 3376, 3331; for a reference to Landwehr's out-of-print book, *Narva 1944: The Waffen-SS and the battle for Europe*, see http://www.uwm.edu/-jpipes/wwboard/messagesnew2/4451.html and, in the same location, 4535.

55. http://www.uwm.edu/-jpipes/wwboard/messagesnew4/30127.html see also in the same exchange, 30134; Franz Kurowski, *Hitler's Last Battalion: The Final Battles for the Reich 1944–1945* (Atglen, Pa., Schiffer Publishing, 1998), pp. 201–22.

56. http://www.uwm.edu/-jpipes/wwboard/messagesnew2/4055.html and 4044, 4043, 4031, and 4029.

57. http://www.uwm.edu/-jpipes/wwboard/messagesnew2/6211.html; see also, in same exchange, 6384, 6216, 6334; http://www.uwm.edu/-jpipes/wwboard/ messagesnew1/639.html, in same exchange, see 718, 724, 744; http://www.uwm

.edu/-jpipes/wwwboard/messagesnew5/2696.html; in same exchange, see 2727, 2714, 2993, 3050, 3106; http://www.uwm.edu/-jpipes/wwwboard/messages/481 .html; in same exchange, see 499, 504, 988; for exchanges that include references to Paul Carrel; see http://www.uwm.edu/-jpipes/wwwboard/messagesnew2/ 6100.html, in same exchange see 6109, 6110, 6121, 6339, 6142, 6102, 6145, 6124, 6150. In one posting, a respondent wrote, "Carell has not only written the best books covering the Russo-German war, but the best books covering WWII at all." For Lucas, see James Lucas, *The Last Year of the German Army, May 1944 – May 1945* (London, Arms and Armour, 1994).

58. http://www.uwm.edu/-jpipes/wwwboard/messagesnew2/6229.html, for the complete exchange, see also 6306, 6300, 6327, 6347, 6381. The individual who accused Erickson of being the ultimate Soviet apologist, Doug Nash, apparently developed a close enough relationship with the veterans of the 5th SS Wiking Division to be invited to a reunion of one of the former unit's tank regiments – see 6347 and http://www.uwm.edu/-jpipes/wwwboard/messagesnew2/4424.html.

59. *See footnote 58.*

60. http://www.uwm.edu/-jpipes/wwwboard/messagesnew4/29363.html; see also in this exchange, 29491, 29712, 29335, and 29398; http://www.uwm.edu/-jpipes/ wwwboard/messagesnew4.29768.html. For discussions of the NKVD, see Michael Kort, *The Soviet Colossus: A History of the USSR* (New York, Charles Scribner's Sons, 1985), pp. 184, 193 196–97 209–10; John Erickson, *The Road to Stalingrad* (New York, Harper & Row Publishers, 1975), pp. 59, 69, 70. As these works make clear, the NKVD also ran an enormous economic empire of slave labor camps. It also played a central role in the purges of the 1930s; see also Robert Service, *A History of Twentieth-Century Russia* (Cambridge, Mass., Harvard University Press, 1997), pp. 219–25.

61. http://www.uwm.edu/-jpipes/wwwboard/messagesnew4/29363.html; see also in this exchange, 29491, 29712, 29335, and 29398; on Eicke, see the exchange at http:// www.uwm.edu/-jpipes/wwboard/messagesnew/2071.html; in the same exchange, see 2077, 2082, 2085, 2088. For a short biographical sketch of Eicke, see Marc J. Rikmenspoel, *Waffen-SS The Encyclopedia* (New York, The Military Book club, 2002), pp. 206–10. For a description of the *Waffen-SS Encyclopedia* and extremely favorable reader reaction see the Amazon site, http://www.amazon.com/ exec/obidos/tg/detail/-/0971765081/qid=1115140053/sr=1-2/refsr12/103-8958436-7746218?v=glance&s=books.

62. http://www.uwm.edu/-jpipes/wwwboard/messages/1686.html.

63. http://www.uwm.edu/-jpipes/wwwboard/messages/1686.html.

64. http://www.uwm.edu/-jpipes/wwwboard/messages/1686.html; For examples of Allied war crimes against the Germans, see http:www.uwm.edu/jpipes/wwwboard/ messagesnew3/15694.html; see also in same exchange, 15702, 15744, 15815, 16037, 15852, 15892, 15879, 15823, 15881,15777; for a discussion of German war cemeteries in Russia and their destruction by the Communists after the war, see http://ww.uwm.edu/-jpipes/wwwboard/messagesnew1/920.html; see also in same exchange, 1045, 933, 939, 941. In the discussion, it is noted that since the end of the Communist regime in Russia, that German organization, in cooperation with locals, has been uncovering German burial sites in the Stalingrad area and

then reburying them in a new cemetery. The commentator noted, "it is a worthy undertaking because these men, like all fallen soldiers everywhere, deserve a decent resting place." (See p. 939).

65. http://www.uwm.edu/-jpipes/wwwboard/messagesnew4/29822.html; see also in the same exchange, 29836, 29834, 29871; http://www.uwm.edu/-jpipes/wwwboard/messagesnew2/6354.html; see in same exchange, 6436, 6357, 6362, 6492, 6356; http://www.uwm.edu/-jpipes/wwwboard/messagesnew4/29347.html; see also in same exchange, 29358, 29365; for other examples see an exchange on what was the "Kampfgruppe," http://www.uwm.edu/-jpipes/wwwboard/messagesnew1.138.html; see also in the same exchange, 130, 134, 144, 152; see an exchange on the "German use of USSR railway network," http://www.uwm.edu/-jpipes/wwwboard/messagesnew1/979.html; see also in same exchange, 982, 999, 1035, 1064, 1066, 1243991; see an exchange on "Who actually beat the Germans, http://www.uwm.edu/-jpipes/wwwboard/messagesnew4/1687.html; see also in same exchange, 1966, 1992, 1973, 22020, 1931, 1806, 1817, 2204, 1866, 2268, 1701, 1741, 1743, 1770, 1781, 1800, 1784, 1819, 1825, 1765; see an exchange on "How rare were religious services in German war areas?" http://www.uwm.edu/-jpipes/wwwboard/messages/759.html; see also in same exchange, 829, 802, 796, 803, 800; see an exchange on "German losses in East vs West Front," http://www.uwm.edu/-jpipes/wwwboard/messagesnew4/30185.html; see also in same exchange, 30208, 30251 and http://www.uwm.edu/-jpipes/stats.html.

66. http://www.uwm.edu/-jpipes/wwwboard/welcome.html; http://www.uwm.edu/-jpipes/bios.html; http://www.uwm.edu/jpipes/wwwboard/messagesnew2/5571.html; http://www.uwm.edu/-jpipes/wwwboard/messagesnew2/4438.html; http://www.uwm.edu/-jpipes/wwwboard/messagesnew2/4476.html.

67. http://www.uwm.edu/-jpipes/wwwboard/welcome.html; http://www.uwm.edu/-jpipes/bios.html; http://www.uwm.edu/jpipes/wwwboard/messagesnew2/5571.html; http://www.uwm.edu/-jpipes/wwwboard/messagesnew2/4438.html; http://www.uwm.edu/-jpipes/wwwboard/messagesnew2/4476.html.

68. http://www.geocities.com/~orion47/. This website address still connects the visitor with the updated site; http://www.geocities.com/~orion47/author.html; http//www.axishistory.com/; http://www.forces70.freeserve.co.uk/; http://home.inreach.com/rickylaw/dictatorship/general/links.html; http://www.InsideTheWeb.com/messageboard/mbs.cgi?acct=mb172947&MyNum=928549264&P=No&TL=928549264; http://www.panzerdiesel.com/eng/e340.html.

69. In one remarkable case, the participant was Russian and his grandfathers fought the Germans all the way to Berlin. The young man complained of the ideological character of the history of World War Two he encountered while in Russian schools. Free from that regime, he now began to grasp the German struggle and experiences; sources 31273, 31251, 31311, 31330, 31277, 31234. (For all the exchanges, see the following Internet sites, footnotes: http://www.uwm.edu/~jpipes/wwwboard/messagenne4/31191.html, add 31556, 31554, 31458, 31417, 31448, 31408, 31330, 31327, 31321, 31311, 31307, 31299, 31298, 31278, 31277, 31272, 31251, 31217, 31214, 31193, 31233, 31215, 31298, 31225, 31195, 31226, 31273, 31232, 31234, 31252, 31276, 31312. The title of the exchange under which the conversations are grouped is "I was wondering, how did everyone get interested in the Wehrmacht in the first place?" April 17, 2000, Monday.

70. http://www.uwm.edu/~jpipes/wwwboard/messagenne4/31191.html;   footnotes 31215, 31225, 31266, 21232, 31234, 31252, 31276, 31307, 31278, and 31272. Ironically, Davies' very first encounter with the Eastern Front came with the purchase of the 1965 Bantam edition of Carell's *Hitler Moves East* within weeks of its release. Its relatively low cost, $1.25, and the author having little knowledge of the Russian participation in World War Two, the product of a keen educational system, led him to buy the book and several hundred more works on the Eastern Front along with several hundred wargames over the next thirty-five years! It clearly had the same impact as recorded by many of the participants in the discussion noted.

71. http://www.uwm.edu/~jpipes/wwwboard/messagenne4/31191.html; footnotes 31193, 31233, 31215, 31298, 31225, 31266, 31232, 31234, 31252, 31276, 31417, 31327, 31397, 31298, 31278, 31272, 31251.

72. http://www.uwm.edu/~jpipes/wwwboard/messagenne4/31191.html; 31214, 31208, 31226, 31234, 31485, 31330, 31272, 31251.

73. http://www.uwm.edu/~jpipes/wwwboard/messagenne4/31191.html;   footnotes 31566, 31327, 31311, 31226, 31448, 31311. By horror, we refer to the Nazi goals of reorganizing and removing whole peoples in the East. At the start of the war, German commanders and soldiers were well aware of Hitler's orders concerning the rules of conduct in war, which govern combat and civilian relations in the West. These would hold no power in the East, the longstanding area for Hitler's Lebensraum. Whole peoples would be reduced, enslaved, or removed. Certainly, the treatment of civilians and POWs as well as the fierceness of combat demonstrated that rules of war were at best a footnote in this brutal theater. See Omer Bartov, *The Barbarisation of War on the Eastern Front, 1941–1945* (New York, St. Martin's Press, 1986).

8. Romancing the War: Reenactors, and "What If History"

1. For a general website that features reenactment groups for World War Two, see "World War II, Reenactment & Historical Links," http://www.anderfront.com/cuslinks.htm. This site also lists links to a Reenactment Event Calendar, "Assorted Reenactment Related Sites," "Assorted Military History Sites," "Sources for Militaria and Books," and addresses of "Reenactment Societies." Thirteen exist within the United States and Two in England. By typing in *Wehrmacht*, Eastern Front, World War 2 on the *aol.com* search engine, twelve sites appeared. These ranged from the World War Two Reenactment/History Links to Military Books Online. Each title has an e-mail address. One word of caution – some sites such as "Assaults on the Truth and Memory: Holocaust Denial in Context – part 1" may offend readers. One can also click the notation, "Show me more like this" for additional, related sites. Netscape turns up different and more numerous sites, plus the availability of different search engines on Netscape, such as Google, turn up more varied sites on this topic. For material on the history of reenacting, see: "*1SS Leibstandarte*," http://www.lssah.com/unit%20hist.html; "World War 2 Reenacting," http://www.reenactor.net/main.htmls/ww2.html & "World War 2 Reenacting: Parent Organization," http://www.reenactor.net/WW2/ww2_orgs.html. For the

growing sophistication of reenacting as of January 2006, see the five pages of websites that serve as an introduction to reenacting, http://ww2reenactors. proboards35.com/. For collector's guides to Waffen-SS memorabilia, see Robin Lumsden, *Collector's Guide to the Waffen-SS* (Hersham, Surrey, Ian Allan Publishing, Ltd., 2000); Lumsden, *A Collector's Guide to the Allgemeine-SS* (Hersham, Surrey, Ian Allan Publishing, Ltd., 2002); Lumsden, *A Collector's Guide to Third Reich Militaria* (Hersham, Surrey, Ian Allen Publishing, 2000), Lumsden, *A Collector's Guide to the Third Reich Militaria: Detecting the Fakes* (Hersham, Surrey, UK, Ian Allen Publishing, 2001); and Chris Ellis, *A Collector's Guide to the History and Uniforms of Das Heer: The German Army 1933–45* (Hersham, Surrey, UK, Ian Allen Publishing, 1993).

2. Jenny Thompson, *War Games: Inside the World of Twentieth-Century Reenactors* (Washington, D.C., Smithsonian Books, 2004), pp. 36–37, 44–46.

3. See "1SS Leibstandarte," http://www.lssah.com/unit%20hist.html; "World War 2 Re-enacting: Parent Organization," http://www.reenactor.net/WW2/ww2_orgs. html; "World War 2 Re-enacting," http://www.reenactor.net/main.htmls/ww2.html. Thompson estimates some 6,000 mostly men belong to twentieth-century reenactment groups. See Thompson, *War Games*, p. xiv. For twentieth-century reenactors recruited mostly from Civil War groups, see Thompson, *War Games*, p. 63.

4. http://www.1saah.com/komm.html; "1SS Leibstandarte" http://www.lssah.com/ unit%20hist.html; "World War 2 Re-enacting: Parent Organization," http://www. reenactor.net/WW2/ww2_orgs.html, "World War 2 Reenacting," http://www. reenactor.net/main.htmld/ww2.html.

5. See: "1SS Leibstandarte" http://www.lssah.com/unit%20hist.html; "World War 2 Re-enacting: Parent Organization," http://www.reenactor.net/WW2/ww2_orgs. html, "World War 2 Reenacting," http://www.reenactor.net/main.htmls/ww2. html.

6. See: "1SS Leibstandarte," http://www.lssah.com/unit%20hist.html; "World War 2 Re-enacting: Parent Organization" http://www.reenactor.net/WW2/ww2_orgs. html, "World War 2 Reenacting," http://www.reenactor.net/main.htmls/ww2.html.

7. *1SS Leibstandarte*, http://www.lssah.com/unit%20hist.html; "World War II, Reenactment & Historical Links," http://www.anderfront.com/enslinks.htm; http://www.lssah.com/news.html; http://www.lssah.com/batt.html. See Thompson, *War Games*, p. 61 for impact of the Internet. See http://www.1ssah.com/.

8. http://www.lssah.com/kt2.html; http://lssah.com/batt.html. Authenticity guided the *1 SS Leibstansdarte*. For this emphasis, see "Die SS Soldat," http://www.1ssah .com/SS%20soldat.html for a discussion of reenactor's "impression" or his uniform, equipment, weapons, and all the accoutrements of a 1940s German's gear and outfit.

9. http://www.geocities.com/ww2_links/axis.html; "World War II, Reenactment & Historical Links," http://www.anderfront.com/enslinks.htm.

10. For societies such as the Northwest Historical Association and the California Historical Group, see http://www.reenactor.net/WW2/ww2_orgs.html; "World War II, Reenactment & Historical Links," http://www.anderfront.com/enslinks.htm; for the Texas Military Historical Society, see http://www.io.com/-tog/tmhs.html. By 2006, reenactment groups had appeared across the globe, from New Zealand to

Europe; see "WW II Reenactors' Nexus," http://www.geocities.com/ww2 links/
societies.html. Often, reenactors are collectors of war memorabilia; see Thompson,
War Games, p. xv and, for a lengthy list of re-enactor vocabulary, see also pp. 289–
95. For a website that covers all areas of reenacting from the Bronze and Iron
Ages to the Present, see "Reenactors World Plus," http://www.reenactorsworldplus
.com/. One can set up a free e-mail account at this site that gives you access to a
wide range of resources. For examples of manufacturers, see http://users.jnlk.com/
militaria/. For pictures of equipment, see http://users.jnlk.com/militaria/
pictures.htm; for an array of diverse products designed for reenactors, see
http://users.jnlk.com/militaria/whatsnew.htm; for advertisements of various manufacturers and suppliers, see http://www.1ssah.com/waffen.html. For a mention
of the first annual convention see, "NEWS," http://members.aol.com/soldaten/
main.htm and http://www.reenactorfest.com/.

11. Thompson, *War Games*, pp. 7–8, 10, 26, 38, 48, 51, 62–63, 77, 79, 84.

12. Thompson, *War Games*, pp. 26–27.

13. Thompson, *War Games*, pp. 50–51, 56–59, 68, 72, 87. For remarks about the hos-
    tility German reenactors provoke, see Thompson, *War Games*, pp. 114, 125.

14. Thompson, *War Games*, p. 58. I make the assumption that the dinner provides
    the occasion to celebrate their involvement in reenacting and commemorating
    the German army. No doubt, the men, and these are almost always men, also
    take great enjoyment from the dinner gathering. Thompson also writes that the
    reenactors are well aware of the view that reenacting is strange and a few even admit
    their own feelings that reenacting is unusual. Mostly, these men believe they are
    "misunderstood." See Thompson, *War Games*, p. 59, 134.

15. Thompson, *War Games*, pp. xx–xxi, 96–97.

16. "Homepage," http://members.xoomco./Falcon.Div/.

17. http://freehosting2.at.webjump.com/02e743cb6/a1/w2hpg/index2.html. The
    group was headquartered in Bensalem, Pa. in 2000. See http://freehosting2.at.
    webjump.com/02e743106/a1/w2hpg/officers.html.

18. "World War II Reenacting: The Parent Organization," http://www.reenactor.net/
    WW2/ww2_orgs.html; see also http://www.io.com/-tog/tmhs.html.

19. Thompson, *War Games*, pp. 104, 108–09.

20. Thompson, *War Games*, pp. 109–11.

21. Thompson, *War Games*, pp. 2–3, 14, 88, 145, 150–51, 164–65, 172–73.

22. "*Waffen-SS* Ranks," http://www.lssah.com/ranks.html. For awards for perfor-
    mance in reenacting events, see "Unit Awards and Decorations," http://www.1ssah
    .com/awards.html.

23. "Rank, Military Courtesy and Organization of the Army, *Dienstgrad* and *Gliederung
    des Heeres*," http://www.reenactor.net/WW2/articles/ger-rank.html.

24. "Vehicles of the LAH," http://www.lssah.com/vehicles.html; http://www.lssah
    .com/field2.html.htm; http://www.1ssah.com/panzerkampfwagen_381.htm;
    http://www.1ssah.com/truck.kubel.222.html.

25. Weapons of the LAH," http://www.lssah.com/LAH%20weapons.html.

26. "German Re-enactor's Appearance," http://www.reenactor.net/WW2/articles/
    appearance_grm.html; "Appearance Standards," http://www.reencator.net/WW2/
    articles/WW2_appear_main.html; "Frundsberg Uniform Requirement," http://
    members.xoom.com/FalconDiv/.

27. "German Re-enactor's Appearance," http://www.reenactor.net/WW2/articles/appearance_grm.html; "Appearance Standards," http://www.reencator.net/WW2/articles/WW2_appear_main.html; "Frundsberg Uniform Requirement," http://members.xoom.com/FalconDiv/. See also Thompson, *War Games*, pp. 210–13.

28. "German Reenactor's Appearance," http://www.reenactor.net/WW2/articles/appearance_grm.html; "Appearance Standards," http://www.reencator.net/WW2/articles/WW2_appear_main.html; "Frundsberg Uniform Requirement," http://members.xoom.com/FalconDiv/.

29. "Re-enactor Items and Collector Reference Books For Sale," http://www.vvm.com/~histpart/books.htm.

30. "W2HPG: Authenticity Guidelines," http://freehosting2.at.webjump.com/3a69490ee/a1/w2hpg/ger1_auth_regs.html and "W2HPG: Authenticity Guidelines," http:freehosting2.at.webjump.com/3a69490ee/allW2hpg/authen.html.

31. http://www.reenactor.net/WW2/ww2_read.html.

32. "Der Rekrut," http://www.reenactor.net/WW2/rekrut.htm; "World War II," http://www.reenactor.net/main.htmls/ww2.html. http://members.aol.com/soldaten/rekrut.htm.

33. "So You Want To Be A German Soldier," http://www.lssah.com/art1.html.

34. *Ibid.*

35. "Die Grundausbildung," http://www.lssah.com/art2.html.

36. "Advanced Impression," http://www.lssah.com/taylor.html.

37. Thompson, *War Games*, pp. 66–67, 212–17. See "'Farbs You Find Everywhere'"; see also Tony Horwitz, *Confederates in the Attic: Dispatches from the Unfinished Civil War* (New York, Pantheon Books, 1998), pp. 10–11. See also "The Definition of FARB," http://www.reenactors.net/WW2/articles/on_farbs.html. For the calendar of events, for reenactors for 2006, see http://www.1ssah.com/events.html.

38. Thompson, *War Games*, pp. 10, 72–73.

39. "Readings," http://www.reenactor.net/WW2/ww2_read.html.

40. *Ibid.*

41. *Ibid.*

42. R. H. S. Stolfi, *Hitler's Panzers East: A Reinterpretation of World War II* (Norman, University of Oklahoma Press, 1991), dust jacket, page facing the Contents page. For a list of some of these alternate accounts see http://www.amazon.co.uk/exec/obidos/ASIN/1853674923/infoline0F-21/202-5682923-6367861. The site lists some nine works that address World War Two. These use several ploys in their accounts of how the Germans win or come much closer to winning. A. Edward Cooper, in his *The Triumph of the Third Reich* (n.p. Agerka Books, 1999), gives the Germans the capacity to produce an atomic bomb that is used on the Allies at Normandy and on the Russians in the East. In the account, disgruntled officers assassinate Hitler and replace him with Field Marshall Erwin Rommel, the good officer who takes over leadership of the German state. In David Downing's *The Moscow option: An Alternative Second World War* (London, Military Book Club, 1979), Hitler suffers debilitating injury in a badly planned landing of his airplane. Hitler was unable to assume his position of leadership when Barbarossa began and direction of the campaign fell into the hands of the professional military. Without his interference, the field marshals led the German armies into Moscow and victory.

Yet, in the end, the Germans suffer defeat at the hands of the United States and the British.

43. See citations and discussion in footnote 1.

44. Maj. Gen. F. W. Von Mellenthin, *Panzer Battles: A Study of the Employment of Armor in the Second World War* (New York, Ballantine Books, 1971).

45. For the planning, see Stolfi, *Hitler's Panzers East*, pp. 15–19 and for tactics, see also pp. 107–17.

46. For assets, see Stolfi, *Hitler's Panzers East*, pp. 15–19.

47. Two pictures facing the title page stress the role of initiative and dynamism in the German army. One shows a Russian KV-1 tank destroyed by the Germans, a tank that surprised the Germans when they encountered it. The other picture focuses on a German anti-aircraft gun, the famous 88' AA, that the Germans adapted to use as a tank killer. The 88' AA showed the flexible nature of the German arms that also depended vitally on initiative at all levels.

48. Stolfi, *Hitler's Panzers East*, pp. 82–83 and, for a general discussion, pp. 77–87.

49. *Ibid.*, pp. ix–xiii, 9–12, 26–32, 41–45.

50. Omar Bartov, *The Eastern Front, 1941–45, German Troops and the Barbarisation of Warfare* (New York, St. Martin's Press, 1986), see chapter 4, "Barbarism and Criminality" and p. 99 for the repeated order that the war in Russia "was no ordinary war, for it was against the Jewish-Bolshevik and Mongol population of Russia." See also his *Hitler's Army: Soldiers, Nazis, in the Third Reich* (New York, Oxford University Press, 1992), see chapter 3, "Perversions of Discipline" for a discussion of the brutality that came to characterize the Eastern Front.

51. The officers declared in their memoirs that although such orders were surely issued, few obeyed them. For example, see General Heinz Guderian, *Panzer Leader*, second edition (Cambridge, MA, DeCapo Press, 2002), p. 152; Field Marshal Erich von Manstein, *Lost Victories* (Novato, California, Presidio, 1982), pp. 179–80.

52. Gerhard Weinberg, *A World At Arms: A Global History of World War II* (New York: Cambridge University Press, 1994), pp. 265–67.

53. Gerhard L. Weinberg, *A World at Arms: A Global History of World War II* (New York, 1994), pp. 188–93, 266–67.

54. *Ibid.*, pp. 268–69.

55. Stolfi, *Hitler's Panzers East*, p. 91. For examples of his discussion of atrocities, see also pp. 80, 90–92.

56. *Ibid.*, pp. 85–96 for a discussion of atrocities and the role of the commissars.

57. See earlier chapters for Manstein and Guderian.

58. Stolfi, *Hitler's Panzers East*, pp. 48–55, 77–78, 113, 115, 119–21. Stolfi does praise Manstein as "cool and brilliant," yet is also critical of Manstein in his action in the northern front in July 1941 and his Kursk battle plan, pp. 48–55.

59. Stolfi, *Hitler's Panzers East*, pp. 85–96. Mellenthin, *Panzer Battles*, p. 244, see p. 233 for a description of Zhukov's drinking habits; Paul Carell, *Hitler Moves East 1941–1943* (New York, Bantam Books, 1967), pp. 105–06. For Manstein's description of the Russian soldier, see his *Lost Victories*, pp. 180–81.

60. Omer Bartov, *Hitler's Army: Soldiers, Nazis, and War in the Third Reich* (New York, Oxford University Press, 1991), p. 83. For a general discussion of the treatment of prisoners of war see also the following pages: 61, 69, 71–2, 75, 83–5, 154–55. See also

Omer Bartov, *The Eastern Front, 1941–45: German Troops and the Barbarization of Warfare*, p. 107 and for a general discussion, see also the following pages, 107–19, 129, 152–54.

61. Stolfi, *Hitler's Panzer East*, pp. 67–71. Actually, Stolfi uses very little evidence and merely argues from supposition. For a description of the revisionists, see Gabriel Gorodetsky, *Grand Illusion: Stalin and the German Invasion of Russia* (New Haven, Conn., Yale University Press, 1999), Preface and subsequent analysis. For an example of the German generals suggesting this idea, see Manstein, *Lost Victories*, p. 181.

62. See Glantz in *What If?*

63. David M. Glantz and Samuel J. Newland, "Hitler's Attack on Russia," in Harold Deutsch and Dennis Showalter (eds.), *What If? Strategic Alternatives of World War II* (Chicago, Ill., Emperor's Press, 1970), pp. 55–67. Newland's section, "What if Hitler had striven to make allies of the Soviet peoples," appears on pp. 62–64.

64. "About the Authors," in *What If?*, pp. 270–72.

65. Newlands, *What If*, pp. 62–64. For an example of a pro-Latvian account of the activities of an allied German unit, see Arthur Silgailis, *The Latvian Legion* (San Jose, CA. R. James Bender Publishing, 1986).

66. Newlands, *What If*, pp. 62–64; "Foreign Volunteers," http://www.axishistory.com/index.php?id=308, pp. 1–2, 9.

67. Newlands, *What If*, pp. 62–64.

68. *Ibid.*

69. "Foreign Volunteers," http://www.axishistory.com/index.php?in=308 and "The RONA and Kaminsky Brigade," http://www.uwm.edu/-jpipes/kaminski.html, pp. 1–2.

Conclusion

1. Helene Keyssar and Vladimir Pozner, *Remembering War: A U.S.-Soviet Dialogue* (New York, Oxford University Press, 1990), p. xi.

2. http://www.soldat.com/

3. http://www.soldat.com/soldbucher.htm. This is part of the *Soldat FHQ* website.

4. http://www.soldat.com/soldbucher.htm.

5. http://www.soldat.com/

6. www.worldwartworhs.org

7. http://www.feldgrau.net/phpBB2/viewtopic.php?t+15126. The list of books on this website notes Hans Schmidt's *SS-Panzergrenadier: A True Story of World War II*, published privately by the author yet widely available, including on *Amazon.com*. It opens with a description of battle that involved the author. The fight pitted young Germans, almost kids, as the author writes, against U.S. soldiers. Schmidt describes the battle and its aftermath as an atrocity of the first order. The account clearly attempts to paint the United States with the same brush used to color the German atrocities.

8. http://www.feldgrau.net/phpBB2/viewtopic.php?t=22.126, http://www.feldgrau.net/phpBB2/viewtopic.php?t=21490, http://www.feldgrau.net/phpBB2/viewtopic.php?t=17784, http://www.feldgrau.net/phpBB2/viewtopic.php?t=17999.

9. http://www.feldgrau.net/phpBB2/viewtopic.php?t=90&sid=b10e4b129c2571d 3dbfb 89627e190d7a.

10. Fritz Bartelmann, "Besieged Outside Stalingrad," *MHQ: The Quarterly Journal of Military History* (Winter 2003), 30–33.

11. Interview by Ed McCaul, "Tank Busting Stuka Pilot," *Military History* (August 2001), 42–49.

12. McCaul, "Tank Busting Stuka Pilot," pp. 42–49.

13. Interview by Roger Steinway, "German Horse Soldier on the Eastern Front," *Military History* (January/February 2005), pp. 34–41.

14. For a scathing analysis of the German soldier and his role in war crimes, see Omer Bartov, *Hitler's Army: Soldiers Nazis, and War in the Third Reich* (New York, Oxford University Press, 1992). Scholars in Germany have also taken issue for some time with the claim of the postwar German generals that they fought a "clean" war. Scholarly criticism was strengthened by the "Crimes of the Wehrmacht" traveling exhibit in the 1990s in Germany. However, this information has only begun to penetrate this country on a scholarly level in English language publications. At the popular level, it has not surfaced at all as yet. See Wolfram Wette, *The Wehrmacht: History, Myth, Reality* (Boston, Harvard University Press, 2006), chapter 6.

Bibliography

Archival Sources:

Bundesarchiv/Militärarchiv Freiburg
    N 252 Nachlass Blumentritt
    N 596 Nachlass Büschleb
    N 220 Nachlass Halder
    N 265 Nachlass Heinrici
    N 447 Nachlass Munzel
    N 422 Nachlass Röttiger
    N63 Nachlass Zeitzler
    MSg1/2454
Cornell Law Library
    William Donovan Papers
Herbert Hoover Presidential Library (HHPL)
    Truman Smith Papers
Hoover Institution Archives (HIA)
    Wedemeyer Collection
Institut für Zeitgeschichte, Munich
    ED 91 Nachlass Geyr
National Archives of the United States (NARA)
    CIA-RDP86B00269R000200010025-1
    CIA-RDP80B01676R002800230011-7
    CIA-RDP75-00001R000400410013-5
    M1270, Roll 6, Page 307
    RG 319, Box 71A, Vol. 5, Folder 3. Seventh Army Interrogation Center, 26
        July 1945; Box 71A, Vol. 4, Folder 1 CIC agent report of 5 June, 1950.
Princeton University, Seeley G. Mudd Manuscript Library
    Wedemeyer Collection
    Allen Dulles Papers
Staatsarchiv Nuremberg
    PS 3798 "Denkschrift der Generäle"
University of Notre Dame Archives (CSHU)
    George Shuster Papers

Contemporary Magazines and Newspapers

American Mercury
Chicago Tribune
Christian Century
Fortune
Liberty
Life
Look
Newsweek
Reader's Digest
Saturday Evening Post
Survey Graphic
New York Times
Time
Times Literary Supplement

Books and Articles

Abenheim, Donald, *Reforging the Iron Cross. The Search for Tradition in the West German Armed Forces* (Princeton, NJ, Princeton University Press, 1988).

Abzug, Robert, *Inside the Vicious Heart: Americans and the Liberation of Nazi Concentration Camps* (New York, Oxford University Press, 1985).

Angrick, Andrej, *Besatzungspolitik und Massenmord. Die Einsatzgruppe D in der südlichen Sowjetunion 1941–1943* (Hamburg, Hamburger Edition, 2003).

———. "Im Windschatten der 11. Armee. Die Einsatzgruppe D," Gerhard Paul and Klaus-Michael Mallmann (eds.), *Die Gestapo im Zweiten Weltkrieg. 'Heimatfront und besetzten Europa* (Darmstadt, Wissenschaftliche Buchgesellshaft, 2000).

Annon, Noel, *Changing Enemies. The Defeat and Regeneration of Germany* (New York, Norton, 1995).

Argersinger, Steven J., "Karl von Clausewitz: Analysis of FM 100–5," *Military Review*, Vol. 66, No. 2 (February 1986).

Bajohr, Frank, *Parvenüs und Profiteure. Korruption in der NS-Zeit* (Frankfurt, S. Fischer, 2001).

Bartov, Omer, *Hitler's Army: Soldiers, Nazis, and War in the Third Reich* (New York, Oxford University Press, 1992).

———. *The Eastern Front 1941–1945: The German Troops and the Barbarisation of Warfare* (New York, St. Martin's Press, 1986).

Bartelmann, Fritz, "Besieged Outside Stalingrad," *MHQ: The Quarterly Journal of Military History* (Winter 2003).

Basinger, Jeanne, *The World War II Combat Film: Anatomy of a Genre* (New York, Columbia University Press, 1986).

Beaumont, Roger A., "On the Wehrmacht Mystique," *Military Review*, Vol. 66, No. 7 (July 1986).

———. "'Wehrmacht Mystique' Revisited," Vol. 70, No. 2 (February 1990).

Bendersky, Joseph, *The "Jewish Threat." Anti-Semitic Politics of the U.S. Army* (New York, Basic Books, 2000).

Benz, Wigbert, *Paul Carell. Ribbentrop's Pressechef Paul Karl Schmidt vor und nach 1945* (Berlin, Wissenschaftlicher Verlag, 2005).

Berkhoff, Karel C., *Harvest of Despair: Life and Death in Ukraine under Nazi Rule* (Cambridge, Mass., Belknap Press of Harvard University Press, 2004).

Bidermann, Herbert, *In Deadly Combat: A German Soldier's Memoir of the Eastern Front* (Lawrence, University of Kansas Press, 2000).

Bird, Kai, *The Chairman: John J. McCloy and the Making of the American Establishment* (New York, Simon & Shuster, 1992).

Blight, David, *Race and Reunion: The Civil War in American Memory* (Boston, Mass., Belknap Press, 2001).

Bohn, Thomas W., *An Historical and Descriptive Analysis of the "Why We Fight" Series* (New York, Arno Press, 1977).

Boll, Bernd and Hans Safrian, "On the Way to Stalingrad: The 6th Army in 1941–42," in Hannes Heer and Klaus Naumann (eds.), *War of Extermination. The German Military in World War II* (New York and Oxford, Berghahn Books, 2000).

Bosch, William J., *Judgment on Nuremberg: American Attitudes toward the Major German War-crime Trials* (Chapel Hill, NC, University of North Carolina Press, 1970).

Bourke-White, Margaret, *Shooting the Russian War* (New York, Simon and Schuster, 1942).

Bower, Tom, *Blind Eye to Murder. Britain, America and the Purging of Nazi Germany – a Pledge Betrayed* (London, Andre Deutsch, 1981).

Bracher, K. D. (ed.), *Deutschland zwischen Krieg und Frieden* (Düsseldorf, Droste Verlag, 1991).

Browder, Dewey, *Americans in Post-World War Two Germany* (Lewiston, NY, Edwin Mellen, 1998).

Bruchner, Alex, *The German Defensive Battles in the Eastern Front 1944* (Atglen, PA, Schiffer Publishing Ltd., 1991).

Burdick, Charles, "Deutschland und die Entwicklung der amtlichen amerikanischen Militärgeschichtsforschung (1920–1960)," in K. D. Bracher (ed.), *Deutschland zwischen Krieg und Frieden* (Düsseldorf, Droste Verlag, 1991).

———. "Vom Schwert zur Feder. Deutsche Kriegsgefangene im Dienst der Vorbereitung der amerikanischen Kriegsgeschichtsschreibung über den Zweiten Weltkrieg. Die organisatorische Entwicklung der Operational History (German) Section," *Militärgeschichtliche Mitteilungen* 10 (1971).

Burleigh, Michael, *The Third Reich. A New History* (New York, Hill & Wang, 2000).

Buscher, Frank, *The U.S. War Crimes Trial Program, 1946–1955* (New York, Greenwood Press, 1989).

Carell, Paul, *Hitler Moves East 1941–1943* (New York, Bantam Books, 1967).

———. *Hitler Moves East 1941–1943* (New York, Bantam, 1965).

———. *Scorched Earth. Hitler Moves East* (New York, Ballantine, 1966).

Carlson, Verner R., "Portrait of a German General Staff Officer," *Military Review*, Vol. 70, No. 4 (April 1990).

Carroll, Wallace, *We're in this with Russia* (Boston, Houghton Mifflin, 1942).

Chamberlin, William H., *The Russian Enigma* (New York, C. Scribner's Sons, 1943).

Chipman, N. P., *The Andersonville Prison Trial. The Trial of Captain Henry Wirz* (Birmingham, Ala., Notable Trials Library, 1990).

———. *The True Story of Andersonville Prison. A Defense of Major [sic] Henry Wirz* (reprinted Iberian Publ. Co., 1991).

Cooper, Edward, *The Triumph of the Third Reich* (Agerka Books, 1999, n.p.).

Creveld, Martin, "Die deutsche Wehrmacht: eine militärische Beurteilung," in Rolf-Dieter Müller and Hans-Erich Volkmann (eds.), *Die Wehrmacht. Mythos und Realität* (Munich, Oldenbourg, 1999).

———. *Fighting Power. Germans and U.S. Army Performance, 1939–1945* (Westport, Conn., Greenwood Books, 1982).

———. "On Learning From the Wehrmacht and Other Things" *Military Review*, Vol. 68, No. 1 (January 1988).

Dershowitz, Alan, foreword to N. P. Chipman, *The Andersonville Prison Trial. The Trial of Captain Henry Wirz* (Birmingham, Ala., Notable Trials Library, 1990).

DePuy, William, Romie Brownlee, and William Mullen, *Changing an Army: An Oral History of General William E. DePuy, USA Retired* (Carlisle Barracks, Pa. and Washington DC, U.S. Military Institute and Army Center of Military History, 1986).

Detwiler, Donald (ed.), *World War II German Military Studies. A Collection of 213 special reports on the Second World War prepared by former officers of the Wehrmacht for the United States Army* (New York, Garland Publishing, 1979).

Deutsch, Harold and Dennis Showalter (eds.), *What If? Strategic Alternatives of World War II* (Chicago, Ill., Emperor's Press, 1970).

Dirks, Carl and Karl-Heinz Janßen, *Der Krieg der Generäle. Hitler als Werkzeug der Wehrmacht* (Berlin, Propyläen, 1999).

Downing, David, *The Moscow option. An Alternative Second World War* (London, Military Book Club, 1979).

DuPuy, T. N., *Generals Balck and von Mellenthin on Tactics: Implications for NATO Military Doctrine* (MacLean, Va., BDM Corporation, 1980).

———. *A Genius for War. The German Army and General Staff, 1807–1945* (Englewood Cliffs, NJ, Prentice-Hall, 1977).

Echevarria II, Antulio J., "Auftragstaktik: In Its Proper Perspective," *Military Review*, Vol. 66, No. 10 (October 1986).

Ellis, Chris, *A Collector's Guide to the History and Uniforms of Das Heer: The German Army 1933–45* (Hersham, Surrey, UK, Ian Allen Publishing, 1993).

Ellis, John, *Brute Force* (New York, Viking, 1999).

Erickson, John, *The Road to Berlin Continuing the History of Stalin's War with Germany* (Boulder, Colo., Westview Press, 1983).

———. *The Road to Stalingrad, Stalin's War with Germany, volume 1* (New York, Harper & Row, Publishers, 1975).

———. *The Soviet High Command: A Military-Political History 1918–1941* (Boulder, Colo., Westview Press, 1984).

Förster, Jürgen, "Das Unternehmen Barbarossa als Eroberungs-und Vernichtungskrieg in Militärgeschichtliches Forschungsamt," in *Das Deutsche Reich und der Zweite Weltkrieg*, Vol. IV, *Der Angriff auf die Sowietunion* (Stuttgart, DVA, 1999).

———. "Hitler als Kriegsherr," in S. Förster, M. Pöhlmann and D. Walter (eds.), *Kriegsherren in der Weltgeschichte. Von Xerxes bis Nixon* (München, 2006).

———. "Hitler Turns East – German War Policy in 1940 and 1941," in Bernd Wegner (ed.), *From Peace to War. Germany, Soviet Russia and the World, 1939–1941* (Providence, RI, Berghahn Books, 1997).

Förster, S., M. Pöhlmann, and D. Walter (eds)., *Kriegsherren in der Weltgeschichte. Von Xerxes bis Nixon* (München, 2006).

Frei, Norbert, *Vergangenheitspolitik. Die Anfänge der Bundesrepublik und die NS-Vergangenheit* (Munich, C.H. Beck, 1996).

Friedrich, Jörg, *Das Gesetz des Krieges. Das deutsche Heer in Russland 1941 bis 1945. Der Prozess gegen das Oberkommando der Wehrmacht* (Munich, Piper, 1993).

Fugate, Bryan, *Operation Barbarossa. Strategy and Tactics on the Eastern Front, 1941* (Novato, Calif., Presidio Press, 1984).

Fyne, Robert, *The Hollywood Propaganda of World War II* (Metuchen, NJ, & London, The Scarecrow Press, Inc., 1994).

Gabriel, Richard A. and Paul Savage, *Crisis in Command. The Mismanagement in the Army* (New York, Hill and Wang, 1978).

Gallagher, Gary W., *Lee and His Generals in War and Memory* (Baton Rouge, La., State University Press, 2000).

Glantz, David M. and Samuel J. Newland, "Hitler's Attack on Russia," in Harold Deutsch, Dennis Showalter, and C. Deytsch (eds.), *What If? Strategic Alternatives of World War II* (Chicago, Ill., Emperor's Press, 1970).

Goda, Norman, "Black Mark: Hitler's Bribery of His Senior Officers during World War Two," *Journal of Modern History* 72 (June 2000).

Gorodetsky, Gabriel, *Grand Illusion. Stalin and the German Invasion of Russia* (New Haven, Conn., Yale University Press, 1999).

Graebner, Walter, *Round Trip to Russia* (Philadelphia, Pa., J. B. Lippincott, 1943).

Greiner, Christian,"Operational History (German) Section" and "Naval Historical Team." Deutsches militärstrategisches Denken im Dienst der americanischen Streitkräfte von 1946 bis 1950, in Manfred Messerschmidt, et al. (eds.), *Militärgeschichte. Probleme-Thesen-Wege* (Stuttgart, Deutsche Verlags-Anstalt, 1982).

Guderian, Heinz, *Kann Westeuropa verteidigt werden?* (Göttingen, Plesse-Verlag, 1950).

———. *Panzer Leader* (Cambridge, Mass., DaCapo, 2002).

Halder, Franz, *Hitler als Feldherr* (Munich, Münchener-Dom Verlag, 1949).

Hansen, Ernst Willi, et al. (eds.), *Politischer Wandel, organisierte Gewalt und nationale Sicherheit. Beiträge zur neueren Geschichte Deutschlands und Frankreich* (Munich, R. Oldenbourg, 1995).

Harris, Whitney, *Tyranny on Trial. The Evidence at Nuremberg* (Dallas, Tex., Southern Methodist University Press, 1954).

Hart, B. H. Liddell, *The German Generals Talk* (New York, William Morrow & Co., 1948).

Hartmann, Christian, *Halder. Generalstabschef Hitlers 1938–1942* (Paderborn, Ferdinand Schoeningh, 1991).

Hass, Gerhard, "Zum Russlandbild der SS," in Hans-Erich Volkmann (ed.), *Das Russlandbild im Dritten Reich* (Köln, Weimar, Böhlau Verlag, 1994).

Hassel, Sven, *Comrades of War*, trans. Maurice Michael (London, Cassells, 2005).

———. *Wheels of Terror*, trans. I. O'Hanlon (London, Cassells, 2003).

———. *SS General*, trans. Jean Ure (London, Cassells, 2003).

———. *The Legion of the Damned*, trans. Maurice Michael (London, Cassells, 2003).

Haupt, Werner, *Army Group Center: The Wehrmacht in Russia, 1941–1945* (Atglen, Pa., Schiffer Publishing Ltd., 1997).

———. *Army Group North: The Wehrmacht in Russia, 1941–1945* (Atglen, Pa., Schiffer Publishing Ltd., 1997).

———. *Army Group South: The Wehrmacht in Russia, 1941–1945* (Atglen, Pa., Schiffer Publishing Ltd., 1998).

Hechler, Kenneth, "The Enemy Side of the Hill. The 1945 Background *Wehrmacht* on Interrogation of German Commanders," in Donald Detwiler (ed.), *World War II German Military Studies. A Collection of 213 special reports on the Second World War prepared by former officers of the Wehrmacht for the United States Army* (New York, Garland Publishing, 1979).

Heer, Hannes and Klaus Naumann (eds.), *Vernichtungskrieg. The German Military in World War II* (New York, Oxford, Berghahn Books, 2000).

———. *War of Extermination. The German Military in World War II* (New York, Oxford, Berghahn Books, 2000).

Heiber, Helmuth and Peter Glantz (eds.), *Hitler and His Generals. Military Conferences 1942–1945* (New York, Enigma Books, 2003).

Herbert, Ulrich, *Hitler's Foreign Workers: Enforced Foreign Labor in Germany under the Third Reich* (Cambridge, Cambridge University Press, 1997).

Herring, George C. Jr., *Aid to Russia 1941–1946. Strategy, Diplomacy and the Origins of the Cold War* (New York, Columbia University Press, 1973).

Heuer, Uwe, *Reichswehr-Wehrmacht-Bundeswehr. Zum Image deutscher Streitkräfte in den Vereinigten Staaten von Amerika. Kontinuität und Wandel im Urteil amerikanischer Experten* (Frankfurt, Peter Lang, 1990).

Higgins, George A., "German and US Operational Art: A Contrast in Maneuver," *Military Review*, Vol. 65, No. 10 (October 1985).

Hillgruber, Andreas, "Das Russlandbild der führenden deutschen Militärs vor Beginn des Angriffs auf die Sowietunion," in Hans-Erich Volkmann (ed.), *Das Russlandbild im Dritten Reich* (Köln, Weimar, Böhlau Verlag, 1994).

Hindus, Maurice, *Mother Russia* (Garden City, NY, Garden City Publishing, 1942).

Hixson, Walter S., *Parting the Curtain: Propaganda, Culture, and the Cold War, 1945–1961* (New York, St. Martin's Press, 1997).

Horwitz, Tony, *Confederates in the Attic. Dispatches from the Unfinished Civil War* (New York, Pantheon Books, 1998).

Hürter, Johannes, "Die Wehrmacht vor Leningrad. Krieg und Besatzungspolitik der 18. Armee im Herbst und Winter 1941/42," *Vierteljahrshefte für Zeitgeschichte*, Vol. 49 (2001).

Hughes, Daniel J., "Abuses of German Military History," *Military Review*, Vol. 66, No. 12 (December 1986).

Ihme-Tuchel, Beate, "Fall 7: Der Prozess gegen die Südost-Generale gegen Wilhelm List und andere," in Gerd Überschär (ed.), *Nationalsozialismus vor Gericht. Die alliierten Prozesse gegen Kriegsverbrecher und Soldaten, 1943–1952* (Frankfurt, Fischer Verlag, 1999).

Jurado, Carlos Caballero, *Breaking the Chains* (Halifax, West Yorkshire, UK, Shelf Books, 1998).

———. *Foreign Volunteers, 1941–45* (London, Osprey Publishing, 1985).

———. *Wehrmacht Auxiliary Forces* (London, Osprey Publishing, 1992).

Just, Günther, *Stuka-Pilot Hans-Ulrich Rudel: His Life Story in Words and Photographs* (West Chester, Pa., Schiffer, 1990).

Karpov, Vladimir, *Russia at War* (New York, Vendome Press, 1987).

Kerr, Walter, *The Russian Army: Its Men, Its Leaders and Its Battles* (New York, Garden City, 1942).

Kershaw, Ian, *Hitler 1889–1936 Hubris* (New York, W.W. Norton and Company, 2000).

———. *Hitler 1936–1945 Nemesis* (New York, W.W. Norton and Company, 2000).

Keyssar, Helene and Vladimir Pozner, *Remembering the War: A U.S.-Soviet Dialogue* (New York, Oxford University Press, 1990).

Knappe, Siegfried and Ted Brusaw, *Soldat: Reflections of a German Soldier, 1936–1949* (New York, Orion Books, 1992).

Knopp, Guido, *Hitlers Krieger* (Munich, Bertelsmann, 2001).

Kopp, Roland, "Die Wehrmacht feiert. Kommanders-Reden zu Hitlers 50. Geburtstag am 20. April 1039," *Militärgeschichtliche Mitteilungen* 60 (2003).

Kort, Michael, *The Soviet Colossus: A History of the USSR* (New York, Charles Scribner's Sons, 1985).

Koschorrek, Günter K., *Blood Red Snow: The Memoirs of a German Soldier on the Eastern Front* (London, Greenhill Books, 2002).

Krammer, Arnold, "American Treatment of German Generals During World War II," *Journal of Military History*, 54 (January 1990).

Krause, Michael D., "Moltke and the Origins of Operational Art," *Military Review*, 70 (September 1990).

Krausnick, Helmuth, "Kommissarbefehl," *Vierteljahreshefte für Zeitgeschichte*, 25 (1977).

Kroener, Bernard, "The 'Frozen Blitzkrieg': German Strategic Planning against the Soviet Union and the Causes of Its Failure," in Bernd Wegner (ed.), *From Peace to War. Germany, Soviet Russia and the World, 1939–1941* (Providence, RI, Berghahn Books, 1997).

Kunz, Norbert, *Die Krim unter deutscher Herrschaft 1941–1944. Germanisierungsutopie und Besatzungsrealtität* (Darmstadt, Wissenschaftliche Buchgesellschaft, 2005).

Kurowski, Franz, *Brandenburg Commandos: Germany's Elite Warrior Spies in WWII* (Mechanicsburg, Pa., Stackpole Books, 2004).

———. *Hitler's Last Battalion: The Final Battles for the Reich 1944–1945* (Atglen, Pa., Schiffer Publishing, 1998).

———. *Infantry Aces* (New York, Ballantine Books, 2002).

———. *Panzer Aces* (New York, Ballantine Books, 2002).

Landwehr, Richard, *Budapest. The Stalingrad of the Waffen-SS* (Brookings, Ore., Siegrunen, 1999).

———. *Fighting for Freedom: The Ukrainian Volunteer Division of the Waffen-SS* (Silver Spring, Md., Bibliophile Legion Books, 1985); 3rd edition in 1993.

———. *Romanian Volunteers of the Waffen-SS 1944–45* (Silver Spring, MD, Bibliophile Legion Books, 1991).

———. *Steadfast Hussars. The Last Cavalry Division of the Waffen-SS* (Brookings, Ore., Siegrunen, 1997).

Large, David Clay, *Germans to the Front. West German Rearmament in the Adenauer Era* (Chapel Hill, University of North Carolina Press, 1996).

Lauterbach, Richard, *These Are the Russians* (New York, Harper, 1944).

Levering, Ralph, *American Public Opinion and the Russian Alliance, 1939–1945* (Chapel Hill, The University of North Carolina Press, 1976).

Lissance, Arnold (ed.), *The Halder Diaries. The Private War Journals of Colonel General Franz Halder* (Boulder, Colo., Westview Press, 1976).

Lochner, Louis (ed., trans.), *The Goebbels Diaries* (New York, Eagle Books, 1948).

Lowenthal, David, *The Past Is a Foreign Country* (Cambridge, Cambridge University Press, 1985).

Lower, Wendy, *Nazi Empire-Building and the Holocaust in Ukraine* (Chapel Hill, The University of North Carolina Press, 2005).

Lucas, James, *Das Reich: The Military Role of 2nd S Division* (London, Arms and Armor Press, 1991).

———. *Hitler's Commanders: German Bravery in the Field 1939–1945* (London, Cassell & Co., 2000).

———. *The Last Year of the German Army, May 1944-May 1945* (London, Arms and Armor, 1994).

———. *War on the Eastern Front, the German Soldier in Russia, 1941–1945* (London, the Military Book Club, 1991).

Luck, Hans von, *Panzer Commander: The Memoirs of Colonel Hans Von Luck* (New York, Dell, 1989).

Lumsden, Robin, *A Collector's Guide to the Allgemeine-SS* (Hersham, Surrey, Ian Allan Publishing, Ltd., 2002).

———. *A Collector's Guide to Third Reich Militaria* (Hersham, Surrey, Ian Allan Publishing, 2000).

———. *A Collector's Guide to the Third Reich Militaria: Detecting the Fakes* (Hersham, Surrey, UK, Ian Allen Publishing, 2001).

———. *Collector's Guide to the Waffen-SS* (Hersham, Surrey, Ian Allen Publishing, 2000).

Lutz, Catherine and Jane L. Collins, *Reading National Geographic* (Chicago, Ill., The University of Chicago Press, 1993).

MacPherson, Peter, "The Photographers of Barbarossa," *Military Historical Quarterly* 2 (Winter 1990), pp. 60–69.

Madej, Victor and Shelby Stanton, "The Smolensk Campaign 11 July–5 August 1941," *Strategy & Tactics* 57 (July–August 1976).

Magenheimer, Heinz, *Hitler's War. Germany's Key Strategic Decisions 1940–1945; Could Germany Have Won World War Two?* (London, Cassell, 1997).

Maginnis, John J., *Military Government Journal. Normandy to Berlin* (Cambridge, University of Massachusetts Press, 1971).

Mansoor, Peter R., "The Second Battle of Sedan May 1940," *Military Review*, Vol. 68, No. 6 (Hune, 1988).

Manstein, Erich von, *Lost Victories. Hitler's Most Brilliant General* (St. Paul, Minn., Zenith Press, 2004).

Manvell, Roger, *Films and the Second World War* (New York, A.S. Barnes and Company, 1974).

Marrus, Michael, "History and the Holocaust in the Courtroom," in Ronald Smelser (ed.), *Lessons and Legacies: The Holocaust and Justice* (Evanston, Ill., Northwestern University Press, 2002).

McCaul, Ed, "Tank Busting Stuka Pilot," *Military History* (August 2001).

Megargee, Geoff, *Inside Hitler's High Command* (Lawrence, Kan., University of Kansas Press, 2000).

———. *War of Annihilation. Combat and Genocide on the Eastern Front 1941* (Lanham, Md., Rowman & Littlefield, 2006).

Mellenthin F. W von, *German Generals in World War II: As I Saw Them* (Norman, University of Oklahoma Press, 1977).

———. *Panzer Battles: A Study of the Employment of Armor in the Second World War* (New York, Ballantine Books, 1971).

Mendelsohn, John, "War Crimes and Clemency," in Robert Wolfe (ed.), *Americans as Proconsuls. United States Military Government in Germany and Japan, 1944–1952* (Carbondale, Ill., Southern Illinois University Press, 1984).

Messerschmidt, Manfred, *Die Wehrmacht im NS-Staat. Zeit der Indokrination* (Hamburg, 1969).

———. (eds.)., *Militärgeschichte. Probleme-Thesen-Wege* (Stuttgart, Deutsche Verlags-Anstalt, 1982).

Meyer, Kurt, *Grenadiers: the Story of Waffen-SS General Kurt "Panzer" Meyer* (Mechanicsburg, Pa., Stackpole Books, 2005).

Moeller, Susan D., *Shooting War: Photography and the American Experience of Combat* (New York, Basic Books, Inc., 1989).

Mitcham, Samuel W. Jr., *Hitler's Field Marshals and Their Battles* (Lanham, Md., Scarborough House, 1994).

Müller, Rolf-Dieter and Hans-Erich Volkmann (eds.), *Die Wehrmacht. Mythos und Realität* (Munich, Oldenbourg, 1999).

Munoz, Anthony J., *Forgotten Legions: Obscure Combat Formations of the Waffen-SS* (n.p., Axis Europa Books, 1991).

Munoz, Antonio J., *Hitler's Eastern Legions, Volume – II The Osttruppen* (Bayside, NY, Axis Europa, Inc., 1997).

Munoz, Antonio J., *Hitler's Green Army: The German Order of Police and Their European Auxiliaries 1933–1945, Volume II, Eastern Europe and the Balkans* (Bayside, NY, Europa Books, Inc., 2005).

Munoz, Antonio J., *Hitler's Green Army: The German Order of Police and Their European Auxiliaries 1933–1945, Volume I, Western Europe and Scandinavia* (Bayside, NY, Europa Books, Inc., 2005).

Naimark, Norman, *The Russians in Germany. A History of the Soviet Zone of Occupation, 1945–1949* (Cambridge, Mass., Harvard University Press, 1995).

Naumann, Klaus, "Godfathers of Innere Führung? German-American Interaction During the Early Years of the Bundeswehr," unpublished manuscript in author's possession.

Nelson, Walter H., *Germany Rearmed* (New York, Simon and Shuster, 1972).

Orlow, Dietrich, *A History of Modern Germany, 1871 to Present*, Fourth Edition (Upper Saddle River, NJ, Prentice Hall, 1999).

Overy, Richard, *Russia's War: A History of the Soviet War Effort: 1941–1945* (Middlesex, Penguin, 1997).

Paget, Reginald, *Manstein. His Campaigns and His Trial* (London, Collins, 1951).

Paul, Gerhard and Klaus-Michael Mallmann (eds.), *Die Gestapo im Zweiten Weltkrieg. Heimatfront und besetztes Europa* (Darmstadt, Wissenschaftliche Buchgesellshaft, 2000).

Petropoulos, Jonathan and John K. Roth (eds.), *Gray Zones. Ambiguity and Compromise in the Holocaust and Its Aftermath* (New York, Berghahn Books, 2005).

Michael Phipps, "A Forgotten War," *Infantry* (November–December 1984).

Pickett, William B., "Eisenhower as a Student of Clausewitz," *Military Review* 65 (July 1985).

Pipes, Jason, "SLOVAKIA! A History of the Slovak Units on the Eastern Front in WWII," *Axis Europa: The Journal of the Axis Forces 1939–1945* (Summer 1998).

Poliakov, Alexander, *The Russians Don't Surrender* (New York, E. P. Dutton, 1942).

Reardon, Carol, *Pickett's Charge in History and Memory* (Chapel Hill, The North Carolina University Press, 1997).

Reuth, Ralf G., "Erwin Rommel–Die Propagandaschöpfung," in Ronald Smelser and Enrico Syring (eds.), *Die Militärelite des Dritten Reiches/27 Biographische Skizzen* (Berlin, Ullstein Verlag, 1995).

Rhodes, Richard, *Masters of Death. The SS-Einsatzgruppen and the Invention of the Holocaust* (New York, Alfred Knopf, 2002).

Rikmenspoel, Marc J., *Soldiers of the Waffen-SS. Many Nations, One Motto* (Winnipeg, Fedorowicz, 1999).

———. *Waffen-SS The Encyclopedia* (New York, The Military Book Club, 2002).

Rippe, Stephen T., "Leadership, Firepower and Maneuver: The British and the Germans," *Military Review*, Vol. 65, No. 10 (October 1985).

Roberts, Alexander B., "Core Values in a Quality Air Force: The Leadership Challenge," *Aerospace Power Journal* (Summer 1994), no page.

Rudel, Hans-Ulrich, *Stuka Pilot* (New York, Ballantine Bal-Hi printing, June, 1966).

Sadoff, Laurence R., "Hans von Seeckt. One Man Who Made a Difference," *Military Review* 67 (December 1987).

Scheiderbauer, Armin, *Adventures in My Youth: A German Soldier on the Eastern Front, 1941–1945* (West Midlands, England, Helion and Company, Ltd., 2003).

Schellenberg, Walter, *The Labyrinth; Memoirs of Walter Schellenberg* (New York, Harper, 1956).

Schoenbaum, David, "The Wehrmacht and G. I. Joe: Learning *What* from History?" *International Security* 8 (1983).

Schubert, Klaus von, *Wiederbewaffnung und Westintegration* (Stuttgart, DVA, 1970).

Schröders, Michael, "Erich von Manstein- ein unpolitischer Soldat?" Forum "Barbarossa": Beitrag 3-2004.

Schwartz, Thomas, *America's Germany: John J. McCloy and the Federal Republic of Germany* (Cambridge, Mass., Harvard University Press, 1991).

Schwendemann, Heinrich, "Strategie der Selbstvernichtung: Die Wehrmachtführung im 'Endkampf' um das 'Dritte Reich,'" in Rolf-Dieter Müller and Hans-Erich Volkmann (eds.), *Die Wehrmacht. Mythos und Realität* (Munich, Oldenbourg, 1999).

Silgailis, Arthur, *The Latvian Legion* (San Jose, CA, R. James Bender Publishing, 1986).

Scott, Glen L., "British and German Operational Styles in World War II," *Military Review*, Vol. 65, No. 10 (October 1985).

Service, Robert, *A History of Twentieth-Century Russia* (Cambridge, Mass., Harvard University Press, 1997).

Sheperd, Ben, *War in the Wild East. The German Army and Soviet Partisans* (Cambridge, Mass., Harvard University Press, 2004).

Shils, Edward A. and Morris Janowitz, "Cohesion and Disintegration in the Wehrmacht in World War Two," *Public Opinion Quarterly* XII (1948).

Short, K. R. M. (ed.), *Film & Radio Propaganda in World War II* (Knoxville, The University of Tennessee Press, 1983).

Smelser, Ronald, "The Myth of the 'Clean' Wehrmacht in Cold War America," in Doris Bergen (ed.), *Lessons and Legacies: From Generation to Generation* (Evanston, Ill., Northwestern University Press, forthcoming).

———. (ed.), *Lessons and Legacies: The Holocaust and Justice* (Evanston, Ill., Northwestern University Press, 2002).

———. "The Holocaust in Popular Culture: Master-Narrative and Counter-Narrative in the Gray Zone," in Jonathan Petropoulos and John K. Roth (eds.), *Gray Zones. Ambiguity and Compromise in the Holocaust and Its Aftermath* (New York, Berghahn Books, 2005).

Smelser, Ronald and Enrico Syring (eds.), *Die Militärelite des Dritten Reiches/27 Biographische Skizzen* (Berlin, Ullstein Verlag, 1995).

Smith, Bradley, *Reaching Judgment at Nuremberg* (New York, New American Library, 1979).

Souter, Kevin, "To Stem the Red Tide: The German Report Series and Its Effect on American Defense Doctrine, 1948–1954," *Journal of Modern History* 57 (October 1993).

Stahlberg, Alexander, *Bounden Duty. The Memoirs of a German Officer, 1932–1945*, trans. Patricia Crampton (New York, Brassey, 1990).

Stein, Marcel, *Generalfeldmarschall Erich von Manstein: kritische Betrachtung des Soldaten und Menschen* (Mainz, von Hase und Koehler, 2000).

Roger Steinway, "German Horse Soldier on the Eastern Front," *Military History* (January/February 2005).

———. "Horse Soldier in Hitler's Army," *Military History* (February 2005).

Stolfi, R. H. S., *Hitler's Panzers East: A Reinterpretation of World War II* (Norman, University of Oklahoma Press, 1991).

———. *Nato Under Attack. Why the Western Alliance Can Fight Outnumbered and Win in Central Europe Without Nuclear Weapons* (Durham, NC, Duke University Press, 1984).

Streim, Alfred, "Saubere Wehrmacht? Die Verfolgung von Kriegs-und NS-Verbrechen in der Bundesrepublik und der DDR," in Hannes Heer and Klaus Naumann (eds.), *Vernichtungskrieg. The German Military in World War II* (New York, Oxford, Berghahn Books, 2000).

Streit, Christian, "Die Kontroverse um die 'Wehrmachtausstellung," *Aufbau*, No. 26, 24 December 1999.

———. *Keine Kameraden. Die Wehrmacht und die sowietischen Kriegsgefangenen 1941–1945* (Bonn, Dietz, 1991).

Sydnor, Charles, *Soldiers of Destruction: The SS Death's Head Division, 1933–1945* (Princeton, NJ, Princeton University Press, 1977).

Syring, Enrico, "Erich von Manstein – das operative Genie," in Ronald Smelser and Enrico Syring (eds.), *Die Militärelite des Dritten Reiches. 27 Biographische Skizzen* (Berlin, Ullstein, 1995).

Taylor, Telford, *The Anatomy of the Nuremberg Trials* (New York, Little, Brown and Co., 1992).

Thelen, David (ed.), *Memory and American History* (Bloomington, Indiana University Press, 1989).

Tiberi, Paul, "German versus Soviet Blitzkrieg," *Military Review*, Vol. 65, No. 9 (September 1985).

Thompson, Jenny. *War Games: Inside the World of Twentieth-Century Reenactors* (Washington, DC, Smithsonian Books, 2004).

Toliver, Raymond F. and Trevor J. Constable, *The Blond Knight of Germany* (Blue Ridge Summit, PA. Tab Aero, Division of McGraw Hill, 1970).

Überschär, Gerd (ed.), *Der Nationalsozialismus vor Gericht. Die alliierten Prozesse gegen Kriegsverbrecher und Soldaten, 1943–1952* (Frankfurt, Fischer Verlag, 1999).

———. *Generaloberst Franz Halder. Generalstabschef, Gegner und Gefangener Hitlers* (Göttingen, Muster-Schmidt, 1991).

Überschär, Gerd and Winfried Vogel, *Dienen und Verdienen. Hitler's Geschenke an seine Eliten* (Frankfurt, S. Fischer, 1999).

Volkmann, Hans-Erich (ed.), *Das Russlandbild im Dritten Reich* (Köln, Weimar, Böhlau Verlag, 1994).

Wegner, Bernd, "Erschriebene Siege. Franz Halder, die 'Historical Division' und die Rekonstruktion des Zweiten Weltkrieges im Geiste des deutschen Generalstabes," in Ernst Willi Hansen, et al. (eds.), *Politischer Wandel, organisierte Gewalt und nationale Sicherheit. Beiträge zur neueren Geschichte Deutschlands und Frankreich* (Munich, R. Oldenbourg, 1995).

———. (ed.), *From Peace to War. Germany, Soviet Russia and the World, 1939–1941* (Providence, RI, Berghahn Books, 1997).

Weinberg, Gerhard L., *A World At Arms: A Global History of World War II* (New York, Cambridge University Press, 1994).

———. *Germany, Hitler and World War Two: Essays in Modern German and World History* (Cambridge, Cambridge University Press, 1995).

Weingartner, James, *Crossroads of Death. The Story of the Malmédy Massacre and Trial* (Berkeley, University of California Press, 1979).

Werth, Alexander, *Russia at War* (New York, Dutton, 1965).

Wette, Wolfram, "Fall 12: Der OKW-Prozess (gegen Wilhelm Ritter von List und andere)," *Der Nationalsozialismus vor Gericht. Die alliierten Prozesse gegen Kriegsverbrecher und Soldaten, 1943–1952* (Frankfurt, Fischer Verlag, 1999).

Wette, Wolfram, *The Wehrmacht: History, Myth, Reality*, trans. Lucas Schneider (Cambridge, Mass., Harvard University Press, 2006).

Westermann, Edward B., *Hitler's Police Battalions: Enforcing Racial War in the East* (Lawrence, University Press of Kansas, 2005).

Wettig, Gerhard, *Entmilitarisierung und Wiederbewaffnung in Deutschland, 1943–1955. Internationale Auseinandersetzungen um die Rolle der Deutschen in Europa* (Munich, Oldenbourg, 1957).

Wieczynski, Joseph (ed.), *Operation Barbarossa: the German Attack on the Soviet Union, June 22, 1941* (Salt Lake City, Utah, C. Schlacks, 1993).

Wolfe, Robert (ed.), *Americans as Proconsuls: United States Military Government in Germany and Japan, 1944–1952* (Carbondale, Southern Illinois University Press, 1984).

Wrochen, Oliver von, "Die Auseinandersetzung mit Wehrmachtverbrechen im Prozess gegen den Generalfeldmarschall Erich von Manstein 1949," *Zeitschrift für Geschichtswissenschaft*, Vol. 46 (1998).

———. "Rehabilitation oder Strafverfolgung. Kriegsverbrecherprozess gegen Generalfeldmarschall Erich von Manstein im Widerstreit britischer Interessen," *Mittelweg 36*, vol. 3 (1997).

———. *Vernichtungskrieg und Erinnerungspolitik: Erich von Manstein – Akteur und Symbol* (Paderborn, Schöningh, 2006).

Yerger, Mark, *Comrades to the End* (Atgen, Pa., Schiffer Military History, 1998).

———. *Ernst August Krag* (Atgen, Pa., Schiffer, 1996).

———. *Otto Kumm* (Winnipeg, Fedorowicz, 1987).

———. *Otto Weidinger* (Winnipeg, Fedorowicz, 1987).

———. *Waffen-SS Commanders. The Army, Corps and Divisional Leaders of a Legend* (Atgen, Pa., Schiffer Military History, 1999).

Ziemke, Earl, *The U.S. Army in the Occupation of Germany, 1944–1946* (Washington, DC, Center of Military History, Department of Defense, 1975).

Internet Sources

Only the major websites used in the book are listed. These account for the vast majority of all websites. In cases such as the German Armed Forces, only the main page is noted. The other pages cited are located through links and clicks. In almost all cases, the authors have copies of the material. The Amazon sites were not included because these are readily available by calling up *Amazon.com* and typing in the name of the author or book. Both of these are listed for all the secondary and what we use as primary citations.

http://eastfront.virtualave.net/
http://en.wikipedia.org/wiki/Hans_Ulrich_Rudel
http://feedback.ebays.com/ws/eBayISAPI.dll?ViewFeedback&userid=sssteiner&frm=1742
http://feldgrau.com/
http:freehosting2.at.webjump.com/3a69490ee/allW2hpg/authen.html
http://freehosting2.at.webjump.com/3a69490ee/a1/w2hpg/ger1_auth_regs.html
http://freehosting2.at.webjump.com/02e743cb6/a1/w2hpg/index2.html
http://freehosting2.at.webjump.com/02e743106/a1/w2hpg/officers.html
http://lexikon.idgr.de/r/r_u/rudel-hans-ulrich/rudel-hans-ulrich.php
http://members.aol.com/soldaten/main.htm
http://members.aol.com/soldaten/rekrut.htm
http://members.aol.com/soldaten/main.htm
http://members.tripod.com/George_Parada/gen8.htm
http://members.xoomco./Falcon.Div/
http://stores.ebay.com/Military-Mugs-and-Models
http://users.jnlk.com/militaria/
http://www.achtungpanzer.com/panzer.htm
http://www.anderfront.com/cuslinks.htm

http://www.anderfront.com/enslinks.htm
http://www.axiseuropa.com/about.php
http://www.axishistory.com/index.php?id=308
http://www.forces70.freeserve.co.uk/
http://www.geocities.com/ww2_links/societies.html
http://www.geocities.com/ww2_links/axis.html
http://www.geocities.com/~orion47/
http://home.inreach.com/rickylaw/dictatorship/general/links.html
http://www.hstrial-derickson.homestead.com/Mugs~ns4.html
http://www.InsideTheWeb.com/messageboard/mbs.cgi/mb47087
http://www.io.com/-tog/tmhs.html
http://www.nazi-lauck-nsdapao.com/
http://www.oradour.info/appendix/landwehr.htm
http://www.ortelli-art.com/militar/mr11.htm
http://www.panzerdiesel.com/eng/e340.html
http://www.randomhouse.com/rhpg/authors/results.pperl?authorid-29510
http://www.reenactor.net/WW2/ww2_orgs.htm
http://www.reenactorfest.com/
http://www.reenactor.net/main.htmls/ww2.html
http://www.reenactor.net/WW2/ww2_orgs.html
http://ww2reenactors.proboards35.com/
http://www.secularhumanism.org/library/fi/cohen_21_2.html
http://www.soldat.com/
http://members.aol.com/soldaten/rekrut.htm
http://www.1ssah.com/
http://www.lssah.com/unit%20hist.html
http://www.11thpanzer.com/index11.htm
http://www.uwm.edu/-jpipes/start.html
http://www.vvm.com/~histpart/books.htm
http://www.wargamer.com/contest/tank.asp
orgs/american/wiesenthal.center/swc.oprep
www.dasreich.ca/ger_oradour.html
www.fliegergemeinchaft.de/main.english/page 5_9_e
www.pointssouth.com/csanet/andersonville.htm
www.ess.uwe.ac/genocide/Halder.htm
www.vho.org/GB/Journals/JHR/2/1/Landwehr59-84.html

Wargames

Wargaming materials: These are part of Edward J. Davies' private collection. They form a part of a large wargaming and wargaming materials collection in the possession of the author.

John M. Astell, Paul R. Banner, Frank Chadwick, and Marc Miller, designers, *Fire in the East: The Russian Front, 1941–1942* (Bloomington, Ill., Game Designers' Workshop, 1984).

Dan Lombardy, designer and David Parham, researcher, *Streets of Stalingrad, Sept–Nov, 1942* (Phoenix Games, 1979).

Dean N. Essig, game and series designer, *Guderian's Blitzkrieg: The Panzer Leader's Last Drive, The Drive on Moscow September 21st to December 20th, 1941* (Homer, Ill., The Gamers, 1992).

Dean N. Essig, game & series designer, *Enemy At the Gates: The Stalingrad Pocket to Manstein's Counterattack Army Group South-19 Nov 42 to 14 March 1943* (Homer, Ill., The Gamers, 1994).

Panzer Blitz: The Game of Armored Warfare on the Eastern Front 1941–1945 (Baltimore, Md.: Avalon Hill Game Company, 1970.

The Last Victory: Von Manstein's Backhand Blow, February and March 1943 (Clash of Arms Games, 1987).

War in the East: The Russo-German Conflict 1941–1945 (New York City, Simulations Publications, Inc., 1974).

Dave Fredericks, game designer and Dean N. Essig, series designer, *Hube's Pocket* (Homer, Ill., The Gamers, 1996).

Magazines

Moves: Conflict Simulation Theory and Technique.
The Grenadier
Command: Military History, Strategy & Analysis
Strategy & Tactics
Fire & Movement
Axis Europa
Axis Europa News Letter
Siegrunen

Wargaming Books

The Editors of *Consumer Guide. The Complete Book of Wargaming* (New York, Fireside Books, Simon and Schuster, 1980).

Index